FLIES

*Their Origin, Natural History, Tying, Hooks, Patterns
and Selections of Dry and Wet Flies, Nymphs, Streamers,
Salmon Flies for Fresh and Salt Water in North America
and the British Isles, Including*

A DICTIONARY OF 2200 PATTERNS

by

J. EDSON LEONARD

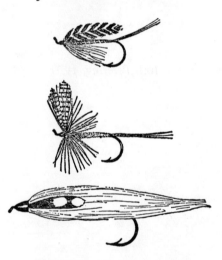

*Illustrated by the Author
Photographs by Jack Leonard and the Cameo Studios*

SOUTH BRUNSWICK
NEW YORK: A.S. BARNES AND COMPANY, INC.
LONDON: THOMAS YOSELOFF LTD

A.S. Barnes and Company, Inc.
Cranbury, New Jersey 08512

Thomas Yoseloff Ltd
108 New Bond Street
London W1Y OQX, England

10th Printing, 1970

ISBN: 0-498-08107-9
Printed in the United States of America

DEDICATION

To my wife, Page, whose unceasing efforts made this book possible, and Little Jack who, we hope, will grow to find happiness in the outdoors by contributing toward the preservation of its riches.

ACKNOWLEDGMENTS

I should like to thank the following persons who contributed so generously of their time and talents to make this book a success:

S. Allock & Co., Ltd. (A. Courtney Williams), Redditch, England, for hooks and information.

Joe Aucoin, New Waterford, Nova Scotia, for salmon and trout flies and information.

Dan Bailey, Livingston, Montana, for information and fly preferences.

Ray Bergman, editor and author, for information and fly dressings.

Bob Carmichael, Moose, Jackson Hole, Wyoming, for favorite patterns and information.

Peter R. Cartile, West Northfield, Nova Scotia, for information and salmon flies.

E. C. Coombes, Tenbury Wells, Worcs., England, for information and trout and salmon flies.

Allen Corson, editor, on the staff of the *Miami Herald*, for information on bonefish flies.

T. J. Courtney, Director, Nova Scotia Bureau of Information, Halifax, Nova Scotia, for addresses and information.

J. T. Cox, Division of Game and Fish, Frankfort, Kentucky, for a list of flies for bass and panfish.

Patrick Curry, Coleraine, Ireland, for favorite flies and information.

Roy M. Donnelly, San Pedro, California, for steelhead flies and information.

Ruth M. Evans (Glen L. Evans, Inc.), Caldwell, Idaho, for many western patterns and flies.

A. W. Marsh (C. Farlow & Co.), for many dressings, especially obscure salmon flies.

Bob Frederick, Allentown, Pennsylvania, for local dressings.

Grace Gabriel-Ray, Bromsgrove, Worcs., England, for trout and sea-trout fly dressings and flies.

Jim Gasque, Asheville, North Carolina, for description of the "Tandem Double Header" and information.

Harold N. Gibbs, Barrington, Rhode Island, information on salt-water fly fishing and "Gibbs' Striper" fly.

Ruth M. Gilmore, Providence, Rhode Island, for contacts.

Earl Gresh, St. Petersburg, Florida, for information about bonefishing, also bonefish flies.

Roderick L. Haig-Brown, Campbell River, B. C., Canada, for favorite flies.

Don Harger, Salem, Oregon, for information and flies for the Pacific region.

C. M. Harrison, Tregaron, Cards, Wales, for fly preferences and trout and salmon flies.

Bill Hart, Carbondale, Colorado, fly selection and information.

M. D. Hart, Commission of Game and Inland Fisheries, Richmond, Virginia, for favorite flies.

W. Haynes & Son (J. B. Haynes), Cork, Ireland, for information and trout and salmon flies.

Fred J. Hogardt, West Roxbury, Massachusetts, information and fly selection.

Herb Johnson, Yarmouth, Maine, for tying the flies sent to me by Ralph M. Plympton.

V. R. Johnson, State Game Warden, Custer, South Dakota, for favorite flies and information.

Joe Kendall, Kamloops, B. C., Canada, for favorite flies and information.

Claude M. Kreider, author of *Steelhead*, Long Beach, California, for favorite flies and opinions about Steelhead.

Francesca LaMonte, Secretary, International Game Fish Association, for invaluable contacts.

Charles Letson, Madison, Connecticut, for contacts.

Neil M. Lindsay, Shalalth P. O., B. C., Canada, for favorite flies and opinions as well as contacts.

R. L. Marston, Beckenham, Kent, England, editor of the *Fishing Gazette,* for addresses and excellent information.

Alex Martin, Glascow, Scotland, for several trout and salmon flies dressed "Parachute" style.

W. R. Maxson, Game Warden, Kelowna, B. C., Canada, for favorite flies and opinions.

Bob Moog, Baltimore, Maryland, for information and a sample Black Ghost dressed Maryland fashion.

O. Mustad & Son, Oslo, Norway, for hooks and technical information.

Dr. Paul R. Needham, Professor of Zoology, University of California, for reading Chapter 13, Aquatic Insects and Crustaceans, and offering suggestions for its improvement.

Charles C. Niehuis, Phoenix, Arizona, for favorite flies and their dressings along with information.

Charles F. Orvis Co., Manchester, Vermont, first for permission to use information from Mary Orvis Marbury's wonderful *Favorite Flies* and for salmon and trout flies together with information.

Ralph M. Plympton, Morristown, N. J. (formerly Pres. of R. C. Nichols Corp., Yarmouth, Maine), for exceptionally accurate information on Maine fishing as well as contacts.

Bert Quimby, South Windham, Maine, for streamer dressings.

R. M. Robertson, Inspector, British Columbia Game Department, for most helpful contacts.

Homer Rhode, Jr., Coral Gables, Florida, for bonefish patterns and interesting opinions.

Dr. Herbert Sanborn, Waterville, Maine, for comments about his originations and several samples.

George Sandiford, Kamloops, B. C., Canada, for fly preferences.

Herbert Sandusky, Outdoor Editor, *Jackson Daily News,* Mississippi, for fly selection.

George F. Schlingloff (George X. Sand), Boca Raton, Florida, for contacts.

C. A. Schoenfeld, Madison, Wisconsin, for favorite flies.

Harold H. Smedley, Muskegon, Michigan, for a copy of his book, *Fly Patterns and Their Origins,* and opinions and fly selection.

Roger P. Smith, Madison, Connecticut, for complete and detailed information, also opinions and fly selections.

Brainerd C. Snider, Ardmore, Oklahoma, for information and contacts.

Emil William Steffens, Rutherford, New Jersey, for information and contacts.

Carrie Stevens, Madison, Maine, for several of her famous streamer flies.

Charles F. Swank, Lewisburg, Pennsylvania, for dressings.

H. G. Tapply, Editor, *Outdoors Magazine,* for invaluable contacts, information, suggestions, and fly selections.

Utah Fish & Game Dep't., Salt Lake City, for recommended fly lists.

Don Webb, Ardmore, Oklahoma, for favorite bass flies.

Herbert L. Welch, Mooselookmeguntic, Maine, for favorite patterns and comments.

Charles M. Wetzel, Newark, Delaware, for fly selections and comments, and the permission to use excerpts from his book, *Practical Fly-Fishing,* should I need them.

Lee Wulff, Shushan, New York, for fly selections and contacts.

Leo W. Young, Durbin, West Virginia, for favorite flies and comments.

Special acknowledgment is given to the following for the privilege of using material previously published:

The Comstock Publishing Co., Inc. for permission to use tables from *Trout Stream,* by Paul R. Needham.

Edward L. Troxell, Director of Trinity College, Hartford, and Superintendent, State Geological and Natural History Survey of the State of Connecticut, for a table which appeared in Bulletin no. 63, Section III, by Dwight A. Webster.

Robert L. Jones, Superintendent, Department of Conservation, The Commonwealth of Massachusetts, for a table which appeared in Fisheries Survey Report, 1942, by Albert H. Swartz.

The State Natural History Survey Division, State of Illinois, for copying the Red-bellied Dace and Shiner minnows appearing in *Fishes of Illinois,* by Forbes and Richardson.

The Charles F. Orvis Co. for certain historical descriptions from Mary Orvis Marbury's, *Favorite Flies.*

PREFACE

Fish in our time are thinning out, and fishing is becoming more competitive every day. Anglers must fish hard and wisely to earn any "net results." Merely mastering the mechanics of wading a stream and casting a line is no longer any assurance that one's creel will contain fish at the end of the day.

Consequently, the angler, to be successful, must have as part of his equipment a variety of information relative to types of flies, their advantages and limitations, what they may or may not simulate in the water, where they are most apt to have a natural counterpart and, finally, how they may most logically be made.

This book deals entirely with this aspect of fishing. Naturally no one human being can be an authority on flies for every section of America, Canada and Great Britain. It would require far more than one individual's lifetime to chronicle all the facts. For this reason I have sought and obtained opinions, records, information of local color, and fly dressings from some of the world's most eminent specialists in fly fishing and these are included in these pages.

The material has taken years to collect and compile, and it is to be expected that there will be certain minor omissions. Nevertheless, I believe that the salient facts are set down here, and that it is reasonable to hope this book will be useful in making fly-tying easier and insect recognition more certain.

Those who understand the ways of fish and the food they eat, and how to make artificial lures to represent that food, are the natural fishermen. They know the why, when and how.

CONTENTS

	PAGE
Acknowledgments	iii
Preface	vii

Chapter I.
HOOK DESIGN 1

Chapter II.
TOOLS OF THE TRADE 16

Chapter III.
MATERIALS 20

Chapter IV.
FLY DESIGN 32

Chapter V.
THE WET FLY 43

Chapter VI.
THE DRY FLY 58

Chapter VII.
THE NYMPH   83

Chapter VIII.
THE STREAMER   93

Chapter IX.
THE SALMON FLY   109

Chapter X.
BASS AND LAKE WET FLIES   124

Chapter XI.
SALT-WATER STREAMERS   133

Chapter XII.
SURFACE LURES   138

Chapter XIII.
AQUATIC INSECTS AND CRUSTACEANS   152

Chapter XIV.
DICTIONARY OF FLY PATTERNS   207

Appendix   287
A collection, with descriptions and illustrations, of the favorite flies by well-known
fly-dressers and fishermen

Bibliography   331

Index   332

LIST OF ILLUSTRATIONS

		PAGE
Plate I	Favorite Wet Flies	Following page 52
Fig. 1	Hook Shapes	3
Fig. 2	Size Variation Showing Gauge and Length Combinations	5
Fig. 3	Hook Parts	8
Fig. 4	Standard Gauge for Hooks	10
Fig. 5	Hook Designs (I)	11
Fig. 5-A	Hook Designs (II)	12
Fig. 6	Tools of the Trade	17
Fig. 7	Fly Nomenclature	37
Fig. 8	Trout Fly Proportions	46
Fig. 9	General Construction Features	47
Fig. 10	Wet-Fly Design	49
Fig. 11	Constructing the Wet Fly	51
Plate II	Steelhead Wet Flies	Following page 52
Fig. 12	Steelhead Wet-Fly Design	55
Fig. 13	Dry-Fly Design (I)	59
Fig. 14	Dry-Fly Design (II)	61
Fig. 15	Constructing the Dry Fly	63
Fig. 16	Fastening Dry-Fly Wings	65
Fig. 17	Constructing Detached-Body Flies	71
Plate III	Favorite Dry Flies	Following page 52
Plate IV	Theory of Streamer Design	Following page 52
Fig. 18	Nymph Design	84
Fig. 19	Special Features, Nymph Design	87
Fig. 20	Constructing the Nymph	89
Fig. 21	Streamer Design, Feather Type	94
Fig. 22	Streamer Design, Bucktail and Other Types	96
Fig. 23	Special Features—Streamer Design	100
Fig. 24	Constructing the Streamer and Bucktail	101
Fig. 25	Salmon-Fly Design	110

Fig. 26	Constructing the Salmon Wet Fly (I)	112
Fig. 27	Constructing the Salmon Wet Fly (II)	113
Plate V	Favorite Streamers	Following page 116
Plate VI	Typical Material List	Following page 116
Fig. 28	Lake-Fly Design	126
Fig. 29	Special Features—Lake Flies	128
Fig. 30	Types of Cork-Body Bugs	140
Fig. 31	Special Features—Cork Bugs	142
Fig. 32	Types of Hair Bugs	147
Plate VII	Favorite Salmon Wet Flies	Following page 116
Plate VIII	Salt Water Flies	Following page 116

Figs. 33-56, FAVORITE FLIES—Between Pages 308-309:

Fig. 33	Four Valuable Flies
Fig. 34	Trout Dry Flies by Orvis
Fig. 35	Salmon Flies by Orvis
Fig. 36	Tandem-Hook Streamers by Sanborn
Fig. 37	Salmon Streamers by Stevens
Fig. 38	Dry Wet Nymphs by Plympton and Johnson
Fig. 39	Special Types by Plympton and Johnson
Fig. 40	Atlantic Salmon Flies by Plympton and Johnson
Fig. 41	Trout Flies by Evans
Fig. 42	Steelhead Wet Flies by Donnelly
Fig. 43	Steelhead Flies by Donnelly
Fig. 44	Pacific Trout Flies by Harger
Fig. 45	Boneflies by Rhode
Fig. 46	Bonefish Flies by Rhode
Fig. 47	Bonefish Flies by Gresh
Fig. 48	Salmon Flies by Cartile
Fig. 49	Hairwing Trout Flies by Aucoin
Fig. 50	Hairwing Salmon Flies by Aucoin
Fig. 51	Featherwing Salmon Flies by Aucoin
Fig. 52	Sea Trout Flies by Gabriel-Ray
Fig. 53	Trout Dry Flies by Coombes
Fig. 54	Salmon Flies by Coombes
Fig. 55	Parachute Dry Flies by Martin
Fig. 56	Salmon and Trout Flies by Haynes

Chapter One

HOOK DESIGN

Since the paleolithic age man has been inventing and making fish-hooks, and for this reason some scientists have stated that the development of mankind can be measured by the improvements in his fish-hooks.

Among the first hooks were those wrought from the bone and the tusks of animals. These were sharpened at both ends and whipped at the center to rawhide or vine lines to impale the fish on both points. Later developments consisted of more ingenious contraptions such as slender, pointed slivers of bone forced at an angle into a wood shaft which somewhat resembled the present-day fish-hook. Many other devices and materials were used: animal claws, pieces of flint ground to shape and sharpened, shells, thorns and even the beaks of birds. But it was not until 4000 B.C. when the Egyptians were producing the first copper implements that metal was used in the manufacture of hooks. It is recorded that the Chinese were using iron hooks as early as 1500 B.C. These hooks must have been quite small and light since they were fastened to the first silk lines and cast by means of a light, willowy reed.

For centuries it was customary, for want of a better method, to bind the line directly to the shank of the hook. Exactly when this practice became outmoded through the advent of the snelled hook is not known, but old English volumes printed before the sixteenth century indicate that snoods and snells were in common use by that time.

Perhaps the most important of all innovations in the design of the hook was the development of the eyed hook shortly before 1880. This led to great advances in fly design and especially to the first serious attempts to construct floating flies. So much has been written about the advantages of the eyed hook over the snelled hook that it is not necessary to repeat them here, except to point out that our present ultra-light dry-fly fishing might never have been possible if it were not for the eyed hook.

Too few anglers know the characteristics of and the proper uses for the many hooks manufactured today. This is a situation that should not be permitted to exist since evidently no other item of tackle is more important than the one making contact with the fish. A knowledge of the characteristics of hooks is of great importance in connection with fly-dressing for an incorrect hook can destroy the effectiveness of any fly or lure.

The kind of fish to be caught, its environment, and the type of fly or lure to be used, determine largely what hook will be most appropriate. A fine wire hook in rough, heavy waters where large fish are expected is as much out of place as a coarse, heavy

1

hook in clear, placid waters. A hook well suited to one fish may be totally unsuited to another mainly because of the diversity of their feeding habits, the nature of their mouth parts, and their environments. Furthermore, different kinds of flies, streamers and nymphs require hooks especially designed for them; no single type of hook is applicable to all fly-fishing conditions.

Fig. 1 illustrates the major hook shapes manufactured today. Certain of these have most desirable features in connection with fly dressing while others have not. The large profile shows a typical hook, the six diagrammed parts of which constitute, in this case, a turn-up, taper-eye type which is widely used for dry and wet flies. These parts vary in shape and design according to the kind of hook, consequently the usefulness of any hook from the fly-dresser's standpoint depends upon the relationship of these parts to each other. For example, it is obviously an error to select a hook with a shallow gape if the body of the fly to be tied must be thick. And it is just as much an error to try to fashion a long-bodied May fly on a short-shanked hook. The selection of the right hook for the fly to be made is one of the first steps toward successful fly-making.

SHAPE

The *Shape* of the hook is the index to the hook pattern. While this term takes into consideration the hook as a whole, it refers more particularly to the return bend from the shank to the barb. The appearance of hooks varies in accordance with the acuteness of this bend. The return bend can be squarish, parabolic or round. Each type of bend has its own respective values, and, when used as a basis for forming the fly most suited to it, will show to best advantage. Shapes most generally used by fly-dressers are the *model perfect, sproat, limerick, sneck, O'Shaughnessy, aberdeen, viking, in-turn* (sometimes called "beak") and the *centripetal*. It should be mentioned here that the term "bend" is sometimes erroneously construed to mean "shape" but, since the bend of a hook really indicates the offset given laterally to the point and barb, the term "shape" has been used here to avoid confusion. Shape does not denote gape, shank length or any other characteristic.

The *Model Perfect* has a common radius from the shank to the origin of the spear and is sometimes known as the round bend. It is one of the best all-purpose shapes in the fly-fishing business and is admirably suited to both dry and wet flies.

The *Sproat* is slightly parabolic in shape but otherwise similar to the *model perfect*. This shape is usually associated with wet flies.

The *Limerick* is the most parabolic in shape of all the hooks, describing an acute angle at the origin of the spear which makes it appear longer than it really is. This shape makes slightly curved bodies possible, a very desirable feature in nymphs and wet flies.

The *O'Shaughnessy* is more parabolic in shape than the *sproat* and has a slight outward swell at the origin of the spear. This is favored for heavy wet flies and is used extensively in salmon and bass-fly types.

The *Aberdeen* is slightly squarish in comparison with the *model perfect* but does not have the severe angularity of the *sneck* described in the next paragraph. This shape is often used in the construction of nymphs, especially the small, light-weight styles, since the entire shank, which is straight, can be used to advantage.

The *Sneck* is square in shape with rounded corners and, because of its near right-

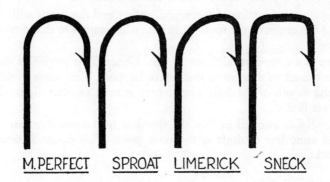

M. PERFECT SPROAT LIMERICK SNECK

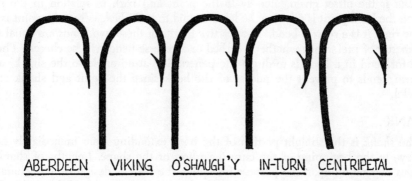

ABERDEEN VIKING O'SHAUGH'Y IN-TURN CENTRIPETAL

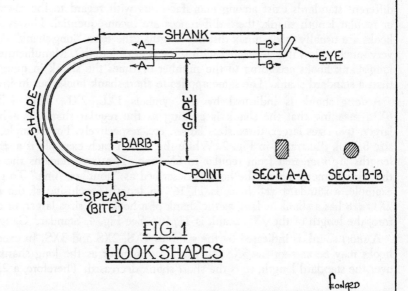

FIG. 1
HOOK SHAPES

LEONARD

angle bends, has a tendency to fracture easily. This was once a standard model in fly-dressing, but today is found in very few well-made flies.

The *Viking* is a combination of the *model perfect* and the *sproat* with a slight additional bend at the origin of the spear. It is somewhat similar to the *in-turn* type but is not so extreme.

The *In-turn* is a comparatively new design. Generally it resembles the *O'Shaughnessy* but has the added feature of the curved-in spear. This tends to drive the point deeper into the mouth of the fish. The *in-turn* is most successfully used in the construction of wet flies.

The *Centripetal* is unusual in that the shank is bent inwardly, putting the leader or line in the same line of draft as the hook point. This design is usually featured in snelled hooks.

BEND

Bend is the offset given laterally to the point and barb in relation to the shank. When the hook point is offset to the left it is said to be *kirbed*. When the point is offset to the right it is a *reverse* bend. The relative merits of these two bends are equal and it is a matter of preference whether a kirbed or a reverse bend will be chosen. The purpose for bend in a hook is to direct the penetration at an angle to the shank, which, in turn, tends to prevent the release of the hook since the point and shank are not parallel.

SHANK

The *shank* is the straight portion of the hook extending from immediately behind the eye to the beginning of the curved portion or the shape. Lengths of shanks are various depending upon the purpose for which the hook is designed. The characteristics and the size of the fly to be tied largely determine the length of the shank. Shank lengths can be divided roughly into three classes—regular, short and long. While different standards exist among manufacturers with regard to the so-called standard or regular length shank, these differences are inconsequential. However, long-shank hooks are usually made in six distinct lengths (the term "long-shank" does not mean very much unless it is associated with some unit of length). Manufacturers label their long-shank hooks according to the number of times the shank in question is longer than a standard shank. The same applies to short-shank hooks but in inverse order.

A *long* shank is indicated by the symbols 1XL, 2XL, 3XL, 4XL, 5XL and 6XL, meaning that the shank is as long as the regular shank of a hook one size larger, two sizes larger, three sizes larger, etc. respectively. For example, consider the size 8 hook illustrated in Fig. 2. While the size in each example is a #8, the shank lengths are increased from regular to 6X long. The gape remains the same as does the wire diameter unless the hook is described as "stout" or "fine." To give a specific example, a standard #8 hook is 11/16" in length (exclusive of the eye) while a 2XL #8 has a shank as long as the shank of a hook two sizes larger, or a #6. Therefore, the length of the 2XL shank is 13/16". See Fig. 4, Standard Gauge.

A *short* shank is indicated by the symbols 1XS, 2XS and 3XS. In exceptional cases hooks may be as short as 5XS. In the same manner as the long shank is increased over the standard length, so is the short shank decreased. Therefore, a 2XS #8 has a

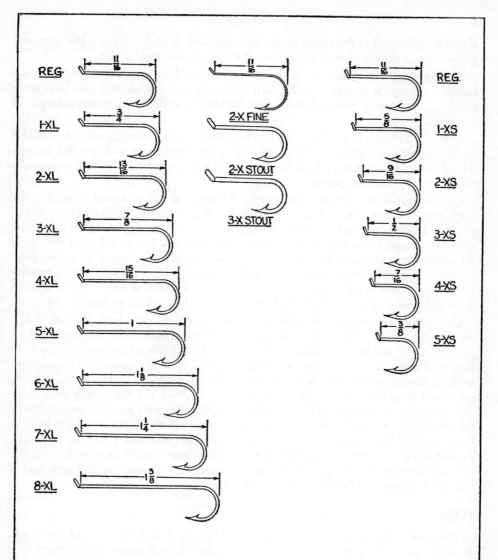

REG.

1-XL

2-XL

3-XL

4-XL

5-XL

6-XL

7-XL

8-XL

2-X FINE

2-X STOUT

3-X STOUT

REG.

1-XS

2-XS

3-XS

4-XS

5-XS

FIG. 2
SIZE VARIATION SHOWING GAUGE
& LENGTH COMBINATIONS
(TYPICAL HOOK, SIZE 8)

LEONARD

shank length equal to the shank length of a standard #10. Here again the gape and wire diameter do not change but remain the same as the regular size.

The *hump* shank is unusual in that there is a bend in the shank which forms a hump. This type is especially useful in the manufacture of cork-body bass bugs since the hump permits a greater bearing area inside the cork and prevents rotation of the body.

The *sliced* shank is fundamentally a bait hook style, although certain shoulder hackle flies without bodies have been dressed on the sliced shank with reputed success. The slices project outwardly from the shank and serve as extra barbs, thus supposedly increasing the hooking power.

Cross-section is the term used to describe the shape of the wire used in making the hook, that is, whether it is round or rectangular, fine or stout. Once again the letter X is suffixed to the numeral indicating the number of times the wire is larger or smaller than the standard size. Generally hooks ranging from 2X fine to 2X stout will serve for nearly every purpose; however, some hooks of extremely heavy cross-section have been developed for heavy salmon and steelhead fishing where it is sometimes necessary to use smaller flies which must still have weight enough to sink and strength to withstand the power of large fish. Such hooks are graded in caliber as large as 4X stout.

Cross-section has much to do with the holding qualities of any hook. A hook of fine wire in the jaw of a fish with a soft mouth is very apt to tear free, while a hook of stout diameter will be difficult to set in the mouth of a fish whose jaws are hard. In nearly all cases the cross-section of a hook is round with the exception of some continental European types which are of rectangular cross-section. Large salt-water hooks are round from the eye to a point a short distance down the shank, but from there the remainder of the hook is flat forged and rectangular with rounded corners. Such construction is required to allow for the utmost strength at the point and the barb. A hook made of fine, round wire with a sliced, narrow barb will penetrate the tough cartilage in the mouths of heavy fish but will fail at some crucial moment because the distance between the spear and the barb is necessarily shallow in this type and a possible backing out of the barb is not unlikely.

GAPE

The *gape* is the distance between the point of the hook and the inside of the shank. In some cases a deep penetration is necessary, especially if the mouth of the fish is excessively fleshy. A wide gape will provide this deep penetration and in addition tend to counterbalance the larger dry flies better than a standard gape will. So-called "wide-gape" hooks have been developed recently, but without limitations a short-shank style of correct size will produce the same result. A hook with standard gape is usually satisfactory for nearly every kind of fishing condition.

EYE

The *eye* of the hook is the ring at the end of the shank. Strange as it may seem, all hooks were eyeless or had straight shanks until shortly before 1880 when the eyed hook was developed. Fly-dressers should pay strict attention to the eyes on the hooks they purchase. Imperfectly formed ends, chips, incomplete closures, and brazing or bronzing that closes the eye, leave a hook useless. No leader, regardless of how well it is tied, will withstand the pressure it should if it is tied over a sharp edge. Eyes are turned up or down or are straight, depending on the type of fly to be tied and the use to which it will be put. Abbreviations generally used to describe the types of eyes are given. (See Fig. 3, Hook Parts.)

Turned-up eye (TUE) is that type of hook having the eye bent upward and above the shank. This type is not so easy to dress flies on unless the fly-dresser has had wide experience in handling materials.

Turned-down eye (TDE) is perhaps the most popular hook for fly-dressing. It permits of maximum clearance for finishing the head of the fly.

Ringed (R) is that type on which the eye is straight and perpendicular to the shape. This type is used for attaching to spinners.

Eyed (E) is that type on which the eye is parallel with the shape. Its purpose is the same as the ringed hook.

Loop-eyed (LE) is the type usually featured in connection with salmon and steelhead flies mainly because it has no sharp edges to fray or cut through the leader knot. The wire is tapered to a narrow edge and bent back parallel to the shank, thus enabling the fly-dresser to cover completely the end of the wire and still leave room for a smooth, tapered and unobstructed head.

Ball-eyed hooks are made of wire having the same diameter throughout and are used for all kinds of wet flies and streamers.

Taper-eyed hooks are mode of wire having a finer diameter at the eye section thus reducing the weight and bulk of the fly at the head. Dry flies dressed on taper-eyed hooks are definitely superior.

Most hooks are manufactured in both taper and ball-eye styles.

ENDS

Hooks without eyes have either plain shanks or shaped ends and are snelled or otherwise wound to leaders and lines. Eyeless hooks are used less each season, although certain, very special kinds of terminal tackle require hooks without eyes. Discounting the archaic types of eyeless bait-hooks which are seldom used, the following shanks and ends are most useful in the construction of eyeless flies and other special tackle.

The *plain* shank and end has no markings or special shape. The snell is wrapped to the shank with winding silk. This is a low-cost snelled hook and is not recommended since only limited adhesion is possible between the windings and the hook.

The *tapered* shank is like the plain shank in that it has no markings, but it is tapered to a finer gauge toward the end. This type is sometimes used in connection with extremely fine snelled tackle.

The *marked* shank is scored at intervals to increase the adhesion between the snell and the hook. This type of shank may be obtained either plain or tapered.

The *flatted* and the *knobbed* types of shank are not useful to the fly-dresser, and therefore need not be discussed here.

The *needle-eye* shank is used principally for the purpose of fishing a minnow. The shank is run through the minnow and the needle eye is then coupled to a flexible snap. This type is most often found on spinner combinations.

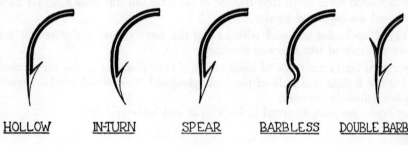

BALL **TAPER** **EYE** **RING** **LOOP** **MARKED** **TAPERED**
UP OR DOWN BEND VERTICAL HORIZONTAL UP OR DWN. & PLAIN & STRAIGHT

EYES ENDS

HOLLOW   IN-TURN   SPEAR   BARBLESS   DOUBLE BARB

POINTS

OFFSET   STRAIGHT

BENDS

FIG. 3
HOOK PARTS

LEONARD

POINTS

The *point* is the extreme forward end of the barb or the part that first contacts the mouth of the fish. The point of a hook is of utmost importance. Many a good fish has been lost because the hook point failed to penetrate properly. High-grade hooks are hollow-ground and their points needle-sharp. Low-grade hooks have inferior points and should be used only when better grades are not available.

The *spear point* is a machine-made point and does not have the curved barb characteristic of high-grade hooks. Fig 3 illustrates the difference between points. Note especially how the barb in the case of the spear point is flat. Even present-day production methods cannot produce uniformity among hook points, and for this reason the spear point is a variable type. Excess thickness of stock at the point, or where penetration begins, is not desirable. Consider the use of extremely fine leaders and the attendant care with which the hook must be set, and the importance of sharp, well-made points needs little if any explanation.

The *hollow point* or *hollow-ground* point is the finest grade for any fly-hook. This point is hand-worked after it leaves the shaping machine and is exceptionally keen and curved at the barb. This insures maximum penetration with the least force.

The *needle point* is made needle-sharp by a machine process which remained a family secret in England for many years. Although the point is excellent the small, sliced barb, which is characteristic of this type, is too shallow to use with confidence.

The *claw* or *beak point* is a hollow-ground point having the added feature of an inward-curving barb. This reduces the gape slightly but tends to drive the hook deeper. It is generally found on hooks with an offset.

The *knife-edge* and *filed points* are somewhat diamond-shaped in cross-section, having sharp cutting edges top and bottom. These points are generally found on hooks used for salt-water game fish having hard, cartilaginous mouths.

BARB

The *barb* tends to prevent the backing out of the hook when a fish is on. Effectiveness depends upon the relative height of the barb, although an abnormally high barb will offer added resistance at the time of striking.

The *double barb* was an English development of years ago and has proved its worth with heavy salmon. The second barb is cut slightly to the rear of and opposite to the conventional barb, and is very useful when playing hard-fighting, leaping fish. Naturally, fine gut cannot be used with hooks which are double-barbed since it requires appreciable force to strike both barbs home.

Another type is the *barbless* hook which was designed to make the release of fish as easy and harmless as possible. The spear has no barb affixed but is crooked at that place where the barb appears in conventional hooks. This is a rather unsafe type if one is fishing "for keeps" but is excellent when angling in protected waters where sport and not meat is the aim.

SPEAR

The *spear* is the return bend of the hook. Some spears are longer or shorter than standard depending upon the gape and the point. Certain salmon trolling hooks and certain heavy, salt-water hooks have comparatively long spears, the purpose being to

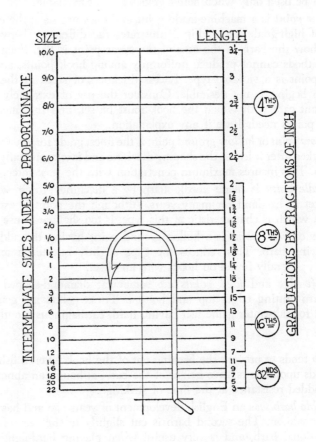

SIZE

LENGTH

INTERMEDIATE SIZES UNDER 4 PROPORTIONATE

GRADUATIONS BY FRACTIONS OF INCH

SIZE	LENGTH	
10/0	3¼	
9/0	3	
8/0	2¾	4THS =
7/0	2½	
6/0	2¼	
5/0	2	
4/0	2⅛	
3/0	1¾	
2/0	1⅝	
1/0	1½	8THS =
1½	1⅜	
1	1¼	
2	1⅛	
3	1	
4	15	
6	13	
8	11	16THS =
10	9	
12	7	
14	11	
16	9	
18	7	32NDS =
20	5	
22	3	

FIG. 4
STANDARD GAUGE FOR HOOKS

Leonard

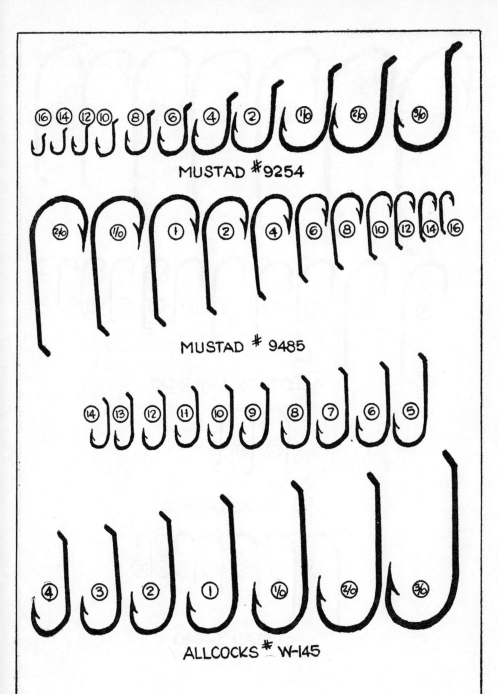

MUSTAD #9254

MUSTAD # 9485

ALLCOCKS * W-145

FIG. 5
HOOK DESIGNS (I)

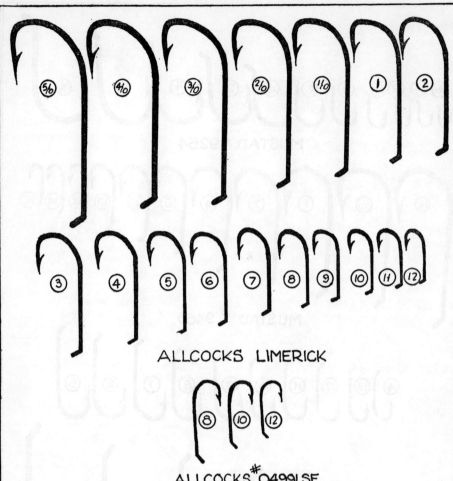

ALLCOCKS LIMERICK

ALLCOCKS # 04991 SF

MUSTAD # 94840

FIG. 5-A
HOOK DESIGNS (II)

Leonard.

penetrate the entire jaw thickness of the fish. Long spears usually feature long points which easily penetrate tough cartilage.

FINISH

There are several hook finishes and these should be understood insofar as their rust-resisting qualities are concerned. If you take this lightly, try using your regular bronze-finish hooks in brackish or salt waters. A good streamer or bucktail costs most of one dollar or even more and it is a sad sight to see an otherwise unharmed lure covered with rust and stains after being used in salt water only because the hook was not suited to such fishing. Generally speaking, bronze hooks are best for fresh water and tinned hooks are best for salt water. High-priced finishes are many and various and if you are willing to invest in expensive hooks you will derive longer service for the added cost. The following finishes are given as examples. The letters (F) and (S) signify the adaptability of each to fresh or salt water or both.

JAPANNED (F) & (S). This is a lacquer finish of blue-black often used on salmonfly hooks. Rust resisting qualities are good.

BRONZED (F). This finish is standard for fresh-water hooks but will not last in salt water.

TINNED (F) & (S). While this finish is usually associated with salt-water hooks it is applicable to any water conditions. Resists rust indefinitely even in the briniest of water.

BLUED (F). This is a heat- and chemically-treated finish best suited to fresh and mildly brackish waters such as tidal rivers in which the salt content is relatively low.

BRIGHT (F). Here again is a finish that will withstand a moderate amount of salinity. It has been used sucessfully on salmon hooks.

NICKEL (F) & (S). This is the finest of all the salt-water hook finishes and will resist deterioration better than any finish so far produced. Heavy-duty hooks are nickel-plated and are inferior only to the solid nickel-alloy and chrome-base hooks.

GOLD PLATE (F) & (S). Gold-plated hooks are used in only the most expensive salmon and steelhead fancy wet flies. The rust-resisting qualities are excellent although discoloration will set in after extensive usage.

It can be seen that in hook design the appointments and finish are almost limitless. Still there is room for improvement. Every angler has wished to discover a hook that would incorporate all the features he believes are ideal. With the appearance each year of new materials in the manufacture of hooks, it is reasonable to expect entirely different designs in the near future. Perhaps plastics, too, may figure in the hook of the future. And it is not unthinkable that the angler may be able to make his own hooks someday. However, until such time, he can select his hooks with more precision, whatever the purpose, whether it be snelling flies, or arranging the simplest of tackle, if he will consider the characteristics of the fish he intends to catch and the nature of the water in which that fish is found.

More fishermen each year are turning to salt-water fly-fishing and usually learn in a very short time that hooks for weakfish must be comparatively broad to prevent tearing through the soft tissues in the mouths of these fish.

Conversely, such fish as the small mouth bass or the wall-eyed pike of fresh waters have fairly hard mouths, and ordinary or even fine-wire hooks can be used with confidence.

For fish with soft mouths use a hook with a deep barb and of stout diameter preferably flatted laterally. If the mouths are also large use a wide-gape hook of the same qualities.

For fish with hard mouths use a hook with an extremely sharp point and a moderately deep barb. The diameter need not be stout. Penetration rather than tenacity is important here.

Some fish are phenomenally quick in striking. Hooks with offset bends and short shanks are ideally suited to this condition.

The following table illustrates proper and customary selection of hooks for all practical fly purposes. This table is based on the characteristics of the fish to be caught, with the usual and some alternate water conditions in which this fish is to be found,

HOOKS FOR FLY DESIGN

(Only bend, shank, eye and weight are shown since finish, shape, etc. are optional.)

PURPOSE & USE	BEND	SHANK	WEIGHT
Dry Fly-Standard	Straight	Std.	Std.
Dry Fly-Light Weight	Straight	1X Fine	Light
May Fly	Straight	2XL	Std.
Fan Wing	Straight	2XL or Std.	Std.
Spent Wing	Straight	1X Fine	Light
Hair Wing	Kirbed	Std.	Std.
Variant	Straight	Std.	Std.
Palmer	Kirbed	Std.	Std.
Bivisible	Kirbed	Std.	Std.
Spider	Kirbed	2XS	Std.
Translucent Drake and May	Kirbed	Std.	Std.
Salmon Dry Fly	Straight	Std.	Std.
Std. Wet Fly & Nymph	Straight	Std.	Std.
Fast Water Wet Fly	Kirbed	2X Stout	Heavy
2X Short Steelhead	Kirbed	2XS	Std.
Featherwt. Streamer	Straight	6XL size 10 } 12 }	Std.
Short Shank Streamer	Kirbed	Std.	Std.
Streamers & Bucktails	Either	2XL - 6XL	Std.
Regular Salmon Wet	Either	Std.	Std.
Low-water Salmon Wet	Straight	1X Fine	Light
Spring Salmon Wet	Kirbed	2XL Stout	Heavy
Spinner Fly	Kirbed	Std.	Std.
Ball Head Minnow, Etc.	Kirbed	3XL	Std.
Hair Bug	Kirbed	As required	Std.
Cork Body Bug	Kirbed	Humped	Std.

EYE	REMARKS
TU or TD Taper	For fast water & quick strikes, kirbed bend.
TU or TD Taper	Usually restricted to slow water & delicate tackle.
TD Taper	If standard wing, taper eye; if fan wing, ball eye.
TD Taper	If large fan wings, ball eye.
TU or TD Taper	Usually restricted to slow water & delicate tackle.
TD Taper	Usually for fast water.
TU or TD Taper	If to be used over fast water, kirbed bend.
TU or TD Taper	Kirbed bend especially for full hackle.
TU or TD Taper	Same as for Palmer.
TU Taper	TU eye gives more clearance.
TD Taper	With long, upturned body.
Loop Eye	Kirbed bend if required.
TU or TD Ball	
TU or TD Ball	Required in turbulent water to sink rapidly.
TU or TD Ball	TU preferred.
TD Ball	Restricted to light tackle and placid water.
TD Ball	
TD Ball	
TU Loop	
TU Loop	Restricted to low water conditions.
TU or TD Ball	For turbulent water & early spring conditions.
Ringed	
Ringed	
TD or Ringed	
TD or Ringed	

Chapter Two

TOOLS OF THE TRADE

There are fundamentally very few tools the fly-dresser needs despite the claims made for the many new gadgets sold in recent years that they are absolutely necessary to the trade. The essential tools are the vise, hackle pliers, scissors, bobbin, whip-finisher and dubbing needle. With these tools all kinds of flies from the tiniest midge to the largest salmon fly can be made with facility. Only the degree of skill of the person making them will determine how nearly perfect the flies will be. Some of the latest developments in tools for fly-making are useful to a certain extent but it is doubtful whether they are responsible in themselves for producing better flies. Good flies are the product of practiced fingers, correct materials and a sense of balance on the part of the fly-dresser. The scarcity of materials during the war years fostered the use of very common feathers, and otherwise disproved the theory that only imported and even exotic plumage should be used in fly construction. Thus, some very excellent patterns were originated and hackled with the neck feathers from the common barnyard rooster, evincing the value of skill and resourcefulness over materials.

Many additional tools are available and, while they may be useful for remote conditions, they are not at all essential. Good fly-dressing results from a minimum of good tools, well-chosen, suitable materials, patience, but most of all, practical "know-how," the overriding importance of which this book stresses throughout.

THE VISE

The fly vise serves one basic purpose: to hold the hook firmly allowing the fly-dresser adequate space to work in and the use of both hands. There are a variety of styles on the market, each supposedly possessing superior qualities and advantages because of added accessories such as mirrors, swivel-joint connections and material holders or clips. These attachments are attractive particularly to the beginner but in most cases they prove awkward to manipulate. It is suggested that the beginner avoid using such vises at least until he has mastered the proper use of the simple vise which, actually, is the best for all conditions.

Some vises feature a chuck shank which is similar to the chuck used to hold a drill. This type puts pressure on the hook by means of a threaded section controlled by a cam-lever or knob which squeezes the jaws shut. It is adaptable to either fine or coarse hooks, holding both firmly. This vise is very popular and requires little mechanical attention.

16

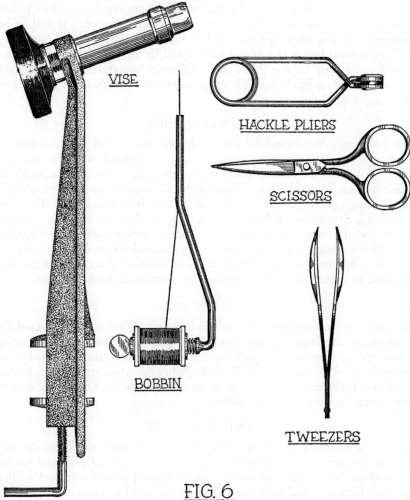

WHIP FINISHER

DUBBING NEEDLE

VISE

HACKLE PLIERS

SCISSORS

BOBBIN

TWEEZERS

FIG. 6
TOOLS OF THE TRADE

A second type is the side-lever vise featuring a side lock operated by a lever. This type is not so adaptable to the larger hooks and the jaws have a tendency to spring if forced to receive too large a hook. However, if small and medium hooks are used, this vise will perform satisfactorily for years.

Another vise in popular usage is the wing-nut type. This is a very simple mechanism consisting of a highly tempered steel rod usually round in shape and tapered, with a narrow saw cut running through the center of the rod for a short distance forming jaws. A wing-nut is threaded through the two jaws approximately one and one-quarter inches from the tips and squeezes shut or opens the jaws as required. Here again the springing of the tips will occur if too much pressure is applied on the wing-nut or if hooks too large are forced into the opening.

Most vises if used properly are satisfactory. If you intend to tie flies of the average sizes, one good vise will serve nicely. If, however, your requirements include everything from size 20 gnats up to huge salmon and striper streamers, it will be to your advantage to use two vises, one for the fine work and the other for the heavy-duty work. Even a small bench vise of the variety sold in the majority of the chain stores will prove satisfactory for the heavy work. Of main importance is the ability of the vise to hold the hook firmly while leaving maximum clearance around the hook for free manipulation of the fingers.

HACKLE PLIERS

Some fly-dressers discontinue the use of this item after a while because their fingers, with practice, develop a sensitivity that cannot be replaced with the most delicate of tools. These pliers are merely spring forceps fastened to the tip of a hackle feather to permit the maximum number of turns of hackle around the fly body while, at the same time, serving as an anchor to keep the hackle from unwinding. Their one disadvantage is their tendency to break the hackle stem when the hackle is being wound. Pliers are useful to begin with but, as soon as the dresser is capable of winding the hackle with his fingers, the pliers should be eliminated except in cases where several hackles are to be wound on at different times. In selecting pliers, be sure that the jaws are rounded to prevent as much as possible the fracture of the hackle stem.

SCISSORS

Two sizes of scissors are needed, small and medium. The small size is used for fine, close trimming, the large size for cutting and preparing materials of coarse texture and dimensions. Manicure or pedicure scissors with the usual crescent curve are exceptionally good for the close work. Triangle-headed wire-cutters are unbeatable for cutting heavy quills and roughly shaping the coarse materials. Once these cutters have become sprung, however, they are useless.

DUBBING NEEDLE

This tool is necessary for many operations—among them, the separation of wing quill fibers preparatory to their being fastened to the hook, picking out finished fur bodies to make them rough and fuzzy, and uncovering wound-over hackle. This tool is best made from odds and ends found in every home. Usually there is a small section of fly-rod tip among the scraps every fisherman treasures. This is ideal for making the dubbing needle. First, whip silk thread at one end of the tip, which has been tapered with a razor blade, then thoroughly cover the windings with lacquer. When this is dry insert the pointed end of the needle to be used into this tapered end. Remove the needle, then drive the head of the needle into the hole already formed, leaving at least one inch of the pointed end protruding. If the broken fly-rod tip is not available, use a meat skewer or the stem of an "all-day-sucker" trimmed to a blunt point. A very handy addition to this tool is to equip the other end with a pin shaped like the end of a botton hook. This can be used to great advantage to hold the hackle back when finishing the head of the fly. A heavier type of dubbing needle for larger work is readily made from a very small screw driver (preferably the kind with a plastic handle) which has been ground to a point.

THE BOBBIN

Although the bobbin is not absolutely necessary it is very useful especially from the standpoint of economy. Several kinds are on the market and one is as good as another provided it has adjustable spring tension. The purpose of this device is to hold the silk working thread taut but allow it to be pulled from the spool as required. Some types feature a light-weight guide-arm which encases the thread. With care, a spool of thread can be inserted into the bobbin and used to the last inch without waste. This of course depends upon the spring tension. A test or two will indicate the correct setting so that any needed tension can be applied as required by any particular fly or condition.

WHIP-FINISHER

The whip-finisher is a most necessary piece of equipment. Any good fly is finished with a whipped head which really prolongs the life of a fly. If there is another short piece of fly-rod tip remaining after the dubbing needle has been made, prepare it in a similar manner by tapering with a razor blade. Wax a section of strong—but not coarse—silk thread and loop it so the two ends straddle the tapered end of the tip. Whip these ends and then lacquer them. Really expert and durable flies cannot be made unless the heads are whipped, thus it is a good policy to make a whip-finisher and learn to use it. Commercially produced metal whip-finishers are offered to the trade but they have the disadvantage of being a little difficult to manipulate. The fine wire often cuts the finest size of working silk and sometimes leaves excess slack around the eye.

Chapter Three

MATERIALS

It would require an entire volume devoted to materials alone to list, classify and grade all of the feathers, wools, furs, flosses, hairs, tinsels, etc. that are used throughout the world in the manufacture of fishing flies. It is the exceptional bird or animal that does not contribute at least a whisker or two to be used in some fly or streamer. From the south pole to the Arctic, on every continent, creatures are hunted for their skins and feathers: gorgeous birds with fabulously long tails, baboons, seals, polar bears, Siberian wolves, leopards, muskrats and Chinese goats, to name but few. The list is unbelievably long and confusing. Why must a certain pattern of fly be tied with three whiskers from the rump of an almost extinct bird or the fringe from the ear of some hideous, sacred dog? Frankly, it is not necessary at all. Years ago, when the art of fly-dressing was safeguarded as a family secret, flies were looked upon as possessing certain mysterious qualities, and the slightest deviation from the strict precedents of that day was nothing short of sacrilege on the part of the fly-maker. It is recorded in old English writings that one fly-dresser went completely mad trying to make a fly to please his client.

Charles Cotton, an English ancient and authority on fly-fishing in his time, wrote at length about the difficulty in obtaining the body material to make the Fiery Brown, which he called the Bright Brown. Cotton wrote of this fly as follows: "the dubbing for which is to be had out of the skinner's lime-pits, and of the hair of an abortive calf, of which the lime will turn to be so bright as to shine like gold," and, "then a brown that looks red in the hand, and yellow betwixt your eye and the sun." It is easily understood why the fly-dressers of that day were plagued with refinements of detail to the extent of becoming physically and mentally ill.

Fortunately fly design has reached more reasonable levels in recent years. No longer is "genuineness of materials" esteemed as the single criterion by which a fly will be judged. Perhaps, according to the original pattern for making a particular fly, plumage from a rare bird was necessary; however, with the technique developed in present-day methods for dyeing materials, many substitute feathers and hairs can be used quite satisfactorily. In some instances, it seems almost a waste of money to purchase the genuine materials, since the word "genuine" usually applies to some feather that is so rare as to make it almost unobtainable, or, in any case, very expensive. Of course if texture, durability or certain floating qualities are found only in the genuine feather, no substitute should be used unless it possesses like qualities. Fly-fanciers are often

20

unreasonable about details of no real importance, and willingly pay exorbitant prices for rare feathers not fundamentally different from several common ones.

All material can be grouped roughly into three classifications: those which are translucent, those which are opaque, and those which reflect light. The following lists are arranged as far as practical with these criteria in mind.

WORKING SILK

Working silk is the thread used to fasten all parts of a fly to the hook. The correct size of thread is important. If the diameter is too fine the silk will break from the slightest pressure; if too coarse it will cause unnecessary bulk making it difficult to form tapered, clean-cut heads. Use the lightest possible working silk at all times. The regular commercial threads come in six sizes.

6-0................special extra fine for delicate, expert work.
4-0................extra fine for hooks size 18 to 22 short shank.
3-0................fine size for hooks number 10 through 16.
2-0................medium fine for hooks size 4 through 8.
A................medium for hooks size 2-0 through 2.
D................heavy for sizes larger than 2-0.

WAX

Wax for fly-making is obtainable in two grades: soft and hard. It is used to add strength and adhesion to the working silk. It is not intended to be used on feathers or hair or for dressing up the fly after it has been made.

HACKLE

Hackle is available from various birds and has two main purposes: to support a dry fly on the water surface, and to impart the semblance of leg action to a wet fly. Almost every kind of bird plumage has been or can be used for hackle. Gamecock and rooster neck hackles are used in the construction of dry flies while hen hackles, bird plumage of many kinds and animal hair are used in the construction of wet flies. Dry-fly hackle should be glossy and resilient and somewhat on the bristly side. Although a hackle feather may contain many fibers it is not necessarily ideal for dry flies. The stiffness of each individual fiber will determine this. Thickness, absorption and strength are required of wet-fly hackles. Saddle hackles are excellent for making wings on streamer flies and the slim, stiffer ones are suitable for some types of dry flies.

The natural colors of gamecock and hen hackle are various among the individual birds, therefore the colors of the hackles can be classified only roughly into two groups: natural solid colors, and natural variegated colors.

THE NATURAL SOLID COLORS

Black: This is not a jet black and has a silver cast to the dull side. Blue Dun: This is a blue-gray color of variable hue from the Andalusian (rare). Brassy Dun: One of several of the Andalusian variations; blue dun with a brassy tinge. Brown: This color includes several shades from dark ginger to dark brown. Cream: This is slightly variable, running from ivory white to pale buff. Dun: Much disagreement exists as regards the true color of dun. The original color consisted of blue-gray with a faint brownish cast, but recent interpretations have eliminated the brown. Most authorities agree on the soft blue-gray shade. *Ginger*: This is another color having variations, but is considered in the terms "light" and "dark" which are correctly descriptive. Light ginger is somewhat darker than cream while dark ginger is between light ginger and brown. *Honey*: Very little difference exists between ginger and honey coloration so far as hackles are concerned and it requires an experienced fly man to detect the very slight bluish tinge in honey hackle. *Mahogany*: This is the true dark red-brown color of the natural wood. *Red*: Red hackle is not crimson or scarlet but is really reddish brown, the color of a Rhode Island Red chicken from which the hackle is taken. *Rusty Dun*: This is another variation of blue dun with a reddish cast. *White*: White hackle is white, and that is all that can be said about it.

THE NATURAL VARIEGATED COLORS

Badger or *Gray List*: This is a whitish or pale-gray feather having a black stripe down the center. *Coch-y-bondhu*: This is similar to the badger but is brown with black tips and has a black stripe down the center. *Furnace*: Furnace hackle has no black tips but is otherwise the same as Coch-y-bondhu. *Grizzly*: This is the hackle from the neck of the Plymouth Rock rooster and is composed of alternately dark-gray and pale-gray bars. *Ginger-Grizzly*: This is a banded hackle consisting of alternately light gray and ginger bands. *Honey-Dun*: Another variation of the badger, having a black center along the stem of the feather and honey tips. *Red-Grizzly* or *Cree*: This is the product of cross-breeding. The feather is alternately red-brown and gray barred. *Speckled Bavarian*: This hackle is either white or ginger with black speckles. *Variant-Grizzly*: Very little difference exists between the variant-grizzly and the red-grizzly. The former is lightly spotted with red-brown in addition to being banded.

There are many kinds of body plumage suitable for wet-fly hackle. Such plumage has been featured in European wet flies for centuries. It is not suitable for dry flies because it is absorbent and must be applied to the hook in a slanting or nearly horizontal position. This sort of hackle is classed as "body hackle" and is taken from birds which are usually speckled or mottled. Some animal hair is used in the same manner— steelhead flies, especially, are often dressed with deer-hair hackle.

The body and hair hackles are: *Badger Hair*; black spots on gray. *Coot*; iron blue dun. *Crow*; near black. *Deer Hair*; mostly gray and brown. *Duck Breast*; white to black with many solid and mottled variations of brown, gray, etc. *Ground-hog Hair*; brownish-black, dark-gray spots on light gray. *Grouse*; mottled brown-gray with some dark brown and black bars. *Guinea*; white polka-dot on pale gray to jet black. *Partridge*; gray, brown, speckled and cinnamon. *Peacock Body Plumage*; brilliant metallic green, yellowish-blue, and blue. *Pheasant Breast*; metallic blue, red, green, brown and mottled brown.

BODY MATERIALS

Nearly every substance that can be wound on the shank of a hook has been used at one time or another for forming the body of a fly. The range is limitless. However, because it is needless to describe every available material, only those materials of practical value are considered here. If a fly body possesses the proper qualities of color and dimension, it can be said that the correct material was used to make it. Whether the material used to make the body has come from a very special bird means nothing except to the purist who is more concerned with the brand and cost than the real quality. The following body materials are described without notes as to their relative merits since certain patterns require these materials whether they are most suited or not.

SILK FLOSS

This is real silk and is usually single or double strand. If carefully handled it makes neat, tapered bodies. The hands should be clean and dry when handling this material; perspiration or gum from other materials will soil the floss. Rayons and some plastics are available, the latter being superb but a trifle more difficult to handle. Manufacturers have a tendency to list their floss with special names for the colors. However, in nearly all cases the colors are reasonably comparable with standard colors, whether they are identified as the color of a particular insect, a number, or merely plain olive, yellow or cream. If you do not know definitely what colors you need, it is advisable to buy an assortment of floss, which is inexpensive, select the piece nearest to the color you want, then order a sufficient amount of it. Otherwise you might become discouraged trying to locate the proper green, yellow or blue-dun.

CHENILLE

This material is round and fuzzy. Silk is the only acceptable material for chenille since it will retain its shape and appearance while other materials such as cotton will not. It is used for bodies of thick, pulpy shape of one color or alternate colors, and for egg sacs on the tips of the bodies of dry and wet flies. Two kinds are popular: sparse for dry flies, and thick for wet flies. The sparse type is especially good for making egg sacs since it is of light weight and has a minimum of absorption. The diameters or sizes of chenille are shown opposite the fly sizes for which they are most appropriate: *Fine*: for sizes 10 to 20. *Medium*: for sizes 2 to 8. *Large*: for sizes 1-0 to 1. *Extra large*: for sizes 1-0 and larger.

TINSEL

Tinsel is made in several finishes: gold, silver, red, copper and blue-green. It is used to rib or form whole bodies, depending, of course, upon the type and pattern of the fly. Some manufacturers claim their tinsels are tarnish-proof, but this is a matter of opinion. All tinsel will discolor after prolonged use, so do not expect the impossible. In addition to the five colors there are eight different types of finishes, although few fly-dressers are required to have all of them unless they are making flies for use from coast to coast. All of the following types are not supplied in every one of the colors already listed. Gold or silver can be obtained in all shapes. The types are shown with the use for which each is best adapted: *Wire*: for ribbing quill body dry flies. *Fine, flat*: for ribbing size 18 to 10. *Medium, flat*: for ribbing size 8 to 2. *Large, flat*: for ribbing size 1 and larger. *Flat, embossed*: for ribbing medium to large salmon and steelhead flies. *Oval, embossed*: for ribbing medium to large flies and streamers. *Round, thread core*: for ribbing small flies. *Three-Strand Twist*: for ribbing salmon flies. In addition to body ribbing, these tinsels can be used to form whole bodies, with the exception of the wire type which is too small for such a purpose.

FUR DUBBING

Nearly all animal skins have some fur which can be made into dubbing. Many animals having long hair are covered with a fine fur close to the skin. A fox tail, for example, contains very rich fur located at the base of the hair. Practically all of the water-frequenting animals, such as the muskrat, have excellent fur for fly bodies. Some fur is more or less translucent, which is sometimes desirable; however, seal, otter, polar bear, and marten furs are the most satisfactory when translucency is needed. Fur is easily dyed and possesses a brilliancy second to none. The standard furs used in the trade are: *Arctic fox*: white, for white to pale gray bodies. *Badger*: cream to pale buff, for light Cahill. *Beaver*: brown. *Capras*, alias *Chinese Goat*: white. *Chinese mole*: light cream for light Cahill. *Leopard*: cream to buff. *Lynx*: various, from white to black. *Marten*: translucent, cream. *Mink*: brown. *Mole* (brown): rich brown. *Mole* (gray): dark bluish-gray. *Muskrat*: dark bluish-gray. *Opossum*: cream to buff. *Otter*: cream, translucent. *Polar bear*: glassy white to cream. *Pribylof seal*: translucent, medium brown. *Rabbit*: various from white to black. *Red fox* (dark): brown and gray. *Red fox* (light): light tan and gray. *Rocky Mt. Goat*: pure white. *Seal*: translucent, black or white. *Sheep*: white to black. (Dyes very well.) *Silver fox*: pale gray.

SPUN FUR

This material is prepared in the same manner as the spun wool. It is easy to work with and, being formed and ready to use, saves time. This precludes the need for spinning the fur for each fly body as it is made.

SPUN WOOL

This is a long-twist material made from wool fibers and is especially recommended for the fly-dresser. It is a finer grade of material than common wool yarns, which incline to separate during the process of being wound on the hook.

ANGORA

This is also known as mohair—a long, soft hair that is easy to handle. It is prepared and worked the same as fur.

RAFFIA

Raffia is a long, smooth-surfaced grass ideally suited to certain fly bodies. It is applied to the hook shank in the same fashion as floss or quill.

STRAW

A material seldom used now, straw, when handled carefully, makes a body that cannot be imitated by any other material. Not durable, it should be ribbed with wire tinsel.

KAPOK

Kapok is known for its buoyancy. Snow white and fluffy, it is used as a filler under floss bodies. Considerable kapok can be compressed in this manner, adding buoyancy to the fly.

OSTRICH PLUME

This makes very attractive herl-bodies. Two strands should be wrapped simultaneously to produce thick, compact bodies.

EMU PLUME

The quill found in emu plumes is stronger than the quill in ostrich plumes and can be used for quill bodies; otherwise it compares with ostrich in every respect.

PEACOCK HERL

This is one of the most generally used of all body materials and is similar to ostrich herl in appearance. It is either metallic green or bronze in color. Except when tying the very smallest of flies, wind two or three, if possible, of these strands together.

PEACOCK EYE

This is the large metallic tip of the peacock tail feather, so named because of the eye-like spot on the end of the feather. The sections are known as herl and, after the fluff has been removed, become striped in appearance, making excellent quill bodies. Interesting effects can be obtained by leaving the narrow band of fluff on the quill, thus producing a body with a very noticeable spiral band.

CONDOR QUILL

These quill feathers are exceptionally large and have wide fibers ideal for quill bodies. The color range varies from white to dark brown. This material is excellent for definitely marked quill bodies.

HERON QUILL

Heron quill is rather narrow and is most suitable for small flies having pale bluish-gray or dun bodies. It must be handled with care.

WING QUILLS

Any wing quill with fairly stiff fibers is useful for making a quill body. Primary and secondary wing feathers from larger birds such as the goose, swan, turkey and others contain fibers which can be used for this purpose. These feathers take dye well and are of good texture.

MOOSE MANE

Moose mane is a coarse, durable hair. It is not appropriate for streamers but makes neat, closely segmented quill bodies and legs for nymphs. Two-tone effects are obtained by winding together a light and dark strand around the shank of the hook. This hair receives dye well.

PORCUPINE QUILL

Porcupine quill is unexcelled for making smooth, buoyant bodies, being durable and easily handled. This quill should be flattened by pulling it between the thumb nail and forefinger before being applied to the hook shank. Its ivory-white color makes it suitable for dyeing.

RUBBER, TRANSLUCENT

This is a fairly recent development toward making translucent may flies. It will adhere only to itself and is shaped by bending over the hook shank, pressing together, then trimming with scissors. The principal disadvantage is its tendency to become tacky during hot weather and for this reason flies made of rubber should be kept one to a compartment. I seriously doubt the claims made for flies featuring this material since it has been my experience that the flies do not float well and strike the water rather heavily.

SILKWORM GUT AND NYLON

Attempts to make fly bodies translucent have produced experiments in the use of silkworm gut and nylon. These materials add weight to the fly but are otherwise as good as, if not better than, most translucent materials. Dyed silkworm gut makes interesting and sometimes effective May-fly bodies. It must be thoroughly soaked in water before being applied to the hook. Large-size gut is difficult to manipulate and is not satisfactory for this purpose.

PLASTACELE

This is a translucent material which can be dyed fairly well. It is available in sheets and is cut in strips preparatory to winding. This makes very effective translucent bodies but is inclined to become scuffed easily. However, it is effective if translucency is necessary.

RUBBER BANDS

Believe it or not, rubber bands in the red, natural and brown finishes make durable and effective bodies.

WING MATERIALS

The wings of an artificial fly can be made from thousands of kinds of wing quills, breast feathers, hair, etc. Certain specific patterns require rare plumage but the majority do not. A variety of substitute feathers having qualities comparable to those of the rare ones can be used where substitution is practical. Fortunately anglers are becoming educated to the really important things to look for in a fly and, more each year, the old, time-worn standards are losing favor. The following wing feathers are arranged in groups to show, at least to some degree, similarities common to each group. It should be added, however, that duck wing-quills are the best of the quill type for trout dry and wet flies. Goose wing-quills, while too coarse for dry flies, are satisfactory for wet flies as are the wing-quills from the various pheasants, grouses, and quails.

WING QUILLS AND TAILS

Black: Crow, raven. *Black and white barred*: Amherst pheasant, zebra pheasant. *Black, white speckled*: Guinea, starling. *Black, white tip*: Turkey tail. *Blue, white tip*: Mallard tips. *Blue and gray barred*: Blue jay. *Bright*: Macaw (red, yellow and blue), Red ibis (light red, light red-black tip). *Brown*: Hen, turkey. *Brown, mottled*: Hen pheasant tail, ring neck pheasant tail, wood duck. *Brown, mottled gray*: Golden pheasant, grouse, owl, partridge. *Brown, speckled*: Cock capercailzie, cock pheasant, hen pheasant. *Cinnamon*: English partridge, pigeon, wood duck (two large back feathers). *Dark gray*: Blackbird, coot, Mandarin, pigeon, plover, ring neck duck, wood duck. *Gray*: Bald widgeon, canvasback, French thrush, gallinule, goose, gray widgeon, heron, lark, mallard, mavis, moorhen, pigeon, pintail, red head, scaup, seagull, shoveler, snipe, starling, teal, turkey, wild pigeon. *Metallic*: Black grouse, copper pheasant, turkey tail. *Metallic, bright blue-green*: Peacock sword. *White*: Goose, mallard, pigeon, seagull, swan, turkey. *White, blue tip*: Mallard flight feather.

BREAST AND SIDE PLUMAGE

Gray, medium, speckled: Blue-wing teal, pintail. *Brown, barred*: Brown mallard grand nashua, scaup. *White*: canvasback, goose, swan satinets, wood duck, *Spotted*: Cinnamon teal. *Lemon, barred*: Egyptian goose, wood duck. *Gray, pale, speckled*: Mallard (drake). *Brown, speckled*: Mallard (hen), widgeon. *Black and white, barred*: Scaup. *Brown and tan*: Shoveler. *Gray, barred*: Teal, widgeon.

STREAMER WINGS

Wings for streamer flies must be flexible yet retain their shape. Saddle hackle and some neck hackle meet this requirement; other feathers with hackle-like qualities are as good. Saddle hackle is used mainly because it has a rich gloss, attractive to fish, and a fine, flexible quill. Saddles from the Plymouth Rock rooster that have been dyed are very lifelike in appearance. The following streamer material is standard to the trade:

Neck and Saddle Hackles: All kinds are suitable so long as they are flexible. *Marabou Feather*: Marabou is very soft and fluffy. When dry it appears large and useless but, after becoming wet, it clings together forming a slender, minnow-like affair very attractive to fish. Large birds such as the turkey and goose have soft, downy feathers near the rump that perform in a similar manner. *Bali Duck Feather (Yanosh)*: This feather is very similar to a long neck hackle but is very closely barred resembling the markings in the finest of mallard feathers. The most attractive imitations of minnows are made with this feather. *Top Knot Feather*: Certain birds have top knots composed of long, slender feathers, sometimes of a metallic color. The wood duck, for example, has such a top knot of rich green feathers which make neat, very active streamers. These can be used for topping on salmon and steelhead flies.

TRANSLUCENT DRY-FLY WINGS

In the interest of producing better and more natural-looking drakes and large May flies, a variety of materials has been used experimentally. Unfortunately, none of these has proved very successful. One of the chief objections to this type of wing is its air resistance. When cast, a fly tied with such wings flutters and sometimes twists fine leader tippets. Two types are in somewhat limited usage, the processed silk and the fish skin. The processed silk wings are machine-cut in one piece, resembling a propeller, and are available in several colors. Fish-skin wings are undesirable, necessitating individual cutting for each pair, and they wilt in a very unpleasant manner.

FANCY BODY PLUMAGE

Certain fancy plumage is necessary. It is used for shoulders, tails, cheeks, topping, and sometimes wings. While dry flies seldom require plumage of this kind other than pheasant tippets for tails, wet-fly patterns call for many different kinds of brilliant and fancy feathers. Fly-dressers could go broke in a hurry trying to stock all of the fancy pheasant skins listed in catalogs, and for this reason it is well to minimize the number of these skins you purchase. With some exceptions many fancy skins possess feathers of the same general description found in others. Before World War II, very fancy and rare plumage was used in the manufacture of salmon and steelhead flies. The need for such plumage in the past few years, however, has been reduced nearly as much as the availability of the feathers. Societies for the preservation of wildlife, extinction of the birds, the substitution of less expensive plumage, and foreign trade conditions, are all factors that have greatly reduced the variety of fancy skins stocked by wholesalers. The skins listed here are useful for general purposes.

Golden Pheasant Feather: Metallic, golden crest; orange and black tippets; gold and red side feathers; a few red and brown barred feathers and some bright, metallic green. *Amherst Pheasant, Lady Amherst, Silver Amherst*: Metallic, scarlet crest; white and black tippets; dark blue-green sides. *Blue Jay*: Brilliant barred light and dark blue feathers next to wing quills. *Jungle Cock*: Blackish cape feathers with wax-white to cream spots. *Blue Kingfisher*: Barred blue and black. *Malay Parrot*: Various, red, green, blue and gray. *Ring Neck Pheasant*: Barred and spotted brown; various mottlings. *Zebra Pheasant*: Black-and-white-striped sides.

HAIR FOR DRY-FLY AND SMALL WET-FLY WINGS

Hair for dry-fly wings is limited to very few animals. Hair does not compress very much, especially when tied with fine working silk to small hooks such as the hooks used for dry flies. Therefore, hair for dry-fly wings must have fine texture, resiliency and strength. Bucktail, bear hair and others customarily used to make streamers and large wet flies are worthless for dry flies. The following are the best kinds of hair for small wings: *Badger*: white to cream, barred. *Groundhog*: gray and dark tan, barred. *Lynx*: white to black. *Monkey*: various, white, cream, barred, black. *Polar Bear*: white to cream. *Squirrel*: various, gray to black.

HAIR FOR STREAMERS AND WET FLIES

There are various animal hairs suitable for streamer flies. Some are really good while others are just something more for the fly-dresser to buy. Any hair to be used to make a streamer must be durable, flexible and, at least to some degree, water resistant. Bucktail, which has been known for years as a standard material for streamers, is not the best because of its tendency to rot after repeated wettings. Bucktail hair is also hollow, which is an undesirable feature, and will break off easily.

Better results are obtained with soft, silk-like and dense hair. Fine, dense hair effects a neater, slimmer fly, making possible a narrow, well-tied head. This cannot be said of bucktail. *Baboon*: The body hair from both the red and orange baboons is fine and silky and ideal for streamer flies. The red baboon has hair a rich cinnamon color. The orange baboon has bright cream hair with black bars at the tips. *Badger*: This hair is barred, flexible and durable, and of excellent texture. *Bear*: Of all the bear hair available the hair from the polar bear is the most effective and useful. This hair possesses a glistening, translucent quality that is not equalled by any other type. Cinnamon bear hair is slightly crinkled and bright. Other bear hair is useful and all are extremely durable, perhaps because of their oiliness. *Bucktail*: Although bucktail has been a favorite for years, it is hollow, absorbs water and tends to break. Because it is compressible it is a little easier to handle than some of the solid hairs. *Capras* (*Chinese Goat*): This hair is widely used by professional fly manufacturers and is often mistaken for bucktail in the finished fly. It is superior to bucktail and cheaper to buy. *Fox Tail*: There are three kinds of foxes possessing hair of excellent quality desirable for streamer making. The Arctic fox tail is white, especially good for wet flies. The red fox tail is brownish and suitable for all light to dark brown flies and streamers. A mottled gray hair comes from the tail of the gray fox and is similar in texture to the hair of the red fox. *Goat*: The long, fine hair from the belly of the goat is finer than bucktail and otherwise stronger. *Impali*: The tail of the impali is reddish-brown with several indistinct dark gray to black bars. In texture it compares with squirrel tail. *Monkey*: This hair is of very fine texture, variable from white to black with barring. *Rolla*: Unusually long and white, this hair is ideally suited to long streamers. It is very durable and will not deteriorate rapidly. *Siberian Wolf*: Tails of Siberian wolves are light tan with medium brown tips and are crinkled. *Skunk*: Skunk hair is similar to bear hair in both durability and texture and is black and white. *Squirrel*: Squirrel tail is standard to the fly trade. It is durable, flexible and available in gray, brown and black.

COARSE HAIR FOR FLOATING BUGS

Bass hair bugs are effective only if they float. Hair for this purpose must be compressible, light in weight and easily worked. Dense, non-compressible hair is not suitable and should be avoided. Deer and caribou hair possess the proper qualities and are most satisfactory for all hair-body bugs, mice and frogs. Obtainable in white, gray and brownish-gray natural colors, this hair also reacts well to dyes.

LACQUERS, CEMENTS AND VARNISHES

Acetate Enamels: are synthetic and can be thinned with turpentine. They make a satisfactory finish for large heads and cork bugs but are inferior to the specially prepared cements for finishing the heads of small flies.

Celluloid-base Enamels: cannot be thinned with ordinary paint thinners. Most supply houses sell a special thinner for reducing the consistency of this enamel. Fingernail polish remover will thin some of them, although a small quantity should be tested before the entire contents are diluted. After repeated dilution celluloid cement inclines to harden rapidly. Every effort should be made to keep the solution air-tight.

Fly-dresser's Cement: is best for dry and wet flies. It is sometimes offered in colors but clear is more satisfactory. It must be thinned with a special agent. Turpentine and other commercial paint thinners only spoil it.

Lacquers: of various kinds are available. While these have been used with moderate success they are not generally recommended for finishing the heads of flies. Their greatest usefulness is the coating of nymph bodies.

Bakelite Varnishes: are inferior to fly cement and the celluloid base enamels. Most bakelite varnishes tend to chip and for this reason are undesirable.

Feather Glazer or *Elixer*: is sold under a variety of trade names, its purpose to prevent the fraying or separation of the wing fibers. The use of this fluid is to be discouraged. Dry- and wet-fly wings are spoiled after being treated with any solution. Wings on flies are intended to appear and act in a natural manner and must compress or open, as the case may be, during casting. When treated so that air cannot penetrate their fibers, they twist, ruining leader tippets, and light on the surface with as much lifelikeness as a wound-up egg-beater. Dry-fly wings, especially, must be sparse and porous to facilitate the use of the new light-weight hooks. Any preparations that close the wing fibers are undesirable.

Ambroid: is one of the most useful preparations for preserving larger surfaces. Large heads covered with Ambroid will retain their shape indefinitely and will not fray or unravel. This composition will serve as filler, base or hardener in a completely satisfactory manner. As a cement for cork bodies it is unsurpassed.

CORK AND BALSA WOOD FOR BUG BODIES

Large surface-bugs having smooth, painted bodies are generally made from two materials, cork and balsa wood. Several shapes of cork and balsa-wood bodies are mass produced and inexpensive. Cork is perhaps the easier to handle. Excellent bodies can be made from medicine-bottle corks by trimming them with a razor blade and carefully finishing with fine sandpaper. Balsa wood is sold in small billets and blanks and is easily cut to shape with an Excello or similar wood-carving knife. A more professional-looking finish is effected by the use of a filler to close the pores or grains before the base coat of enamel is applied.

GLASS EYES

Glass eyes add to the attractiveness of a streamer or floating bug, from the fisherman's standpoint, although it is a matter of conjecture as to whether the fish is aware of them. These eyes are fastened to soft wire stems which can be bent around the shank of the hook or cut to the length of a short pin and driven into the body. The former method applies to hair-body bugs, the latter to cork or balsa-wood bugs. The eyes are clear but a drop of enamel on the inside surface will produce any desired color.

DIVING DISCS

Diving discs are metal plates similar to the plates on casting lures but are necessarily lighter. A triangular extension is fastened to the bottom side of the shank by winding tight with the working silk. Then it is bent slightly to the desired angle. These discs are available in several sizes ranging from small, for streamers size 10 and 8, to large, for streamers and surface bugs size 1 or larger.

DYES AND CLEANERS

There is one advantage to buying fly materials from a reputable house: the materials are clean, ready to use and dyed when required. However, the subject of dyes is cause for disagreement in many cases, especially if the fly-dresser is trying to duplicate an off-shade or odd color. For this reason many tyers prefer to dye their materials in their own shop.

Many materials in the rough such as hair on the skin, fur, some hackle necks and duck skins are quite oily and must be thoroughly cleaned before dyeing. Warm soapy water will remove much of the surface film. Then if the material is rinsed several times, squeezed dry and dipped in high-grade naptha it will become oil-free, after which it should be washed with soap again and rinsed thoroughly before being exposed to the dye solution.

It pays to use dyes especially compounded for dyeing feathers and hair; there is just no substitute for good dyes. The drug store variety does not penetrate the fibers and leaves the material a very washed-out, pale shade of the color you intended it to be. By all means purchase your dyes from reputable houses catering to fly-dressers.

Chapter Four

FLY DESIGNS

It may come as a surprise to learn that angling with the artificial fly is not the comparatively modern sport it is claimed to be but was popular centuries ago. Homer, who perhaps recorded the first accounts of fishing, relates that the anglers of Greece as early as 1000 B.C. used "insidious food" for bait. To several authorities on the history of fishing this indicates the first use of artificial flies; at least it illustrates that some sort of artificial bait was fairly common in that day.

The Macedonians are credited with first having used artificial flies when, in the river Astraeus, located between Thessalonica and Boroea, they cast their feathered hooks intended to represent "Hipporous," an insect similar to the bee or wasp. Claudius Aelian, famous historian of that day, wrote at great length about the Macedonians and their imitations of Hipporous. In his *De Animalium Natura* Aelian writes: "These fish feed on a fly which is peculiar to the country, and which hovers over the river. It is not like the flies found elsewhere, nor does it resemble a wasp in appearance, nor in shape would one justly describe it a midge or bee, yet it has something of each of these. In boldness it is like a fly, in size you might call it a bee; it imitates the color of a wasp, and it hums like a bee." It is interesting to know that Aelian wrote this sometime around 200 A.D. and that his description is considered the first written account about an artificial fly.

In consideration of Hipporous, Aelian again writes: "They do not use these flies at all for bait for the fish; for if a man's hand touch them, they lose their color, their wings decay, and they become unfit for food for the fish. For this reason they have nothing to do with them, hating them for their bad character; but they have planned a snare for the fish, and get the better of them by their fisherman's craft." The imitation of this fly is then described. "They fasten red (crimson) wool round a hook, and fit on to the wool two feathers which grow under a cock's wattles, and which in color are like wax." This description is especially interesting since it describes a fly closely resembling our own favorite red-hackle.

Other ancient volumes allude to the use of artificial lures, although whether these creations were flies or not is a matter for conjecture. Theocritus, Greek poet, around 300 B.C. wrote of fishermen using "the bait fallacious." Exactly what this means has been a source of dispute among anglers and historians for many years, since Theocritus did not describe the shape or color of the bait. Nevertheless it is not inconceivable that the "bait fallacious" may have been some sort of feathered lure. Undoubtedly then,

32

as now, anglers enjoyed discussions about their favorite lures and methods. What a treat it would be to turn back the clock to a crisp, clear spring morning 200 B.C. and hear a typical streamside conversation. Imagine the sages of the river Astraeus discussing the virtues of the Boroean Bivisible, Thessalonican Terror or perhaps a Royal Charioteer.

Records on fly-fishing, especially, and all fishing, generally, are quite spotty and vague. For several centuries after the birth of Christ very little information on fishing is recorded and, but for the occasional non-informative line or two appearing in a volume of history, poetry or philosophy, we have few authentic accounts until the fifteenth century. Then, in England, were published the first of countless volumes dealing with fishing as both a vocation and a recreation. Many were devoted to fly-fishing almost exclusively and were descriptive of the fly patterns of that day which, it must be added, have endured through the years without major change.

One of the first books to be printed in England was written on the subject of fishing. This was the often-quoted *A Treatyse of Fysshynge With an Angle,* written by Dame Juliana Berners, the prioress of the Benedictine Nunnery of Topwell, near St. Albans. This wonderful tome was originally hand-wrought since its writing preceded the printing press. It was not press-printed until 1486 when William Caxton, the father of English printers, was producing the first cumbersome volumes of that day. This book was exceptional for its descriptions of trout and grayling flies, one of which was almost identical to the descriptions written by Aelian for the fly we accept to be the original red-hackle of the Macedonians. The names of these ancient flies alone remind us of various present-day patterns. The prioress named them the Dun fly, Stone fly, Yellow May, Black Louper, Dun cutte, Maure fly, Tandy fly, Wasp fly, Shell fly and Drake fly.

Near the middle of the seventeenth century many books on fly-fishing were published, each one contributing interesting lore on the flies then used and how to make them. Thomas Barker's *Art of Angling,* published in 1651, was a valuable piece of literature in its day, dealing with the problems met on English trout streams and the flies of "greatest creddit." Barker explained the values of Palmer flies and contended they were more effective than the winged patterns, an opinion maintained by many experts living today.

John Denny's *The Secrets of Angling* appeared in 1652. This book was notable for containing the first illustration of a fishing fly. Then in 1653, that arch-angler of all time, Izaak Walton, published his literary classic, *The Compleat Angler.* This book, replete with lore of the stream and the spirit of angling, encourages all men to fish and love it. Walton described nymphs, especially the caddis, and the way to use them. Most outstanding, however, is his analysis of the necessary flies for trout fishing. He described the "twelve kinds" of artificial flies to his heel-tagging friend and pupil, Venator, in terms familiar to even modern fly-dressers. Surprising, too, is his reference to dry flies when he explains that the twelve kinds of flies are to be used on the top of the water. This is considered by many authorities the first allusion to dry-fly fishing. While the true identities of the patterns Walton described are somewhat obscured by the vague and fanciful names he gave them, they can still be recognized as being similar to some of our modern counterparts. He even went so far as to thoroughly explain the procedure for tying a fly—a procedure not unlike the one followed today. The flies he described we recognize as the antecedents of many of our popular patterns: Dun flie, Dun fly, Stone fly, Ruddy fly, Yellow or Greenish fly, Black fly, Yellow flie, Moorish fly, Tawny fly, Wasp fly, Shell fly, Drake fly, May flie, Oak flie, Hawthorne and Grasshopper.

In 1662 more techniques were expounded in the *Experienced Angler* by Venable. Perhaps the largest number of flies to be classified in that period was the list compiled by Charles Cotton, later follower of the errant Walton, and published in 1675 with a supplement to the fifth edition of Walton's *Compleat Angler*. More elaborate in the description of flies than previous books and even differentiating between plain and palmer hackle-type flies, Cotton's *The Art of Fly-fishing* became a recognized standard. He described the legendary "fiery brown" at length but under the name "bright brown," and particularized the "peacock fly," progenitor of the famous brown-hackle-peacock.

It was about this time that the soldier-palmer became well known, and so named because its solid red body resembled the color of the jackets worn by British soldiers.

The trend toward treating fly-fishing as a science began with *The Fly-Fisher's Entomology* written by Alfred Ronalds, an Englishman, shortly before the middle of the nineteenth century. A very able student of the stream, Ronalds patterned artificial flies after the natural insects appearing in the waters with which he was familiar. Many of these patterns remain unchanged to this day and undoubtedly will be popular for years to come. About this same time T. G. Hofland further amplified fly-fishing in his book *The British Angler's Manual*. Another contribution of outstanding value was G. P. R. Pulman's *Vade Mecum of Fly-Fishing for Trout* published in 1851. This work, which construed dry-fly fishing, contained many otherwise unrecorded dressings of flies with instructions on how to make them.

One of the truly great books describing flies was written by F. M. Halford, exponent of the dry fly. His *Dry-Fly Fishing in Theory and Practice* has been accepted as a standard. Halford is credited with several innovations in connection with dry-fly fishing. His development of the artificial may fly resulted in the first fan-wings, detached bodies and fish-skin wings. An advocate of eyed hooks, he did more, perhaps, to expedite the snell-less hook than any of his contemporaries, and his "quill gnats" were the bases for the popular quill-body flies.

The continued popularity of hackle flies is evident in the book *Yorkshire Trout Flies* written by T. E. Pritt, who refers to the impressionistic values of hackle flies,

W. C. Prime favored very sparse wet flies and spiders, emphasizing sparseness of hackle but keen definition of body color and shape. American authors were of similar bent. L. B. France claimed he could take a gray or brown hackle and be fully equipped for any trout fishing.

Angling books of all descriptions became increasingly abundant as the nineteenth century came to a close. New and different theories in regard to fly-fishing spurred inventions. Colored plates and line drawings of infinite value appeared. Meanwhile American writers had already started to classify the fish of our continent and this led to hundreds of brilliant books on the subject of fly-fishing. Although the English had been fishing with dry flies since Walton's time (this is a matter of deduction based on Walton's own writings), American anglers did not turn to the sport seriously until a few years after the twentieth century. There are isolated cases, certainly, where conventional dry flies had been used, or where wet flies had been especially treated to remain on the surface, but, for the most part, dry flies were a rarity. Confirmation of this is shown in the comparatively late appearance in 1912 of the first American book covering dry flies, *Practical Dry-Fly Fishing*, written by Emlyn M. Gill. However, British types and patterns of flies prevailed for trout and salmon until the later development of flies for bass fishing unleashed a stampede of radical departures from British standards. New and various materials were tried, streamers and bucktails appeared, and orthodox usage was amended to suit the fishing conditions on this continent.

American Indians were able fly-fishermen. Records, although very incomplete, show convincingly that the North Carolina Indians had been making deer-hair flies long before the Civil War. Apparently these floaters were fabricated from narrow strips of deer skin with the hair untrimmed. With this material the Indians made a spiral-shaped bug of many legs, not entirely unlike our present-day bass bugs. Some authorities on flies have referred to these creations as the prototypes of modern reverse-hackle flies.

To reduce fly-dressing to a formula has been the aim of anglers and correspondents for centuries. The art has, however, been so much involved with theory and whim that it has escaped simplification. In the last decade so many variations and alternate designs have become recognized as to make exceedingly difficult the tabulation of even a fair percentage of existing fly patterns. There are many classes, groups and kinds of flies, depending on shape, color, size and individual peculiarities. This book is an attempt to show the classifications, groups and kinds to which all flies belong.

Fundamentally, artificial flies are made according to two schools of thought. The first, the Impressionistic, believes that approximate size, general appearance and color are sufficient to lure a trout under all conditions, while the second, the Realistic, demands precise duplication of an insect. Actually, no artificial fly can be termed an exact duplication of an aquatic insect. Materials so far developed do not transmit light as does the natural fly, nor are they as sparse and delicate. Well-dressed flies will, however, prove adequate to whet a trout's appetite and curiosity provided, of course, they are skillfully handled.

If credit for minimizing the number of fly patterns can be attributed to either of these schools of thought, it should be given to the Impressionistic group. According to one of their theories, several patterns can be incorporated into one, thus reducing the need for many similar patterns. Another theory stresses the superiority of simulating size more than color. Unfortunately, however, there are limits to even such reasonable deductions as these.

Flies made according to either the Impressionistic or Realistic conceptions must look right to the fish or they will be useless, regardless of theory, technique or anything else. Fish have notions, too, and are sometimes imbued with as much obstinacy as your best fishing companion, experts to the contrary notwithstanding.

Color is the source of much discussion among anglers and fly-dressers. However, color must be associated with the translucency and opacity of the object to which it is applied. With the sun as a background, a dry fly with an opaque green body may seem black to a fish, while one with a translucent green body will appear to some degree greenish—as we know it—to the fish. Translucency is desirable in dry flies since flying insects are seldom opaque. Fur is composed of many connected particles which permit the penetration of light and for this reason is perhaps the best material for dry-fly bodies when translucency is desired.

Another consideration worth noting is the difference between the back and the abdomen of an insect. Quill which supposedly imitates the segmented bodies of natural insects is the same color throughout its length, whether dyed or natural. However, for the sake of comparison, examine a may fly; the back is usually much darker than the abdomen. When viewed from the top the may fly appears similar to many commercial patterns but when seen from the underside it compares with very few. This explains why so-called imitations of a hatch in progress are not really imitations at all from the viewpoint of the trout, though they may be from the viewpoint of the fisherman. Still some anglers contend they are using an "exact" imitation. From this it could be deduced that the color of the abdomen of a dry fly is far more important than the color of the back.

Wet flies, while they are tied according to the same patterns used for dry flies, embody different principles, namely, opacity and strength of color. A wet fly, with water as a background, must reflect light, thus showing its color. The greater its reflection potential, the more intense will become its color.

There are basically two kinds of artificial flies: those which float are known as dry flies, and those which sink are known as wet flies. Of the dry and wet categories there are many subdivisions which will be considered at length a little later. But for the present it can be said that the designs of all flies are based on:

(1) aquatic and a few terrestrial insects.

(2) minnows and other aquatic creatures other than insects.

(3) eye-appeal—color, shape, symmetry, etc.

The method of dressing them, the quality and kind of materials used, the proportions and style are different; therefore no single rule is applicable to all of them.

Aquatic and terrestrial insects are represented by nymphs, dry and wet flies. Minnows and other aquatic creatures other than insects are represented by streamers, bucktails, large wet flies and large nymphs. Flies whose design is based on eye-appeal are various and depend on color combinations which have proved effective or on shapes which, to some degree, are attractive in profile or create a definite action in the water. The large bass bugs, while originally designed to simulate the appearance of mice, huge moths, frogs and other creatures, have become monstrous of late, and embody peculiar shapes and garish colors, although it seems these oddities increase their effectiveness.

FLY NOMENCLATURE

AFT BODY: See *BODY*.

BODY: In most cases that portion wound around the shank of the hook and extending from the origin of the tail fibers to the base of the wing. Fore and aft bodies are those portions extending in each direction before or behind the center joint.

BUTT: A ruff of herl or chenille located at the tail end of the body.

CENTER JOINT: Similar to the butt in appearance but located midway on the shank. It is not necessarily the same material or color as the butt and is characteristic of many salmon and fancy lake flies.

CHEEK: Usually a narrow, short feather such as jungle-cock, blue-jay, etc., tied over wings or shoulders. Also the outside feather immediately behind the eye.

FORE BODY: See *BODY*.

HACKLE: A group of fibers from any bird feather, a single feather wound circum-

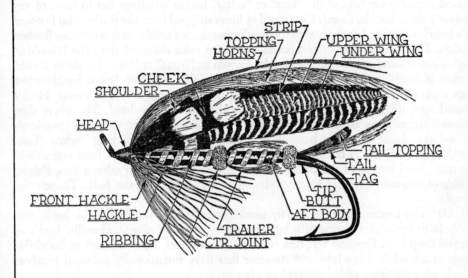

FIG. 7
FLY NOMENCLATURE

Eonard

ferentially and together around a hook, several feathers wound circumferentially and together around a hook (vertically or horizontally), a tuft of animal hair, combinations of feathers and hair, nylon fibers, shredded wood or fur, strips of metallic cloth, strips of rubber, and many other substances fastened to the body of a fly. Location depends entirely upon the individual type of fly and may be at the head, on the sides, beneath, all over, spiral-like. Hackle may be subdivided for clarity as follows: *Backing*: Hackle wound immediately behind the "face" or "collar" hackle windings but in front of any body or Palmer hackle. *Beard*: Composed of fibers stripped from the feather and fastened in a bunch below and to the rear of the head; sometimes a single section of wing feather. *Collar*: The hackle (usually but not always) of a color different from the "shoulder" hackle and wound nearest the head. Also known as "front" or "face" hackle in consideration of bivisibles and salmon flies. *Face*: See *Collar*. *Palmer*: Spiral hackle windings around the body increasingly wider spaced near the head. *Reverse*: Hackle wound with the dull side (inside) of the feather toward the head. The fibers slant forward rather than backward. *Shoulder*: The hackle feather wrapped completely around the shank near the base of the wings; also called "backing" when "face" hackle is used. *Split*: A hackle feather having all the fibers stripped from one side of the quill; used largely in the construction of sparse wet flies and salmon flies. Palmer hackle of two colors wound together should be split to reduce the bulk. *Throat*: See *Beard*.

HEAD: The foremost part of the fly immediately behind the eye of the hook; generally built up with working silk but frequently made of plastic, chenille, herl and clipped deep hair. Dry and wet flies necessarily have neat, tapered heads or no visible heads at all, while large lake and streamer flies have intentionally enlarged heads to which are sometimes added painted or glass eyes.

HORNS: A single pair of feather fibers (not sections) tied on at the head and extending over the wings or topping.

JOINT: See CENTER JOINT.

OPTIC HEAD: The head of an artificial fly that is equipped with painted or glass eyes.

RIBBING: Spiral windings over the body; generally tinsel, twisted fibers, thread, etc.

SHOULDER: That area on each side of the fly behind the head; also short matched feathers in same place.

SPLITS: See STRIPS.

STRIPS: Matched pairs of feather sections, usually long and slender, placed near the top edge or in center of wing.

TAG: The tag is a narrow winding of silk, tinsel or fur located at the rear of the body and *under* the tail fibers; *not* synonymous with "tip" which, although disputed by some authorities, is always in front of the tag winding and immediately behind the body. See also TAIL TAG and TIP.

TAIL: Composed of either several fibers or a whole feather and is fastened to or near the tip of the shank.

TAIL RUFF: See BUTT.

TAIL TAG: This is quite commonly called "tag" and, therefore, develops another source of confusion as to whether it is the same as "tag" which it is not. For this reason I have added the word "tail" to differentiate between the two. A tail tag is usually a short piece of wool replacing the conventional feather tail, but can be floss.

TAIL TOPPING: In salmon and other fancy flies, that short upper section (usually of contrasting color) placed above the tail proper; generally made with gold pheasant tippet.

THROAT: A theoretical portion on the underside of the fly directly under and slightly aft of the head.

TIP: A tip is any winding such as floss or tinsel located immediately behind the body and may or may not be accompanied with a tag which is always *under* the tail fibers whereas the tip always *encircles* the tail fibers. See *TAG, TAIL TAG.*

TOPPING: The topmost feathers which edge the wing proper; almost always pheasant crest and peacock sword.

TRAILERS: Matched feather sections such as short pheasant crest, one above and the other below the body, tied on at the center joint.

WING: Composed of various materials and tied behind the head of the fly; fundamentally single, double, or combination. In fancy and salmon flies there are several wing sections. These are best identified as upper and under wings—regardless of the diversity of materials or colors. The following break-down is useful as a key to the recognition of wing types: *Bunched*: See *Rolled. Closed*: Paired quill sections having concave sides together; tied over the back but in vertical plane. *Dee*: Salmon-fly type; similar to flat but slightly divided. *Divided*: Paired quill sections (either single or double layers) having convex sides together and tied upright as dry-fly wings; generally but not necessarily with single layer wings tied in vertical plane but over the back, as wet-fly wings. *Down*: Often associated with imitation of caddis flies. Wing sections are arranged roof-like over the back; sometimes tied *Reverse* (which see). *Fan*: Made of two matched, fan-shaped breast feathers tied with their convex sides together and in an upright position. *Fish-skin*: Variously shaped; a substitute for conventional materials when translucency is considered essential. *Flat*: Sections tied to rest horizontally, one over the other, over the back of the fly; closely parallels the wing appearance of the natural stone fly. *Forward*: Loosely any dry-fly wings set well forward but actually the "divided" or "upright." *Hackle tip*: A type of material; not alone descriptive of position. Hackle tips are substituted for nearly every other wing material and are especially effective as *Spent* wings (which see). *Hair*: A type of material; not alone descriptive of position. Most frequently used in rolled, split style for dry-fly wings and in down style for wet flies. *Hair split*: As regards dry flies only. Tied as rolled, split wing. *Inner Wing*: The innermost layer of wing fibers, single or married; typical of extra-fancy salmon flies. *Married Feathers*: Two or more unlike, longitudinal feather strips so joined together into a single wing as to interlock the barbules of each strip. This is accomplished by stroking the fibers between the fingers. Lefts and rights cannot be married very well; use fibers with same curvature. *Outer Wing*: The outermost layer of wing fibers, single or married. See *Veil. Reverse*: Sections of feather tied on by their tips rather than their butts and extending over the back of the fly in a vertical plane. *Rolled*: Breast feathers rolled between the fingers to remove the natural lay of the fibers and tied on the hook in a bunch. See *Bunched Wing. Rolled-split*: Same as rolled but split with working silk to form paired wings; this term generally applied to dry flies. *Sail*: Single hackle-tip upright style for dry flies. *Spent*: Said of wings which simulate the wings of dead drakes and spinners. Usually tied with hackle tips but not uncommonly made of feather sections. Should be at right angles to the body and prone. *Split*: See *Rolled-split*. *Spoon*: Breast or side feathers tied spoon-shape over back of fly and in vertical plane; usually double feathers, closed. *Translucent*: Wings made of processed material (also fish-skin) to simulate drakes, etc.; tied variously as required. No special position. *Upright*: Any wing tied in an upright or nearly upright position. *Veil*: Generally the breast and side feathers through which the inner wing partially shows; not a dense feather. See *Outer Wing*. *Vibrator*: Hackle tips cocked so far forward they are nearly parallel with the shank, thus vibrating when the fly is set in motion by either the current or the retrieve. *Upper*: Usually, in salmon flies, that part which comprises the upper portion of the whole. Not to be confused with "topping" which is merely edging. *Under*: That part which makes up the under or lower portion of the whole; sometimes referred to as the "base wing," a term rather vague for a definition.

COMMON DIFFICULTIES

The following tips are useful in the construction of any fly. Certain variations are possible and should become evident during the construction of individual types of flies. However, many rules of the thumb can be established by following these suggestions as progress is made.

SIZING A FLY: Trout Fly Proportions, Fig. 8, are based on the relationship between the wings, body, hackle, tail and hook of both dry and wet flies. The proportions used are especially important. If each part is not reasonably well-balanced with the others, the finished fly will be unsatisfactory in one or more respects. Dry flies particularly must be properly balanced to insure correct behavior on the surface. Top-heavy wings, hackle of incorrect spread, tails too flimsy or short, and lumpy bodies all reduce the efficiency of the fly and can render it absolutely worthless.

DIMENSIONING WINGS: It is surprising that the error of making the wings too large occurs with fly-dressers of considerable experience. This practice causes unbalance and a most unsatisfactory fly. It is better to make the wing too small than too large; at least the fly will not be top heavy if a dry fly or inclined to float if a wet fly. The fibers in oversized wings will collapse under pressure of the working silk while the fly is being tied. Natural curvature of the feather should point toward the rear of the fly; pointed toward the front it will cause splitting of the fibers.

TAPERING THE BODY: Fly bodies should be smoothly tapered not only for appearance but for durability. A rough or open section is vulnerable to being caught by the tooth of a fish or torn loose during false casting and rough handling. There should be no knobs or lumps in a body made of tinsel, floss, quill and similar materials, since the longevity of such bodies is dependent on slight overlapping of the fiber at each preceding turn during construction. This neat overlapping is impossible, of course, if irregular surfaces exist.

APPLYING TAIL FIBERS: The tail sections have more than a slight part to play in balancing the completed fly, although they are often regarded lightly. Otherwise excellent dry flies are useless if their tail fibers are flimsy, short or absorbent. When the correct material is being fastened to the hook, care should be taken that the fibers do not rotate out of position. Tails should be parallel to the shank in wet flies, and either parallel or bent slightly downward in dry flies. Hold the sections on top of the hook shank when tying them and do not let them slip laterally while performing other work.

OBTAINING EYE CLEARANCE: Perhaps the most noticeable error in fly-making is the badly finished head. This is actually the result of several errors: often the use of coarse working thread, too much material, improper proportions, but usually the cramming of so much material toward the eye of the hook that there is little if any space left to finish the fly neatly. This error can be avoided easily by using less material and keeping the work more toward the rear of the hook. It became a custom a few years ago to dress all dry flies a trifle short with the result that 1/64 or so of an inch of uncovered shank behind the eye showed plainly. In some instances this was instrumental in achieving balance and is still good practice. It also permits of clean-cut and compact terminal knots, and gives the fly-dresser an opportunity to really show his capabilities.

WINDING HACKLE: Over-dressing a dry or wet fly with hackle makes it bulky and unnatural in appearance. Use only enough hackle to correctly fulfill its need—float the dry fly or add leg action to a wet fly.

WORKING SILK: One of the most difficult but necessary habits to acquire is always to leave the silk thread hanging ahead of the materials to be applied or wound. One of the best methods to accomplish this is to wind the thread to the eye of the hook before each successive operation, then return it by unwinding to the place where the material will be fastened. Care must be taken to prevent unnecessary bulk resulting from superfluous winds.

CLEANING FLUFF FROM PEACOCK QUILL: Hold the single strand between the thumb and forefinger, the thumb nail against the quill. Stroke gently several times until the green fluff has been removed. Another method is to place the quill section on the fly-table, and rub it with a rubber eraser. This removes the fluff quickly, but will break the quill if too much pressure is applied. Use definitely marked sections of quill. Good fibers have clean-cut, longitudinal stripes.

CLEANING FLUFF FROM HACKLE: Hold the feather in the left hand and run the thumb and forefinger of the right hand against the grain of the feather. It will be noticed that the sections toward the butt are soft and lack strength. Remove these by stripping toward the end. Look for gloss and resiliency in dry-fly hackle and absorbent but strong qualities in wet-fly hackle. Wet-fly hackle can be coarser than dry-fly hackle without ill effects.

MAKING DUBBING: Wax the working silk thoroughly. Trim the fur from the skin by clipping small portions into fine bits. Mixed colors can be prepared in the same fashion, as can solid off-tones so useful at times. Spread fur sparingly over the waxed silk thread, then roll the fur and thread together over the table top by stroking with the finger tips back and forth, until the fur has adhered to the silk, and a uniform diameter has been formed. Always leave a little excess thread on both ends of the dubbing for fastening to the hook and for rotating around the shank to form the body. This material will separate if handled roughly before the whole body has been formed. Then it becomes durable.

REMOVING SEGMENTS FROM A WING FEATHER: Select that portion where the feather is smooth, elastic and free from extraneous matter. Hold the dubbing needle close to the quill in the center of the feather, separate the fibers, then separate them again to the width of the desired wing. Matched wing quills should always be used since the curvature of the right wing quill is the opposite to the curvature of the left wing quill.

WHIP-FINISHING HEADS: Any fly is as good as its head knot is strong. Half-hitches and similar knots are unsatisfactory mainly because they are external and may become unraveled easily. The whip-finish, however, is an internal knot, or one which is tightened from the inside, leaving no windings to become uncoiled.

The whip-finish is easily learned and should be applied to all flies. With the left hand place the loop of the whip-finisher in a position extending beyond the eye of the hook. Wrap the working silk at least five or six turns around the loop and fly head, letting the whip-finisher hang vertically. Pressing the thumb of the left hand against the fly head to prevent unraveling, cut the working silk a convenient distance from the fly. Insert the tip of the working silk through the loop and draw snug. Place the right thumb over the head of the fly and, with the left hand, grasp the whip-finisher, which has been hanging by its loop. Drop the loop through and under the five or six turns wrapped around it. This pulls the end of the working silk inside the windings. Clip off the extra inch or two of working silk remaining and apply a drop of cement to the windings. Heads finished in this manner will usually outlast the fly.

Chapter Five

THE WET FLY

Categorically a wet fly is any fly fished under the surface. General usage, however, has construed the term to apply to any fly, either winged or wingless, generally resembling an insect, thta is dressed sparsely enough to sink quickly. Originally the wet fly was designed to represent a drowned surface fly, but through the years it has become widely diversified. To trout and salmon fishermen the wet fly is a means of representing (1) pupae emerging at the water's surface, (2) an adult insect submerged to deposit eggs, (3) small crustaceans and shrimp, and (4) drowned surface flies, generally "spinners." Nymphs, bucktails and streamers, while classed basically as wet flies for their physical properties, are, nevertheless, quite different and are best considered separately.

The proper construction of wet flies is based on five factors: sparseness, absorption, profile, a hook heavy enough to insure sinking of the fly, and color. Sparseness gives freedom of movement to each individual hackle and tail fiber, at the same time allowing the wing to move as willed by the current. Materials must be absorbent to prevent even the slightest tendency the fly may have to float. Nothing is more provoking than a wet fly that persists in staying on or near the water surface. While it may sometimes take trout in this condition, it is not intended to float. The profile should approximate the general contour of the fly or creature being simulated, and the hook should be made especially for wet-fly design. Generally wet flies are dressed on ball-eye hooks for their slightly added weight, although de luxe flies are sometimes made on heavy-weight hooks with tapered eyes. Color has much to do with the "net" results of any wet fly. Body colors are quite recognizable in a submerged fly. Color retains most of its values under water and, under some conditions, may even become intensified.

As has been pointed out before, regardless of materials, a fly that has been constructed out of proportion will not perform properly. And since all fly-dressers are primarily interested in the behavior of every fly they manufacture, they must be concerned with best proportions possible to build into any fly. Turn to Fig. 8, Trout Fly Proportions, and notice how the illustration of the wet fly shows the relationship of the materials as they are properly assembled. First notice that the tails (A) are equal to the body length, or the distance from the point where the head will be located to the origin of the bend in the hook. The body, therefore, will extend from the point where the tails are fastened to where the head will be located. The hackles indicated by the letter (C) should be long enough to just touch the tip of the hook point. This makes it comparatively easy to select a hackle of the correct size by fanning the feather around the shank where the hackle will be tied. The wings (D) are compared in a horizontal line to the length of the hook. In nearly all cases the wings should extend to the hook-bend. Dimension (E) is very important. It measures the amount of head clearance as one eye-length. This distance is left clear to facilitate the strong, neat leader knot necessary for correct terminal connections.

The characteristics and behavior of any wet fly must be as correct as those of the dry fly. Even though the dry fly must float and appear alive and as natural as possible, its perfection is no more important than that of the wet fly. As a matter of fact, I have contended for many years that it requires more absolute skill to dress a wet fly than a dry. This can be verified by comparing both types of flies manufactured by the same individual, provided the samples are in the same price classification.

Wet-fly hackle must be absorbent but strong, and the whisks as large a diameter as possible to properly simulate an insect's legs. This will tend toward sparseness, requiring fewer turns of hackle, and still retain lifelike "leg" appearance. Partridge hackle is the nearest approach to the ideal in hackles. Its color is mottled brown and grayish-buff and blends well with nearly all body and wing combinations. A similar hackle is the neck feather from the guinea. The polka dot white-on-black becomes an attractive banding after the hackle is wound.

The profile of the wet fly depends for the most part on the natural insect. Keep in mind that the profile of a wet fly can be viewed very critically by the feeding fish. If the nymph that is appearing has a pulpy body, the wet-fly imitation should have a reasonably similar body. The opposite applies in the same way. Fur is superb for pulpy-bodied flies, not alone for the fact that it can be spun to a large diameter, but because many little ends of the fur trap air particles as well. When the fly is drawn through the water, these air particles lend the illusion that the body is translucent and thick. Quill bodies, on the other hand, are smooth and are best suited to representing the slim, banded bodies of slender insects.

Wet flies are so very necessary to good angling that it will be good policy to construct your wet patterns as true to life as you possibly can. So long as the silhouette is a fair counterpart of the shape of the natural fly you are attempting to imitate, and the coloration reasonably close, your product will be worth your confidence.

Wet flies are usually classified according to the characteristics of their wings. The following cross-sections of the many types are arranged accordingly. Keep in mind that wet-fly dressings must be sparse. It is a mistake to overdress wet flies, especially. All wet flies having wings are constructed according to the following sequence of materials: first the tails are tied on, then the body is wrapped, after which the hackle is added either by being wound around the shank or placed in a bunch below the shank. The wings are tied on last, slightly forward of the hackle. Ribbed bodies, multi-colored tails and hackles and shouldered wings may require more operations, nevertheless the same sequence applies in nearly every case.

Fig. 10, Wet-Fly Design, illustrates the many styles of wet flies in general usage, exclusive of the streamer, bucktail and salmon types, which are dealt with in their respective sections. Here we will treat the wet fly as a separate and distinct type, suited to many fresh water and some salt water fish.

DIVIDED-WING

In this type the wings are dressed to allow for the greatest amount of flexibility. Sections of a wing-quill are used to make the wings and must be carefully paired, that is, with the natural curve of the feather—or the concave side—pointed outward. This imparts some movement to the wings during the retrieve. Narrow wings are more active than wide ones.

CONSTRUCTION, Preparation of Materials: It is advisable to lay out as much material as possible before attempting to tie a fly. Select the hackle, flank, or crest feather from which the tail fibers will be cut, the feathers to make the wings, and the body and hackle material. Where it is possible to select these materials according to proportionate measurement, use Fig. 8 as a guide in making the selection. For example, place the hackle feather with the dull side facing the rear of the hook, and bend the feather over the hook shank to spread open the fibers. If the longest fibers extend approximately to the point of the hook, the hackle is correct. Body material must be proportionate to the hook size. To illustrate, let us assume you will tie a fly having a quill body. How large, you may ask, shall the quill be? The only reasonable answer to this question is based on the number of revolutions the quill must be wound to properly cover the hook shank. As a general rule, eight revolutions of quill should properly form the body, including a fractional part of an inch for the over-lapping of each turn. Therefore the quill should be approximately one-eighth as wide as the body will be long. This does not mean that a body composed of ten revolutions is not as good. However, wider quill makes stronger bodies. The wings should not be cut until the other parts of the fly have been completed.

Setting up the Work: Place the hook in the vise so that the point and barb are beyond—not within—the jaws. Wax the working silk and fasten it to the hook shank at that point directly above the barb. Winding is always done with the right hand.

Tying on the Tails: See Fig. 11, No. 1. Select three or four fibers from the material chosen to make the tail, grasp them between the thumb and forefinger of the left hand and hold them against the hook shank, meanwhile sliding the fingertips downward to hold the hook shank as well. Check the overhang of the tail fibers (they should extend beyond the hook one body-length) then fasten them with three or four turns of working silk.

Fastening the Body Material: See Fig. 11, No. 1. Hold the narrow or tapered end of the body between the thumb and forefinger of the left hand and tie it in place, winding it at close intervals to prevent lumps or irregularities which would destroy the appearance of the finished body windings.

Winding the Body: See Fig. 11, No. 2. Continue the windings forward to that point where the body will be terminated, or approximately where the hackle will be fastened. Wind the body material, which is quill in our example, slowly and evenly, using the left hand to wind on the near side, and the right hand on the far side. Be certain each succeeding turn slightly overlaps the preceding turn. This strengthens the body since the overlapping prevents tearing the edge of the quill and subsequent unraveling of the entire body. When making a body of wool, dubbing or floss, handle the body in a similar manner. Tie down the forward end of the body with a half-hitch and apply a drop of cement.

Fastening and Winding the Hackle: See Fig. 11, Nos. 3 & 4. Split the hackle and

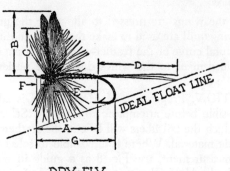

A = SHANK LENGTH
B = A
C = APPROX. ¾ B
D = G
E = APPROX. ¾ A
F = 1 EYE LENGTH

IDEAL FLOAT LINE

DRY-FLY

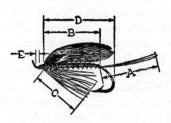

A = B
B = BODY LENGTH
C = TO HOOK POINT
D = TO HOOK BEND
E = 1 EYE LENGTH

WET-FLY

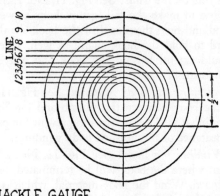

HOOK*	LINE*		
	REGULAR	VARIANT	SPIDER
20	1		
18	2		
16	3	6	7
14	4	8	9
12	5	9	10
10	6		
8	7		
6	8		
4	9		
2	10		

LINE 1 2 3 4 5 6 7 8 9 10

2"

DRY-FLY HACKLE GAUGE

FIG. 8
TROUT FLY PROPORTIONS

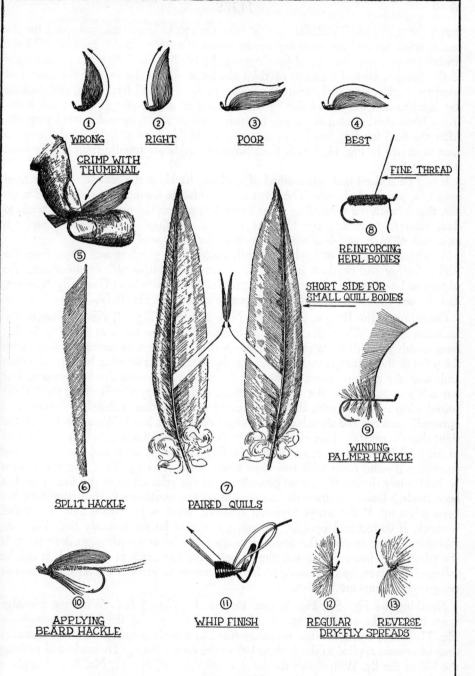

① WRONG ② RIGHT ③ POOR ④ BEST

CRIMP WITH THUMBNAIL

FINE THREAD

⑧ REINFORCING HERL BODIES

⑤

SHORT SIDE FOR SMALL QUILL BODIES

⑥ SPLIT HACKLE ⑦ PAIRED QUILLS

⑨ WINDING PALMER HACKLE

⑩ APPLYING BEARD HACKLE

⑪ WHIP FINISH

⑫ REGULAR ⑬ REVERSE
DRY-FLY SPREADS

Eonard

FIG. 9
GENERAL CONSTRUCTION FEATURES

fasten the tip, or small end, far enough from the eye to leave sufficient space for the hackle windings and the fastening of the wings. To split a hackle feather, hold the feather between the thumb and forefinger of the left hand and strip against the angle of the feathers with the fingers of the right hand. Grasp the butt of the stem and wind the hackle, alternately using the fingers of the right and left hands, and stroking the fibers toward the rear of the fly with the thumb and forefinger of the left hand. If the fibers twist toward the front, unwind as far as necessary and rewind properly. After the final winding has been made and the hackle appears right, bind down the stem as shown in Fig. 11, No. 5. Four turns of hackle are usually sufficient for most trout wet flies.

It will be noticed that this method of applying hackle is the reverse of the method used to apply dry-fly hackle. There is a reason. Hackle wound in the described manner, that is, with the succeeding fibers being longer than the preceding ones, tends to slant rearward, covering the fibers of the first windings. Split hackle occupies a minimum of space and does not form bulk behind the eye of the hook.

An alternate method of applying wet-fly hackle is to pluck several fibers from the hackle feather and tie them in a bunch directly to the underside of the shank. Tie additional bunches of fibers to obtain greater fullness if necessary. Generally, however, flies dressed with hackle beards are purposely sparse. See Fig. 9, No. 10.

Fastening on the Wings: See Fig. 9, Nos. 3, 4, & 7; Fig. 11, No. 5. Cement the hackle windings. While the cement is hardening, choose the area of wing feather from which you will cut a section, or one-half the fly wing. Separate the fibers with the point of the dubbing needle.Determine the width of the fly wing by approximation and, with the dubbing needle, space off this width, separating the fibers again. Cut out this section. Repeat the same procedure with the opposite feather. Hold these paired wing-segments (with the natural curve of the feather inclined downward and outward) between the thumb and forefinger of the left hand. With the nail of the right thumb crimp the base of the wing sections at that point where they will be tied to the hook. Place the wings as shown in Fig. 11, No. 5, on top of the shank—not straddling it—and cover with two loose turns of the working silk. (The wings must be held firmly during this entire procedure and not released until the final turn has been made.) Gradually increase the tension on the working silk until the slack has been taken up. If the wings have not revolved, wind two or three more turns and re-check. If correct and upright, the wings can now be permanently tied down. At this stage of construction the finished product can be classified as good or poor. If the wings have become distorted, the fly will have lost much of its appeal. It can be salvaged, however, by unwinding as far as necessary to make whatever corrections or wing replacements are required.

Finishing the Fly: See Fig. 9, No. 11; Fig. 11, Nos. 5 & 6. With a single-edge razor blade make a tapered cut slanting toward the eye of the hook as shown in Fig. 11, No. 5, and make the necessary turns to completely cover the butt fibers. A drop of cement applied to these fibers before the final windings are made will prolong the life of the fly. Whip-finish the head as indicated in Fig. 11, No. 6, and apply a last drop of cement to seal all possible open places.

If you have been making a large wet fly with proportionately heavy working silk, it is still possible to form a neat, tapered head. After you have tied down the wings do not attempt to taper the head with the heavier silk, but secure it with a half-hitch

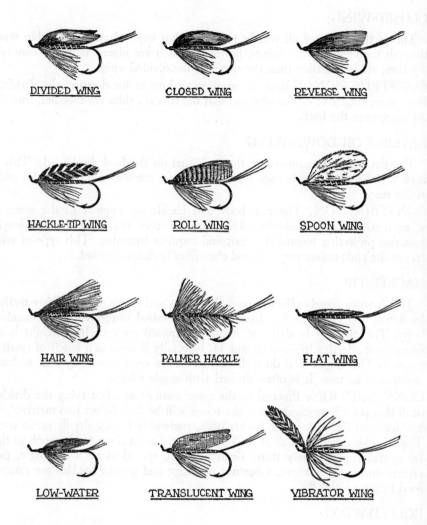

DIVIDED WING   CLOSED WING   REVERSE WING

HACKLE-TIP WING   ROLL WING   SPOON WING

HAIR WING   PALMER HACKLE   FLAT WING

LOW-WATER   TRANSLUCENT WING   VIBRATOR WING

FIG. 10
WET-FLY DESIGN

Leonard

and apply cement. Then, while the cement is still tacky, fasten gossamer or very fine working silk over the heavier base winds, taper the head and whip-finish. Very large flies can be finished in this manner.

CLOSED-WING

This is the oldest of all wet-fly types and has enjoyed an unassailable reputation through the centuries. Its wings, however, which are placed with the concave sides together, are less flexible than the wings of the divided-wing.

CONSTRUCTION: Follow the same procedure as for dressing the divided-wing, but reverse the curve of the wings so that the concave sides are together, thus forming a closure over the back.

REVERSE OR DOWN-WING

The down-wing is unusual in that it is tied on the hook backwards. This type is used to imitate the female caddis fly whose wings are somewhat triangular and larger at the rear.

CONSTRUCTION: The tail, body and hackle are applied in the same way as when making the divided-wing. The wing, however, is tied by the tips, leaving the butt end projecting toward the rear, and requires trimming. This type of wing will fray at the ends unless very soft and close-fiber feathers are used.

HACKLE-TIP

This is an extremely effective type. Tied slim and sparse, this fly fairly rivals nature for action and will take fish from the hardest-fished waters with phenomenal regularity. The ultimate in delicacy, it can be dressed on very light-weight hooks and seems most effective in sizes 16 and 14, especially if there is a hatch of small flies in progress. The angler will do well to concentrate on this wet fly and to know and understand its uses. It is often dressed with single wings.

CONSTRUCTION: Proceed in the same manner as when tying the divided-wing until that point is reached where the wings will be tied. Select two matched, resilient hackles from the base of the hackle neck, preferably from a dry-fly grade cock neck. These hackles should be short, stiff and glossy. Fasten them to the hook so that they are spread approximately thirty degrees. Being spaced at such an angle, they will vibrate during the retrieve. Chestnut partridge and guinea hackles are exceptionally good to use on this fly.

ROLLED-WING

In this type the wing is composed of flank, side and breast feathers from such birds as the mallard, wood duck, teal and widgeon. These materials are finely barred, banded or speckled and give a very lifelike appearance to the fly.

CONSTRUCTION: The same procedure is followed as when making other wet flies, with the exception of the treatment of the wings. Remove the fluff from the base of the feather and break off the center section at the top. Place the feather between the palms of the hands and rub it briskly, removing all the curvature peculiar to this kind of feather. Pinch together as many of the fibers as necessary to make the wing and, holding them tightly, strip or cut them, whichever method is more convenient,

mcginty

golden demon

railbird

black demon

rogue

silver doctor

Plate II
Steelhead Wet Flies

Eonard

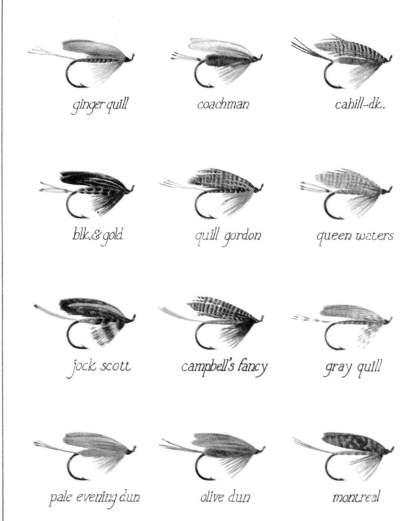

ginger quill   coachman   cahill-dk.

blk.& gold   quill gordon   queen waters

jock scott   campbell's fancy   gray quill

pale evening dun   olive dun   montreal

Plate I
Favorite Wet Flies

LEONARD

from the feather. Place these fibers on the shank and tie them down securely, after first having applied a drop of cement to their underside.

SPOON-WING

The spoon-wing is seldom seen today except as a spinner fly for bass, in which form it has been a successful lure for many years. However, certain salmon and steelhead patterns are dressed with spoon-wings on turn-down-eye hooks. The spoon-wing is weaker than other wings, in that its main support is a fine quill center which is the most vulnerable part of the fly. As soon as this center is fractured the wing will break off. It does make up into a beautiful fly, however.

CONSTRUCTION: Follow the same procedure as when making the divided-wing types except for the wings. These will be whole paired feathers taken from under the wings or from the breasts of the various ducks. Breast feathers from the wood duck, mallard and others are unbeatable for this purpose. In addition to the duck plumage, partridge hackle, guinea breast and crow breast, to name but a few, are widely used. Place the butts of the wing feathers so that they straddle the hook, and wind several turns of the working silk around the butts until the wings are snug. Before whipping the head be certain the wings are not set at an angle; they should be flat, together, and vertical.

HAIR-WING

This is an American variation which has become popular in the past ten years. In reality it may be no more than a midget bucktail dressed in standard or special patterns. However, when correctly made, the hair-wing is the most durable of all the wet flies. A variety of animal hair is available for making this fly, giving it unlimited possibilities. Ordinarily it is dressed with bucktail and squirrel-tail wings, the former in plain white and natural brown plus the many dyed colors, the latter in mottled-gray or barred-brown. These kinds of hair can be used to make wings for nearly every standard pattern, and the finished fly will closely represent the fly dressed with original feather wings.

CONSTRUCTION: Here again the single difference between standard types and this one is in the application of the wing. After having wound and fastened the hackle, trim off the tips of a section of bucktail, or whatever hair is to be used, and lay them on the top of the body. Take two or three turns with the working silk, then check that the hair has not rolled out of position. Take several more turns and finish with the whip-knot. Sometimes it is difficult to make hair-wings remain in place, and at such times it is advisable to touch the butts of the wings with Ambroid cement before they are applied to the hook.

PALMER

It is not possible to dress all standard patterns without being familiar with the Palmer style of hackle. Patterns such as the Wickham's Fancy, Flying-Caddis, Queen of the Waters, Silver Sedge and others require this type of hackle. Some years ago the Palmer style was so popular that one of the best known tackle houses dressed this fly on a #8 hook and sold it under a special trade name. It was made in one pattern and size to serve one purpose: to lure big brown trout from the deep holes. It did catch big trout and has continued to do so for years.

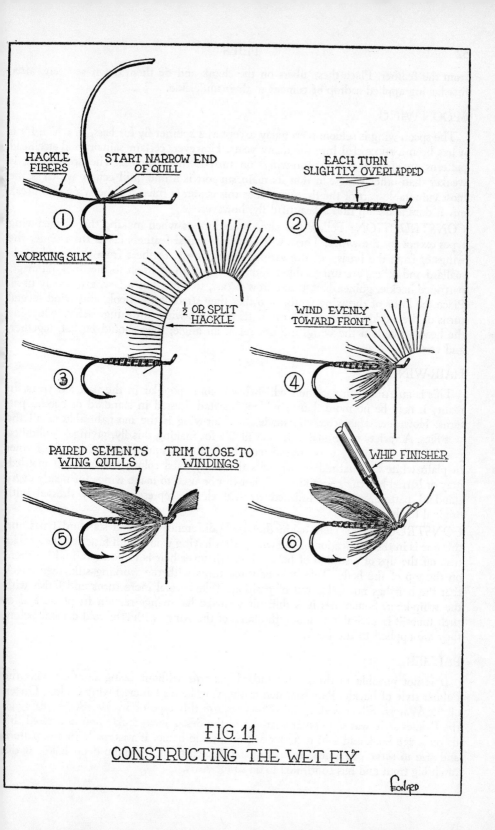

HACKLE FIBERS START NARROW END OF QUILL

① WORKING SILK

② EACH TURN SLIGHTLY OVERLAPPED

③ ½ OR SPLIT HACKLE

④ WIND EVENLY TOWARD FRONT

⑤ PAIRED SEMENTS WING QUILLS TRIM CLOSE TO WINDINGS

⑥ WHIP FINISHER

FIG. 11
CONSTRUCTING THE WET FLY

Leonard

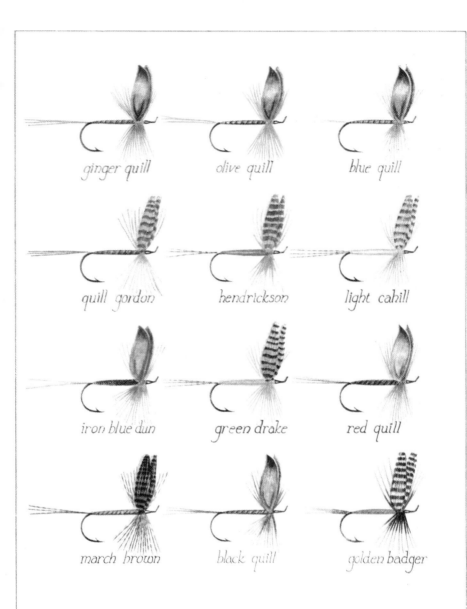

ginger quill

olive quill

blue quill

quill gordon

hendrickson

light cahill

iron blue dun

green drake

red quill

march brown

black quill

golden badger

Plate III
Favorite Dry Flies

Rodger

red-bellied dace

shiner

Plate IV
Theory Of Streamer Design

Eonard

CONSTRUCTION: Fasten the tail fibers in the usual manner. Split a hackle lengthwise as already described and secure the tip end slightly forward of the tail windings. Fasten the body material and wind it the required distance up the shank of the hook, leaving the hackle feather hanging free. Wind the hackle at even intervals and tie with one or two half-hitches. The shoulder hackle should be of slightly wider spread and restricted to three turns. Complete in the usual manner.

FLAT-WING

Undoubtedly this was one of the first of the artificials tied to represent a submerged female stone fly. With its wings folded close over its back, it does resemble this insect endeavoring to deposit eggs. This type is more effective if tied with mottled or barred wings similar to the wings of the natural insect than with flat gray or brown wings.

CONSTRUCTION: Dress this fly in the same way as any standard type of wet fly, but fashion the wings folded over the body. At first these wings will be troublesome because they will have a tendency to elevate at the rear, and perhaps curl downward over the hackle. Sometimes this results from an attempt to apply too much wing. A good method to prevent elevating of the wings at the rear follows: After the hackle has been wound and fastened, rub a little dubbing material on the winding silk. Wind this dubbing where the wings will be located. This will form a cushion so that when the wings are tied down the windings will surround a larger surface and thus prevent the curling and elevation of the wings. I have used this method with many different types of wet flies and really believe it simplifies the dressing of wings difficult to handle, particularly the wings of the hair fly, already described, and this, the flat-wing. In selecting wings, choose pairs having the flare of the tips pointed inward to form a natural closure similar to that of the natural insect.

LOW-WATER

This fly is the development of several fly-makers who sought to construct a wet fly that would sink quickly and have the maximum of hooking power but, at the same time, retain the size and shape of the standard dressing. This need was occasioned by adverse fishing conditions on salmon waters. When low water necessitated the use of the smallest size of flies and their proportionately small hooks, holding a fish became very doubtful. A hooked fish often meant a lost fish due to the lack of holding power of the hook, itself. Consequently the short-dressed fly, on a hook two or three sizes larger than ordinarily would have been used, was developed. This amounts to a size #8 fly dressed on a hook size 4, or a size 6 fly on a hook size 2. Many steelhead anglers use this type of fly for the additional hook power alone; although trout fishers are inclining toward similar arrangements for use in rough, heavy streams.

CONSTRUCTION: This is merely a standard wet fly dressed small for the size of the hook. It is best to proportion this fly two sizes smaller than the hook size, although certain localities have established other precedents concerning this proportion.

TRANSLUCENT-WING

This is mainly a large brown-trout fly of slim appearance and medium-sparse dressing to simulate the female May fly descending below the surface to deposit her eggs. This fly features the egg sac at the tip of the abdomen, and fish-skin wings.

CONSTRUCTION: The procedure is standard with the exception of fastening the wings. These wings are machine-cut in one piece and resemble a propeller. Fold the wings in the shape of a "V" so they straddle the hook. Take several laps with the working silk, meanwhile holding the wings upward and toward the rear. Finish in the usual manner.

VIBRATOR-WING

The purpose of this type is to obtain the maximum of wing action. This is accomplished by fastening two glossy and resilient hackle-tip wings pointed toward the front immediately behind the eye. The water resistance causes these wings to bend outward and backward with great activity.

CONSTRUCTION: Follow the same procedure as when making the hackle-tip but incline the wings well forward, even in a straight line if necessary.

STEELHEAD WET FLIES

Steelhead wet flies are perhaps the most recent addition to the list of specialized flies. Rivers of the Pacific slope are rough, fast, and punctuated regularly with falls and rapids. Normal conditions mean a heavy volume of water, which, incidentally, is no deterrent to the steelhead. These big, lightning-fast fish are perfectly comfortable in such water and usually stay close to the bottom; consequently the wise steelheader fishes deep, letting his fly sweep behind the boulders and into the pockets.

A wet fly dressed according to eastern standards is definitely a misfit for steelhead, mainly for the reason that it is too lightly dressed on hooks usually too small, and is too drab. The great majority of eastern wet flies are based on natural insects; steelhead flies are not. It is an unpleasant thought to picture a steelhead hooked on one of the whisp-like wet flies commonly used by brown-trout fishermen.

Claude M. Kreider, one of the best informed steelhead specialists in the Pacific area, and author of the excellent book *Steelhead,* is definitely an advocate of large flies. Kreider believes in three things which, considered as a whole, are nothing less than a maxim: big water—big flies—big fish. And Claude is a most practical fisherman.

The weight of the fly is one of the first considerations. It must be heavy enough to stay *deep*. The second consideration is color. These flies are as bright as clowns when compared with eastern natural-looking patterns. Yellow and orange are the predominating colors, with red, off-shades of red, and black almost as popular. Durability is the third consideration and a most important one. Atlantic salmon flies probably could be used regularly for steelhead if it were not for the abuse that steelhead give a fly. Even so, certain patterns having comparatively durable bodies and wings have been and are still being used successfully. Present trends show that fly-dressers are concerned about building durable flies: wing fibers have been replaced by strong polar-bear hair; bodies, instead of being the more delicate floss, are now harder, longer, wearing materials like reinforced tinsel, chenille, and even brass and copper wire.

The sinking properties of steelhead flies depend on the hook weight alone; not very much can be done to keep a fly deep by merely adding more material to the wings, hackle or tail fibers. Therefore, extra weight is made possible by two means: by using hooks of heavier calibration or larger size without increasing the size of the fly itself, or by wrapping heavy wire around the hook shank. Both methods are popular; each has its own individual merits.

6/6
REGULAR

SIZE 6 FLY-STD. #6 HOOK

6/6 2X STOUT
EX-WEIGHT
NO SIZE INCREASE

SIZE 6 FLY-2X STOUT #6 HOOK

6/2 3X SHORT
EX-WEIGHT
WIDER GAPE
NO SIZE INCREASE

SIZE 6 FLY-3X SHORT #2 HOOK

6/2
EX-WEIGHT
WIDER GAPE
NO SIZE INCREASE
USELESS EXTRA LENGTH

SIZE 6 FLY-STD. #2 HOOK

FIG. 12
STEELHEAD WET FLY DESIGN

LEONARD

Fig. 12, Steelhead Wet-Fly Design, illustrates a single pattern, the Silver Demon, dressed standard in every respect, and three alternate dressings of the same pattern on different hooks. It will be noticed that the *fly* is the same size in each case; that the *hook* is the single element changed. These four different hook sizes have always been a source of confusion to many anglers, principally because most people expect to see a difference in the size of the fly or some other alteration in it when the terms "2X short" or "dressed short" are affixed. Actually, the fly is not altered at all. But the *hook* is.

The standard-size hook has a gape proportionate to the hook size. Consequently the size of the fly corresponds to the hook. However, it is not always logical or practical to go to a larger-size fly simply to have the fly sink deeper. The solution is to increase the hook weight without effecting a change in the size of the fly.

The fly labeled A in Fig. 12 is a fly of standard size throughout. Fly B, however, is the same fly dressed on a 2X stout or strong hook. Except for the calibration of the wire, the hooks are identical in every department. Fly C is again the same size fly dressed on a short shank hook of larger gape but having a *shank* equivalent to the shank length of the standard. This means, of course, that the wire is heavier and the gape wider, each condition being ideally suited to steelhead flies. Fly D is this same fly dressed on a standard hook having the gape and wire diameter the same as the short shank hook in Fly C. Since the hook is standard, however, its shank is necessarily longer than required for the fly and a portion of it remains unwrapped.

The foregoing description has been prepared with the thought in mind that it might be possible to have some stronger tendency toward standardization in the future than we have today. To this end, a proposed system for the designation of hook and fly relationships follows.

When the fly dressed on a standard hook is in proportion to that hook, let us assume that the fly size denotes the hook size; for example, a Royal Coachman size 6. However, to establish certainty, we could go one step further and denote both sizes in this manner: Royal Coachman size 6/6. In keeping with this plan, we would write the size of fly B in Fig. 12 in this manner: Silver Demon size 6/6-2X stout; fly C, 6/2-3X short; fly D, 6/2. This would forever eliminate the doubt in the minds of fly-fishermen about the definite and important relationship between hook and fly.

Wire-wrapped bodies are being featured on many of the newer patterns. The wire adds appreciable weight to the fly and, for this reason, is recommended for use with standard-weight hooks. Some patterns are dressed extra heavy, that is, on stout hooks with the additional weight of the wire wrapping. These flies probe the very depths of a river regardless of the current conditions, thus increasing the percentage of strikes.

Steelhead flies cannot be classified into definite groups like the majority of other wet flies. The obvious differences between two or more patterns are not attributable so much to the details of construction as they are to the combinations of colors. Whether a fly has hackle or not does not particularly assign that fly to a distinct class of hackled or hackleless flies; this is a difference in pattern only. In like manner, a wire body instead of a tinsel body would not classify wire-body flies to the exclusion of flies having tinsel bodies.

CONSTRUCTION: Steelhead wet flies are constructed in the same way as trout wet flies. The greater number of patterns have hair wings, slightly stiffer hackle than that used on trout flies, durable chenille and tinsel bodies, and thick hackle-fiber tails. The dressing, itself, is on the full side but is not bushy. Beard hackle is used infrequently since saddle hackle wound in the collar style is gaining prominence. However, copper and brass wire, especially when it is to be the body proper instead of a covered part, is prepared and applied a little differently from orthodox materials.

The wire is wound around the hook shank immediately after the shank has been covered with winds of working silk and lacquered. No other work precedes this. To prepare the wire, taper the edge to be tied to the shank by filing carefully with a fine jeweler's file. Place this on the shank and slowly wind the wire around the tapered tip and up the shank to a point slightly farther from the eye of the hook than ordinarily. This wire has no spring, consequently will remain in position. Next rub a little jeweler's rouge on a fine brass-bristled polishing brush and buff the wire to a high luster. With a similar brush entirely free of rouge or other polishing agent, buff the wire again to increase the luster and to remove the few remaining particles of rouge. (Silver polish and similar cleaning and polishing agents are sometimes recommended but these do leave a deposit or film on the wire that tends toward discoloration.) Finish with a coat of lacquer.

Now tie on the tail fibers. While this is in inverse order, it is the most satisfactory for the reason that a knob would be formed by the wire wrapping if the wire were wound over any material on the end of the shank. Tail fibers must be much thicker than usual. Use a whole hackle feather if necessary, stripping off the fibers into a bunch. After the tail is in place, taper the juncture between body and tail by carefully winding the working silk into a tight cone.

If the pattern requires it, apply the hackle accordingly.

The wings, which are generally hair, are tied on last, unless shoulder trim such as jungle-cock eyes, chatterer, or strips of contrasting color are necessary which, of course, would follow the application of the wings.

By all means use cement wherever logical. Moreover, coat the head several times to insure its permanency.

Steelhead flies are still undergoing development and improvement. Undoubtedly many books to come in the near future will contain invaluable information, better patterns, better methods of construction. At least they will be twentieth century techniques and may set entirely new precedents in fly-dressing.

In the pattern dictionary, Chapter 14, steelhead patterns are listed in an individual group. This list does not include every steelhead pattern because it is doubtful whether the majority of such patterns have been tabulated or not. However, the list does include a reasonable cross-section of the patterns you will find most anglers using.

Chapter Six

THE DRY FLY

The dry fly is essentially just what the name implies: a dry or floating fly, bug, beetle or spider often referred to as "driftfood." These creatures come to the stream surface voluntarily, by emerging from the stream-bed to molt and eventually fly away, if not consumed by a feeding trout, involuntarily falling on the water or by being swept into the stream by freshets. High waters reach into the network of weeds and soil lining the river and wash away many of the small, hiding land-inhabitants. Showers cast caterpillars and other immature insects to the surface where they drift helplessly. These insects rarely drown, however, and this is one of the strong points for the dry-fly fisher.

It is reasonable to believe that any dry fly must have a certain likeness to the natural floating insect. This is especially true in the matter of behavior. Behavior, or floating quality, is dependent upon three primary factors: light hook-weight, balance in design, and buoyancy of materials. Here sparseness is included with the second factor, and does not require individual mention. Taken in sequence: the dry fly should be dressed only on hooks made for dry flies; the eye should be finely tapered; the shank round and fine; and the shape either sproat or round. The tapered eye reduces hook weight in a critical area and minimizes the size of the head. Be particular about the eye on any hook you use, and the more emphasis you place on the perfect suitability of dry-fly hooks, the better. Sharp edges, imperfectly turned eyes and coarse plating are all enemies of fine leader points. The taper should graduate evenly from the full diameter of the shank into the finer wire size at that point where the wings will be tied in, or approximately one-fourth the distance of the shank from the eye.

DRY-FLY PROPORTIONS

Not enough emphasis can be placed on the importance of correct proportions in dry-fly design. Regardless of how beautiful the colors might be, if the wings are too long, or the hackle too small or too large, or the body is improperly dressed, the finished fly will not perform satisfactorily. For example, wings too long will twist light leader tippets during casting. Or if the hackle should be dressed too long, the chances are the fly will fall forward on its head. These and many other conditions are a detriment to good angling and are all too common in dry-fly design. Any single, unbalanced portion of a dry fly can destroy the value of that fly, itself. It will require effort to develop the proper technique, but the results of consistently well-balanced

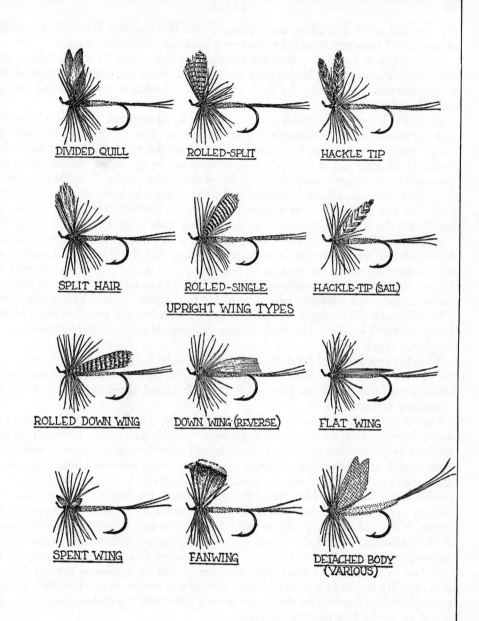

DIVIDED QUILL   ROLLED-SPLIT   HACKLE TIP

SPLIT HAIR   ROLLED-SINGLE   HACKLE-TIP (SAIL)

UPRIGHT WING TYPES

ROLLED DOWN WING   DOWN WING (REVERSE)   FLAT WING

SPENT WING   FANWING   DETACHED BODY (VARIOUS)

FIG. 13
DRY-FLY DESIGN (I)

Leonard

dry flies will repay that effort many times. Fewer flies properly balanced, regardless of hue, are of infinitely more value than grosses of the hit-or-miss variety.

Turn to Fig. 8 and notice how the relationship of one part of the fly affects the other parts. Proportioning begins with the first operations and continues throughout every successive phase until the fly is completed. All comparisons are based on the shank length (A).

The wing length is expressed as (B) which is equal to shank length (A). Notice that the wings are set far enough behind the eye to allow for forming the head of the fly without cramming. This also makes possible the tying of clean, neat leader knots. The hackle radius (C) is readily determined by spreading the hackle at the base over a pin which is held at the center of the circle entitled "Hackle Diameter." The Dry-Fly Hackle Gauge is indexed by line numbers which are identified with the hook size. For example, let us assume that a hackle feather fanned around the pin would describe a radius extending to line 4. We wish to make a standard dry fly. Therefore, with the radius #4 shown opposite hook size #14, we determine that the hackle feather in question is suitable for a size #14 dry fly only. In most cases the Hackle Gauge will be used in inverse order, that is, the size of the fly will be known, and it will be necessary to select the hackle to match it. Notice also that the gauge indicates the different relative radii for the regular, variant and spider types. The tail length (D) is equal to the total hook length less the eye, this latter length being described as (G). The body length (E) equals approximately three-quarters the shank length (A).

The characteristics and behavior of a dry fly can be judged by a simple test. Toss the fly into the air and watch its descent. If it lights on the table top in an upright position with just the hackle legs and the tips of the tail fibers supporting it, the fly is properly balanced.

Hackle spells the success or failure of any dry fly, whether or not the other materials have been well chosen. Its purpose is twofold: to provide buoyancy to the artificial, and to simulate as closely as possible the legs of the natural insect. Actually this latter consideration is not important enough to be too much concerned with, since an insect has six legs, and it is self-evident that an artificial with six hackle legs would be almost useless as a floating fly. However, the application of too much hackle destroys the illusion to the fish, and does not assist in floating the fly as first thought might indicate. Hackle of dry-fly quality is necessarily elastic with a maximum of resistance to absorption. To support the weight of the dry fly properly, these fibers should bend without penetrating the water surface. Once the water film has been pierced, the fly will lose its buoyancy. A good demonstration of surface tension is the old trick of floating a dry needle in a glass of water. Similarly, a minimum but sufficient amount of hackle points bending on the water surface will cause the surface tension to support a fly in the best possible manner.

The butts of the hackle placed between the heavy ends of the wing base brace the wings and, at the same time, are concealed when wound over by the body material. This tends to taper the foundation for the fly body. If two hackles are to be used, they should be placed with the convex sides together. The rear one should be wound clockwise, the front one counter-clockwise. This cross-winding tends to brace the wings and the hackle.

Those who are especially mindful of exact duplication will be interested in the

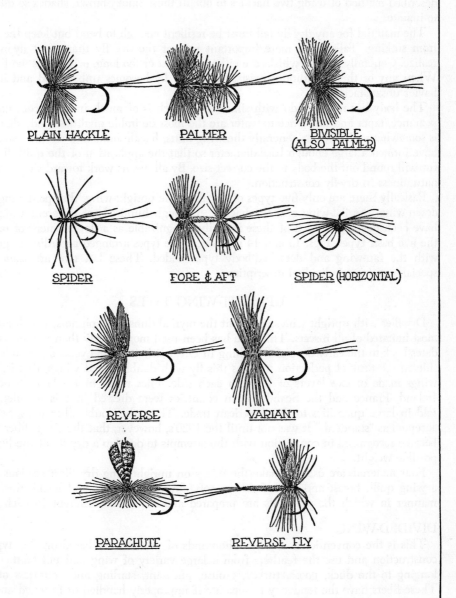

PLAIN HACKLE   PALMER   BIVISIBLE
(ALSO PALMER)

SPIDER   FORE & AFT   SPIDER (HORIZONTAL)

REVERSE   VARIANT

PARACHUTE   REVERSE FLY

FIG. 14
DRY-FLY DESIGN (II)

LEONARD

described method of using two hackles to obtain those smoky-brown shades so difficult to imitate.

The material for any dry-fly tail must be resilient enough to bend but keep the hook from sinking. Tails are a more important part of the dry fly than most fly-makers realize. Generally the tail whisks are either too short or too long, or perhaps too flimsy. When any of these conditions exists, the whole fly becomes unbalanced and its behavior unsatisfactory.

The body has much to do with silhouette, which is of much importance. Slim appearance, taper and resistance to water are the most desirable qualities. Body diameter is somewhat variable, but generally the wing butts, hackle butts and working silk will have formed a large enough base diameter so that the application of the quill, floss or fur will round out the body to the correct size. By all means work toward slimness and naturalness in dry-fly construction.

Basically there are only five types of dry flies: the upright-wing, the spent-wing, the down-wing, the flat-wing and the hackle. Although hundreds of different variations have been developed, each of these is easily recognizable as a development of one of the five basic types. Figs. 13 and 14 illustrate these types arranged according to groups with the fan-wing and detached-body types added. These last two are somewhat special, requiring individual descriptions.

UPRIGHT-WING TYPES

Dry flies with upright wings represent the myriad duns and spinners, which are the most imitated of all insects. This type has been used more widely than any other and dates back to the early days of fly-fishing in Great Britain. Some years ago it was considered the peak of perfection to dress this fly with double-paired wings, that is, with wings made of two layers of fiber on each side. Flies made in England, Scotland, Ireland, France and the Scandanavian countries were dressed in this manner, and sold in large quantities to the American trade. Thus, the double-fiber wing became accepted as "standard." It was not until the 1920's, however, that the single-fiber wing became recognized in connection with the attempts to develop a dry fly of the lightest possible weight.

Four materials are used to make the wings on upright-wing dry flies: sections from a wing quill, breast and flank feathers, soft, fine animal hair, and hackle-tips. The manner in which the materials are prepared and applied is different in each case.

DIVIDED-WING

This is the conventional dry fly. Thousands of patterns are based on this type of construction and use the feathers from a large variety of wing and tail feathers belonging to the duck, goose, turkey, grouse, pheasant, starling and countless others. These fibers have the tendency to separate if improperly handled or fastened and for this reason should be tied with the natural curve of the feather inclined toward the rear of the fly. This will prevent to a minimum the separation of the fibers during construction and fraying of the tips after repeated false casting.

CONSTRUCTION, *Preparation of Materials*: Lay out the required materials generally according to the same plan described for constructing the wet fly and the proportions illustrated in Fig. 8. Materials for dry flies are necessarily water-resistant and resilient to a practical degree. Keep this in mind when selecting hackle, especially. Fig. 8 shows the re-

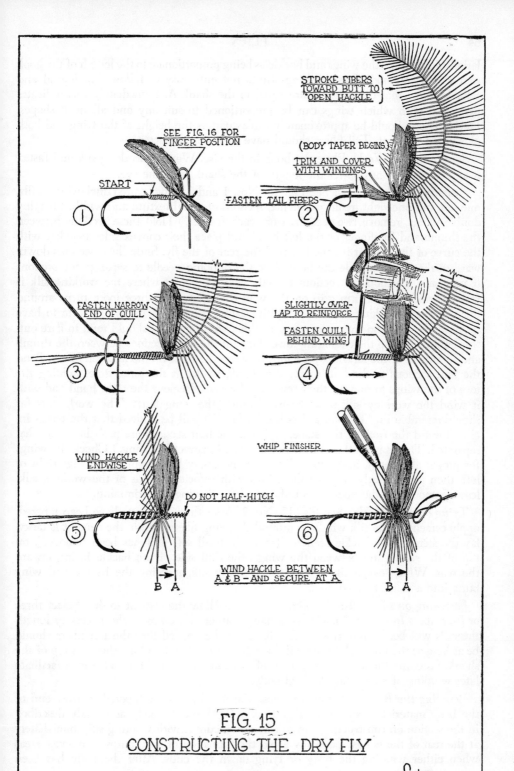

FIG. 15
CONSTRUCTING THE DRY FLY

lationship between the wings and hackle as being proportionate to the length of the hook shank. This method of establishing size is not only easy to follow, but logical and reliable. Note that the wings B are equal to the shank A. Immediately this indicates the speed with which wings can be proportioned to suit any and all hook shapes. Hackle fibers should be approximately three-quarters the height of the wing and both glossy and resilient. Tail fibers should have the same character.

Setting up the Work: Place the hook in the vise. Wax the working silk and fasten it approximately one-quarter the length of the shank from the eye.

Fastening on the Wings: See Fig. 16, Nos. 1 and 2. From paired duck-wing quills, one left and one right, remove matched sections of equal texture and width. (If tying double wings, remove two sections from each feather.) Hold these sections between the thumb and forefinger of the left hand and place their convex sides together with the curve of the feather inclined toward the rear of the fly. Slide these sections downward so that they straddle the hook. Use the dubbing needle to separate the sections if necessary. Position the sections directly over that point where the working silk is fastened and, with a firm grip on the wings, wind two or three loose turns around them with the working silk. Draw up the slack gradually. If the wings seem to have set properly, wind on two more turns; at this point the wings should tend to flare outward a little. Grasp the extending lower butts of the wing sections between the thumb and forefinger of the left hand, the tops between the right thumb and forefinger. Bend the butt sections to the left, under the shank, while, at the same time, holding the tops of the wings to prevent their revolving forward. Remove the right hand and with it wind the working silk several turns around the wing butts. The work thus far should resemble Fig. 16, No. 2, less the hackle. (It will be noticed that the wings incline toward the front at this stage, and that the butt sections are probably somewhat separated. This is natural and does not indicate incorrect handling.) Check the wings for proper alignment, make any adjustment necessary by pressing the wings right or left, then permanently emplace the wings with sufficient winds of the working silk, leaving enough of the fiber butts unfastened for shaping and trimming.

Tying on the Hackle: See Fig. 15, No. 2. After the wing butts have been tapered, apply cement to the silk windings around the wing fibers. While the cement is tacky, lay the stem of the hackle feather (from which all soft fluff has been removed) on top of the shank and between the wings, the dull side of the hackle facing toward the rear. Wind several times with the working silk, merging the hackle and wing butts into a solid, tapered area.

Fastening on the Tails: See Fig. 15, No. 3. Allow the cement to dry. Select three or four fibers from a stiff hackle or a flank feather and estimate the necessary length the tails will be, by referring to Fig. 8. It will be noticed that the tail fibers should be as long as the hook. Hold the tail fibers in the left hand and lay them on top of the shank, fastening them with three turns of working silk. Avoid excess turns to facilitate later winding of a smoothly tapered body.

Winding the Body: See Fig. 15, Nos. 4 and 5. Fasten the tapered, narrow end of the body material as shown in Fig. 15, No 3. Wind the body as already described in the section on constructing the wet fly and secure it with working silk immediately at the rear of the wings. Carefully avoid the formation of any lumps or uneven areas when either winding the body or tying down the ends. After the body has been

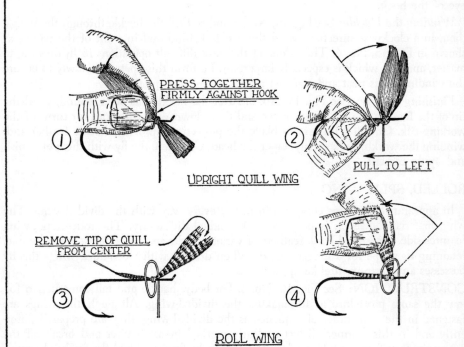

PRESS TOGETHER
FIRMLY AGAINST HOOK

① ②

UPRIGHT QUILL WING

PULL TO LEFT

REMOVE TIP OF QUILL
FROM CENTER

③ ④

ROLL WING

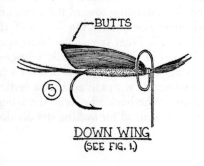

BUTTS

PRESS WITH THUMB

⑤ ⑥

DOWN WING
(SEE FIG. 1.)

FLAT WING

FIG. 16
FASTENING DRY-FLY WINGS

Leonard

wound and permanently tied down, trim off the excess, wind the working silk to the eye of the hook.

Winding the Hackle: See Fig. 15, Nos. 5 and 6. Pull the hackle through the wings; then, in a clockwise direction, wind the hackle behind and in front of the wings, as shown in Fig. 15, No. 6. This is one of the most difficult operations in fly-dressing to master, and one which is especially important. Perform this operation slowly to ensure the winding of as neat and compact a hackle spread as possible.

Finishing the Fly: See Fig. 15, No. 6. After the hackle has been wound, wind the tip of the feather behind the hook eye and tie it down with three or four turns of the working silk. Cut off with a razor blade the projecting tip of the hackle feather and, winding the working silk evenly, taper the head. Complete the fly with the whip-finish and apply cement.

ROLLED, SPLIT-WING

In appearance this type compares in nearly every way with the divided wing. The wing material, however, is prepared and handled differently. The rolled, split-wing features side, breast and flank feathers of various ducks and is, perhaps, more durable, retaining its shape for a longer period. When dressed with wood-duck wings this fly possesses an uncanny, lifelike appearance.

CONSTRUCTION: See Fig. 16, No. 3. For body, hackle and tail construction follow the same procedure as for making the divided-wing. Although the wings are fastened in the same order of sequence as the divided-wing, they are prepared differently and in this manner: Select a clearly marked breast feather and break off the center tip, thus forming a V notch in the end of the feather. Hold the feather between the palms of the hands and rub briskly several times. This removes any curvature. Press the feather against the top of the shank, the tips extending toward the front, and fasten with the working silk at a point approximately one-quarter the length of the shank from the eye. This is illustrated in Fig. 16, No. 3. Next spread the fibers apart until they are equally divided and, with several turns of the working silk, criss-cross between the divided sections. Pull back on the wing tops, making several turns with the working silk in front of the wings. This will incline the wings in an almost vertical position as shown in Fig. 16, No. 2. Fasten the butt of the hackle between the wings, then continue in exactly the same manner as already described for making the divided-wing.

HACKLE-TIP WING

This is a very lifelike variation, especially good for imitating the many delicate flies frequenting slow streams. Interesting colors can be obtained by dyeing the barred hackle tips. This offers a very wide range of colors from pure white to black, including many banded alternate colors. The tiny neck hackles which make the wings for this type of fly are found at the top of the cape behind the cock's comb and some are found on the sides at the top of the neck. These are ideally shaped, being round, glossy and resilient, with a surprisingly strong center quill. Usually they are slightly cup-shaped.

CONSTRUCTION: Select a pair of hackle feathers about the same length as the sections you would cut from a wing feather, depending, of course, on the size of fly to be tied. Match these with their convex sides together, placing them in position in the same manner as when making the previously described flies. Take two or three loose turns with the working silk, size the wings for height, then take all the slack out of the working silk. Bend the two butts back along the underside of the hook shank and trim off the surplus. Continue to finish the fly in the usual manner. Never trim the round tips to shorten or true a wing. It is better to proportion the wings first, even if it requires a longer time.

Certain and special patterns may require a different arrangement of these wings. It is not uncommon to use double wings, meaning that there are double layers on each side; and it is fairly ordinary to have to dress a long-shank fly, the wings of which are in tandem, one pair behind another. In the former case, the wings are merely doubled—right and left—one over the other. In the latter case, the rear wings are tied in first, a short portion of body added, then the front wings are fastened.

The hackle-tip wing type of fly can be dressed extremely sparse and thin, making it superb for heavily cast-over waters.

SPLIT, HAIR-WING

This type closely resembles the rolled split-wing in every respect. For durability this fly is unsurpassed. Such patterns as the Royal Coachman and White Wulff tied with split hair-wings have acquired a deserved reputation for attracting trout, small-mouth bass and salmon.

CONSTRUCTION: The hair for making this wing is restricted to comparatively few animals. Deer hair is too coarse, and most other animal hair is difficult to fasten to the hook. Badger, groundhog, lynx and polar-bear hair are the best for this purpose. With scissors, snip off a small patch of hair close to the skin. Pull out all the loose hair and, with a tooth brush, comb out the fine surface fuzz at the base. With working silk fastened in the usual place and well-coated with cement, place the prepared hair over the hook in the same manner as when constructing the rolled split-wing. After fastening the hair securely and dividing it with the working silk, make a tapered cut slanted toward the rear with a razor blade to eliminate any chance of forming a lump where the butt of the hair terminates. Finish the fly in the usual manner.

SINGLE ROLLED WING

This is a good fly to use up the odds and ends that accumulate on any fly-dresser's table, and is very acceptable in small sizes even to the severest crank. The wing is made from the center tip which has been removed from a breast feather in the construction of the rolled split-wing.

CONSTRUCTION: Fasten the single wing in an upright position and finish the fly in the usual fashion.

SAIL-WING

The sail-wing is often featured on certain hackle and bivisible types. It is an easy type to begin with and makes a very satisfactory fly.

CONSTRUCTION: Select a single hackle tip and remove the slight curve by drawing the feather over the thumb nail. Fasten with the working silk on the far side of the hook, place the hackle in position, and finish in the regular manner. This wing can be fastened on top of the hook down-wing style, and then bent upward and held in position by winding the hackle behind it.

DOWN-WING TYPES

Dry flies featuring down-wings represent principally the sedges or caddis flies and the alder flies. It could be said they are similar to wet flies in appearance with the single exception of the hackle, which is wound like all dry-fly hackle.

Three materials are used to make the wings on down-wing flies: sections from a wing quill, breast and flank feathers, and soft, fine animal hair. Hackle tips are not the correct shape and are inclined to assume an upright position.

Down-wings have one thing in common: the wings are tied on before the hackle.

ROLLED WING

This is the easiest of the down-wings to dress. The dark-barred flank feathers from the wood duck make exceptionally effective wings, closely simulating the mottled brownish wings of the natural alder fly and some caddis flies.

CONSTRUCTION: All down-wings are tied in inverse order compared with other dry flies in the respect that the tail, body, wing and, finally, the hackle, are applied in that order, a sequence entirely unlike any other. The reason for this is obvious. Since the wings extend over—but close to—the back, they must be tied on before the hackle. Complete the tail and body in the same manner as when making a wet fly. Secure the working silk with a half-hitch, and apply a drop of cement to the area where the wings will be located. Select a flank feather having the required barring or mottling, fold it so the sides are pinched together, and set it in position above the windings behind the eye of the hook. Make one turn with the winding silk and check the position of the wings. If they are satisfactory tie them down securely and knot the working silk with a half-hitch. Select a hackle feather according to correct proportions and fasten the butt end under the body, with the dull side toward the rear. Trim off the excess of the butt, then half-hitch the working silk immediately behind the eye. Wind the hackle carefully, keeping it from piling up at the eye. After sufficient winds have been made, complete the fly with the whip-finish.

REVERSE QUILL-WING

This fly also represents the alder and caddis flies, but is made with the segments from various wing and tail feathers. It is an excellent imitation of the wing-over-the-back flies, although it is not so durable as the rolled-wing.

CONSTRUCTION: Follow the same procedure as when making the rolled down-wing, up to and including the finishing of the body. Then cut two-wing segments from matched quill feathers, placing their concave sides together. Holding these segments between the thumb and forefinger of the left hand, turn the butts toward the rear of the fly, bringing the tips immediately above the windings behind the eye of the hook. See Fig. 16, No. 5. Fasten the tips with the working silk, tie on the hackle, and finish with the whip-knot.

HAIR-WING

The hair-wing closely resembles the rolled down-wing and is exceptionally durable, outlasting the majority of types many times over.

CONSTRUCTION: This fly is dressed in exactly the same manner as the rolled down-wing. Sufficient cement must be applied to the base of the wing to insure its permanence.

SPENT-WING TYPES

Spent-wing dry flies fulfill the need for delicate imitations of dead drakes and spinners. When sparsely dressed, they light on the water surface delicately with their wings outstretched. Spent-wings are most effective during the evening hours when the trout are rising very quietly to fallen spinners. Since they must be more or less restricted to placid waters, where imperfections show so noticeably, spent-wings should be dressed accurately and lightly. The ideal fly of this sort would have wings resting on the water surface and hackle consisting of so few turns as to bend under the weight of the fly. This is not a rough-water fly and performs best on water for which it was designed—pools of quiet character.

HACKLE-TIP, SPENT

The hackle-tip is the accepted standard of the spent-wing variety. The material from which the wings are made is flexible and light, making sparse dressing and delicate casting possible. This type of fly is often affectionately called "airplane" for its profile.

CONSTRUCTION: Follow the same procedure as when making the upright hackle-tip wing with the following exception: Wind the working silk in criss-cross fashion between the wings, while holding the wings downward. Usually this will place the wings in the proper position, but a drop of cement added to the shank where they are fastened will maintain their position. Strive for sparseness particularly in the dressing of the hackle. If the fly should ride too high over the water surface, it will detract from the illusion that it is lying flat.

ROLLED WING, SPENT

Sometimes it is necessary to dress spent-wing flies with wood duck, teal and mallard wings. Patterns such as the Quill Gordon, Cahill Quill, Light Cahill and others are especially effective when tied with original wood-duck wings tied spent.

CONSTRUCTION: The same procedure for making the rolled split-wing is followed in this case. After the wing has been split it must be secured with criss-cross windings. This treatment arranges the fibers in an outstretched position. Be sure they are neat and uniform.

QUILL WING, SPENT

Although this type of spent-wing is the least durable of all types, it is sometimes required. However, nearly every pattern to be tied with standard, quill-fiber wings can use hackle tips plain or dyed to advantage. The Royal Coachman, for example, while dressed with white duck-wing fibers according to original pattern, is best made with hackle-tip wings. Spent-wing flies dressed with wing-quill fibers are not durable mainly because the fibers tend to separate after being bent horizontally.

CONSTRUCTION: Follow the same procedure for constructing the divided upright wing, but bend the wing sections downward and wind the working silk between them to emplace them permanently.

FLAT-WING TYPE

The flat-wing was designed to provide a counterpart of the stone fly, an insect infrequently seen. It resembles the down-wing slightly but has wings entirely flat and folded over the back. Fiber sections from wing and tail feathers are well suited to this type since they do not elevate at the tips after being tied down.

CONSTRUCTION: The flat-wing is tied more like a wet than a dry fly. First tie on the tail fibers in the same manner already described for dressing the wet fly, then the body material. Cut two sections from a wing or tail feather, placing one over the other, with concave sides curved downward. (These should be from a right and left feather for symmetry.) Place a drop of cement on the front tip of the body and, holding the wings firmly between the thumb and forefinger of the left hand, lay these on top of the hook, securing them firmly with the working silk. A good trick is to wind a little dubbing immediately in front of the body to act as a cushion for the base of the wings; this prevents curling of the fibers and elevation of the wings at the rear. Fasten the butt of the hackle and wind it in the same manner as when dressing any other dry fly.

FANWING TYPE

It has been claimed by certain writing anglers that the fanwing is designed to represent the various moths and butterflies. In my opinion this claim is very questionable. Nevertheless, the fanwing has been used for years with definite success and especially in the Royal Coachman pattern. But if any angler has ever seen a moth or butterfly that in any manner compared to a Royal Coachman, he is a much better informed person than I. The Royal Coachman has been an enigma for many years, with all sorts of speculation as to the effectiveness of the fly on most streams. Certainly no other pattern of fanwing has enjoyed a reputation comparable to the Royal Coachman. Generally it can be said that fanwing flies more or less simulate the larger drakes and may flies. Such large insects as the gray, brown, green, and yellow drakes have been dressed as fanwings for many years, in spite of the fact that drakes come to the water surface with their wings folded over their backs in a vertical position. Still the fanwing remains the favorite imitation of drakes, although other types such as the hackle-tip wing, the hair wing and even wingless styles have been used with reasonable success. Perhaps this preference for the Coachman is due to the beauty of the feather wings.

It is more difficult to balance the fanwing than the regular types of dry flies. The wings are very large in comparison with the other parts of the fly and, consequently, offer much more resistance during casting than do the other types. If the hook is too light for fanwing construction it will cause the fly to rotate, perhaps twisting the leader tippet. Therefore it is well to tie fanwings on standard-weight hooks, and in some instances on wet-fly hooks, especially if the fly is size 12 or smaller.

CONSTRUCTION: Select a pair of matched breast feathers, paying special attention to their curvature and shape. Do not trim the tips to even the feathers if one wing is slightly longer than the other because this will unbalance the fly intolerably. It is much better to find an exact pair. Place the butts of the feathers so that they straddle the shank at that point where they will be fastened. Wind two or three tight turns of working silk from the left and over the butts of the feathers. This will pull the butts slightly forward. With the thumb and forefinger of the left hand pull the butts

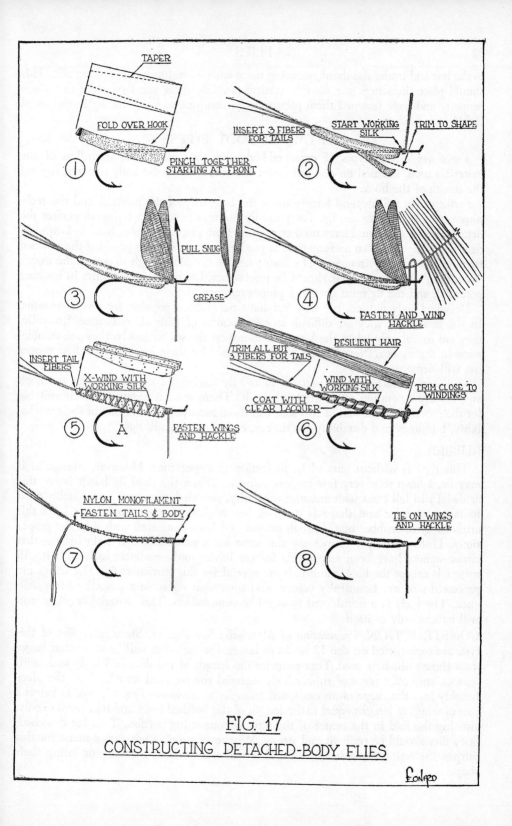

FIG. 17
CONSTRUCTING DETACHED-BODY FLIES

to the left and under the shank, securing them with several turns of working silk. This should place the wings in a directly vertical position. After you have sized the wings properly and have fastened them permanently, continue to finish the fly in the usual fashion.

DETACHED-BODY TYPES

There are several types of detached-body flies, but each type, regardless of the materials used, is based on one principle: the extension of the body material beyond the length of the hook.

Performance will depend largely upon the buoyancy of the material and the technique used in making the fly. For years fly fanciers have been trying to perfect the detached-body drake and have used everything from pieces of rubber band to lacquered deer hair. Anyone's own preference is as good as the next fellow's provided the finished fly meets certain requirements. The body must be flexible enough to permit the trout's "mouthing" the fly, the hook should be unobstructed to give the maximum in hooking potential, and the fly must float in a proper manner.

Detached-body flies are not new but have never been popular, for several reasons. In the first place, they are difficult to cast because of their air resistance. Secondly, they are useful only when the large drakes are on the water. Lastly, they are troublesome in the fly box. Nevertheless, there is a place for these huge flies as their proper use will demonstrate.

The term "detached-body" pertains to any fly having a body longer than the hook and usually extending at an angle above it. There are numerous materials suitable for the construction of flies of this sort, but those most popular because of their workability, buoyancy and durability are rubber, cork, hair and silk floss.

RUBBER

This type is without parallel in perfection of appearance. However, strange as it may be, I have seen very few anglers using it. When the shad fly hatch is on, this artificial will kill trout with amazing regularity, provided, of course, a reasonably good imitation of color and shape is used. A few anglers of my acquaintance hold this artificial fly or "rubber bug" in high esteem and have done well with it at the proper times. Unfortunately I cannot say the same for myself, although I do believe that circumstances have been responsible for my having only mediocre luck with it. All materials except the hackle and tails are special for this particular fly. The wings are processed silk, are beautifully veined, and somewhat resemble a propeller in appearance. The body is a translucent sponge-like composition. This material is pliant and will adhere only to itself.

CONSTRUCTION, *Preparation of Materials*: See Fig. 17. Since most flies of this type are constructed on size 12 hooks or larger, the materials will be somewhat larger than those ordinarily used. First estimate the length of the detached body and, with scissors, snip off a piece of rubber body material the required length. Trim the piece roughly into the shape of an elongated triangle, as shown in Fig. 17, No. 1. Select a pair of wings of lengths equal to the length of the finished body and fold them evenly, creasing the fold in the center of the narrow connecting portion. Tails for detached-body flies should be resilient and strong. Whenever possible use moose mane for this purpose, selecting three strong hairs that will flex without breaking or losing their shape.

Setting up the Work: Place the hook in the vise, leaving as much clearance as possible between the vise and the shank of the hook for maneuvering the body into position. It is not necessary to locate the working silk on the hook at this time, since the body and tails are fastened without it.

Attaching the Body: Fig. 17, No. 1. Double the material lengthwise so that it resembles a roof, then place it over the hook as shown, holding it at an angle approximating the position of the finished body. With the fingers of the right hand pinch the forward end of the body together. Be sure the fold at the rear of the body is not sealed. This would prevent the insertion of the tail sections.

Fastening in the Tail Fibers: Holding the three pieces of moose mane, or whatever material you have chosen for the tails, between the thumb and forefinger of the left hand, insert them into the fold at the rear of the body. Place these as close to the top of the body as possible, then squeeze the fold together.

Shaping the Body: See Fig. 17, No. 2. After you have permanently emplaced the tails, squeeze the entire body together by pressing the bottom side firmly between the thumb and forefinger. The use of pliers will make it possible to compress the body edge into a solid section. Trim the lower edge with scissors, but do not trim so close to the edge as to cut through the seal formed by the two sides.

Fastening on the Wings: See Fig. 17, No. 3. Wind several turns of working silk around the shank immediately in front of the body and coat with cement. Grasp the tips of the wings between the thumb and forefinger of the left hand, slipping the loop formed by the lower portions over the hook eye and as far back as the end of the body. Tilt the wings slightly toward the rear, at the same time pulling upright until the narrow neck below the hook is snug. With the right hand wind several turns of working silk around the base.

Winding the Hackle: Tie down the butt of the feather and wind the hackle in the conventional manner.

Finishing the Fly: Apply the whip-finish.

CORK

This was the original detached-body fly tied with trimmed fish-skin wings. F. M. Halford is credited with having made the first fly of this sort in his many attempts to devise the perfect imitation of May drakes. Although cork-body flies of this kind have lost some of their popularity because of their comparatively fragile bodies, they are, nevertheless, excellent floaters and reasonably effective dry flies. Cork, of course, is opaque and for this reason cannot be compared with the translucent rubber body.

CONSTRUCTION: The formation of the body is the exception in this case. Otherwise the fly is made according to the outline for constructing the rubber-body type. From a smooth, clean cork billet slice two symmetrical pieces approximately the shape of the fly body. This is illustrated in Fig. 17, No. 5. Trim these two sections to the exact shape required, being careful to make the inside surfaces as smooth and true as possible. Next fasten the tip of the working silk at the end of the shank and wind it in criss-cross fashion, ending a short distance behind the hook eye. (The working silk must be the same color as the cork body, either natural or stained.) Coat the inside surfaces of the two sections of cork liberally with cement and wind two or three turns of working silk around the front end of the body. Continue to wind the working silk at fairly wide intervals (to effect a criss-cross winding instead of a close, even one) until the silk is slightly to the rear of A, as shown in Fig. 17, No. 5. At this point, separate the two sections with the dubbing needle just wide enough to permit the insertion of the tail sections. Position these sections then squeeze the two sides of the body together, continuing to wind the working silk toward the rear. Return the windings to the front of the body, keeping the same interval. Allow the cement to set, then finish the fly as already described for constructing the rubber-body type.

DETACHED-BODY, HAIR

This type is the most difficult to make and perhaps the least satisfactory of all the detached-body-type flies. However, very large drakes can be constructed from various sorts of hair and for this reason they are sometimes popular with fishermen interested in huge brown trout and river smallmouth bass. For the average trout angler they are not especially useful.

CONSTRUCTION: Select approximately fifteen to twenty resilient hairs and tie the butt ends immediately behind that point where the wings will be located. Moisten the fingers with a thinned solution of cement or lacquer and spread it lightly over the hair, keeping the tips as free from the solution as possible. Wind separate wrappings at six or seven intervals as shown in Fig. 17, No. 6. Very carefully trim all but three of the hair tips which will form the tails. Apply a bit of the thinned cement around each individual wrapping and at the extreme end of the body or at the base of the tails. Finish the fly in the same manner as when making the rubber-body type.

SILK FLOSS

Neat and even small flies can be made after the pattern of the silk floss detached-body fly. These are dressed on hooks as small as size 16 and fished with surprising success. In all fairness, however, I do not believe that these flies will raise trout that other conventional types would not have raised. One advantage of this type over other detached-body flies is the adaptability of this fly to standard patterns. When tied with translucent wings it makes the most lifelike artificial known to fly-dressers.

CONSTRUCTION: Cut off a short section of nylon leader material of the same diameter as the shank of the hook. (In some cases it may be necessary to use nylon of a diameter exceeding that of the hook.) With the working silk tie this firmly to the hook shank as shown in Fig. 17, Nos. 7 and 8. Clip off any of the nylon that may be in excess of the desired body length. Apply a drop of cement to the tip of the nylon and fasten on three tail fibers, after which tie on the tip of the silk floss or wool yarn which will form the body. Holding the nylon between the thumb and forefinger of the left hand, gradually wind the body material, alternating pressure from first the thumb held on the near side to the index finger held on the far side when making each revolution. With the exception of the place where the body is located, no difference exists between this and the conventional type so far as the body windings are concerned. Interesting effects can be obtained by ribbing with tinsel, thread, or other colored materials.

HACKLE TYPES

Hackle-type flies are, for the most part, impressionistic, representing pupae emerging from the water, duns shedding their nymphal cases, and other small miscellaneous surface creatures. They are comparatively easy to dress since most of the hackle flies are wingless.

The red hackle of the Macedonians was the first hackle fly recorded in history. It was later named the Bonny Red Heckle in England and became the basis for the many hackle flies of our time. Certain authorities have eulogized hackles to the exclusion of all other types, claiming that if trout will not take a hackle, they will take nothing so far as flies are concerned.

There is at present a trend toward hackle flies that may alter the flies of the future. More anglers each year are relying on sparse, wingless standard patterns. The Ginger Quill, Blue Quill, Cahill and others dressed without wings are very effective, attesting to the worth of the wingless flies.

It should be understood, however, that a few types of flies are classed as hackle flies, not because they are wingless, but because their hackle treatment makes them peculiar. The variant, for example, has hackle nearly as long as the hackle on a spider but, in every other respect, is like the so-called "standard" dry fly. Therefore, a true definition for a hackle fly might be: any wingless fly, or a winged fly having peculiar hackle arrangement.

PLAIN

Plain hackle flies are dressed with hackle at the shoulder only and are especially effective when dressed on size 18 and 20 hooks. This type is excellent for the beginner to start with because it is not involved and is relatively simple to construct.

CONSTRUCTION: With the single exception of the omission of the wings, this fly is tied exactly like the conventional dry fly.

PALMER

The Palmer hackle was originally designed to imitate caterpillars and other fuzzy creatures which have fallen to the surface. The hackle is always one color regardless of how many feathers are used, making the fly distinguishable from bivisibles and other multi-color hackle flies.

This is a wingless fly as a rule, although standard patterns such as Wickham's Fancy and others feature the Palmer style of hackle. It is a fly of high-riding qualities and fish-getting appeal, by virtue of its hackle legs extending throughout the length of the body. As a matter of fact, this type of hackle treatment will give almost any fly better floating quality, without appreciably altering the pattern. The extent of the hackle depends greatly upon whether the fly-maker wishes to produce a full Palmer effect or only a thicker span of hackle at the shoulder. In the true sense of the word, a Palmer-type hackle fly requires that the hackle be wound around the full length of the body—not closely, but with an interval between each wind. Certainly it can be seen that the added hackle legs will lend support on the water surface and tend to keep the fly high enough to resist absorption. Still, this type can be dressed as sparsely as desired. Generally two hackles are required, however, one extending the length of the body, with the mentioned intervals between each wind, and the other tied at the shoulder in the conventional manner.

CONSTRUCTION: Fasten the tail at the rear of the shank. Secure the body ma terial and tip end of the hackle immediately in front of the tail. Work the body material forward to the same place that the wings would be located on a winged fly. Wind the hackle (butt end in fingers) toward the eye of the hook, at the same time spacing the hackle winds evenly. Fasten the hackle with working silk. Apply the shoulder hackle, wind and trim off the end.

When extra sparseness is desired, it is well to tie Palmer flies with a split hackle, meaning that either the hackle has been split lengthwise, or the fibers have been removed from one side of the quill. This reduces bulkiness and makes for neater hackle application.

In the case of upright-winged flies dressed with Palmer hackle, the wings and shoulder hackle are applied exactly the same as the wings and hackle in the conventional types.

An interesting variation of the Palmer is the reversed front or shoulder hackle. Instead of winding the hackle with the shiny side toward the front and the dull side facing the rear, wind the hackle in reverse order. This will cause the front hackle to cup slightly frontward. When properly tied the reverse hackle is undoubtedly the finest floating fly made. Almost impossible to upset, it is the best all-purpose dry fly manufactured and is strictly an American adaptation.

BIVISIBLE

The bivisible fly was designed to serve a dual purpose: provide visibility to both fish and angler under exactly opposite conditions. At times, particularly in the evening, the required color of the fly pattern may be dark or true black. But this dark or black color may be next to impossible for the angler to see. Therefore, while a Palmer or hackle-type fly of the darker colors might be appropriate from the trout's standpoint, it may be entirely wrong from the angler's. Consequently, a white or light bit of hackle at the eye of the fly is the answer. The original design for the bivisible was based on this condition. But, as usual, certain other modifications changed the hackle combinations until today it is not uncommon to find almost any colors in sections or even blended. Therefore, they become "trivisibles" or whatever term you wish to give them.

Often a bivisible dressed on the Palmer lines will be seen. It is then a deviation from the true bivisible standard.

CONSTRUCTION: Fasten a dark and light hackle by the butt end at the shoulder. (Face the light hackle with the dull side toward the front if a reverse hackle is desired.) Wind the working silk back to the tip of the shank and fasten in the tail, which often consists of the tip ends of two hackles. Wind on the body in the conventional manner and secure with the working silk. Wind the dark hackle (with the dull side toward the rear) two or three turns at the shoulder, then proceed toward the tail by taking two or three turns more. Be careful to wind the hackle so that the turns are close together and leave no intervals between winds. Return to the starting point by winding back through the hackle already in place. Tie down the tip with working silk, and finish the work by winding on the front hackle.

PALMER BIVISIBLE

The Palmer Bivisible is dressed in the same way as the Palmer hackle fly but has the added feature of the dual-hackle effect of the bivisible.

SPIDER

The Spider is a comparatively new style of dry fly and has established a fine record for taking trout in waters that have become increasingly hard-fished. The acme of sparseness and delicacy, the Spider is ideal in connection with the extremely fine 6X and 7X leader tippets, and offers practically no resistance to the air when cast. The Spider is truly the answer to the problem of catching brown trout in many of our eastern streams.

There are two types of Spiders. One floats with its hook point in the usual horizontal plane (like other dry flies) and the other comes to rest on the water surface with its hackles spread out radially and the hook dangling vertically in the water. Of the two types the latter is generally considered more productive for one particular reason. The hackle arrangement makes it possible to produce an illusion that is most excellent. For example, consider the badger hackle, which has a black stripe running down the center of the feather. The outside portion is usually a dirty white or palest gray. When this type of hackle is wound on the shank and is then spread radially on the water surface, the black center streak becomes a very small black dot while the lighter, outside portion becomes hardly noticeable. On warm June nights when the tiny black gnats are worrying your eyes and nostrils, this little Spider will sometimes fill your creel.

CONSTRUCTION: The conventional type of Spider is dressed in the same manner as any hackle fly, except that it is extra sparse. Body coloration is generally silver or gold tinsel. The first step is the fastening of the tail whisks, and these must be long and stiff. Wind the silver or gold tinsel body, but leave sufficient space for winding the hackle. Take two or three turns with the hackle, tie down and whip as with other types of flies. It is important that the hackle be stiff and resilient since there are so few hackle legs to support the weight of the fly.

The Spider with the hackle that rests radially on the water surface differs from the conventional type Spider in one respect. It has no tail sections. This, of course, is to permit the hook weight to incline the fly so that the hackle is in a horizontal position. Sometimes the absence of any body whatsoever is beneficial in that it reduces to an absolute minimum the size of the Spider. The stripe in the hackle is the main feature. Two—and never more than three—turns of hackle are sufficient.

FORE-AND-AFT

The Fore-and-Aft hackle fly is simply a fly with two sections of hackle, one at the shoulder and one at the tip of the body. This is a very high-riding fly but has one disadvantage in its tendency to roll on the surface, thus placing the hook point in various positions. It is seldom seen today except when used on salmon and very rough and fast waters.

CONSTRUCTION: Tie on the tail sections in the usual manner, then fasten the butt end of a hackle feather (with the dull side facing the rear) at a point immediately over the tail windings. Wind the hackle closely and secure the working silk with two or three half-hitches. Fasten and wind the body material as far as the shoulder of the fly, securing it with half-hitches. Tie on the shoulder hackle, wind it in the customary manner, and finish the fly with the whip-finish.

REVERSE HACKLE

This fly can be winged or wingless and rates special mention only because its hackle is applied in a reverse manner; that is, the fibers tend to bend toward the front instead of toward the rear. This makes the fly very difficult to upset on the water.

CONSTRUCTION: Follow the same procedure as when making the standard winged or hackle flies except that the hackle should be fastened with the dull side of the feather facing toward the front.

VARIANT

The Variant is purely an American version of the dry fly, but does not pertain to any especial type; rather does it pertain to a type of hackle which, in turn, could be substituted for the hackle on most dry-fly types to obtain a variant condition. The Variant type is dressed with a hackle several sizes larger than regular. See Fig. 8. Sometimes Variants are fashioned on short shank hooks, and in isolated cases are superior to the regular, although it has been my experience that the short-shank fly is difficult to float properly and seems to miss strikes with annoying regularity.

The neatest Variants are tied with hackle-tip wings a little shorter than the wings of a regular fly, cocked approximately midway between the position of the spent-wing and the upright.

A large number of Variants are tied with gold and silver tinsel bodies, purely the fancy of their designers.

CONSTRUCTION: Follow the same procedure as for tying the upright hackle tip with the single exception of using a hackle of larger diameter, the size of which is shown in Fig. 8.

MULTI-COLOR VARIANT

The Multi-color Variant, a Western innovation, is dressed with several hackles of contrasting color or a single hackle, either dyed or plain, containing bars or irregularly dark and light areas. These bars are various, following no particular pattern, and are found in feathers from birds of crossbreed only. Flies dressed with several hackles of this sort are usually a little gaudy in appearance but are, nevertheless, quite effective at times.

CONSTRUCTION: This fly is tied like any other winged dry fly. When using three or four contrasting hackles, one behind the other, restrict the number of turns to as few as possible to prevent unnecessary bulk. For example, three turns of each hackle should be sufficient for tri-color Variants, and either three—or preferably two—turns for four-hackle Variants.

PARACHUTE

This is a radical among dry flies and is fast gathering a following. The construction embodies an entirely new idea in hackle treatments and for this reason provides the maximum of surface tension without surplus hackle fibers. The name "Parachute" is indicative of the character of this fly, as the first cast will prove. No other fly casts so easily nor planes in so lifelike a manner as this innovation, which comes to rest on the water surface as delicately as a lazy snow flake. Certain physical advantages are obvious in this kind of construction, notably the stability of the fly as affected by the horizontal hackle which projects radially from the base of the wing. Likewise, this fly floats *on* the surface not *above* it—that is the body, the entire hackle and the tails all contact the water instead of only the tips of the hackles on the bottom side and the tails, which is typical of conventional flies. This suggests immediately the advantage of little if any arching of the leader in a critical area—the six or eight inches near the hook eye. Another excellent feature is the position of the hackle. The hackle on conventional flies, if neatly wound, is limited to a comparatively small area under the wings and does not simulate the straddle-legged appearance of natural insects, whereas the Parachute style of hackle dressing more closely imitates this appearance, in that the fibers extend circularly in all directions.

For hard-fished waters the Parachute is a welcome change that will often bring trout to the landing net that were otherwise uninterested in anything with a hook in it. CONSTRUCTION: Several attempts to produce an ideal hook for the Parachute have been made. Pre-war efforts included shanks with a short pin rising above the hook and modifications of the numerous hump-shank types. However, none of these special hooks is necessary; the plain shank hook, when properly used, is equal to any hook so far developed. The main principle of this fly is the winding of the hackle in a horizontal plane, which is in complete opposition to conventionally wound hackle. And, although there are numerous ways to produce a Parachute effect, the following method is the least involved and, for that reason, is recommended.

In the first place, the Parachute is best made with breast-feather rolled wings because the quill in the center of the feather is a support for the hackle windings. Select a breast feather having strong fibers, roll it between the fingers to remove the lay of the feather and fasten it to the hook shank on the upper side with quill or butt end pointing toward the rear of the hook. Next select a hackle of sufficient spread to reach at least to the tip of the hook shank and tie this in a vertical position with the butt of the feather projecting at least one-quarter of an inch above the shank. The butts of the hackle and the wing must be close together for a most important operation later on. With the working silk tie the tail section and the body material to the hook in the usual manner, applying immediately afterward two or three half-hitches in front of the unfinished wings. Place a drop of lacquer or cement between the butt of the wing feather and the butt of the hackle and, when this is tacky but not yet dry, wind the two together with a few turns of working silk to develop a firm, upright base for winding the horizontal hackle. (You may have to experiment a little in regard to forming this base, since the flexibility and other characteristics of feathers are not constant.) If necessary, coat the joined butts with a second coat of lacquer or cement. Carefully wind the hackle around the upright butts in a clockwise direction with the dull side of the hackle feather facing upwards. Tie down the hackle tip. Be sure to wind clear of the wing tips, which are yet in the unfinished stage and projecting forward. The one big difficulty is preventing the hackle from creeping up the butts. The tendency of the hackle to creep can be minimized if you will make slow turns close to the hook, and apply as little hackle as possible. Understand that all, repeat all, of the fibers will lend support and, therefore, fewer turns than ordinarily taken when making conventional flies will prove adequate. Apply a very small drop of cement to the base of the hackle windings, being sure that none spreads onto the fibers themselves. At this stage the upright butts will be surplus and the wing tips will have remained forward yet unfinished. Turn to the butts first and, if these are completely hardened from the cement, clip off the excess length—not so close as to cut the topmost hackle winding, but close enough to eliminate their spine-like appearance. Now for the wing. With the working silk build up a narrow section in front of the wings (behind the eye of the hook) to act as a brace, meanwhile inclining the tip in a near-vertical position by pulling rearward with the thumb and forefinger of the left hand. After the wing has assumed an ideal position, it should be carefully split with the working silk and made permanently divided with criss-cross winds. Since the hackle is already fixed, a little difficulty may be experienced in keeping it free of the wing during this operation. However, its management will be less troublesome after several flies have been tied. Complete the work with the whip-finish, cement the head, then get your rod and waders and catch some trout.

REVERSE FLY

The reverse fly was designed for one very special condition: to imitate a fly in upstream flight. An angler fishing in the customary manner will be facing upstream and the drift of his artificial fly will be toward him. This means each cast will place the fly headed downstream, or in the direction opposite to that of the insect in flight. Whether it is of importance to have the artificial to reproduce the flight of the natural fly is a matter of opinion. However, there are other considerations with regard to balance that make the reverse fly noteworthy. For example, the standard type of dry fly is dressed with the hackle supporting the lightest part of the hook, and the tails supporting the heaviest portion. This is entirely in reverse so far as logic is concerned, but because flies have been tied in this manner for so many years, the chances are they always will be. The reverse fly is dressed with the tails extending over the eye of the hook, and with the hackle at the curved or heaviest portion. Consequently the fly will come to rest in a very natural position. But with this different style of balancing the fly come attendant evils. The wings are more easily crushed than the wings dressed on standard types since they will be the first part of the fly to enter the fish's mouth. (Usually a trout is caught with only the bend and barb in its mouth.) In addition, the reverse fly is somewhat more difficult to tie.

CONSTRUCTION: Place the hook in the vise in the customary manner, then simply construct the fly in reverse order. Fasten the wings directly above the barb of the hook and tie in the butt of the hackle. Wind the working silk toward the eye of the hook, fastening on the tail fibers. Attach the tip end of the body material, wind it toward the wings and secure it with several turns of working silk. Wind the hackle and whip-finish the head. Difficulty may be encountered when finishing the fly because of interference from the barb and point of the hook. However, by working slowly you will be able to effect a neat, compact head.

MISCELLANEOUS TYPES

Several types of flies, sometimes classified individually, are in reality nothing more than slight variations of conventional types. The Flying Ant, for example, is fundamentally a spent-wing and the short- and the long-shank-body flies merely variations in length from the standard types. However, because some of these are so well known and are often referred to as "types," they are included here.

FLYING ANT

Both the red and black ants are semi-floating flies but are cast and handled in the same manner as dry flies. This type is best suited to slow currents, pools and backwaters, the natural places for the congregation of these insects and, for this reason, is necessarily of sparse dressing. Ants are especially effective when permitted to sink just below the surface film of the water. Fishing thus requires watchfulness on the part of the angler because some strikes may pass undetected, particularly during an upstream cast, unless, of course, the angler is well-versed in wet-fly tactics.

CONSTRUCTION: This fly should be made in two stages: first the preparation of the body and second, the winding of the hackle and the placement of the wings. Wind either black or red floss on the shank, graduating the size so that the body is bulbous toward the rear. The floss body is preferably lacquered to simulate the shiny chitin of the ant. Allow the lacquer to dry thoroughly. Next select two hackle tips that are resilient and narrow. Place these with their convex sides together, fasten with the winding silk in the same manner as when making the hackle-tip spent-wing, and arrange the wings to lie flat by criss-cross winding the working silk between them. These should be approximately the length of the hook shank. Next fasten on the butt end of a stiff, short neck hackle with a three-quarter inch spread. Wind only three turns of this hackle, fasten and clip off the surplus. Pluck out with tweezers all the hackle projecting above the hook, leaving only those few fibers below. Whip-finish and cement the head.

HUMP-BODY ANT

This is a most lifelike creation and is especially so because of the hump-shank hook. While I was gathering information from all parts of the United States and Canada relative to regional peculiarities in fly design, I received dozens of authentic styles and patterns exclusively for Western waters from Ruth M. Evans, production manager for Glen L. Evans, Inc., Caldwell, Idaho, famous fly manufacturers. Among the many special patterns were three hump-body ants of surprisingly realistic appearance. These flies, in addition to having bulbous bodies, feature the very slender crooked neck typical of the ant, which adds much to the naturalness of their appearance. Wingless and sparsely hackled to advantage, and with lustrous bodies, they are examples of well-planned fly design.

CONSTRUCTION: The body is largely the same as the body of the Flying Ant already described, with the exception that it is narrowed at the hump in the shank and is wound as far as the end of the return bend of the hump. The head is wound extra large of black working silk. Plastacele, a translucent material, is ideal for making the body if translucency is necessary.

WHITEFISH MAGGOT

While this is not strictly a type of dry fly so much as it is a type of body only, it is described here for the benefit of those living in Montana and Washington who are partial to it. Actually the maggot is a plain hackle fly with a plastacele body and no tails.

2X LONG-SHANK DRY FLY

This was the predecessor of the present-day artificial may fly and is still fairly popular in certain regions of New York and Pennsylvania. It is generally made up as a Fan-Wing or Rolled Split-Wing in patterns such as Female Beaverkill, Cahill (light and dark), Yellow May, and Green Drake. Several firms dress this type in all standard patterns, which more or less attests to its popularity. It can be dressed as a large Spent-Wing, in which form it is most useful during drake hatches.

CONSTRUCTION: Exactly the same procedure is followed for dressing any of the other types of dry flies with which this long-bodied fly is to compare. The length of the body alone is the single contrasting feature.

2X SHORT-SHANK DRY FLY

Certain authorities claim the shorter-bodied fly has merits superior to the merits of conventional styles, especially in hard-fished waters. While this may be pure hypothesis, the Short-Shank fly will take trout, especially brown trout, when dry-fly fishing has dwindled down to a mere nothing; although the spiders are perhaps better during this time.

CONSTRUCTION: Follow the same procedures used to dress any of the other fly styles, but use the short-shank hook.

Chapter Seven

THE NYMPH

A nymph is construed by fly-fishermen to mean any type of the many larvae, small crustaceans and immature insects which are water-inhabiting. Technically this definition is incorrect, since larvae and crustaceans are not nymphs. It is acceptable, however, for the single purpose of generalizing the construction of these underwater creatures which, from the viewpoint of the fly-maker, have certain characteristics in common. Complete details on the characteristics of, and the differences between, nymphs and larvae are contained in Chapter 13.

According to some authorities, nymphs and larvae comprise as much as 85 per cent of all the food eaten by trout, which is one reason why the artificial nymph is one of the most effective lures yet developed. In addition, these aquatic animals are phenomenally ubiquitous in the stream, although certain kinds prefer to congregate in specific regions and strata of the stream. Therefore, nymph-fishing is not limited to any especial type of water. One or another sort of nymph or larvae exist in every pool, rapids and backwater. This would lead one to conclude that nymph-fishing should be the most popular variety of fly-fishing.

Actually, however, nymph-fishing has been the least popular with fly-men, undoubtedly because it is not so spectacular, for example, as fishing with the dry fly. Perhaps a second and more exact reason for the unpopularity of the nymph is the difficulty met when fishing it. Usually the fisherman cannot see the nymph he is using and, unless he is familiar with the currents controlling the course of his lure, may find it impossible to establish its position. This immediately suggests the evil of slack line which is so frequently the cause of missed or even undetected strikes.

Any sort of fly-fishing is plagued with short strikes; therefore nymph-fishing should be expected to produce its share of this annoyance. However, it is possible to reduce the number of misses by keeping a tighter line. Watch for the belly in the line, especially when casting upstream. If it inclines toward one side, exert pressure on the rod in the opposite direction. Holding the rod tip high is a helpful means of keeping as much line off the water as possible, which reduces to a minimum the chances of creating excess slack. If you can possibly estimate the position of the nymph, do it by all means, being watchful for the slightest flash from a trout anywhere within two or three feet of where you think the nymph may be. A trout will not roll on his side, thus creating a flash, *until he has mouthed the object he is after.* Consequently, when you see this flash, strike, even though the flash may appear a considerable distance

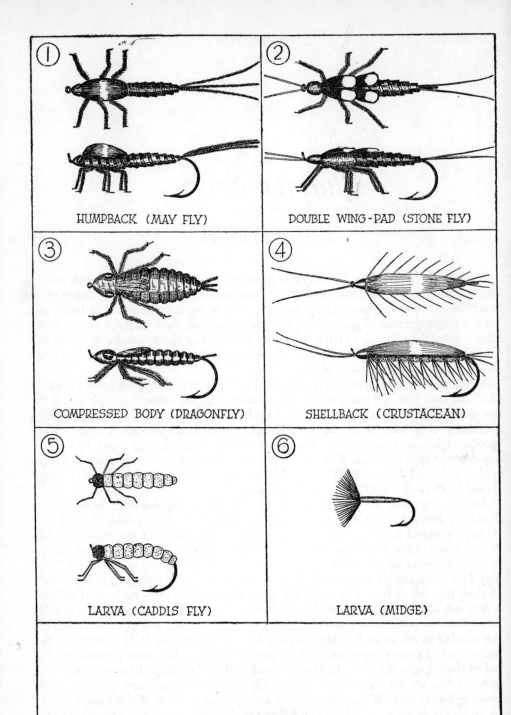

HUMPBACK (MAY FLY)

DOUBLE WING-PAD (STONE FLY)

COMPRESSED BODY (DRAGONFLY)

SHELLBACK (CRUSTACEAN)

LARVA (CADDIS FLY)

LARVA (MIDGE)

FIG. 18
NYMPH DESIGN

LONARD

from where you think the "business end" of your cast may be. The chances are you will be fast to a racing trout.

Fly-dressers are largely responsible for encouraging interest in nymph-fishing. More each year they are becoming familiar with the metamorphoses of natural insects and less interested in the brilliant creations based on eye-appeal alone. Plastics, processed materials, and the discovery of new uses for various feathers have founded entirely new principles for the construction of nymphs. Certainly the translucent materials available from nylon and other innovations produced by chemistry will develop further varieties in nymph styles, thus making the simulation of underwater creatures more nearly perfect.

Nymphs should be made to sink quickly. Heavy wire hooks can be used to advantage, in this respect, and are superior to regular-weight hooks wound with fine lead strips. When you plan to use a deep-going nymph in strong currents and intend to tie it heavily enough to preclude the use of split shot, try some of the small but heavy-wire steelhead hooks. These hooks are of sufficient weight to take the nymph to the very bottom where it should be. Nymphs are best fished deep since the "naturals" spend most of their time clambering over the rocks and debris covering the stream bed. Therefore, materials which are water-resistant enough to impede quick sinking of the nymph should not be used, unless their weight will offset whatever buoyancy they may have.

Nymphs are not easily reduced to any category since there are so many kinds in which shape, color, size and habitat are the determining factors. However, for the benefit of the fly-dresser, there are six types of nymphs which form the nuclei of all nymph and larvae construction. Combinations of any part or parts of these six types make possible the development of any special type when required. Fig. 18 illustrates these six types, showing both side and plan views.

SPECIAL FEATURES

The construction of successful nymphs is largely dependent upon the ability of the fly-maker to invent different and unusual treatments of materials for the purpose of grafting more lifelike effects onto what he is making. These treatments may consist of a slight variation in the method of trimming or shaping a feather, lacquering or not lacquering a certain part, or forming the legs, wing pads, tail sections or abdominal gills in an unorthodox fashion. Nymph-making involves no fixed rules. Amazing things can be accomplished with feathers, plastics, rubber and thread, thus making materials adaptable to any individual condition.

Fig. 19 illustrates various uses for some materials. These uses are merely suggestive of what can be done with the materials illustrated. Many materials other than the ones shown can be substituted with resultant, equal effectiveness. For example, No. 1 illustrates the customary arrangement of tails found on some May-fly nymphs. Ordinarily, fly-dressers prefer to use trimmed hackle feathers for tails—mainly because they are more durable. However, this does not mean that herl and similar materials are to be excluded. On the contrary, herl is a very useful material for the construction of nymph tails.

Legs can be made from a great variety of materials. Generally the effect to be produced determines why a particular material is more suited to the construction of a certain type of leg than of another. Fig. 19, No. 2, for example, illustrates four similarly shaped legs which nevertheless differ in appearance because the treatment and materials were not alike.

The leg bearing the claw at the tip is a good example of variety in the treatment of material. It is merely a hackle feather stripped of all the fibers with the exception of a very few on the end. Naturally this same treatment can be applied in the construction of tail sections having webbed or enlarged tips. The fringed leg in Fig. 19, No. 2, is a hackle feather trimmed with shears. However, herl is very similar in appearance and can be used for the same purpose, although it is restricted to patterns having dark legs because of its dark greenish color. The plain type made of moose mane or horse hair is the simplest to handle and requires hardly any preparation. No. 2 also illustrates one use of several hair fibers handled as a unit. As many fibers as necessary to create sufficient bulk are fastened to the body and then wound at the proper places with silk thread to form the joints. The joints are then lacquered or cemented to insure permanency of the leg shape.

Some nymphs possess gills along the sides or on the back. Trimmed hackle feathers or herl simulate such appendages nicely and are fastened at each juncture in the body. This is shown in Fig. 19, No. 3.

Quill-bodied nymphs with lacquered backs produce interesting and effective two-tone combinations, effectually representing the bodies of many May-fly nymphs. Most quills have light and dark stripes, generally ranging from ivory-white to pale buff and from light to dark brown. Lacquer to be applied to the backs should be the same color as the dark stripe in the quill forming the bodies. This color arrangement is evident in a large number of aquatic insects.

It is profitable to study the larval and pupal stages of the insects appearing in the streams you frequent. The more you know about nymphs and larvae, the more accurate your imitations of these creatures will become.

HUMPBACK

Nearly all May-fly nymphs are constructed according to this pattern. Variations in size and perhaps certain other features may be necessary as determined by the dimensions of the natural nymph being copied.

CONSTRUCTION, *Preparation of Materials*: It should be understood at this time that no specific materials are required to make any one type of nymph. Many combinations of materials can produce the desired effect. For example, Fig. 19 illustrates four different types of legs which can be used on any nymph, depending upon the purpose the fly-dresser has in mind. The same applies to body materials, wing pads and tail fibers. Nymph design is very flexible, having few if any rules controlling construction. For the purpose of illustration, let us construct a humpback nymph having fringed legs and tails, a very common type. Nymphs have six legs, so it will be necessary to select three medium-size hackle feathers with stems strong enough to retain their shape after being bent. With scissors trim all the hackle fibers from the stem, leaving just a very slight stubble remaining close to the stem. See Fig. 19, No. 2. Select three more hackle feathers having fine fibers for the tails, trimming them in the same manner. Next take any flank or shoulder feather having a fairly thick stem and a dark stripe on one side and strip the fibers from it. Then, holding it between the thumb nail and forefinger, flatten by stroking it several times in such a way that the dark stripe appears next to the light stripe, not behind it. See Fig. 19, No. 4. In the same manner that you would

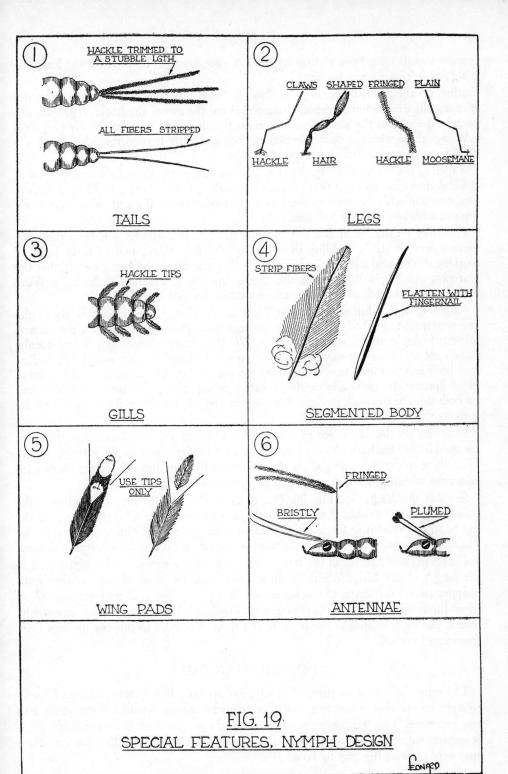

① HACKLE TRIMMED TO A STUBBLE LGTH.

ALL FIBERS STRIPPED

TAILS

② CLAWS SHAPED FRINGED PLAIN

HACKLE HAIR HACKLE MOOSEMANE

LEGS

③ HACKLE TIPS

GILLS

④ STRIP FIBERS

FLATTEN WITH FINGERNAIL

SEGMENTED BODY

⑤ USE TIPS ONLY

WING PADS

⑥ FRINGED

BRISTLY

PLUMED

ANTENNAE

FIG. 19·
SPECIAL FEATURES, NYMPH DESIGN

Leonard

prepare a quill wing for a wet or dry fly, cut a segment (to be used for the hump or wing-pads) from a wing feather.

Setting up the Work: See Fig. 20, No. 1. Place the hook in the vise. Wax the working silk and fasten it a short distance behind the eye of the hook. Wind the silk back to the end of the shank and fasten on the three tail sections already prepared. (Arrange these with the center section extending slightly beyond the other two.) Tie on a piece of cotton thread to taper the body.

Tapering the Body: See Fig. 20, No. 2. Wind the cotton thread smoothly, tapering the abdomen gradually. At that place corresponding to the thorax, build up a slightly larger section with the cotton thread and, after tying down the end, secure the working silk with two or three half-hitches.

Fastening on the Back: See Fig. 20, No. 3. Place the segment cut from the wing feather over the body, holding the fibers by the tips. Wind two or three turns of working silk around the butt ends of the feather and the body, being certain that the rear-most winding is directly over the edge of the enlarged section of the body. Wind the working silk back to the place where the tails are tied on.

Fastening and Winding the Body: See Fig. 20, Nos. 3 and 4. Tie the tip of the prepared quill to the body in the usual manner. Coat the entire body with cement and allow it to dry until the cement is tacky. Wind the body material slowly and evenly, but do not try to overlap each preceding turn as when making wet- and dry-fly bodies. The body material used to make nymphs is tough and does not require such treatment to reinforce it. Be especially careful, when winding around the humped section and on both sides of the back feather, that no gaps appear. Tie down the front end of the body as shown in Fig. 20, No. 4.

Fastening on the Legs: See Fig. 20, No. 5, and Fig. 19, No. 2. Arrange the three trimmed hackle feathers, already prepared to form the legs, in a single, parallel section. Hold these under the enlarged section and, with the working silk, fasten them with criss-cross windings until they extend at right angles to the body.

Shaping the Back: See Fig. 20, No. 6. Bend the back feather forward over the enlarged part and toward the eye of the hook. Hold it tightly with the fingers of the left hand and bind it to the hook with the working silk. Whip-finish the head in the usual manner and, with a razor blade, cut the surplus part of the feather from the head.

Finishing the Legs: Trim the legs on each side of the nymph to a length equal to the length of the body. With the thumb nail kink the stem of each feather until it approximates the shape of the leg shown in Fig. 20, No. 7. If necessary use pliers to set the bend in the stem. Apply cement to each bend and allow to dry thoroughly. Touch the leg windings at the body with a drop of cement to prevent the legs from becoming loosened.

DOUBLE WING PAD

The stone fly is characteristic of this type of nymph. It is quite similar to May-fly nymphs except that it has two sets of wing pads, two—instead of three—tails, and two antennae. This nymph is dressed to best advantage on medium-size hooks since it involves numerous operations requiring considerably more space than the operations necessary to make the may-fly type.

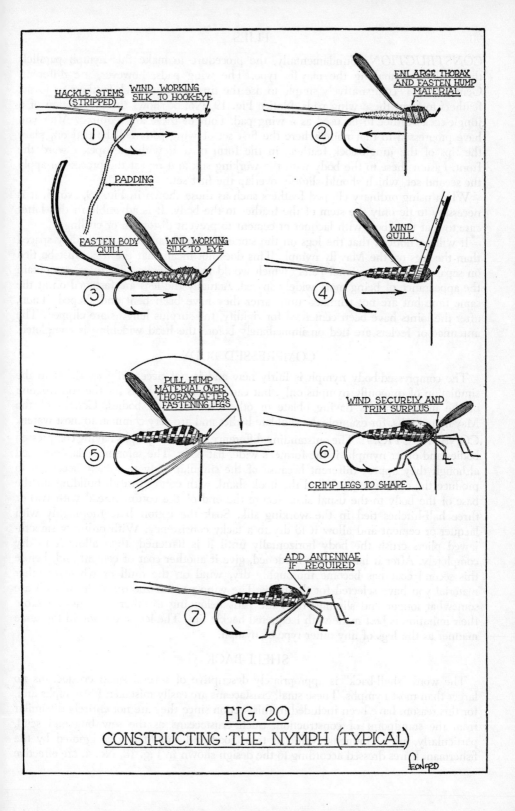

HACKLE STEMS
(STRIPPED)

WIND WORKING
SILK TO HOOK-EYE

① →

PADDING

ENLARGE THORAX
AND FASTEN HUMP
MATERIAL

② ←

FASTEN BODY
QUILL

WIND WORKING
SILK TO EYE

③

WIND
QUILL

④ →

PULL HUMP
MATERIAL OVER
THORAX AFTER
FASTENING LEGS

⑤

WIND SECURELY AND
TRIM SURPLUS

⑥

CRIMP LEGS TO SHAPE

ADD ANTENNAE
IF REQUIRED

⑦

FIG. 20
CONSTRUCTING THE NYMPH (TYPICAL)

LEONARD

CONSTRUCTION: Fundamentally, the procedure to make this nymph parallels the method of making the may-fly type. The wing pads, however, are different. Generally, it is comparatively simple to use the tips of jungle-cock feathers or breast feathers to form these wing pads. Notice Fig. 19, No. 5, shows the preparation of a jungle-cock feather to be used as a wing pad. Four of these are required. After you have progressed to that point where the first set of wing pads will be tied on, place the tips of the jungle-cock feathers in the form of a V with the apex toward the front. Fasten these to the body with the working silk and repeat the process to apply the second set, which should slightly overlap the first set.

When using ordinary clipped feathers such as those shown in Fig. 19, No. 5, it is necessary to tie only the stem of the feather to the body. It is advisable in this latter case to coat the fibers with lacquer or cement to prevent distortion or curling.

It will be noticed that the legs on the stone-fly nymph appear more widely spaced than the legs on the May-fly nymph. This does not mean that the legs must be tied on separately or in sectional pairs (which would incur obvious difficulties), to obtain the appearance of being more widely spaced. Actually the legs are fastened on at the same time but are not trimmed until after they have been bent and shaped. Then, after the joints have been cemented for rigidity, the surplus lengths are clipped. The antennae or feelers are tied on immediately before the head widening is completed.

COMPRESSED BODY

The compressed-body nymph is fairly new and is not necessarily restricted to the simulation of dragonfly nymphs only, but can be used as a basis for the construction of the many nymphs having oblate or otherwise flattened bodies. Certain of the May-fly nymphs, for example, have oblate bodies and are very common to most waters.

CONSTRUCTION: The outstanding difference between nymphs having compressed bodies and other nymphs is the former's wide, flat body. The same materials are used although they appear different because of the singular body treatment necessary to produce the oblate shape. Wind the hook shank with cotton thread, building up the base of the body to the usual size. Secure the end of the cotton thread with two or three half-hitches tied in the working silk. Soak the cotton base thoroughly with lacquer or cement and allow it to dry to a tacky consistency. With ordinary smooth-jawed pliers crush the body horizontally until it is flattened, then allow it to dry completely. After it has become hardened, give it another coat of cement and, before this second coat has become thoroughly dry, wind on the quill or whatever other material you have selected for the body. The wing pads of the dragonfly nymph are somewhat longer and slimmer than the pads belonging to other nymphs, therefore their imitation is best made with lacquered hackle tips. The legs are made in the same manner as the legs of any other type of nymph.

SHELL-BACK

The word "shell-back" is appropriately descriptive of several small crustaceans no larger than most nymphs. These small crustaceans are easily mistaken for nymphs and, for this reason, have been included in this section since they are not entirely dissimilar from the standpoint of construction. Such crustaceans as the sow bug and scud, particularly, are of immense value as trout food and should not be ignored by the fisherman. Lures dressed according to the design shown in Fig. 18, No. 4, are effective nearly everywhere. Several firms advertise similar creations as being nymphs, which, of course, they are not. Nevertheless, they are used in the same way as a nymph and have been responsible for many a heavy creel of trout.

CONSTRUCTION: Certain fly-dressers have offered various versions of the shell-back to the trade. Some of these have been fashioned from cellophane, plastic and similar materials. Each material has it merits and makes the superiority of any one type generally a matter of opinion on the part of the user. I prefer firstly, durability of materials and, secondly, simplicity of construction. Therefore, I have found the following dressing most satisfactory from these two standpoints:

Fasten the working silk at the tip of the shank and tie on three short tail sprigs. Tie the tip end of a section cut from a wing or tail feather to the tip of the shank, or approximately where the tails were tied. Next select a hackle feather consisting of long, extra-thick fibers and trim these fibers the length you wish the finished legs to be. Tie the tip end of the hackle feather to the end of the shank. If the body is to be pulpy it should be made of chenille. Generally chenille is the best material for making the body for a shell-back fly, since it is of large diameter yet compressible. Tie the tip of the chenille, or whatever material you have selected, at the same place where the other materials have been tied. Wind first the chenille around the shank, leaving a slight space behind the hook eye for securing the other materials, then the clipped hackle, spacing each revolution evenly. Five or six turns of hackle will be sufficient. Tie down the hackle stem at the front of the hook with two or three half-hitches. Now bend the feather, which is to form the back, toward the eye of the hook. This will force the hackle fibers extending above the body to become bent downwardly, extending to the left and right of the body. Secure the front end of the back with several turns of working silk. Finally, tie two fibers of moosemane or similar material to the head of the fly. These antennae should not exceed the length of the body. Carefully build up the head of the fly with working silk and finish with the whip knot.

LARVAE

Larvae of the hellgramite, alder fly, fish fly, caddis fly and two-winged flies are taken in great quantities by trout. What angler has not used the hellgramite or "clipper" as a bait for smallmouth bass or has not seen the "stick-worms" of the caddis fly crawling sluggishly over the large, flat stones covering the stream bed? Larvae are extremely abundant in all sizes, ranging from the tiniest of worms to creatures such as the hellgramite which attains lengths of three inches or more. It has been my experience, that imitations of the smaller larvae are effective if dressed neatly and durably, but that facsimiles of the larger ones are not very productive of fish. I have seen many imitations of the hellgramite which, from the standpoints of eye-appeal and technique, were unassailable. However, careful use in the hands of veteran fly-fishermen proved these artificials absolutely useless, which seems to substantiate the theory that if you want to use a hellgramite, find a real one.

For the most part, larvae are worms with or without legs. The caddis-fly worm is an example of the type having legs, while the larvae of the midges are examples of the type without legs. Certain larvae are actually large, making imitation exceedingly difficult and undesirable and for this reason no mention is made of them in this section.

CADDIS

For years imitations of the caddis worm have been made with a white chenille body and a black chenille or herl head. Observant fly-dressers, however, have developed improvements over this first imitation, achieving even a natural translucency through the use of plastics and rubber body material. Imitations of the caddis are prerequisite lures. Learning to use them is an added assurance of catching more fish.

CONSTRUCTION: A short-shank hook with a fairly wide gape is desirable for this lure because the curvature of the shank adds naturalness to the body which is otherwise unobtainable. Place the hook in the vise, but leave as much clearance between the shank and vise as possible. With scissors, cut a strip approximately the width of a rubber band from a piece of translucent rubber body material generally used in the construction of may flies and drakes. Taper one end and tie it to the hook midway between the barb and the shank. Wind this tightly around the shank, leaving sufficient space behind the hook eye to form the head. Fasten the end with working silk and trim off the surplus rubber. Cut three (3) strands of moose mane to one inch in length and tie them on the underside of the body, leaving equal lengths extending on each side. Next shape the head by building it up with working silk and coating it with lacquer or winding black ostrich herl around the space between the front of the body and the rear of the hook eye. Finally shape the legs by kinking them in the places where joints would be found on the "natural" and apply a drop of lacquer on each joint to retain its shape.

MIDGE

Midges are undoubtedly the most numerous of all stream inhabitants and, while seemingly infinitesimal, they are, nevertheless, important trout food. This may seem difficult to believe since some midges are merely a fractional part of an inch in length; however, any reliable post-mortem will prove convincingly that midges are abundant and that trout like to eat them. It is good policy to have at least a few imitations of midges in size 18.

CONSTRUCTION: Essentially this larvae is nothing more than a smooth-bodied hackle fly dressed with a very small-diameter reverse hackle at the head. A thin coat of lacquer over the body will bring out the color to full advantage and add the sheen which is peculiar to midge bodies.

OTHER TYPES

There are many other combinations of the types already described that will be found useful. With the knowledge gained from the descriptions of the six basic types of nymphs and larvae, the fly-dresser can make whatever alterations are necessary to produce any sort of imitation he wishes. Chapter 13 describes in detail the many aquatic insects the angler should know even to the extent of indicating dimensions and coloration. Using this as a guide plus the information learned so far, the fly-maker should have no difficulty with the construction of any type of nymph or larva.

Chapter Eight

THE STREAMER

According to certain very obscure accounts on fly-fishing, the first streamer fly was produced by accident. It seems that a fly-dresser had made several hackle patterns of wet flies for one of his clients, a very adept fisherman, but had been a trifle careless with the details of finishing the head of one fly. The fisherman, upon arriving at the stream, happened to select the very fly having the imperfect head and commenced fishing, totally unaware, of course, that he was about to introduce a new kind of fly.

Repeated casts soon caused the hackle to unwind and trail behind the rest of the fly. Shortly thereafter the fisherman struck and landed a heavy trout and, after examining his terminal tackle as all good anglers will, realized what had happened to the fly which now no longer possessed hackle but instead had acquired a streamer. The fisherman immediately assumed that the fly had been "roughed" by the trout and that it was useless. Unwound hackle bespeaks poor workmanship and for this the fisherman privately denounced the fly-dresser. Changing to a second fly the irate angler placed cast after cast in perfect style over the best of the pools and rapids without raising a fish. He tried a third fly, a fourth, then a fifth, with the same result. In desperation he opened his fly-book in search of a well-chewed favorite and happened to glance at the "unwound hackle" just as a gust of wind swept across the stream. The breeze ruffled the hackle, which now lay straight over the body of the fly, causing it to vibrate like a thing alive.

In a few moments this strange fly was re-tied to the leader and cast into the same pool from which the angler had caught his solitary large trout. On the second cast a powerful fish struck and was creeled shortly afterward. Several more trout which had ignored the conventional type of flies previously cast came from hiding to take this "unwound" fly with unusual boldness.

As the story goes, the fly-maker was apologetic about his carelessness, but the angler was so enthusiastic over his creel of fish and the performance of the improperly tied fly that he ordered more flies dressed exactly like the one with the "unwound hackle."

This story may be true. The same thing has happened to me with one exception: I did not catch fish with the "unwound hackle." Undoubtedly it has happened to many anglers but whether this incident was really the founding of the streamer fly or not is highly debatable.

According to authentic records, Herbert L. Welch of Mooselookmeguntic, Maine, is reputed to be the originator of the streamer fly. Welch states he dressed the first

LONG-SHANK STREAMER
WITH BEARD HACKLE

SHORT-SHANK STREAMER
WITH SHOULDER HACKLE

TRAILER HOOK (SANBORN DESIGN)

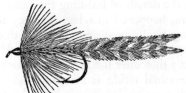

PALMER STREAMER

WOUNDED MINNOW

BY-PLANE

PLYMPTON-JOHNSON TYPES

FIG. 21
STREAMER DESIGN, FEATHER TYPE

Eonard

streamer in 1901 and designed the Welch Rarebit, Black Ghost, Jane Craig, Welch Montreal and Green Spot, the last of which is often erroneously listed as Green's Pot.

Streamers and bucktails are as standard as dry and wet flies to the fly-fisherman of today. Few if any serious anglers are unaware of the values of the streamer-type lure, not only for salmon and bass, but for practically every game fish. The longer flies are becoming more depended upon every year by anglers from coast to coast.

In recent years striped bass and sea trout (weakfish) have been added to the list of those fish which will take the streamer. For years enterprising fly enthusiasts have been catching baby tarpon on streamers and bucktails. Many anglers cast the spinner-streamer combinations with either the fly or plug rod, catching everything from panfish to muskies. Therefore, it might seem that the streamer is the nearest approach to universality so far as flies are concerned, since no other single type of lure equips the fly-man to catch so many different kinds of fish. From the three-quarter inch midgets to the five-inch long-toms, streamers are the most useful individual lures made and are limited only by the ability of the angler using them.

Generally, a streamer or bucktail is any long, slim lure composed of feathers or various kinds of hair and fished underwater to imitate a minnow. Nearly all streamers and bucktails are designed to look, when wet, like minnows. Some, however, are intended to represent other creatures such as large nymphs. Streamers are not radically different from bucktails, since they are constructed similarly. The main difference between the two is the material used to make the "streamer" or trailing portion which extends beyond the rear of the hook. The streamer wing consists of neck or saddle hackle feathers, while the equivalent in the bucktail is usually deer hair or the hair from other animals. Actually the word "bucktail" is misleading. One would think that flies labeled with the word would necessarily be constructed of bucktail. This is not so. One of the materials most widely used in the construction of bucktails is Chinese goat hair. In other words, any animal hair can be used to advantage, so long as its general properties are similar to those of bucktail.

Originally only deer tail hair was used. Fly-makers, who are never content with anything they have made, began to experiment with other kinds of material and discovered there were numerous kinds of hair far superior to bucktail. Today the material for a hair streamer is selected according to the value of its oil content, its degree of translucency and opacity, the amount of crinkle it possesses, and its resistance to rot and breakage.

Any streamer or bucktail must be flexible to the extent that it will vibrate and undulate when retrieved, because these lures are largely dependent upon activity for their effectiveness. The perfect streamer should have (1) a streamlined silhouette when wet, (2) maximum action, and (3) appearance reasonably similar to the object it is intended to represent.

Invariably streamers are identified with long-shank hooks on which the many trout, bass, and salmon patterns are dressed, to provide longer bodies and a consequent means of hooking "short strikers" or those fish which elusively strike only at the rearmost part of the lure. Conversely, circumstances alter cases in this respect and require short- or regular-shank hooks for catching those fish which tend to strike at the head end of the lure. Smallmouth bass are often inclined to approach the streamer from the side and then strike it a glancing blow near the front. This peculiarity seems

BUCKTAIL - OPTIC HEAD   BUCKTAIL - PLAIN

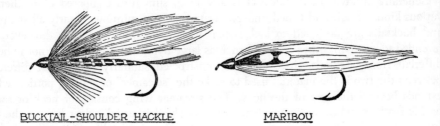

BUCKTAIL - SHOULDER HACKLE   MARIBOU

COMBINATION (VARIOUS)   MALLARD MINNOW

FIG. 22
STREAMER DESIGN, BUCKTAIL & OTHER TYPES

to exist throughout adverse fishing times and is tormenting to say the least, especially when streamers with long-shank hooks are used.

A dual-purpose type was developed, featuring the addition of a trailer hook having its point concealed in the tips of the streamers. This gave double protection against losing hard-to-hook fish. Variations of this lure are common. Although the original type was made with a piece of silkworm gut connecting the trailer hook to the shank of the main hook, modifications have used wire in place of the silkworm gut and even light-weight, long-shank hooks coupled to the main hook by silk windings or solder. It has been my own observation that this lure is most successful when made with nylon leader material, which produces desired flexibility in so long a lure. An inflexible, long lure assumes the character of a lever in the mouth of a fish and is frequently worked loose.

Dr. Herbert Sanborn was the originator of the trailer hook or double-hook trolling streamer. Dr. Sanborn claims he lost many good salmon trolling with a single long-shank hook and therefore developed the two-hook type. Sanborn designed the nine-three and has this to say about it: "The nine-three is my own creation, although I've heard of many others that claim to have originated it. I've been told many times how *I* tie it, but *nobody* will tie it the way I do and that is where they make their mistake. This has been the most effective color combination I have found and when it is tied correctly for fish and not for the fisherman's eye it will work well. Bucktail (white); three green feathers tied on flat and two natural black edgewise or the regular way; silver tinsel body and jungle-cock on sides."

Jim Gasque, ace bass fisherman, North Carolina guide and author of *Bass Fishing,* has developed a lure which parallels Dr. Sanborn's double-hook trolling streamer but is considerably larger and more heavily dressed. This lure is constructed with an extra-long bucktail wing and is as large as a plug. Jim has used his Tandum Double-header in competition with practically everything in fly-rod tackle, out-fishing the other lures by a broad margin. The Tandum Double-header is, however, definitely not the lure for the neophyte with a cheap rod.

When the water has reached its annual low it makes the fishing of any natural or artificial bait a troublesome, and oftentimes fishless, business. The ordinary streamer would be much too heavy for the extremely light leaders necessary at this season. Therefore, extra-light streamers have been developed to make possible the use of 2X and 3X leader points for fish such as salmon and bass which, otherwise, would be leader and lure-shy. These extra-light or midget streamers and bucktails are merely sparse miniatures of the larger ones. A few whisks of bucktail or other suitable kind of hair, a slender tinsel body, a tiny patch of hackle at the throat, perhaps jungle-cock shoulders, and the fly is finished. Midgets are deadly and will often bring big trout otherwise untouched and unseen to the landing bow.

In devising effective streamer lures one can let one's imagination be unconfined. It is very possible that most of the streamers must have been developed in this manner, since it would require a far more informed angler than I to recognize anything akin to nature in several of the patterns which have proved so effective. However garish, they are, nevertheless, consistent killers of all popular game fish.

As in most cases, locality and preferences peculiar to various fishermen determine the usefulness of streamers or any other lure. For this reason, the reduction of all streamer-type flies to a common formula is not a simple undertaking. However, I have classified the many kinds into groups, with the thought that they may at least be referred to some kind of common denominator.

STREAMER PROPORTIONS

Rules for proportioning the streamer and bucktail are more variable than the rules pertaining to other flies. Several factors determine hook sizes, streamer length, hackle spreads, and trimmings. We do know, however, that the fundamental purpose of the streamer is to simulate a minnow, and the proper length is the most important consideration. If the average minnow of the type in question should measure three inches, the streamer dressed to imitate it should approximate this same length as measured from the front of the head to the tips of the feather or hair streamers. A word about hook length with respect to the feathers: if the hook should be too long, the streamers, during repeated false casts, will whip around the rear of the hook and consequently spoil the retrieve. As a general rule it is advisable to use a hook approximately two-thirds the length of the streamers. This seems to be a happy medium. The gape of the hook depends largely on the characteristics of the fish sought. To best illustrate this, let us consider the design of a streamer to be used for smallmouth bass. We wish to make this lure about two and one-half inches long. Therefore, the hook length should be approximately one and three-quarter inches. If we refer to Fig. 4, Standard Gauge, we can see that a standard hook 1¾ inches long would be size #3/0. A lure only 2½ inches long tied on a hook this size would be entirely out of proportion. Besides, the hook would be oversize for most smallmouth bass. By maintaining the same shank length but using a 3X or 4X long-type hook, however, we can obtain a more balanced arrangement. For example, a 3X long-shank hook 1¾ inches in length will have a gape equal to the gape of a #1½; a 4X long shank equal to the gape of a #1. Either of these hooks will be satisfactory unless the water is in such condition as to make fine leaders necessary. It is not at all uncommon to find smallmouth bass and salmon extremely cautious and leader-shy. In this case the 6X long shank will reduce the wire diameter without sacrificing any of the length and minimize the hook weight. Incidentally, it should be mentioned that the extra-long-shank hooks in the smallest sizes, while they may be of sufficient length in the shank for some streamers, are dangerously flimsy and bend easily. For this reason it is well to dress streamers on long-shank hooks no smaller in the gape than #8 especially if they are to be used for such fish as the tough-jawed smallmouth. Light wire hooks that will bend easily have no place in fishing for powerful, leaping fish unless, of course, they are used with soft-action rods. Rods designed for bass fishing have more backbone than light trout rods and exert greater pressure on the terminal tackle, thereby prohibiting the use of the extremely fine-wire streamer hooks.

Both shoulder and Palmer hackle used in streamer design must have sufficient spread to extend beyond the width of the hook gape. Generally shoulder hackle is long enough to slant toward the hook point and blend with the streamers so that no abrupt beginning and ending of any one material or color is evident, thus streamlining the profile of the lure.

When mallard or teal are used to lend the aspect of scales, they must be tied with their slight natural curve bending toward, rather than away from, the body. Single strips or, in some cases, a few fibers, tied on over the other materials, will add the appearance of separated scale rows, a sometimes desirable feature.

In considering the location of jungle-cock eyes, study the general appearance of the minnow on which your imitation is based and affix the jungle-cock so that the white spots will be located in that place best comparing with the location of the eyes in the minnow. Small streamers will require the shortest of jungle-cock feathers taken from the top of the neck.

SPECIAL FEATURES

Small streamers made of long mallard or teal feathers look very much like those tiny white chubs of which brown trout are especially fond. Eyes can be painted directly on the side feathers but must be close to the head on lures so small.

Many streamers with weighted bodies bear the brand name of various well-known tackle houses and, although a little hard on fly rods, they are excellent in deeper waters. These are relatively simple lures to make. The hook, for example, is nearly completely covered by the side feathers and is not wound with the usual materials for this reason. A thin strip of lead is coiled around the hook shank to provide the added extra weight for which these lures are famous, then three or four hackle streamers are fastened midway up the shank. Guinea and mallard are generally used for the side feathers, although other feathers from pure white to black are sometimes featured on lures of this type. Painted optic heads complete the construction. A streamer characteristic of these weighted-body lures (the Mallard Minnow) is shown in Fig. 22.

FEATHER STREAMERS

A feather streamer is fundamentally any wet fly dressed with extra-long feather wings. Consequently all standard patterns *can* be made up as streamers, although many such patterns are not suited to such construction. For example, a Ginger Quill tied on a long-shank hook and having long hackle streamers would be a rather sad-looking affair. Other patterns, however, would be entirely in order dressed as streamers provided, of course, that their make-up permitted their adaptation to the longer hooks.

Feather streamers, like any other type of streamer, are dressed on either long- or short-shank hooks. The prevailing fishing conditions will determine which shank length is most suited to your own fishing grounds. As to the construction of the streamers themselves, this will depend fundamentally on whether long or short hooks are to be used.

Fig. 21 illustrates the feather streamer with beard hackle dressed on a long-shank hook and a similar streamer dressed with shoulder hackle. Either beard or shoulder hackle can be used in connection with any streamer or bucktail regardless of the length of the hook.

CONSTRUCTION: Because streamers are fundamentally wet flies with extra-long hackle-feather wings, they are dressed in the same way as wet flies up to and including the application of the hackle. See Figs. 21 and 24. In the case of streamers having very long bodies, it is well to wind cotton thread around the entire shank length to form a suitable base for the body. Tinsel bodies, especially, should be prepared in this manner, since the slightest irregularity in the winding of the tinsel will develop into a knob or a separation with sharp edges. This can be prevented completely if each preceding turn is slightly overlapped by each additional turn.

It will be noticed that the last four figures on Fig. 24 are divided into two groups—

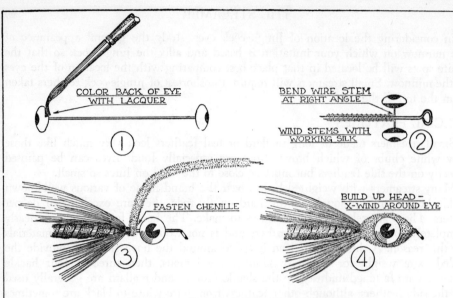

COLOR BACK OF EYE WITH LACQUER

①

BEND WIRE STEM AT RIGHT ANGLE

WIND STEMS WITH WORKING SILK

②

FASTEN CHENILLE

③

BUILD UP HEAD — X-WIND AROUND EYE

④

CHENILLE HEAD WITH GLASS EYES

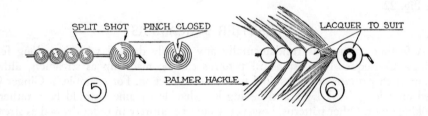

SPLIT SHOT   PINCH CLOSED

⑤

PALMER HACKLE

LACQUER TO SUIT

⑥

WEIGHTED BODY WITH PAINTED EYES

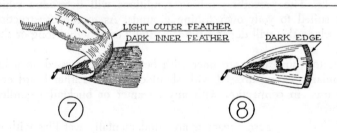

LIGHT OUTER FEATHER
DARK INNER FEATHER

⑦

DARK EDGE

⑧

HEAD AND GILL DESIGN

FIG. 23
SPECIAL FEATURES—STREAMER DESIGN

LEONARD

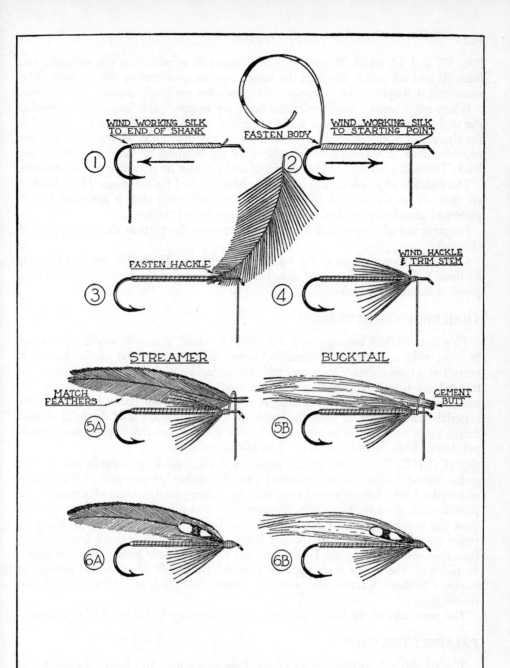

WIND WORKING SILK
TO END OF SHANK

FASTEN BODY

WIND WORKING SILK
TO STARTING POINT

① ②

FASTEN HACKLE

WIND HACKLE
& TRIM STEM

③ ④

STREAMER

BUCKTAIL

MATCH
FEATHERS

CEMENT
BUTT

5A 5B

6A 6B

FIG. 24
CONSTRUCTING THE STREAMER & BUCKTAIL

LEONARD

Nos. 5A and 6A which illustrate the final stages in constructing the streamer, and Nos. 5B and 6B which illustrate the same stages in constructing the bucktail. This arrangement simplifies the exposition and eliminates needlessly repeated descriptions.

When tying feather streamers to the hook, try to match the feathers by arranging the slight, natural curve of one feather opposite to the curve of the other. Whether the tips curve in or out seems to make little if any difference. When tying patterns requiring four or six individual feathers, tie the feathers as matched pairs to the hook. This will keep the streamer balanced and improve its efficiency and appearance.

The addition of jungle-cock shoulders is often standard for streamers. These feathers are fastened on the sides of the streamer or bucktail wing after it has been tied in place and completely finished except for the winding of the head.

Frequent use of cement will insure permanency of the parts as they are applied to the hook.

Cain River streamers are of the feather-streamer type. The bodies are slim (usually all tinsel). The hackle is wound shoulder style in front of the streamers and is composed of two separate colors.

TRAILER-HOOK STREAMER

This lure, while it may appear to be a little involved, is simply two flies connected by wire, silkworm gut or—preferably—nylon. The main portion of the lure is in every respect an ordinary streamer, with the exception of having no tail fibers. The trailer hook is generally smaller than the front hook and dressed in any way that suits the fancy of the person making it. Most patterns have trailer hooks tied with materials that harmonize with the entire streamer, although it is doubtful if such details make much difference to the fish. The chances are that a plain hook would not detract from the fish-luring qualities of the streamer.

CONSTRUCTION: First tie an unlooped snelled hook of suitable size for the trailer, then dress the hook as a wet fly. (The relationship between sizes of the streamer and trailer hooks follows no set rule, thereby making combinations of various hooks possible and effective. Generally, however, the trailer hook is several times smaller than the streamer hook.) Place the streamer hook in the fly vise. By holding the trailer snell in the fingers of the left hand, approximate the overall length of the lure, then with working silk fasten the snell to the streamer hook. The snell should be tied with the trailer hook uppermost so the point will be concealed among the streamer feathers. Cement the windings around the snell and allow them to dry thoroughly.

The remainder of the lure is dressed like any streamer fly having feather streamers.

PALMER STREAMER

The wiggling, breathing action of the Palmer streamer has been effective for all kinds of sport fish for years. One of the best lures I have ever used is a streamer of this sort tied with black body hackle and yellow hackle streamers. Coupled to double nickel spinners this is one of the most reliable of streamers. Because it combines maximum bulk with the lightest possible weight, the Palmer streamer is used as a fly-rod lure for the largest of fresh-water game fish. It is doubtful that a better spinner lure exists.

CONSTRUCTION: Because bodies are not important in the construction of this type of streamer, emphasis is placed on the thick hackle wound the entire length of the hook shank and on the two or more streamers extending aft of the hook. First fasten the streamers to the end of the hook shank. Tie the tip end of a large hackle immediately over the streamer windings and wind it as closely as possible up the shank. Several hackles, each of which must be tied separately, will be necessary to cover the entire length of the shank. Use care when tying down the butt end of the hackle stems to prevent unraveling. Finish the head in the usual manner and cement it thoroughly.

WOUNDED MINNOW STREAMER

A rather odd and recent departure from the usual type of streamer is the Wounded Minnow, which is dressed on one side only and has a corkscrew action in the current. When you first examine this lure you are inclined to think that the streamers have revolved out of position and that the fly was poorly made. A second glance, however, will reveal that the streamers are intended to be on one side only, the purpose being to cause the lure to plane erratically. This is a development of Ralph M. Plympton of New Jersey and Herbert Johnson of Maine.

CONSTRUCTION: See Fig. 21. The single major difference between this and other feather streamers is the location of and method of tying on the streamer feathers. Instead of placing them over the body, tie them with their concave surface facing inwardly and on one side of the body only. Hackle of the beard sort is best suited to these lures.

BY-PLANE STREAMER

Another interesting variation in streamers popularized by Johnson and Plympton, and one destined to make fishing history, is the By-Plane. This is, perhaps, the most outstanding and completely different streamer tied today. Bert Quimby of South Windham, Maine, is credited with having originated this fly for Chief Needahbeh. The feathers which make up the wing are not tied on vertically in the usual manner but are fastened "flat-wing" style or, horizontally. This makes possible the imitation of those narrow stripes common in many minnows. For example, the combination of dun over blue over dun produces a grayish-blue background with a very narrow blue stripe, one of the most effective color arrangements for streamers.

CONSTRUCTION: See Fig. 21. With the exception of the described wing arrangement, the By-Plane is otherwise like conventional streamers having beard or shoulder hackle and other usual features.

BUCKTAIL STREAMERS

It has been explained that the word "bucktail" is very loosely used by fishermen and has little meaning other than to identify any streamer tied with animal hair. Streamers tied with long hair wings are very dependable lures, as witness the Edson Tiger light and dark patterns, the Mickey Finn, the Warden's Worry, and others. Their action is somewhat different from the wriggle of feather streamers, being more the "breathing" or open-and-close type of motion.

CONSTRUCTION: Bucktails or hair streamers are constructed according to the same plan for making feather streamers. Beard hackle, shoulder hackle, long and regular length hooks, optic heads, trailer hooks and all other individual features of the feather streamer can be included in the design of hair streamers at will by the fly-maker. To illustrate this point refer to Fig. 22. The Optic Bucktail is simply a hair streamer with or without throat hackle but having a slightly enlarged head equipped with lacquered eyes. The addition of shoulder hackle entirely encircling the lure behind the head would not necessarily alter the fly. Nor would the absence of any hackle at all. Likewise, the lure would still remain an Optic Bucktail if a trailer hook were added. The same would apply in the case of jungle-cock shoulders. Thus it can be seen that many combinations are possible. No one type of streamer is a criterion.

A simple hair streamer is tied in this manner: Construct the body according to the description for making the feather streamer and apply the kind of hackle you prefer. Cement the windings and, while waiting for the cement to become tacky, snip sufficient hair to make the wing from the skin. Coat the butts of the hair with cement and place the hair over the fly body after gauging the exact location of the wing. Wind two or three loose turns over the base of the hair wing as shown in Fig. 24, No 5B. Apply a little more cement between the wing and the body, then draw the working silk tight, while at the same time holding the wing between the thumb and forefinger of the left hand. Wind the working silk around the head until all spaces are closed, complete with the whip-finish, then cement the windings.

OPTIC BUCKTAIL

Although originally designed for trout and bass, the Optic Bucktail has been adapted to nearly all kinds of fly-fishing in recent years. It is a very dependable lure and has established an impressive record. The name "Optic" is traceable to the painted or glass eyes featured in this lure. The formation of the head, however, is generally a little larger than the average, being purposely enlarged to provide space for the eyes. It is worth repeating at this point that the optic feature usually associated with bucktails need not be restricted to bucktail streamers alone and can be used in conjunction with any type of streamer lure.

CONSTRUCTION: See Fig. 23, Nos. 1 to 4. Since it differs from other streamer lures only so far as the head is concerned, the Optic can be constructed generally according to any plan for streamer or bucktail. The space for forming the head must necessarily be greater, to accommodate the additional materials used, however, and must be proportionate to the other parts of the lure. Various materials are useful for building up the head. If the fly is more or less small, such as the midget trout bucktails, it will not require special materials for this purpose. The working silk will build up the head size satisfactorily in this case but should be wound neatly to avoid any possibility of creating slack or irregular surfaces. If the lure is medium to large size, chenille will form the head quickly and compactly. Clipped deer hair is another material frequently used for this purpose, although it is more suitable for surface and semi-surface lures.

When making small optics, wind the head the necessary size and coat it with lacquer of the proper color. Allow the first coat to dry thoroughly, then apply a second coat. Any irregularities appearing after the second coat has been applied can be reduced, if not entirely eliminated, by the addition of a very light coat of lacquer thinner, which dissolves and smooths the surface film. A very professional and lustrous finish results from a final coat of clear lacquer.

Coloring the eyes consists merely in applying a drop of lacquer held on the tip of the dubbing needle to each side of the head. The pupil, which frequently is the color of the head, is applied in the same manner. Color combinations for the head, iris, and pupil are a matter of preference, although too elaborate arrangements tend to destroy the effect of a simple pair of eyes. For example, a black head and pupil, and a yellow or white iris, produce an excellent contrast, as does the same combination applied in reverse order. A white head, however, looks well-finished with yellow and black, red and black, yellow and red, or red and white eyes. The colors for the head and eyes are governed largely by, and should be in harmony with, the color of the whole lure.

Optics of larger size having heads made of chenille generally feature glass eyes. Fig. 23, Nos. 1 to 4 show these eyes in the different stages of preparation and application to the hook. Since these glass eyes are formed on soft wire stems which can be bent and shaped to suit any condition, they are prepared quickly for application to the hook shank.

It is assumed the streamer or bucktail is complete thus far with the exception that the eyes have not been tied nor the head wound. Select a pair of eyes and paint the back surface with lacquer of suitable color for the pattern. (Pupils in glass eyes are black, therefore no color other than the one used to paint the iris is necessary.) When the lacquer has become dry, bend the stem immediately under the eye into the shape of an L. Prepare two eyes in this manner, then place them opposite each other, one on each side of the head. Estimate the length the stems must extend toward the rear of the lure and clip off the surplus with wire cutters. Tie these eyes to the hook by winding the working silk the entire length of the clipped stems. Fasten the tip of the chenille as far back of the eyes as the other work already completed will permit. Wind the chenille tightly in close even coils until it completely covers the space allotted to the head. Tie down the end of the chenille with several turns of working silk and complete with the whip-finish.

MARABOU STREAMER

Marabou plumage, when dry, branches out from the main stem of the feather erratically, appearing fluffy and deceptively useless. When it is wet, however, it becomes streamlined and very effective. The fibers, which are limp and absorbent, cling together, giving the marabou a long, tear-drop appearance which is ideal and produces the best facsimile of swimming possible to obtain with feathers. Body color is not important because the entire hook shank is enveloped with strands of marabou which leave little, if any, body to show through. Usually a few fibers of mallard or teal over the back add much to the appearance of the lure. Mallard, for example, is delicately and closely mottled, lending the aspect of the tiny scales of minnows of which the streamer is an imitation. With the addition of soft, fine-feathered shoulders, jungle-cock eyes, or a narrow, dyed center section, marabou streamers can be dressed in various ways to produce most lifelike imitations of minnows.

CONSTRUCTION: (At the outset keep in mind that any lure made of marabou plumage will appear too fluffy. This is natural and cannot be avoided.) First pluck several strands from the main stalk of the feather and arrange these with the butt ends together so that the tips will extend approximately one-third the shank length beyond the rear of the hook. Tie these to the shank at a point immediately behind the eye of the hook, and continue to build up the streamer until the hook is entirely covered. Add the mallard or teal fibers over the back, shoulders, or jungle-cock eyes if these are desired, then finish with the whip-knot.

COMBINATION STREAMERS

Numerous streamers, such as the Supervisor, nine-three, Gray Ghost, Green Ghost, and Moose River, which are used principally for salmon and large trout, are neither true feather streamers nor true "bucktails" but are really combinations of both types. These lures are more complex than plain feather streamers or bucktails and resemble the European long-shank wet flies. Some may be dressed with Palmer hackle wound the entire length of the shank, an underwing of bucktail or other hair, an upper wing of feather streamers, topping of pheasant crest or other metallic feather, shoulders of pheasant tippet, jungle-cock eyes, and a body containing several colors and materials, plus, perhaps, an optic head. This is merely characteristic of some patterns and should not be accepted as the general rule.

Combinations are almost always based on effects produced by the blending of the many feathers and hairs of which they are made. This blending is most noticeable when the streamer has become wet and all the parts cling together. It is true that the appearance of some streamers of this sort tax the imagination and seemingly represent nothing that ever lived. The Supervisor, for example, is reputedly an imitation of the smelt, but other patterns are not even vague representations of anything in nature. Nevertheless, the ornate, combination streamer is a lure of unassailable merit.

CONSTRUCTION: Perhaps the best way to demonstrate the construction of a combination streamer is to select a minnow and devise as close an imitation of it as good judgment and practicability will permit. Naturally every individual feature will not be defined. If, however, the finished product compares as a whole with the minnow from which it was copied, it will be satisfactory. Plate 4 was prepared especially to illustrate the possibilities for selecting materials best suited to the imita-tions of two very common minnows, the red-bellied dace and the shiner. Always keep in mind that we are interested in the overall appearance of the streamer when it is in the water. A dry streamer inclines toward bushiness and does not present the same streamlined profile nor the total blending of materials that it presents after it is wet. For this reason it is advisable to become familiar with the properties of the materials when they are both wet and dry to facilitate the best possible streamlining of the lure.

The red-bellied dace is an interesting model for two reasons. Firstly, it is a brilliant minnow clearly marked. Secondly, it has contrasting, longitudinal stripes which are the outstanding color scheme. Let us assume this minnow is in an aquarium on the work table. At once we notice the red stripe on the belly, the yellow center band be-tween the two black stripes, the dark olive-brown color of the back, and the yellowish fins. Now the problem becomes: what is the quickest method to develop the best and most durable streamer of generally similar appearance? Where to begin?

At first it might seem a good plan to build the streamer around a black body repre-senting the black stripes next to the belly. This, however, would make any simulation of the yellow fins quite difficult. The red stripe of the belly would then have to extend below the black body of the streamer, preventing the fin material from showing to any advantage. Therefore, it would appear that the shank covering should be red to represent the belly stripes and that hackle wound Palmer style could well represent the fins. With this as a basis around which to form the entire lure, we can now select and proportion the many materials to be used. First, however, the length of the streamers must be established and the most suitable hook chosen. For the purpose of illustration, consider 3 inches as the overall length. It is well to know the overall length of any streamer or large wet fly for the reason that some feathers, while they may be ideally marked and colored for a particular condition observed in the minnow being copied, might be too short to extend the required length.

Preparation of Materials. Gold pheasant crest is bright and metallic and therefore is superior to most materials for the formation of the tail. It is not necessary to try to trim or shape materials so that they describe the shape of the tail; color is sufficient. The body must be deep orange-red. This suggests the use of floss silk or wool. Since the fins along the belly are yellow they should be represented by Palmer hackle wound the entire length of the shank. The spread of this hackle should be wide enough to extend below the point of the hook. The streamer portion is shown to consist of four longitudinal colored sections—a yellow section between two black ones and the whole topped with dark metallic-green peacock sword. Hackle streamers are not ideal because they are not easily tied in the manner necessary to provide a yellow stripe between two black ones. Bucktail, or preferably polar bear or Chinese goat hair, is adaptable to the building up of several layers of different colors. However, do not clip any hair from the skin until ready to fasten it in place, to avoid any error in estimating the proper length of each section. The same applies to the peacock sword. The shoulder material may be one of several kinds of feathers. Since the single purpose of the shoulder is, to a reasonable degree, the imitation of the head of the minnow, the shoulder should be selected with this thought in mind. Notice that the head of the natural minnow is olive-green on top and white on the sides. We can stretch a point and say that the peacock sword will serve well enough for the top portion, but what about the white sides? Silver pheasant tippet is white with a black edge and will do very nicely. So will white goose breast. Remove several fibers from the upper side of the shoulder feather to allow, later on, the greenish color of the peacock sword to show. Jungle-cock eyes are usually tied too long. In reality, these feathers, by virtue of their wax-color spot near the tips, represent the eyes of the minnow and should be fastened in such a position that the whitish spot approximates the location of the real eye.

Dressing the Streamer: The dressing of streamers has been covered adequately and requires little if any further comment. However, it may be worth a second thought to consider that game fish, while reputedly stupid about some things, are remarkably intelligent about the kinds of things they usually eat. Spurious-looking artificials may produce some strikes, but more lifelike lures are bound to produce more. Using a little logic in the construction of streamers will contribute much toward their final success.

The shiner minnow, a widely distributed and consequently popular live-bait, is illustrated in Plate 4 with a suggested imitation. Essentially the same procedures already described in connection with the red-bellied dace apply. The materials, of course, are somewhat different. The fins are made of ice-blue or bluish-white hair, the body is either cream-yellow floss or gold tinsel, and the back consists of mallard fibers dyed slate-blue. Notice that the fins are represented by several fibers of hair fastened to the underside of the shank, and that the yellowish central stripe corresponds to the yellow covering of the hook shank. Because the shiner is principally bluish-white, the hair space-filler between the body and the mallard back should be of similar color. The shoulders consist of overlapped feathers—pale gray over red—and are arranged in such a manner that the outer, pale gray feather is slightly shorter than the inner red one. By this method the simulation of open, red gills is effected.

Chapter Nine

THE SALMON FLY

Salmon flies, which are fashioned from the plumage of the world's most beautiful and exotic birds, call for the ultimate in skill, artistic ability and color sense on the part of the fly-dresser. Strict adherence to purity of pattern as determined by locale over many years has made some of the traditions which govern the construction of these flies seem inexplicable. But precedents have been so interwoven in the techniques of dressing salmon flies that even the slightest violation of any one of them is apparent to the connoisseur and, moreover, is considered intolerable by those perfectionists who demand absolute authenticity. Thus it can be said that salmon flies are fit for a king if for no other reasons than the cost and the painstaking efforts necessary to produce them. Anyone can sit down to the fly-maker's table and tie a bunch of feathers together that might occasionally deceive a fish, but not everyone can make a genuine salmon fly.

Some patterns are dressed with as many as twenty or thirty different feather materials. Consequently the dressing of these patterns is not entirely simple, even taking account of the current trend to modify the original patterns by skimping or even entirely omitting several materials. When making flies of such an involved nature as these, one must know the correct procedures and be able to proportion the work, otherwise there will not be sufficient space on the hook to accommodate all of the materials.

To many persons, salmon flies appear needlessly brilliant and gaudy. Actually this appearance is necessary in many cases. When the waters are high these large, bright flies serve as attractors. Naturally they must be visible for many yards since they are used in heavy, deep water. Small, dull flies would be of little value until later in the season when the water has thinned and the salmon have become selective.

The explanations given for the color combinations found in salmon flies are, for the most part, mere assumptions. Interesting histories have been written at great length about salmon flies but, while they are voluble as regards the inventer and the reputed success of his invention, they do not indicate the bases for the fly patterns themselves. Of course, it must be taken into consideration that a large number of salmon patterns were developed in the early nineteenth century when, perhaps, representation of some specific creature that a salmon would eat was of lesser importance than some imaginative angler's conception of what a salmon would like based on color and symmetry alone. The Candlestick-maker pattern, for example, be-

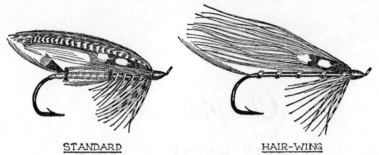

STANDARD   HAIR-WING

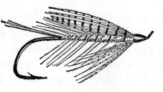

LOW-WATER   MINIATURE

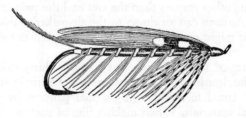

DEE

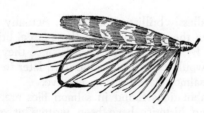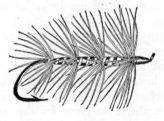

SPEY   GRUB

FIG. 25
SALMON FLY DESIGN

Lonard

cause its colors were extremely bright, was often spoken of as something brilliant enough to light the salmon bed. The Durham Ranger, another bright fly, was recommended for its ability to be seen from comparatively great distances under the water surface.

Whether the originators of these flies contrived them to be imitative of natural creatures or merely intended them to stand as classic examples of the fly-dresser's art may never be known. While certain of the old, fancy patterns may have been intended to simulate shrimp and prawns, their names would not lead one to think so—being fanciful in most cases and outright mysterious in a few. It was the general rule during the early years of fly-making to entitle fly patterns after the surname of the originator, the title of a tradesman, occasionally the name of a river or loch, or, too frequently, by an entirely irrelevant name, as witness the Popham, Butcher, Inver Green, and the Black Dose respectively.

Some patterns have been based on the color of salmon eggs, in accordance with the old and still-credited theory that salmon, when spawning, are especially diligent about salvaging eggs which have become detached from main egg clusters. The male, in his effort to prevent the escape of these scattered egg groups, which would be washed downstream and lost, seizes them in his jaws to return them to their former place. This same theory accounts for the use of actual salmon eggs as bait and, perhaps, for the frequency of bright yellow-orange in salmon flies.

Salmon flies are made in two types: wet flies, which are very involved to make, and dry flies, which are usually of either the bivisible or the parachute class.

WET FLIES

Salmon wet flies have been so affected by local influences as to make their general classification somewhat vague and inaccurate. For this reason, any semblance of standardization is probably too much to hope for, although several serious attempts have been made in this direction. Ordinarily, flies, such as trout wet flies, are identified by the shape of the wings, the treatment of the hackle, and overall appearance. Not so, salmon flies. The dressing of any individual, standard-pattern salmon fly may be tied variously, depending upon the region where it was made. Well-known as it is, the Silver Doctor is recorded as being tied in many ways but is still recognizable as a Silver Doctor in any one of its several dressings. One fancier may prefer to leave out the green strips in the wings, while another might like the addition of blue strips; or one might like more guinea hackle than the "standard" calls for, while another might want a solid blue hackle. These preferences establish local precedents which, in turn, become regional standards until, in time, there is such conflict as to what is standard and what is not that the task of tabulating even a nominal percentage of these divers flies seems hopeless.

In Great Britain, for example, a salmon fly is dressed according not only to the pattern dressing, but according to the preferences of local anglers who believe their ideas concerning hackle arrangement, wing positions, etc., improve the original pattern. Flies dressed for the rivers Spey, Dee, Helmsdale and Grimersta are typical; those for each river vary slightly, for the most part in styling rather than color.

American types are no less individualized. One group of flies known as the Margaree type and named after the famous salmon river of the same name is special in that it features hair wings. It follows from this that any standard pattern might be classified

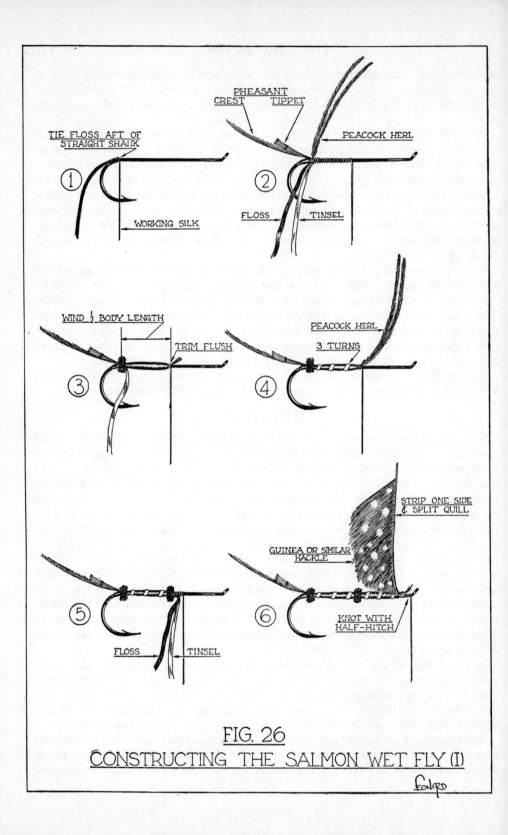

FIG. 26
CONSTRUCTING THE SALMON WET FLY (I)

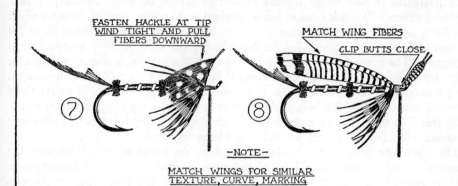

7 — FASTEN HACKLE AT TIP
WIND TIGHT AND PULL
FIBERS DOWNWARD

8 — MATCH WING FIBERS
CLIP BUTTS CLOSE

—NOTE—

MATCH WINGS FOR SIMILAR
TEXTURE, CURVE, MARKING
AND RESILIENCY

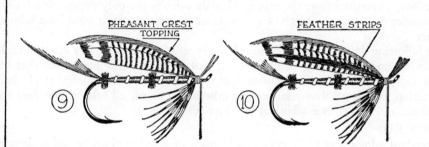

9 — PHEASANT CREST
TOPPING

10 — FEATHER STRIPS

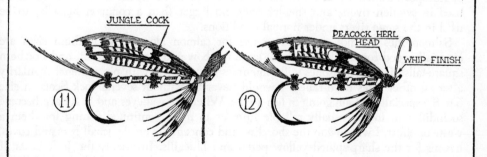

11 — JUNGLE COCK

12 — PEACOCK HERL
HEAD
WHIP FINISH

FIG. 27
CONSTRUCTING THE SALMON WET FLY (II)

Eonard

as a Margaree if hair wings instead of feather wings are used. Actually, almost identical effects will result from either a standard or Margaree type of dressing when the fly is wet. Let us suppose that you have been making a Parmachene Beau for salmon and have everything tied on but the wings. Shall it be a standard or a Margaree? The conventional dressing includes white wings with narrow red feather strips up each side, and jungle-cock eyes. When wet, this fly will be white-winged with a narrow red center. This same effect can be produced if you will tie on three layers of suitable hair—first white, then red and, finally, a top layer of white. Essentially this fly is the same as the standard in both proportion and color, but is, according to correct classification, of the Margaree or Hair-wing type.

There are four basic types of salmon wet flies: the Standard, the Miniature, the Low-water, and the Hair-wing. Each of these has as many aliases as a Chicago crook, making recognition difficult unless the characteristics of the four types are known. Streamers, which are so effective for salmon, are used too universally to be classed as a salmon-fly type. The majority of trout and bass streamer patterns are suitable for salmon, although special patterns are more popular, possibly because they have been more widely advertised than the others. Usually price is the only dependable index. If a streamer costs twice as much as a good trout or bass pattern, it must be a salmon streamer.

The following descriptions of the four basic types of salmon wet flies are the result of checking and re-checking many lists. At first it might seem impossible that all salmon flies could be classified into so few types, but from the standpoint of their construction, which involves relationships otherwise unseen, all salmon wet flies are dressed according to rules established for these four types.

STANDARD

A standard salmon wet fly is meticulously made of genuine plumage and is dressed fully but in proportion to the size of the hook on which it is tied, which may range from size 10/0 to not smaller than size 6. This is the original salmon fly, one which has been used throughout the world, embodying all the characteristics and principles of European salmon-fly design. I have seen flies of this sort, the size of a wren, to be used in swollen rivers, and smaller ones, no larger than a common horsefly, to be used in the same rivers under normal conditions.

Salmon flies are not restricted to use for salmon alone. The medium sizes are especially good for smallmouth bass, large rainbow and steelhead trout, and northern square-tails. The smaller ones will sometimes take panfish with phenomenal regularity after all other lures have failed. I would never be without several Jock Scots in size 6 to 8, especially if I am going to fish a lake. When the walleyes and bass have become so indifferent to the usually reliable lures as to make continued fishing for them a waste of effort, I will row to the shoreline and concentrate on the small bars and coves, havens for the sharp-spined yellow perch and bluegills. Invariably the Jock Scots, if neatly cast into the proper spots, will bring forth several of the frisky little fellows.

CONSTRUCTION: The description that follows is of general application. See Fig. 26 and Plate VI. At the outset the construction of the salmon fly will require the best efforts of the fly-dresser. The materials are so varied in texture and the operations so numerous that heed must be paid to each step. Special care must be taken to prevent bulkiness, or the fly when finished will turn out to have been a total waste of time and materials.

After the hook has been set in the vise, the rearmost material must be fastened and wound. Most patterns will have a short section of floss or tinsel tied at the beginning of the bend in the hook. Keep in mind that there are to be many pieces of material fastened but not wound, throughout the entire procedure, until the work has progressed to more advanced stages. Notice in Fig. 26 that the silk floss is fastened a short distance beyond the straight portion of the shank. The floss is then wound to that point where the tail sections will be tied in. Generally this is at the very end of the straight shank. Secure the floss with a half-hitch and apply a drop of lacquer. Immediately tie in the longer section of tail, which often is golden pheasant crest. Tie in the shorter tail section, which may be golden or silver pheasant tippets. Fig. 26, No. 2 illustrates this operation. Many patterns require chenille or herl at this point. Peacock herl is shown in this example. It is well to wind two strands at the same time and then wind back through the herl with fine working silk to prevent the herl from unwinding or breaking. While it may be difficult at first to secure the butt end of the herl and the silk and tinsel at the same time as shown in Fig. 26, No. 2, it will improve the body construction to do so. After the chenille or herl base has been formed at the tip, wind the silk as far forward as is specified for the particular pattern. The example we are following in the illustration requires that the silk must extend only halfway up the shank. This too is common in salmon-fly design. After the silk has been wound and cinched with a half-hitch at the mid-shank point, wind the tinsel with even spacing and secure as is shown in Fig. 26, No. 3. If the pattern calls for it, and most will, fasten two strands of herl or one of chenille as before, and form the center ball or joint. Tie in silk floss and tinsel again in the same fashion as you did previously in No. 2. This color may contrast with the first section of silk or it may be the same, depending upon the pattern. The next operation is the application of the hackle. Let it be understood that hackle in salmon-fly design may be a combination of breast feathers, tippets, crests and other brilliant plumage. For the sake of illustration we will consider the guinea hackle wound shoulder style, which is frequently used.

First split the guinea feather with a razor blade to reduce the thickness of the center quill. Clean out the remaining pith. This will leave the feather more flexible and suitable for winding. For small flies remove all the fibers from one side, then split the quill. Fasten the feather by the tip end as shown in Fig. 26, No. 6. If two hackles of different colors are to be used, tie these together at the tips. Wind the hackle slowly, meanwhile directing the position in which the hackle sections will lie by pushing downward with the thumb and forefinger of the left hand. Such hackle as guinea can be wound safely only about two-thirds the length of the feather, because the stem is rather stiff beyond this point and has a tendency to break. Tie the hackle down securely with the working silk and clip off the excess. A second hackle should be wound in the same fashion, but seldom at the same time with the first hackle. Fig. 26, No. 6, and Fig. 27, No. 7, illustrate the application of the hackle and the approximate extent to which a guinea hackle can be wound. Wing selection is very important. Only those feathers which have a strong body and good texture should be used. This does not mean they must be stiff and unwieldy. On the contrary, they must possess resiliency to prevent separation and splitting. Perhaps the best feathers for this purpose are white swan quills which can be dyed any desired color, wood duck, mallard dyed or plain, teal and hen mallard side feathers, pheasant body and side plumage and the swan favillions and fleeches. Tied in combination or with thin sections tied over the base wing (these are known as splits) these feathers will constitute a good portion of all salmon fly wing materials. To continue with the illustration, it will be seen that paired barred wood-duck side feathers are used. These are tied in directly over the hackle windings as shown in Fig. 27, No. 8. After the wing butts are well tied down, and the working silk has been cinched with a half-hitch, the surplus butts should be clipped neatly. Care should be taken to allow sufficient space behind the eye for addition of several more materials. It is usually about this point in the process of construction that most flies will indicate the dresser's ability or lack of it. Fig. 27, No. 9 illustrates the fastening of the topping, which in most cases is golden pheasant crest. This feather is extremely glossy and metallic in appearance and does much to improve the general appearance of the fly. It must be tied with its curve facing the wings, never away from them. In Fig. 27, No. 10, the method of fastening the "splits" is shown. Usually these splits are plain, dyed feathers or pheasant crests. In some cases tippet shoulders may be added first, or perhaps a combination of hackle tips. In our example the two splits are carefully paired, then placed with their concave sides toward the wings. The excess at the butts is trimmed. If two or more sets of splits of different colors are to be added, these should be tied one pair at a time, with only the fewest turns of working silk wound between pairs. Finally the jungle-cock trim is added in precisely the same manner as a single pair of splits. Strangely enough, some patterns call for the jungle-cock tied short, or with the eyes close to the head windings. Others, for example the English "Dandy," require that the feather extend beyond the tip of the wing. For the most part, the jungle-cock shoulders are dressed short to medium. The heads of many patterns are finished with herl or chenille, as illustrated in Fig. 27, No. 12. Two herl sections or a single strand of chenille are used for this, and are applied in the same manner as the materials for forming the tip and center balls or joints. Whip-finish the final windings, touch with cement and the fly is completed.

If you have come this far and have had sufficient room to perform all the operations near the head of the fly, it can be claimed you will have no more than average difficulty in dressing salmon flies. If the work appears crammed at the eye, and the materials are not neatly blended into one complete unit, the chances are the body material was extended too far forward, which is, incidentally, the most common error that will be made in dressing most fly styles. Consider salmon flies nothing more than large, fancy wet flies, and the job of making one may become easier.

THE POPHAM

Because the Standard wet fly is often very involved, requiring many materials and operations, I have chosen for a specific illustration the Popham, a rather complicated pattern which involves practically all of the different operations necessary to dress any salmon wet fly. Plate VI shows there are twenty-three separate operations in the make-up of the Popham pattern and, while this does not represent the maximum number for all patterns, it does include nearly every combination of material types found in most patterns.

Preparation of Materials: If possible, all materials should be laid out in sequence on the work table. Plate VI denotes both the materials and their sequence for making the Popham. Where materials are used for a second and third time reference is made

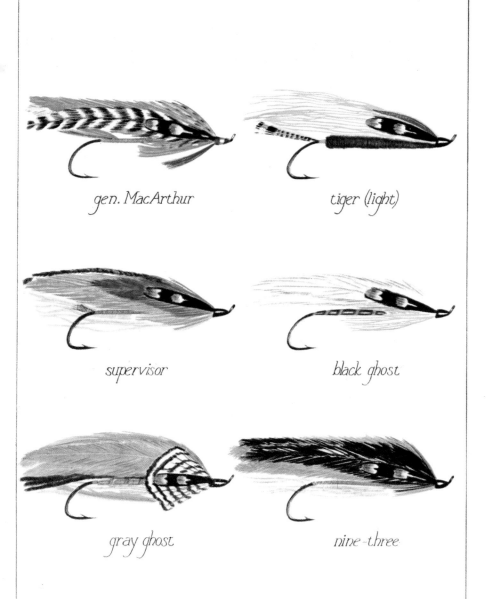

gen. MacArthur

tiger (light)

supervisor

black ghost

gray ghost

nine-three

Plate V
Favorite Streamers

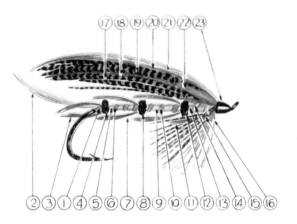

THE POPHAM

1. gold tinsel tag
2. gold pheasant crest tail
3. silver pheasant crest trailers
4. black ostrich herl butt
5. yellow floss body
6. gold tinsel rib
7. same as 3
8. same as 4
9. same as 5
10. same as 6
11. same as 3
12. same as 4
13. same as 5
14. same as 6
15. quinea hackle applied "beard" fashion
16. blue hackle applied "beard" fashion
17. brown mallard grand nashua or Egypt. goose
18. red feather strip
19. same as 17
20. bright blue feather strip
21. gold pheasant crest topping
22. blue-jay cheek
23. head (black working silk)

Plate VI
Typical Material List

FONARD

jack scot

silver doctor

durham ranger

black dose

dusty miller

silver wilkinson

Plate VII
Favorite Salmon Wet Flies

Leonard

gibbs' striper

gresh red-yellow

gresh red-white

rhode's shrimp

Plate VIII
Salt-water Flies

EONARD

to the preceding operations which include the same materials and treatment.

(1) Gold tinsel tag. Tinsel for tags and ribbing for flies the size of our example, which, let us say, is a size 1/0, should be medium or medium-large and embossed. With scissors taper the end to be tied to the hook. Locate the tapered end slightly aft of the barb, fasten it with winding silk and wind three or four turns up to that point where the tip will be located.

(2) Golden pheasant crest tail. Select a full, thick crest feather which, after being tied to the hook, will be approximately the length of the body. Tie this, with the natural curve of the feather pointing upwards, to the hook at that place where the tag winding was terminated.

(3) Silver pheasant crest trailers. Select two matched, short crest feathers and tie one on the top side and the other on the bottom side of the hook so that the concave sides face inwardly.

(4) Black ostrich herl butt. Usually tip or butt windings are narrow, two—or, at the most, three—windings being sufficient. Fasten a short piece of fine working silk the same color as the herl to the hook and, after the herl has been wound, wind the working silk once or twice through the herl to insure its permanency.

(5) Yellow floss silk. Choose a rich, yellow floss and, if it is of the two-strand variety, separate the strands. Fasten the tip of one of these to the hook. If your vise is equipped with a material clip or clips, place the floss in one of them to prevent soiling and damaging the floss. If your vise is not equipped with material clips, be careful not to scuff the surface of the floss.

(6) Gold tinsel rib. Taper the edge of the end of the tinsel and fasten it as close to the herl tip winding as possible. Wind the floss tightly and neatly, slightly tapering this section by making extra turns toward the front if necessary. Secure the floss with the working silk then rib with the gold tinsel.

(7) Silver pheasant crest trailers. These are applied in exactly the same manner as (3).

(8) Black ostrich herl center joint. See (4).

(9) Yellow floss silk. See (5).

(10) Gold tinsel rib. See (6).

(11) Silver pheasant crest trailers. See (3).

(12) Black ostrich herl front joint. See (4).

(13) Yellow floss silk. See (5).

(14) Gold tinsel rib. See (6).

(15) Guinea hackle applied "beard" fashion. From a clearly marked guinea breast-feather pluck several fibers and tie them approximately two fly-head lengths behind the eye of the hook. Thick, bushy hackle is not necessary on salmon wet flies; a little goes a long way. This portion of hackle is known as "backing," principally because it is rearmost.

(16) Blue hackle applied "beard" fashion. This is stripped from the feather in the same manner as the guinea already tied and should be applied to the front. This is generally called "face" hackle, a self-explanatory term.

(17) Brown mallard Grand Nashua or Egyptian goose breast. Either one of these two materials is satisfactory for the wing in the Popham, although the latter is more ideally marked. Golden pheasant tail fibers, while a little more difficult to handle, are marked quite like Egyptian goose breast. Place a drop of cement on the final hackle

windings and, while it is drying, remove several sections from an Egyptian goose breast feather. Tie these on immediately in front of the hackle.

(18) Red strip. This material can be tied on in one of two ways: by tying it between the main wing sections as they are built up or by adding them to the outside of the finished fly. For the purpose of illustration we will use the former method and tie a single section from a large wing feather dyed red directly over the wing fibers already in place.

(19) See (17). This consists of fastening on the upper portion of the wing fibers.

(20) Blue strip. See (18). Any material similar to that used for the red strip is satisfactory. The blue should be brilliant and the strip tied over the wing fibers—not on the side.

(21) Golden pheasant crest topping. The majority of salmon wet flies are topped with golden pheasant crest. Actually this feather does add brilliance to the fly because it is metallic in appearance. Select two full-bodied feathers and attach them to the hook with their concave sides facing downwardly.

(22) Blue-jay cheek. This is another material frequently used to add the final touch to salmon flies. It is dressed short with the concave sides of the feathers facing inwardly. As a general rule when patterns do not call for jungle-cock eyes they do require blue-jay or chatterer cheeks.

(23) Material for head. Salmon flies often feature chenille, herl, dubbing, or silk floss heads. No especial rule governs the use of any one of these materials, although a balanced appearance is desired in every case. Black, for example, is acceptable for practically all patterns. However, red is usually used on the Silver Doctor. So long as the color of the head more or less harmonizes with the general color scheme of the entire fly, it will be correct.

MINIATURE

The miniature is the most difficult to dress of all the fly types primarily for the reason that, small as it is, it contains as many parts as its bigger counterpart, the standard, and is constructed according to the same strict principles governing the construction of the latter. In reality the miniature is not an individual type at all, so fas as method of manufacture is concerned but, because very small wet flies are especially popular and useful during those times when the salmon are annoyingly selective, it has become recognized as such. This type, because it was designed for adverse fishing conditions, requires the finest of salmon leaders, the tippets of which may be as small as 3X. Such small flies and fine leaders demand the utmost in rod technique. Fishing with miniatures for full-sized salmon is ticklish business. After the fish has struck and the barb has been driven home, the outcome is never decided until either the leader has parted or the fish has been killed.

The majority of Miniatures range from size 8 to size 12, although it is probable that some enterprising fly-dresser, for the purpose of demonstrating his skill, has actually made smaller ones. The most satisfactory sizes are 10 and 8. British and some American manufacturers list miniatures in odd sizes: 7, 9, and 11.

CONSTRUCTION: Exactly the same procedure for dressing the standard is followed.

LOW-WATER

The Low-Water is a slim, sparsely dressed fly tied on a hook several sizes larger than ordinarily would be used. Such a fly appeals to a salmon when he is selective in much the same manner as the miniature but has the advantage of greater hooking power. Low-water conditions demand that the hook be strong enough to turn and hold a fighting fish, that it sink the fly properly, and that it have sufficient gape to penetrate into the tough parts of the jaw. These flies, which are used for "greased line" fishing, are deadly when properly used. Patterns generally are not standard; nearly every region where salmon fishing is done has contributed several special patterns which seem to be superior to standards.

These flies are classified according to the size of the fly rather than the size of the hook and almost always are favored in sizes 2 through 8. The size relationship between the fly and the hook is not uniform among fly-dressers. As a rule, the fly is two or three sizes smaller than the hook, although this is not a true guide by any means. Some localities prefer 2X or 3X long-shank hooks, to make the matter even more involved. In this connection, it might be worth giving some thought to devising a system to designate low-water flies something like this: pattern, Blue Charm, size 8/4— meaning that the fly is size 8 and the hook size 4. Likewise, if long-shank hooks are to be used, the length of the hook could be suffixed in the same manner; therefore, the same fly tied on a 2X long-shank hook would be described like this: pattern, Blue Charm, size 8/4-2X.

The following patterns represent a fairly accurate cross-section of the favorites dressed as low-water flies: Black Spean, Blue Charm, Fiery Brown, Gled, Inky Boy, Jeannie, Jockie, March Brown, Lady Caroline, Lemon Gray, Logie, Pink Lady, Prosser's Black, Rankin Special, Silver Blue, Sir Charles, Silver Doctor and Thunder and Lightning.

CONSTRUCTION: The low-water is dressed the same as the standard with the exception that, as stated before, it is sparse and short for the hook size.

HAIR-WING

The hair-wing is an American departure of merit, having proved its worth on both the Atlantic and Pacific salmon, steelhead, and trout. In appearance it resembles a short streamer dressed in proportion to the hook. This type has become very popular on the Atlantic coast around the region including Maine and northward where the spectacular Atlantic salmon make their inland runs.

Hair-wing flies may be tied in all standard patterns, although patterns having many wing materials will be necessarily bulky regardless of how carefully they are tied. The following patterns have excellent reputations and are dressed on hooks ranging from size 10 to 3/0: Abbey, Black Bear, Black Bomber, Brown Bomber, Captain, Coachman, Cosseboom, Grizzly King, Jock Scott, Major Griggs, McGinty, Mystery, Parmachene Belle, Professor, Royal Coachman, Ross Special, Silver Doctor, Silver Grey Bomber, Yellow Bucktail (Silver Body).

CONSTRUCTION: The wings are applied in the same fashion as bucktail and other hair wings. Most patterns are tied with shoulder hackle but are frequently made up alternately with short hair hackle tied beard fashion. The bodies, of course, are dressed in the usual manner.

SPEY

Coincidentally the word Spey is the name of a type of natural hackle located behind the saddles on a gamecock and is also the name of a river in England. Authorities disagree as to whether this style was named for the river or the hackle. It seems a logical deduction that both the style of fly and the hackle were named after the river.

A salmon fly tied "spey" fashion is recognizable principally for its thin, smooth body and long, sparse hackle. Some fly-dressers claim that spey flies are traditionally without tail fibers. This seems to be borne out by the majority of dressings.

CONSTRUCTION: Features rather than constructional differences set this fly apart from others. Hooks are generally 3X long. The wings are the down-wing type and on some patterns the butts are thinned out, leaving a few fibers projecting downward; these are then fastened like hackle in front of the Palmer windings. Most of the patterns are dressed with flank or side feathers which are flexible.

GRUB

The absence of both wings and tail help to identify the Grub. This would seem to indicate that Grubs are nothing more than a body and hackle, which is exactly the case. Frequent mention is made that Grubs are Palmer-hackled, and perhaps in some localities this may be the rule. However, some of the original Grub patterns do not bear this out in that they are sectionally hackled—that is, the hackle is wound at intervals, leaving the body exposed between the separate hackle windings. Another recognizable feature is the rather narrow spread of the hackle; the fibers, according to exactness of pattern, are slightly shorter than the gape of the hook is deep. Preference generally is for dark bodies with closely wound tinsel ribbing.

CONSTRUCTION: There are no wings or tail. The body is wound in separate sections—usually three or four—where a hackle is fastened and wound. Do not attempt to wind the hackle Palmer-fashion. It must be restricted to the areas between the body sections. Hackle for Grubs frequently is fancy body plumage such as tippets, pheasant body feathers, etc.

DEE

The Dee is variously named; Long Dee, Spring, and Spring Salmon are the most common aliases. Wings are the identifying feature since they are flat, narrow, and slightly divided. The bodies are correctly tied slim. Several imitations of the Dee have been made and, perhaps, may be equal to the Dee in every respect save one: they are not authentic. Whether authenticity makes any particular impression on a salmon is a question only the salmon can answer. Anglers are often too fastidious about seeming trifles and too unconcerned about other things of importance. However this foible makes fly-fishing, fly-making, and fly literature, all the more interesting.

CONSTRUCTION: Dress this fly slim and divide the narrow wings slightly.

DRY FLIES

Salmon dry flies are simply enlarged trout dry flies: regular winged uprights, bivisibles, hackles, fore-and-aft hackles, and the more recently developed gliders and parachutes. Sizes range from 8 to 2 on both regular and long shanks. The regular upright types in these sizes are more difficult to hackle and balance properly than the smaller ones and for this reason fly-dressers have devised such excellent innovations as the fore-and-aft and the glider, both of which are more widely used each season.

Although they are constructed in the same way as the smaller ones for trout, these large dry flies are usually more brightly colored. To the trout fisherman, who is necessarily of more conservative taste than the salmon fisherman, these bright candy-striped flies are worthless. On the other hand, the salmon caster needs them as much as the trout fisher needs a Black Quill or a Coachman.

Special attention must be given to the hook. Loop-eye hooks are unsurpassed for salmon dry flies; a low-water type, size 6, is ideal. The best grades of taper-eye hooks are satisfactory but must be examined for rough edges which would cut the leader tippet. Low-water, loop-eye hooks eliminate this possibility.

STANDARD WINGED

Regular trout dry flies in the larger sizes, 6 and 4, are used by many salmon fishermen. Some years ago the idea of adding hackle to the rear of the fly for additional support proved to be an advantage in floating these heavier flies. As a result the fore-and-aft became a "standard" in several sections of the country.

The following patterns represent a cross-section of the favorites used by salmon fishermen nearly everywhere. Keep in mind that these patterns are tied with or without the aft hackle as determined by local preferences and prevailing fishing conditions: Cahill, Cinnamon Sedge, Greenwell's Glory, Gray Wulff, March Brown, Montreal, Montreal Silver, McGinty, Pale Evening Dun, Parmachene Belle, Professor, Queen Waters, Reuben Wood, Royal Coachman, Royal Wulff, Silver Doctor, Whirling Dun, White Wulff and Yellow Sally.

HACKLES AND BIVISIBLES

These flies have long been popular and will probably remain so for years to come. Although newer developments are gradually gaining favor with many fishermen, the chances are they will never completely outclass the hackle flies. The list which follows is the result of painstaking effort to tabulate the most favored patterns: Black Bivisible, Brown Palmer (dark and light), Colonel Monell, Gray Palmer (dark and light), Gray-hackle Yellow, MacIntosh (brown and gray), Mole Hackle Bivisible, Pink Lady Bivisible, Red Hackle, Royal Coachman Bivisible, Seal Hackle and Soldier Palmer.

PARACHUTES AND GLIDERS

Parachutes, which are described in Chapter VI, and Gliders, so named for their true gliding appearance, are quite similar in respect to their construction and effectiveness. Gliders are dressed with upright hackle-tip wings which fairly twitch of their own accord and help the fly to plane with rare delicacy to the water surface. The ordinary fly having hackles tied at right angles to the body, especially when larger than size 8, will strike the water with some disturbance, definitely putting the fish "down," whereas the Glider will not. Another advantage appreciated by careful anglers is the stability of these flies. Built to ride the water with a minimum of fly rising above the surface and aided by every hackle fiber lending support, the Glider is difficult to upset even on windy days. Consequently, it remains afloat for surprisingly long periods. Too, because the fly lies so close to the water surface, it permits the leader to straighten out over the water without any arching at the eye of the fly.

Gliders are the development of Ralph M. Plympton of New Jersey and Herb Johnson of Yarmouth, Maine. While I was familiar with the Parachute, I was wholly ignorant of the excellent Glider series until it was introduced to me by Ralph "Brick" Plympton who, with Herb Johnson, one of the canniest Down-East Yankees ever to tie a fly, spent many hours perfecting it. The Glider is a durable, well-balanced and otherwise ideal dry fly.

Mr. Alex Martin, manufacturer of deluxe fishing tackle, of Glasgow, Scotland, sent me an unusual, beautifully tied standard-pattern salmon fly dressed with parachute hackle. The pattern, a Silver Wilkinson, contained each and every part and feather found on the standard dressing. It was indeed a rare specimen among flies. Mr. Martin made an interesting comment concerning the Parachute, as follows: "This firm was responsible for development here of the fly dressing method invented by Mr. Brush of Chicago which we called the Parachute. Its feature is tying in a plane parallel to the hook shank to achieve flotation, and correct orientation either in or on the water." This indicates the usefulness of salmon wet flies dressed with parachute hackle. It is quite reasonable to think that a sinking fly dressed with parachute hackle would be more visible to a fish than the conventional fly.

CONSTRUCTION: The key difference between the Parachute and the Glider lies in the wing arrangement. Ordinarily the Parachute is dressed with either breast feather or hair wings, whereas the Glider is topped with long hackle-tip wings. Undoubtedly your own favorite patterns dressed as Gliders would perform as well as those patterns already established as aces for salmon by Plympton and Johnson. I have always been slightly hesitant to use the extremely bright patterns but realize that in many cases these "Christmas-tree" flies are absolutely necessary. However, to make the description of the Glider series complete, I have included, on page 123, the original patterns as tied by Herb Johnson. (Incidentally, these patterns are favored in size 6.)

GLIDER FLY PATTERNS

	Wings	Hackle	Body	Tail
Black Fairy	white hackle tips—upright	black	peacock herl silver rib	blue & red hackle fibers
Blue Highlander	white hackle tips—upright	blue & white	peacock herl silver rib	red, blue & yel. hackle fibers
Brown Fairy	brown hackle tips—upright	cochy-bon-dhu	peacock herl gold rib	cochy-bon-dhu
Pheasant	metallic grn. pheasant body feathers	badger	peacock herl silver rib	red & badger hackle fibers
Rainbow	white hackle tips—upright	red & blue	orange wool silver rib	blue & red hackle fibers
Silver Doctor	griz. hackle tips—upright	blue, red & white	white wool gold rib	blue, red, white hackle fibers
Thunder and Lightning	red & yellow hackle tips—upright	red & yellow	peacock herl silver rib	blue & red hackle fibers
Yellow Miller	yellow hackle tips—upright	yellow	yellow chenille copper rib	red & yellow hackle fibers

Chapter Ten

BASS AND LAKE WET FLIES

In Chapter 4 it was mentioned that the design of some flies is based on eye-appeal only and the emphasis is placed on color, shape and symmetry rather than on any attempt to imitate something in nature. This can be truly said of bass and lake wet flies and, for that matter, of salmon flies, which, generally, are so much like lake flies as to make distinguishing between them difficult to many anglers. A few of these larger flies vaguely suggest resemblances to creatures such as huge bees (McGinty), perhaps over-size moths (various—gray, white, brown, etc.), or crayfish—if you can stretch your imagination a bit. Most of them, however, are just beautiful creations and look no more like living creatures than a traffic signal or the grille of a new Buick. Neverthe-less, and for reasons known only to the fish, they are as reliable for bass and landlocked salmon as worms are for bullheads.

While many of the patterns for both lake and bass flies are more than half a century old, there has never been any way of determining why certain patterns are traditionally considered strictly landlocked salmon or lake flies and others strictly bass flies. Out-wardly, the patterns appear to be much the same.

In other words, you would use ancients such as the Bishop, Frank Gray and Owner for bass but the Tomah-Jo, New Lake and Prince Edward for landlocked salmon.

The fullness of the wings, the manner in which the hackle was applied, the charac-teristics of the body and the tails were practically the same for both types of fish. If any single factor could be traced as a cause for this vagary, it might be to the salmon fly influence from New England. American versions of the true salmon fly were, for the most part, direct copies of the British patterns which were very involved and beautiful examples of craftsmanship. Therefore, it seems reasonable to assume that this basis of pattern styling would be taught and practiced throughout most of New England and Canada. On the other hand, fly-dressers in other sections of the country, where there were no landlocked salmon, were developing innovations of their own for both large and smallmouth bass. Fundamentally, these flies for bass were con-structed along the same lines as the British flies, and were different only insofar as the color combinations of the pattern were concerned. Hook size was no real index—even flies for trout were often size 1/0 and larger.

To look at the Academy pattern, for example, is to recognize obvious resemblances to certain salmon-fly dressings. However, it was first made by Professor T. A. Wil-liamson of Leesburg Academy, Virginia, in 1878 and designed for Potomac River black bass. This pattern is obviously like the Governor Alvord, which has been used successfully for landlocked salmon, and the Bob-White—a variation of it.

Good examples of vagueness in the classification of these larger flies are the Premier, a "bass" pattern, the Parmachene Belle and No Name, both of which are "lake" flies. The Premier was named in 1878 by the brother of Mr. C. F. Orvis, who thought its colors resembled the raiment worn by the Prime Minister of England. This brilliant fly soon became popular but, since it was designed especially for bass fishing, did not appear in the lists of "lake" flies. For some reason, it seemed that a fly made for land-locked salmon was not appropriate for bass and vice versa. This is especially inter-esting in the consideration of the two other patterns of the "lake" variety for land-locked salmon which bear such a striking resemblance to the Premier as to be mis-taken for it by many.

The Parmachene Belle was concocted by Mr. Henry P. Wells sometime about 1885 and named after Parmachene Lake, Maine. It was thought that the red in this pattern approximated the color of the belly-fin of the trout, supposedly a killing bait, while the No Name, developed in 1880 by Mr. Orvis to be a variation of the Professor for a particular customer, was based on eye-appeal alone.

Each of these three flies is predominantly red and white. Each resembles the other two. However, one of them, the Premier, was set apart as a bass fly while the others were designated as "lake" flies. If fullness of wing, type of hackle, or body treatment had determined the classification of these three patterns, there would be no need for questioning them. The flies, however, are similar in every department and show no single or outstanding feature to differentiate them. Comparisons among such flies are endless and good cause for madness. If you consider there are tabulated in this book thirty-one dressings for the Coachman flies, eight for the Professor, twelve for the Cahill, nine for the Montreal, and nine for the March Brown, you will appreciate the expression: "It's not the pattern, it's who made it."

During the time I was spending hours on end in research on fly patterns, I hap-pened to find mention of the Romany Rye and the Romany Ree. At first, the names seemed to indicate the possibility of British origin; however, so little information was available, I began a search in an effort to find at least additional mention of the name. Eventually two references were found; one alluded to the probability that the flies were named after the nicknames given by the English to a Gypsy man and woman, while the other suggested the likelihood that they were of American origin. *Favorite Flies,* a masterpiece in the exposition of fly lore, written by Mary Orvis Marbury, con-tained an account explaining that these flies were the inventions of Mr. William J. Cassard of New York City who also designed the Matador and the Cassard. The Orvis people of Manchester, Vermont, were kind enough to cooperate by searching their files for further clues to the true dressing of these two flies. Mr. C. W. Shafer, then treasurer of the Orvis Company, explained that he had succeeded in finding one Romany Rye which had been tied for the exhibit of the Orvis line of flies at the World's Fair in 1893, and that he would have one tied according to the original pat-tern. I received this shortly thereafter and entered the dressing in the *Dictionary of Patterns* exactly according to this sample. Unfortunately the Romany Ree, a variation of the Romany Rye, is nowhere described in the reams of notes I have collected nor in any of the volumes at my disposal. Since the sample sent to me by Mr. Schafer was tagged, "Romany Rye" or "Romany Ree," I indexed the two flies accordingly.

REGULAR   BALL-HEAD MINNOW

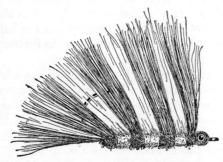

WEEDLESS HAIR WING   SPOON WING

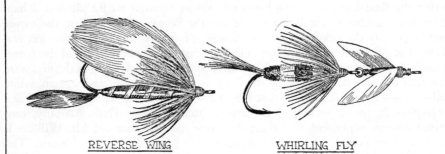

REVERSE WING   WHIRLING FLY

FIG. 28
LAKE- FLY DESIGN

LEONARD

In years past, lake and bass flies were huge things made from spoon-shaped swan and goose feathers, the rump feathers from the turkey, and the side feathers from under the mallard's wing. Generally, any fly smaller than size 1/0 was considered improper. Patterns looked more like creations from a milliner's shop than fishing lures; nearly all had red feather tails, thick silk bodies ribbed with tinsel and a little chenille for contrast, hackles the size of a silver dollar, and multi-colored wings. The gaudier they were, the better. Usually they were double-snelled on gut heavy enough to beach a Chesapeake striped bass.

In recent years, however, the trend has been toward more sparsely dressed flies having flexible wing parts such as the breast feathers used on trout wet flies. Such materials offer less resistance to the mouth of a striking fish than do the stiff, unyielding materials having a center quill. This is an important advantage. Any part of a fly too resistant to pressure is apt to force the hook away from the mouth of the fish in the same manner that a lever will.

Various new patterns have proved themselves effective despite their lack of resemblance to anything a part of normal fish diet. The multiple-color hair flies are in this class and are usually labeled "weedless" hair flies. Notice the illustration, Weedless Hair Wing, Fig. 28. This is typical of one style only and there are hundreds of others. There is plenty of scope for invention in the hair, wet-fly class.

There are five important kinds of lake and bass wet flies: the eyed wet fly, the spoon wing, the reverse wing, the weedless hair-wing, and the whirling fly. Irrespective of which of the five kinds interests you, it should be built around these fundamental principles: The hook, if for use with spinners, should have a large, clean eye; if for snelling, it should have a marked shank. The wings should be resilient as practical. Flies of this size can be missed easily by a striking fish, especially if the wings are stiff enough to deflect the strike. Materials must be sufficiently brilliant in color to be strongly visible for many yards. Full dressing is desirable, although this does not connote over-dressing. The finished fly will be correct so long as its several parts are in proportion. Durability should be emphasized. These flies take a beating and must be dressed as strong as possible. The frequent use of cement to terminate and seal each operation will be helpful.

It should be pointed out at this time that the following flies are commonly dressed as: (1) wet flies with turn-down or turn-up eye hooks for use without spinners, (2) snelled flies, (3) ringed flies for coupling to spinners.

REGULAR

This type is simply a large edition of the trout wet fly. As a rule the wings are paired sections from large goose quills or folded breast and side feathers from the mallard, teal, wood duck and similar birds. In this one respect the regular differs from the spoon-wing, which has roundish feather wings with quill centers.

CONSTRUCTION: (Ref. Fig. 11, Constructing the Wet Fly.) Follow the same procedure described for dressing the trout wet fly. However, beard hackle is not recommended for flies so large as lake and bass flies. Full shoulder hackles are superior and give better proportions.

SPOON WING

Many of the older patterns such as the Beaufort Moth, Cheney, Cleveland, Bishop,

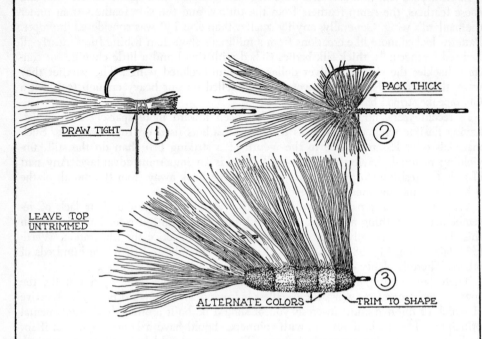

DRAW TIGHT ①

PACK THICK ②

LEAVE TOP
UNTRIMMED

ALTERNATE COLORS — TRIM TO SHAPE ③

WEEDLESS HAIR-WING TYPE

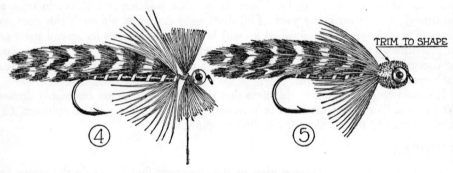

④

⑤

TRIM TO SHAPE

BALL-HEAD MINNOW TYPE

FIG. 29
SPECIAL FEATURES—LAKE FLIES

LEONARD

Juno, Prince Edward and Parmachene Belle were dressed with large, spoon-shaped wings in the then popular "Henshall" style—meaning the concave sides of the feather faced outwardly. Dr. James A. Henshall of Cincinnati preferred bass flies with wings curved to the outside like the "Henshall," a pattern he designed in 1872, as well as others he invented. More popular, however, are flies having the concave sides facing inwardly. This tends to brace the entire wing section, preventing ultimate breakage of the center quills of the feathers.

Flies of this sort are pretty in the hand but have two disadvantages: they offer considerable wind resistance during casting, with attendant "fluttering," and they risk being deflected from the mouth of a striking fish due to the stiffness of their wings.

CONSTRUCTION: Follow the same procedure for making the Spoon Wing as described in Chapter 5. If thicker bodies are desired, build up the body base with wool or cotton thread, then apply the outer body in the usual manner.

REVERSE WING

The Reverse Wing, although it is seldom seen today as a fly-rod lure, is still made with a weighted body for plug-rod spinner fishing especially for largemouth bass.

CONSTRUCTION: Place the hook upside down in the vise and dress the fly exactly like a Spoon Wing.

WEEDLESS HAIR-WING

The word "weedless" is used because this fly is designed to keep the hook free from weeds and lily pads. This type of fly can be used in spots which would ordinarily foul other sorts of lures. With its alternate colors and high back it makes a very buggy-looking affair especially good for taking largemouth bass. I have found this fly most effective when connected to the smallest of spinners, primarily because it seems to perform best when near the surface, and for this reason should not be weighted too heavily.

CONSTRUCTION: See Fig. 29. Place the hook upside down in the vise. Wind two or three turns of strong nylon or silk tying-thread on the tip of the shank. From the hair you have selected, which is usually deer or caribou hair, clip a section the diameter of a soda straw. Hold this section firmly between the thumb and forefinger of the left hand and, with the dubbing needle held in the right hand, remove the downy hairs found at the base of the section before applying it to the hook. Place this section, with the natural tips pointing rearward, on the shank as shown in Fig. 29, No. 1, then bind it down with the working silk. The butts facing toward the front will now fan outwardly at right angles to the hook. Hold the working silk tightly in the right hand and, with the thumb and forefinger of the left hand, bend these butts to the rear as shown in No. 2.

Clip another section of hair from the hide, remove the fuzzy hairs at the base, and fasten it on the hook as far rearward as the previous work will permit. Again bend the butts rearward and secure them with two or three turns of working silk in front of, but not around, the hair. Repeat this procedure as many times as necessary to extend the hair body the full length of the hook, meanwhile frequently pressing the enlarging body toward the rear to make it as compact as possible. This prevents the appearance of "bald" spots. If such spots do appear, however, they can be covered by patching with small tufts of hair wound on over the bare spot.

At this stage the fly may look like a horrible mass of whiskers the size of a golf ball. This is both natural and desirable, since a thick, buoyant body depends upon the maximum quantity of hair being crowded into the smallest possible space.

It will be noticed that Fig. 29 illustrates the construction of a weedless hair-wing having alternate bands of color. Here the method of construction is fundamentally the same, although the sections are alternately red and white, black and yellow, or gray and brown as desired. Hackle feathers can be used in combination with the first section of hair to form the tail. Frequently this particular style of dressing features tail combinations such as grizzly hackle and red hair; black hackle and yellow hair; red hackle and gray hair. Likewise, various colors commonly used in the make-up of the body are: solid black for the body and back with white or yellow tail sections; solid yellow for the body and back with red and white tail sections. Combinations are too numerous to try to list and it is really unnecessary to do so. The fisher's own opinions on color are usually as valid as those of the experts.

If the body is as full as you wish it to be, finish the work with the whip-finish and lacquer the head; no other tying is necessary. Grasp the top of the lure and remove from the vise. With scissors roughly trim the underside. Next trim the sides in a vertical plane, leaving sufficient stubble from which to make the final shape. The lure will now look somewhat like a thick comb.

Finally round off the bottom as evenly as possible by clipping off small portions at a time to avoid forming rough or flat surfaces. After this operation the lure should be narrow, have a rounded bottom and a high fuzzy back in which the hook is entirely concealed. Do not trim the back hair; it should be naturally shaggy. In general the finished product should look like Fig. 29, No. 3.

Flies of this sort are often tied with large heads and either painted eyes or eyes having pliable wire stems. The latter are fastened to the shank of the hook before the winding of the hair has been started. Since the hair is fastened on after the eyes have been tied to the hook, they are necessarily covered until the hair has been trimmed into the shape of a head and the stubble trimmed from around the eyes. For details of the application of glass eyes see Fig. 23 and for painted eyes see Chapter 8, Constructing the Optic Bucktail.

BALL-HEAD MINNOW

The Ball-Head Minnow is a semi-surface lure especially effective for small and largemouth bass. Generally it is dressed on turned-down eye hooks for use without spinners since, when made on large hooks, it is nearly as heavy as most streamer-spinner combinations. Because the clipped hair head, full hackle, and streamers give this fly considerable buoyancy, it works very close to the surface. If retrieved fairly fast, it will cause a disturbance just under the surface which is most attractive to bass. Glass eyes are favored for this lure and add much to its appearance and effectiveness. Although it is quite similar to the various Optics, it is more heavily dressed.

CONSTRUCTION: See Fig. 29. In this case, the glass eye must be tied on first. Select a pair of eyes and, if you wish to color the iris, coat the back surface of each eye with a stroke of lacquer. After the lacquer has become dry, bend the wire stems of the eyes at right angles approximately one-eighth to three-sixteenths of an inch below the eye. Next approximate the length the wire stems must be to allow for sufficient winding to the hook shank. Fasten these wire stems on the shank by winding with working silk but be certain there is ample room in front of the eyes for the application of enough hair to finish the head. Next wind the working silk back to the tip of the shank, then wind the body. Body material is variously silk, chenille, tinsel or combinations of these, and is wound after the manner of other types of fly bodies. Tails are optional.

The hackle streamers are tied on immediately in front of the forward end of the body and may be as many as six feathers. As a rule, combinations of grizzly and plain dyed feathers are most effective. Keep in mind that it is important to leave sufficient space for forming the head; in other words, do not crowd the work toward the eyes.

Hackles for flies as large as the Ball-Head Minnow must be widely spread and, consequently, are only found on the necks of large roosters. These long-fiber hackles are difficult to wind unless they are tied tip-first to the shank. This method of winding permits the successive turns of hackle to incline slightly toward the hook point, thus preventing the necessarily thick stem from adding needless bulk to an area which the hair head should occupy.

The construction of the head consists of tying several tufts of deer or caribou hair in the space from behind the hook eye to the front of the hackle windings. At first, this will seem a troublesome business because presence of the eyes, the limited space, and the proximity of the work already done hamper the operation. The best way to be certain of forming a full head is to tie short clippings of hair in rather thick bunches, starting close to the hackles and adding as necessary until the entire area is well covered. Before attempting to shape the head with scissors, first flatten the hackles and streamers between the thumb and forefinger of the left hand and, holding the lure in this manner, remove it from the vise. It is necessary to keep the hackle fibers away from the untrimmed hair in order that they will not be cut unintentionally while the head is being shaped. With the scissors begin to shape the head by trimming toward the front, removing only a little with each clipping, until the head appears to take on shape. Aspire toward roundness and, when the head is approximately the proper size, carefully trim the stubble around the eyes. See Fig. 29.

Clever manipulations in trimming make odd and interesting shapes possible: owl-like and froglike faces, flat and grooved heads, hammerheads, etc. Your own ingenuity is the best guide in this respect. Whether or not such effort is truly worthwhile is a question. However, some very "buggy" looking gadgets often become the best fish-getters.

WHIRLING FLY

The Whirling Fly is certainly unorthodox in more than one respect, as Fig. 28 will indicate. Many attempts to produce a fly that would make at least some kind of struggling motion have been tried, but few of these attempts have ever succeeded. The one reproduced, for which I have some claims to authorship, is very effective. The fly is not only interesting to watch; it is dynamite to lethargic fish, especially of the lake variety. During the hour of twilight, when the lengthening shadows finger their way among the snags and deadheads, the Whirling Fly will perform to best advantage, whirling and fluttering like a large moth trying to lift itself from the water surface.

One very special use for this fly is locating fish. Trout will sometimes reveal their whereabouts by darting uncertainly after a fly of this kind. Even if they do not "take" they will have shown themselves long enough for the angler to make a mental note of their presence. These fish may be coaxed later on into accepting a fly more to their liking. In this respect, therefore, it could be said that the Whirling Fly is a "fish-finder."

CONSTRUCTION: It is necessary to make this lure in two stages: first, the tying of the fly proper on a ring-eye hook and second, the construction of the revolving head which consists of two trimmed feather sections tied obliquely on the barrel of a swivel. The color is a matter of preference, although I have found all white and all yellow the two colors most quickly taken by large and smallmouth bass, black and white crappies, yellow perch (jacks), rock bass, and large bluegills and sunfish. A third pattern, which will sometimes work well during the heat of the day, is the McGinty, which features a thick, puffy, chenille body.

For the sake of illustration let us model an all-yellow fly. First tie a plain hackle fly having yellow tails, chenille body, and hackle. After the head cement has hardened, carefully open the ring eye with a pair of duck-bill pliers. Match two wing feathers dyed yellow and clip off approximately 1¼ inches of the tip end. Remove as many of the fibers from the clipped end as necessary to leave each end approximately one-half to two-thirds the length of the entire fly body. It will be noticed that these ends have a slight flare on the soft side of the feather which will act like the trailing edge of a propeller. The short stubbly fibers on the opposite side, however, are useless and should be removed by being stripped against the grain of the quill. The two sections should now represent the blades of a propeller. For obvious reasons it is necessary to place these sections exactly opposite each other on the swivel and bind them tightly with the working silk. Adjust their positions until they are oblique to the center line of the swivel. Carefully lacquer each section, avoiding the separation of any of the fibers. Allow the lacquer to flow around the windings but do not permit even a small amount to touch the bearing surfaces at the ends of the barrel of the swivel. Connect the swivel ring to the eye of the hook, then close the eye carefully with the pliers.

The combinations possible in lake and bass fly construction are absolutely limitless. Hackle-tip wings, detachable pork-rind trailers, numerous variations of hair-wing design, and the use of cork and balsa to make rotating heads can all be used to stimulate invention. The old saw, "What is one man's meat is another man's poison," is perhaps one of the most cogent reasons why there are thousands and thousands of different flies. After having spent many years in an exhaustive and comprehensive research on fly patterns and their origins, I am of the sincere opinion that it is virtually impossible to concoct a pattern or devise a fly that has not been made at least once before. Some of the latest developments, according to the real histories, are not new at all but are, in more than a few instances, merely new names applied to patterns as old as seventy-five years or more.

Chapter Eleven

SALT-WATER STREAMERS

In late years interest has increased in the use of the fly rod and streamer flies for catching striped bass, weakfish, baby tarpon, channel bass, shad, and other salt-water fish that can be handled on fly tackle. Very recently the bonefish, reputedly the fastest fish known, has been added to the list. Perhaps the most available of all these to the majority of fishermen are the striped bass and weakfish in the east and the weakfish and baby tarpon in the south, especially in Florida.

Casting for "stripers," those fish of phenomenally quick strikes and surging power, with a bass or light salmon rod and suitable streamers, gives fly casting a new flavor. In many cases, particularly when inland fishing has been discouraging or limited to over-fished streams, casting for "stripers" with such tackle offers the angler an opportunity to satisfy his yearning to hook something long enough and heavy enough to really bend the rod.

In some sections along the Atlantic coast the "stripers" and weakfish are not infrequently found together. One can wade out among the sand bars and, having plenty of room for backcasts, shoot the streamer or spinner-and-fly far out into the incoming tide, never quite knowing whether the lure will be taken by a racing striped bass or a bucking "weak." It is indeed an unforgettable experience to connect with one's first tide-running weakfish or "trout" finning his way into the broad marshy estuaries.

"Follow the gulls" is an adage of great importance to salt-water anglers and their boatmen, for the gulls are the key to locating the fish. Like the fish, gulls, too, are vigilant in their search for alewives and smelt. Hour after hour, craning their bony necks in every direction to spot some morsel to eat, the gulls glide easily on the breasts of rising air currents. Then, when they have spied a school of the forever-plagued alewives, they will plummet into the river to emerge quickly with struggling fish in their beaks, thus unintentionally giving the watched-for signal that school fish are about.

What a sight it is to watch the systematic encirclement of these school fish by the slashing "stripers." Gradually the school withdraws into itself until it becomes a frightened, compact mass of flashing gold. The bass attack it savagely from all sides until in desperation the alewives leap in concert into the air, making a ruffled sound like the spatter of heavy raindrops. All will be quiet for a moment; then the fluttering fish will surge up again. In almost measured cadence this maneuver will be repeated many times until the alewives have been thinned out or, usually, until the "stripers" have satisfied their appetites.

When striped bass and weakfish are running they are interested in three principal foods: the alewife or branch herring, the smelt, and the shedder or peeler crab. When they are feeding on peelers, striped bass, especially, and weakfish, generally, will not stir for any kind of substitute. But when they are attacking schools of hapless alewives and smelt, if they are within reach of your cast, they will smash your streamer with a vengeance.

So far as shape and construction concerned, streamers for salt-water fishing are not different from other streamers; even the colors are frequently the same, since salt-water game fish are somewhat impartial in matters of color. If any differences between fresh- and salt-water streamers do exist, they are chiefly in the size and finish of the hook. Bronzed hooks, which are made primarily for fresh-water fishing, are not satisfactory in brackish waters and cause rapid deterioration of the fly or at least discoloration of the body materials. Tinned hooks, being more serviceable in salt water, are adaptable to all conditions.

Roger Smith of Madison, Connecticut, has used flies in brackish waters for years and is of the opinion that tinsel-body flies should be avoided as much as possible because, in the presence of salt water, an electrolytic action is set up between the hook and the tinsel which corrodes the hook. My experience has been the same as regards the tinsel becoming discolored. Salt air and water work fast on brilliant metal surfaces. When the flash of a bright body is needed, it is well to use the bare shank for this purpose. Though the body may not have the brilliance of tinsel it will retain all the luster of the hook plating.

It seems that fanciful designs in flies, or those that are based chiefly on color and little else, have not yet invaded the salt-water field to any great extent. Although there has been much experimenting in Florida with the colors of bonefish flies, the facts are that most fly dressers are trying to produce imitations of the small school fish on which the game fish feed. This tendency is recognizable in the majority of salt-water streamers. To look at a well-made streamer is to identify in some measure the minnow it was intended to represent, usually the smelt, the alewife, the young shad and others. While it would be straining the imagination to try to associate some of the "killers" with an individual species of fish, some of the most unnatural looking gobs of hair and feathers become, when wet, suprisingly realistic imitations of shrimp and small school fish.

If you wish to start from scratch to make a pattern of your own, it is not too difficult to capture one of the school minnows to serve as a model. In some instances this may not be practical and for this reason the natural colors of three very important food-fish are included here.

ALEWIFE (Branch Herring): Back, olive; upper sides, indistinct blending of pale blue and pink; lower sides, bluish silver; head, golden yellow on sides with irregular pale blue surfaces. When viewed from a distance this fish appears to be a pale yellow.

SMELT: Back, brownish-olive with an indistinct bluish sheen; sides, mixed areas of silver and light buff suffused with pink; head, slightly darker than back with pale bluish cheeks.

YOUNG SHAD: Back, bluish silver; sides, silver gray; head, silver gray with some pink near the gills.

These colors immediately suggest several combinations of feathers and dyed hair that would work very well. Remember that an exact imitation is neither necessary nor very practical. Mixed portions of hair of two or more colors will often suffice to produce the proper effect. This is also true of streamer feathers placed one over the other.

In passing, it might be worth mentioning that golden pheasant crest, a material widely used in the manufacture of salmon flies for its brilliant hue, is excellent for the simulation of metallic "brights" common to most small food-fish. I doubt that any other feather can be seen so far under the water surface as this one.

Although the adaptation of the fly rod to salt-water fishing is largely a recent development, the sport of fly fishing in brackish waters is known to have started in the nineteenth century. Among the first records of salt-water flies and their use are in the writings of George Trowbridge of New York City, and the never-to-be-forgotten bass enthusiast, Dr. James A. Henshall, author of the famous "inch for inch, pound for pound" assertion in praise of the fresh-water black bass. These two able fellows must have discovered the possibilities in fly casting for salt-water fish almost simultaneously since each wrote within a year or two of the other of the effectiveness of certain patterns for taking coast fishes that would rise to the fly. George Trowbridge must have been an adventurous angler in his time, for he wrote in 1885 of having caught on the fly surprisingly large salt-water fish one would hardly expect to find interested in taking flies of any sort. Both Henshall and Trowbridge are credited with having been the real pioneers in exploiting the fly rod in coastal waters but there is every reason to believe that other contemporary anglers might have been doing the same thing without writing about it.

Dr. Henshall designed the Golden Dustman in 1883 and had already established for it an enviable record among the popular flies of that day for killing fresh-water bass before he put it to use in Florida salt waters. Henshall particularized the Golden Dustman for the metallic flash of its body and wings, claiming this flash was essential. Trowbridge was most systematic in his analysis of fly patterns and developed combinations based on the slow but very effective method of trial-and-error. His Cracker pattern is a classic example. This fly was developed after much experimenting in an effort to include many colors for the purpose of giving the fly the greatest visibility. The Cracker was named for the natives of Florida and presumably also Georgia. Allusions have been made to the possibility that Trowbridge gave the fly this name because it was so "crackin'" good, although the former derivation seems more justifiable. However, the fly was "crackin'" good; in fact so good that Trowbridge caught with it what is believed to have been the first tarpon ever to be taken on fly tackle, as well as channel bass weighing as much as 20 lbs, weakfish (sea trout) of unusual size, bluefish, and mackerel.

Both the Golden Dustman and the Cracker are more or less reminiscent of many of the bass flies designs of the 80's. Neither approached the profile of present-day streamers; each could be defined loosely as falling into the category of a salmon fly. The Golden Dustman was predominantly brown and brilliant yellow, the Cracker surprisingly like a miniature Star-Spangled Banner with a hook concealed within its folds. I have not the slightest doubt that these old patterns would still galvanize a worthy fish into a strike even today. Their records in the past speak for themselves.

There are dozens, possibly hundreds, of flies designed for salmon and bass that would make excellent lures for salt-water species. Patterns such as the Supervisor,

Silver Ghost, Black Ghost, and a host of others have caught and will catch practically everything worth while having fins. However, comparatively few streamers or flies of any sort, for that matter, have been designed especially for striped bass, weakfish, tarpon and the other coveted game fish. In the majority of cases, anglers have used their regular flies.

One streamer resulting from efforts to produce the ideal striped-bass fly is the "Gibbs' Striper," which can be fished with confidence in any waters where striped bass abound. This fly is the final product of a series of experiments by Harold N. Gibbs, former Fish and Game Administrator for Rhode Island and present chairman of the Pollution Abatement Committee of that same state. This is a beautiful streamer having a long white bucktail wing, a bright blue feather center strip, short black-barred cheek, silver body, and red throat. Its value is firmly established since it has taken striped bass weighing more than 16 lbs. Harold Gibbs has designed other flies for this type of fishing but it is doubtful if they will ever become as popular as the "Gibbs' Striper."

Roger P. Smith, one of Connecticut's most capable fly fishermen, has introduced fish such as the shad, "buckie" (a kind of herring or alewife), hake, whiting, sand dabs, flounder, blackfish, porgy, sea robins, and kingfish to fly casters, who might never have known them otherwise. Smith has spent much time experimenting with colors and shapes in fly design and, consequently, has interesting and worthwhile findings. The Enfield shad fly with colored beads attached is his favorite fly for shad. This is a rather plainly made fly consisting of a yellow wing in front of which are three glass beads threaded on the leader. The color of the beads is important. Red, yellow, and orange should predominate, while other colors, namely blue and green, have been used at times with some success.

Smith has also found that white-winged flies are especially effective. In addition to the Enfield shad fly, he also considers the White Miller, Royal Coachman, and Parmachene Belle key flies. His favorite streamers are the Parmachene Belle, Dark Edson Tiger, and others of the regular salmon type.

Perhaps no other state offers so much to the salt-water fly caster as Florida. For years a few fishermen have tried to sell the public on the value of fly casting for the excellent "fly-fish" along the coast of Florida. Unfortunately the sport had never become accepted seriously by more than a few until, a very short time ago, when it was learned quite by accident, according to Allen Corson, that the bonefish would take the fly.

Bonefishing has lured major anglers from most everywhere in the country. Lee Wulff, for example, definitely one of our best-informed and experienced trout and salmon fishers, found that the bonefish is in a class by itself. Lee considers Homer Rhode's Shrimp Fly the most effective he knows for *albula vulpes*. Rhode, himself, has this to say about the Shrimp Fly and bonefishing in general:

"My favorite all-year fly is my Shrimp Fly that I developed nineteen years ago after taking my first bonefish. These flies have a yellow, barred rock, and white stiff neck feather (rooster) in each wing with a heavy salt and pepper yellow and white hackle.

Next, I like a barred rock divided-wing streamer fly with a yellow or a yellow and white hackle.

Straw-color divided-wing streamer flies with yellow or white hackles or a combination of the two are good. A white or barred rock feather between the two straw-color feathers is also very effective.

After a lapse of around twelve years, deer-hair flies in white, and yellow and white, with a heavy yellow, yellow and white, or white hackle are again coming into use and are very effective. A variation of the deer-hair-type fly consists of the same color combination using polar bear hair with a heavy yellow, white, or yellow and white hackle."

Earl Gresh of St. Petersburg, Florida, is an ace fly-dresser with more than thirty years of salt-water fly-fishing experience. He has definite and interesting views on the subject of bonefish flies and shows preference for red-and-white combinations. His background consists of fishing for Nipigon brook trout, "coasters" off the shore of Lake Superior, and "bright" salmon of the Miramichi, New Brunswick, in which province he once lived. He has also caught "slungling" big rainbow trout in Wyoming, Montana, and Idaho. So his opinions are certainly supported by first-hand experience. Few anglers really have the opportunity to pursue both fresh- and salt-water fishing. It is for this reason that Gresh's comments are especially valuable. With all this inestimable fishing to his credit, Gresh states: " . . . until you have hooked into an albula vulpes, bonefish to you, you don't really know the meaning of Atomic Energy."

In reply to the author's question inquiring about the color combinations he might have found especially good, Gresh replied:

"My manner of dressing is the result of thirty years of fly fishing for salt-water fish and I have come to the conclusion that any colors will do just so they are red and white. I tie white polar bear hair on a red wool body, or dyed red polar bear hair on a white body. However, I have used an all-white fly with just a small red check very effectively for, after all, as I have said before, there is no such thing as a fly-feeding fish in the Florida salt water, so, as I see it, the idea is to excite the fish in order to make it take the lure. Using the red-and-white combination, I have caught thirty-four different species of salt-water fish; therefore, I really believe it is the presentation of the lure and the manner of retrieving that catch fish."

The field of salt-water fly fishing is hardly touched. While there are a handful of anglers who could write volumes on the subject, there are thousands more who do not know about the unlimited possibilities of the fly rod in the many tidal rivers, bays, coves, and salt ponds of our coastline. Unfortunately, the majority of fishermen who have not discovered this phase of fishing think in terms of clotheslines and winches when the word "salt-water fishing" is mentioned. This supercilious attitude has prevented many sportsmen from exploring one of the most exciting and really satisfying kinds of fishing known.

There is another very worthy aspect to the encouragement of fly fishing in salt water. Every angler who might divert his attention from the fresh-water places he regularly frequents—if for only a time long enough to try salt-water fishing—would be practicing conservation of the best sort while at the same time striking and netting so many fish in one day that his casting arm will ache. This cannot be considered lightly by those anglers of our day who find inland-water fishing so highly competitive as to make a normal catch something of a rarity.

It is my opinion that, with the disheartening thinning-out of our inland-water fish population and the pressures from industry on our streams and rivers becoming greater each year, a large majority of fresh-water fishermen will turn to salt water in the near future. Perhaps to some worthwhile degree such a turnabout might improve the outlook for fresh-water fishing in the years to come.

Chapter Twelve

SURFACE LURES

Surface lures are creations of cork, balsa wood, hair, or combinations of these, designed to represent moths, mice, frogs, crawdads, grasshoppers and, frequently, wholly imaginary creatures. Actually, imitation is not important; but color, size, and action are. Joe Abel, a veteran fisherman of the Delaware River, has a pet term for one of the hair bugs made by the writer—"That red-eyed bow tie." Nevertheless, the "bow tie" has caused many a tight line and bowed rod for Joe Abel. The last time I saw it, it was eyeless, chewed into a terrible condition and rusty—evidence of faithful service.

Whether these lures are made of cork or hair depends, for the most part, on your own preference. Some anglers swear by each type; others swear at them. However, there is one saving grace about these bugs: they are more fun than a chimpanzee to watch. A well-made plunker properly handled will gurgle and "talk" the full length of the retrieve, while an all-hair bug of the Henshall type will sneak along through the weeds in a manner that will make the skin on your neck prickle.

These lures do catch fish. Largemouth bass, especially, are susceptible to them, smallmouth frequently take them, trout respond to the smallest sizes, and some salt-water fish will strike them in shallow waters. These bugs are to the fly-rod man what the popping plugs are to the plugger. Their use is becoming more widespread each season.

One of the most important things to remember about making either cork- or hair body lures is to have sufficient space between the bottom side of the finished lure and the inside of the hook barb. Many otherwise excellent lures are spoiled simply because they do not have enough hook exposed to hook the strikes. Another good point about having enough hook exposed is the attendant ballast it gives the lure. Nothing is more irritating than a bug which persists in settling upside down on the water.

Bodies made of hair should be as compact as the maker can possibly tie them. This tends to insure durability. The Emerson Hough type of bug is shaggy and seemingly anything but compact. However, this shagginess is deceiving. The bug is quite compact but untrimmed, thus giving the appearance that it is sparser than it really is.

If a bug is intended to float, it should be made throughout with this thought in mind. Several factors tending to reduce the buoyancy of surface bugs are: hooks too large and too heavy, skimpy bodies, cement accidentally brushed on the hair, and too sparse tail sections. Of these it seems too sparse tail sections are most frequently the cause of poorly balanced, hence drowning, surface bugs.

Because these lures are so large when compared to trout flies, they require good workmanship and sense of proportion on the part of the fly-maker. Neat trimming of the hair, careful shaping, smoothing and sanding of the cork, clean-cut painting, etc., cannot be done in a hurry. Consequently, it takes time to make an attractive, balanced, and, most of all, useful surface bug.

Classification of these lures is necessarily general only and they can best be divided into two types: hair bugs and cork bugs. So many varieties of each kind have been developed in the past ten years that they cannot be confined to a single chapter. However, since there is a large amount of invention connected with bug-making, it is necessary to know only the fundamentals to design practically any kind of bug or lure one would need in a whole lifetime. The following descriptions are for the sole purpose of showing what can be done with cork and hair and are not intended to cover all the types of bugs.

CORK-BODY LURES

Although there are others, the majority of cork-body bugs are based on three shapes, called flathead, tenpin and plunker. A fourth shape, the diver, is merely the plunker shape having the slanted head in reverse position. Some lures such as small grasshoppers are often made up with bodies having corrugations, but any one of the mentioned three shapes with ridges cut in it will be satisfactory. In other words, there is very little that cannot be done with these three as a basis. The flathead, for example, is used for the various moths, spent hair-wings and surface minnows with hackle streamers; the tenpin for mice, hair-winged bugs, and, when turned end for end, for crawdads; the plunker for a limitless additional assortment.

Cork bodies are easily available and are inexpensive. For this reason it is advisable to buy them already shaped unless you happen to have a "yen" for experimenting. Ordinary medicine corks have caught plenty of bass, it is true, but are a little too small for proper shaping and finishing unless the bug is to be a small one.

Shaping the body is a fairly easy matter. Use a light-weight file, a razor blade (single edge), and coarse sandpaper for roughing the body into shape. Do not concentrate on one side or one area for too long a time; it is very easy to work a cork billet down to nothing. Instead, develop the entire shape gradually by repeatedly going over the body as many times as necessary. This will minimize the tendency to file flat spots and irregular surfaces. Sanding should be done over a clean space on the work table so the dust can be saved for mixing with cement to make a filler. Preparations especially for this purpose are no better than this easily made cement which is about as fine a filler as you can use.

After the body is sanded to the proper shape it should be surfaced. If any pits appear, fill them with cement and cork dust. Incidentally, the filler will have the tendency to shrink while it is drying, so pack the cork dust on thick. The surplus is removed easily with sandpaper after the filling has dried.

Locate the spot where the hook will be and mark it with a lead pencil. Insert a dull hacksaw blade upside down in a small bench vise then, holding the cork firmly between the fingers, carefully saw the slot for the hook by sliding the cork back and forth over the saw blade. Another method of preparing the cork for the hook is to make a longitudinal V cut in the cork, and removing the V section. The hook is then placed in the opening, the V section replaced and cemented, and the body

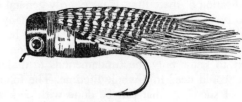

FLAT HEAD *(QUIET)*

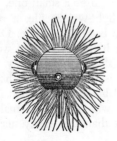

TEN-PIN *(SWIMMING)*

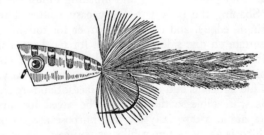

PLUNKER *(NOISY)*

FIG. 30
TYPES OF CORK—BODY BUGS

LEONARD

allowed to dry overnight. This, however, is not as easy as the former method, and has no particular advantage over it.

The method used for attaching the wings depends largely upon the material used to make them. Feathers are generally tied on with working silk. Hair, however, is either tied on or wrapped with thread and forced into drilled holes.

A cork bug is as good as its finish. It is a waste of effort to spend valuable time preparing a smooth body, placing and securing the wings and tails, and otherwise doing a good job, if the finish is dull, unattractive and poorly applied. If for no other reason than to show consistency and good workmanship, it is well to be neat and particular with the details of painting or lacquering the body and pinning on or painting the eyes. These things are done after the body is finally smoothed with rottenstone rubbed on with a damp cloth, then buffed with a small shoe brush. The pits will have been filled and the plugs smoothed to match the contour of the body; the wings and tails tied on. If the bug looks right, give it a thin coat of clear lacquer or celluloid enamel. This will permanently seal the pores of the cork and furnish a smooth base for the colored enamel. It is important to have the prime coat as thin as possible. The finish coat (or coats) depends upon your own notions: spots, streaks, stripes or ribs—whichever you prefer. In this connection, it is well to use these sparingly until you have acquired the knack of proportions. Most bugs need no more than either three or four circumferential stripes or six spots on the back.

Allow several hours between coats of enamel or lacquer regardless of the stated drying time of these materials. It is added life to the bug to apply two finish coats of clear enamel or lacquer over the colors.

Actual construction is detailed in the descriptions of the various types of cork bugs to follow.

FLATHEAD

The flathead is the most common cork bug. It is usually made as a feather-wing moth but is often featured as a hair spent-wing or a wounded minnow. This type has a flat, slightly rounded type of head which creates little disturbance on the surface; thus it is known as the "quiet" type. Actually this shape will plop or "chugg" when properly manipulated, and for general surface fishing will perform as well as most bugs. CONSTRUCTION: See Fig. 31. First shape and sand the cork billet to the proper size. Saw the slot in the bottom side for the hook in the manner described in the previous section. If this saw cut is too deep, the hook will be too near the top of the body, leaving insufficient space between the inside of the barb and the bottom of the body. Therefore, cut the slot approximately one-third as deep as the body is thick. Try the hook (the hump-shank type) for clearance and, if it appears to be in the correct position, remove it from the slot and cover it with working silk, winding from the rear toward the front, then back again. Put a drop of cement on the end of the shank and fasten on the hair tail. Next coat the windings on the shank with thick cement and, while the cement is becoming tacky, fill the slot in the body with cement. When the cement begins to get cloudy force the hook into the slot as far as it will go. Do not rotate the cork on the hook once the hook is in position, for this would loosen the seal and require repetition of the whole process. Mix a little cork dust with cement and plug up the space remaining in the slot. Set the body aside to dry thoroughly.

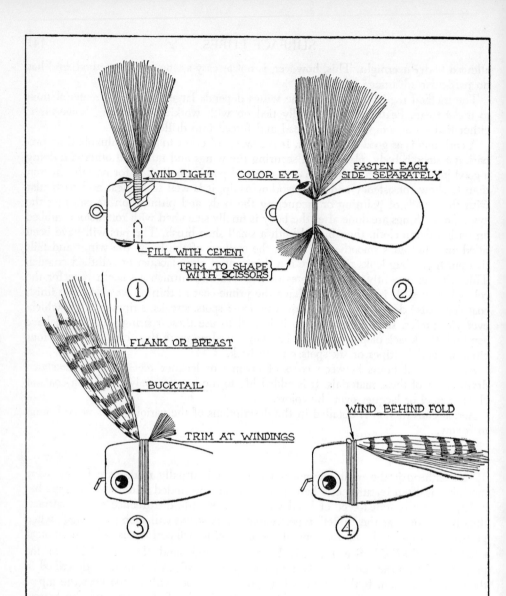

FIG. 31
SPECIAL FEATURES — CORK BUGS

LEONARD

When the cement has become dry and hard, smooth the surface of the cork filler in the slot until there is no irregularity.

Approximate the position of the eyes. In the case of flatheads, the eyes are usually placed on the end rather than on the sides, but this is not necessarily a rule. It depends on the size of the bug body and the size of the eyes. However, for the purpose of illustration, let us place the eyes (glass type) on the front of the body. It should be mentioned here that glass eyes have appreciable weight and can effect the stability of the bug. Therefore, set them as low in the head as is practical. In the opinion of many persons this adds to the attractiveness of the finished bug, although some sad facial expressions often result.

With the dubbing needle or bodkin mark holes into which the stems of the glass eyes will be driven later. Try to mark these holes in the same horizontal plane; lopsided floating will be the result if one eye is set nearer the water line than the other eye. Enlarge the hole just enough to locate it easily, then set the eyes aside. Incidentally, the stems of the eyes should be clipped to proper length and the points sharpened with a file to prevent any bending or buckling when the eyes are being set in place.

With a countersinking drill held in the hand (not a brace) lightly spin the drill with its point in the marked hole. Do this with care so as not to make the base for the eye too large. Check for depth by holding the stem of the eye in the fingers and pressing the eye into the hole. A little less than half of the eye should sink into the hole—no more. If the countersinking is correct, the body is ready for coloring.

Celluloid enamels are a boon to the bug-maker. They have luster and flow well from the brush, blending into a hard, shell-like protective finish. The key to applying them well is to control their consistency by the use of the thinner specifically designed for such enamels. Do not try to mix thinner for one brand with the color of another brand. Chemistry will not permit it. In this connection it is logical to purchase both colors and thinners from the same manufacturer.

Reduce the color you have selected for the base to the consistency you think is right. Then brush it on a test piece of the same material the bug body is made of; this will indicate what to expect. Thinning too much is as bad as thinning too little. Stroke the color on in full, clean sweeps and do not attempt to repair the strokes once they are made. If necessary, the imperfect areas can be sanded again and re-colored. Try to keep the countersunk holes for the eyes as free from enamel as possible since these will be filled with heavy cement immediately prior to the application of the eyes.

Putting on the spots, stripes or streaks is the next operation. Since the flathead features feather wings tied down-wing style, it will not require very much if any coloring of the back. Therefore, estimate the covered portion of the back and begin to color the bug accordingly. When making banded bodies such as the bee type, you will find it an advantage to extend the bands completely around the body for the purpose of keeping the bands even and of the same width throughout. A very useful material for this purpose is masking tape, the kind in general usage in engineering offices for repairing blueprints, etc. Carefully cut strips of the masking tape and place them in position according to the width of the bands. These strips will prevent the colored enamel from covering the spaces between the bands and will enable you to work faster without undue concern over irregular edges. When the enamel has hardened, remove the masking tape carefully and you will find the two-tone bands are nearly perfect.

Interesting stencils are made in masking tape with the aid of sharp whittling and cutting tools. Even a single-edged razor blade can be used with facility. Diamond, square, round or oval shapes of all sizes can be arranged irregularly or placed in neat rows. A single row consisting of patterns of the same shape graduated in size from large to small makes a practical and attractive design. The varieties of these arrangements are limitless.

Give the body at least one and preferably two coats of clear enamel. This will harden the surface of the colored layer and achieve certain protection for the whole body.

Next is the application of the wings. This operation appears more difficult than it really is. Actually the wings may be fastened on in several ways, any one of which is correct so long as the wings remain in place. Perhaps the simplest method is to lay the wing material over the back of the body, approximate the length necessary, trim the butts of the feathers or hair accordingly, then tie the wings by winding the working silk completely around the wing butts and the bug body. Alternate methods vary from bug-maker to bug-maker, making it difficult to state whether there are any right or wrong ways of attaching wings. However, one of the most durable wing applications is done as follows. It is a method used by fastidious bug-makers.

Soak the butts of the feathers to be used for the wings in water to remove the stiffness in the center quills. Meanwhile, with a sharp razor blade, cut a shallow channel for the winding silk completely around the head of the bug body. This must be made in the exact place where the working silk is to be wound. Carefully pick out the thin slice of cork between the slits made by the razor blade. Touch up the naturally rough surfaces with fine sandpaper until a uniform depth results.

By this time the feathers should be pliable enough for attachment to the body. Start the working silk against the rear edge of the channel by taking two turns. This will keep the tip of the thread from slipping. Place the two wing feathers upside down (or with the concave surfaces uppermost) with the butts pointing toward the tail of the bug. This is shown in Fig. 31, No. 3. If you want to use bucktail or hair under the wings, which is good practice, place a thin layer of hair on top of the wings. Take one turn with the working silk, hold it snug, and coat the butts of the feathers and the hair with heavy cement. Wind the working silk toward the front edge of the channel until the wings are anchored.

With pressure on the working silk, bend the wings over the back. Now bind the wings into their proper position. This is illustrated in Fig. 31, No. 4. If you have done this correctly, the windings will be smooth and even, just filling the width of the channel cut in the head. Always secure the thread with the whip-finish.

Notice that the working silk replaces the thickness of cork removed from the channel cut. This prevents piling up of thread around the body and effects a neater finish. In most cases, especially at first, the tendency is to make the channel a little too deep (cork compresses easily) and for this reason a slight depression may be formed. Practice will determine the proper depth for this cut. Once the tier has learned the "feel" of cork he will have little further difficulties.

For permanency, coat the windings with cement, let them dry thoroughly, then enamel them the same color as the body.

The described method is only one of many methods useful in applying wings. However, until you have become an adept, you will do well to follow the outline given.

Fig. 31, No. 1, shows an excellent method for the application of hair wings tied "spent." Hair which otherwise could not be used because of its texture and characteristics will serve as well for this type of dressing as any other type of hair, thus effecting a worthwhile saving. Likewise, combinations of colors or types can be prepared which make use of odds and ends which, ordinarily, would be thrown away.

As shown in the illustration, this method consists of winding the butts of the bunches of hair with working silk. First, of course, the hair is given a coat of thick cement at the ends around which the working silk will be wound. A time-saving device is the electric drill, which should be passed completely through the bug body. If possible, the drill should be held stationary and the bug body pressed against it. This will give better control to the drilling and result in a smooth, clean hole. Some dressers use a heavy bodkin, pressing it into the cork from each side; this, however, has certain disadvantages.

With the hole drilled through the body, there remains merely to insert the already prepared wings into the hole. First fill the hole with thick cement, then force the wings into position.

The positioning of the eyes is the last operation. Since the holes have been countersunk and are ready to receive the eyes, they now require only a coat of cement. Allow the cement to set slightly, then press the eye firmly in place. If they are not rotated or otherwise moved once they have been located, they will remain fast for the life of the bug.

TENPIN

The name tenpin is derived from the shape of the cork billet from which it is fashioned. This shape is most useful since two entirely different actions in the water are obtainable by reversing it end for end. The finished bug illustrated in Fig. 30 is the type made with the small, knobbed end at the front. This arrangement imparts a slight swimming action resulting from a steady retrieve. Reversing the body gives the bug a widely swinging movement. As shown, the tenpin is made up with the knob toward the front.

CONSTRUCTION: The tenpin arrangement is different from the flathead only insofar as the construction of the wings and eyes are concerned. Here the wings and eyes are combined, the eyes being fashioned from the hair wing butts tapered and rounded to shape and then enameled the desired color. This bug is the essence of simplicity and a consistent getter of bass and especially bluegills. Whether its appeal is due to the large pop-eyes or the shape of the billet is a question. Very possibly it is due partly to both.

Fig. 31, No. 2, illustrates how simply the wings and eyes are fashioned. After the painting has been done, wind the working silk around the neck of the billet. Clip a bunch of hair from a bucktail or whatever kind of material you are using, and place it on the side of the bug body where the neck swells into the main body. Wind the working silk one or two turns, check the position of the hair and its spread, then cement the windings at the wings. Repeat the procedure on the opposite side, using cement freely. Keep the windings as neat and even as possible to prevent unnecessary and unsightly piling up of the thread. Whip-finish the thread.

With sharp, curved scissors clip off the butts of the hair, and shape them into roundish eyes. Do this as accurately as you can, paying special attention to trimming the outer edges. When these are as neat as can be expected, coat them with thin cement, applying at least two and preferably three coats. This will prepare the butts for painting. Next brush on the base color (usually black or yellow) and allow it to dry thoroughly. Color the center with a tiny drop of enamel held on the tip of the dubbing needle.

PLUNKER AND DIVER

Both the Plunker and Diver are made from the same billet; that is, the Plunker is tied with slanted front receding toward the bottom, while the Diver is tied with the slanted front receding toward the top. This reversal of position results in (1) surface disturbance in the case of the Plunker and (2) planing downward in the case of the Diver. Fig. 30 illustrates the Plunker, a dependable and popular style. Color scheme of this bug approximates the frog, various wounded minnows and other surface creatures. Certain color combinations are reputedly effective for night and dark water but these properties are in my opinion strictly the notion of the bug-makers. Your own good sense will determine the needs for your own fishing grounds.

CONSTRUCTION: Fig. 30 represents the Plunker tied with streamer tails and a thick ruff of hackle. This design is suited to the simulation of a wounded minnow and, with the hackle tails separated and arranged widely forked, the action of a small frog.

The streamer tails or legs, whichever the case may be, are fastened to the hook first. The winding of the hackle ruff follows. The body is cemented to the hook in the same manner as any cork body, and then the eyes are either painted on or pushed into place.

Hair is frequently used to form the streamer section, especially in the construction of frogs, in which case the hackle ruff is eliminated.

A better plunking effect is sometimes achieved by cupping out the front surface of the head. This creates a water trap which produces a gurgling sound as the lure is drawn through the water.

It should be understood that there are few do's and don't's in bug-making. So do not hesitate to put your own ideas to work at the vise. People give various reasons for making fishing tackle a certain way. Nine times out of ten the real reason is the same: they catch fish with it.

HAIR LURES

Dr. James A. Henshall did more, perhaps, to exploit the first bass hair bugs than any other angler. He is credited with having made the original hair bug, one which bears his name to this day. Copies and modifications are numerous, but none are basically different from his original "Henshall" bug. Whoever invents a worthwhile thing usually finds the market immediately flooded with "better than the original" imitations. And this was the case with the Henshall bass bug. Practically every manufacturer offers to the trade a similar lure. Any one of them will catch bass. But from the standpoint of durability and easy casting, nothing so far developed is superior to the Henshall type.

More recent uses of hair for surface lures include making imitation frogs, crawdads, mice, and nearly everything palatable to a fish. For the most part, one is about as effective as another so long as shape, size, and general color approximate the original. For example, the fundamental in frog imitation is the long, spread legs. If the body

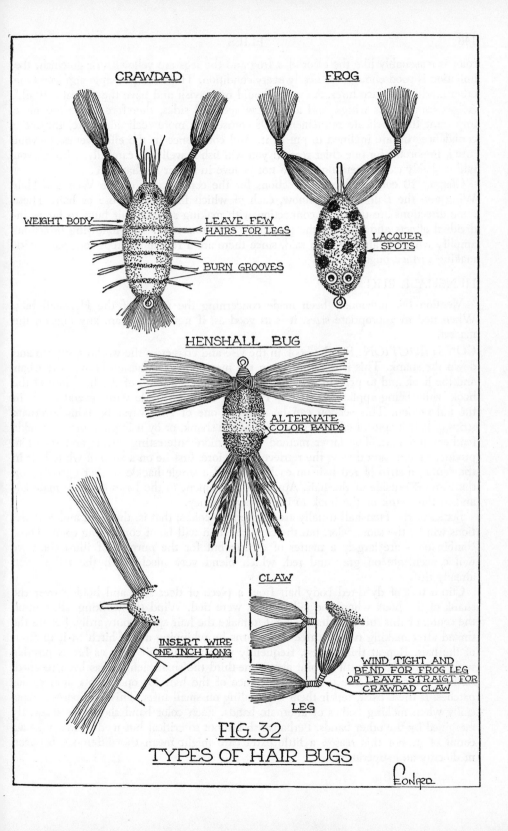

CRAWDAD

FROG

WEIGHT BODY

LEAVE FEW
HAIRS FOR LEGS

BURN GROOVES

LACQUER
SPOTS

HENSHALL BUG

ALTERNATE
COLOR BANDS

CLAW

INSERT WIRE
ONE INCH LONG

WIND TIGHT AND
BEND FOR FROG LEG
OR LEAVE STRAIGT FOR
CRAWDAD CLAW

LEG

FIG. 32
TYPES OF HAIR BUGS

Eonard

color is reasonably like the color of a frog and the legs are yellowish or greenish, the imitation is good enough for nearly every condition. The same principle applies to the other kinds of surface lures. A mouse should be grayish and have the typical "rattail." A bug usually has wings, and a minnow speckled sides; therefore, these are more important than delicate refinements. Of course, the more realistic a lure, the more confidence you are inclined to put in it. And confidence in the effectiveness of your lure is important for one chief reason: you will fish it well and carefully, whereas you will probably cast something you do not believe in rather haphazardly.

Chapter 10 contained brief directions for the construction of the Weedless Hair Wing and the Ball Head Minnow, each of which involves the use of hair. These same directions are useful in connection with making surface hair bugs so far as individual effects and some of the procedures are concerned. The following directions amplify what has already been said, since there are a few more steps connected with making surface bugs.

HENSHALL BUG

Mention has previously been made concerning the merits of the Henshall bug. When tied in appropriate sizes, it is as good as, if not better than, any bug on the market.

CONSTRUCTION: Set the hook in the vise and criss-cross the working silk up and down the shank. This is done to obtain the maximum of adhesion between the hair and the hook and to prevent as much as possible the spinning of the hair around the hook while being applied. Generally Henshall bugs are made with several colors in the tail section. This section can be made in one of two ways: by tying alternate strips of hair longitudinally over the back of the shank, or by using mixtures of hackle feathers and hair. The latter method creates more interesting effects and seems to produce more action during the retrieve. Therefore, first tie on a strip of white hair in the center, a strip of red hair on each side, and a single hackle feather (grizzly) on the extreme outside of the hair. Apply a little cement to the bases of these materials and to the shank of the hook to insure permanency.

Bodies of the Henshall usually are of alternate colors; that is, the front and rear sections will be the same color, but the center section will be of contrasting color. These combinations are largely a matter of choice; but for the purpose of illustration we will concentrate on gray and red, which blend very nicely with the tail section already tied.

Clip a tuft of dyed-red body hair from a piece of deer skin and hold it over the shank of the hook where the tail sections were tied. Wind the working silk around the center of this tuft and draw it tight to make the hair spread outwardly. Secure the thread after making two or three more turns by whipping a half-hitch in it in front of the hair. Repeat this process, frequently pushing the hair back as far as possible with the thumbnail until a point about one-third the shank length has been reached. At this point, check the general appearance of the hair for open spots or irregular patches. If these exist, repair them by winding on small tufts. This is important especially when making bodies of alternate bands. Each color band should be distinctly margined by the other bands. Perhaps fish are not so critical but men cannot take account of it. For this reason a little extra care might mean the difference between mediocrity and superiority.

Apply the center band of color, which, in this pattern, is the natural gray color of the deer hair. Wind this on in the same manner until a point about two-thirds up the shank has been reached. Again check for bald spots or other irregularities and, if they exist, repair them as formerly described. The last third (exclusive of the wing area and the tapering of the head) is built up with red hair.

The bug body at this stage will be a mass of hair requiring shaping. Whip two half-hitches in the thread in front of the front red section and remove the bug from the vise. With sharp scissors trim the body to shape until it resembles the illustration in Fig. 32. It is better to have the body a little too large at first since further trimming will reduce it to the exact size suitable for the hook. When trimming the body, cut from the rear toward the front. The hair naturally inclines slightly toward the rear and for this reason is trimmed more easily if cut in the opposite direction.

The wings are tied on in several ways, but are best fastened on the hook in this manner. Clip a large, full section of bucktail and place it over the bug body down-wing style. Each wing section to be bent into place should be slightly longer than the body. Therefore, estimate the length proportionately. Cement the thread windings in front of the body and the underside of the hair tuft. Wind the hair tightly to the hook, tapering the winds as much as possible. At this stage the wings-to-be will be a solid section over the back of the body.

When the hair is firmly bound and anchored, secure the working thread behind the eye of the hook with a half-hitch. Allow the cement holding the wings in place to dry thoroughly. Then divide the hair into two approximately equal sections. Holding the sections divided, pass the working thread between them, at the same time pulling outward on one section at a time. Carefully wind the working thread around the base of one wing section and then the other, until each projects outwardly at right angles to the body.

Cement the bases liberally as the work proceeds; do this at frequent intervals rather than all at one time. Taper the head and finish with the whip-knot.

Henshall bugs are often tied with wings the same color as the center band. This is not a fixed rule but seems to give the bug a pleasing appearance from the standpoint of color balance. Yellow and black, red and gray, black and white, red and white seem to be the most widely used colors. And for night fishing the all-black bug will always be unbeatable.

FROGS AND CRAWDADS

At first there might seem to be little if any similarity between a crawdad and a frog. From the standpoint of construction, however, there is much. The legs of the frog compare with the claws of the crawdad. Each travels in the same way—that is, the crawdad scuttles along backwards with his claws trailing, while the frog, of course, moves head first with his rear legs trailing. As for the differences, there are relatively few, namely: the crawdad has antennae which are not necessary on the artificial and its legs and tail are strictly a matter for the scissors; the frog has front legs, of course, but these, too, are unnecessary on the artificial. Consequently, the main differences between these two are their shape and the color.

The following description covers the construction of both the frog and crawdad.

CONSTRUCTION: (Ref. Fig. 32) Prepare the hook by criss-cross winding the shank with working thread. Clip a long, full section from a bucktail (not a section of deer body hair) and place it on top of the shank with the butts facing the rear. Securely bind the bucktail to the hook. The short butts will now spread outwardly around the rear of the hook, and the longer ends will tilt upwards. If the short ends are at all sparse, bind on a similar section on the bottom side of the hook. Bring the working thread forward beyond the long sections and secure it with a half-hitch. Remove the work from the vise and trim the short section to shape. If making a frog, trim it short and round. If making a crawdad, leave a few stray pieces of hair remaining at the center. Addition of hair to form the body will cause the legs to incline rearward in a natural manner.

Notice the arrangements of the legs of the frog and the claws of the crawdad. If legs or claws with a definite angle in the joints are desired, set a piece of fairly stiff, fine-gauge wire in the hair where the joint will be. Tightly wind over this wire and the bucktail around it and terminate with the whip-finish. Coat the windings with cement and allow to dry. It is worth mentioning here that the joint windings should be the same color as the bucktail. The nippers on the ends of the crawdad claws are easily imitated by whipping another joint close to the end of the claw, separating the tips of the hair and cementing them apart. The feet of the frog's legs are made similarly but are not separated at the tips. Instead, they are flattened, trimmed round, then cemented. To retain this flattened shape, place a spring-type clothes pin on each flattened end and leave it there until the cement has hardened.

The legs projecting from the sides of the crawdad are simulated by untrimmed sections of hair. Crawdads have ten legs (hence the name decapod), five on each side. These need not be long. The tail is also produced by a mere trimming operation. Clip the hair near the eye in such a manner that the untrimmed pieces extend downwardly over the eye of the hook.

Color is debatable among bug makers. Some like frogs very greenish, while others prefer yellow and white combinations. In either case, the necessary mottled effects are obtained by tying in alternate patches of hair, especially on the back. Generally the belly is white to cream-yellow; the back is green with either black or brown spots. Crawdads are more reddish than one is inclined to think. For this reason it is well to use deer hair dyed a bright brown (fiery brown).

Enamel is sometimes used to make the spots on frogs, thus making it possible and therefore convenient to use only two colors of hair: green for the back and cream-white for the belly.

STRIP-SKIN BUG

This lure is fundamentally of Indian origin, according to an authoritative source. The North Carolina Indians first made it years before our Civil War and used it successfully for generations. In general appearance it resembles a thick Palmer fly with spent wings. Whether the Indians bothered with the wings or tied the fly without them is a question. Nevertheless, the principle of tying the body has carried on to this day and, while the great majority of fly-makers have dropped this bug entirely or never carried it to begin with, flies made with strip-skin bodies are as effective now as they ever were.

CONSTRUCTION: The body is the single departure from other types of hair bugs. From an untreated deer skin, preferably the skin from the shin bones, cut pieces approximately six inches square. Flesh these out as thinly as possible until the skin is entirely free from fleshy tissue. This can be done by scraping the piece with a strong fish scaler. Cut strips about the width of a shoe string from the six-inch pieces and soak them in a brine solution for an hour. Then remove them, press out all moisture and allow them to dry. They can then be stored in a box lined with moth preventative, preferably crystals or flakes.

Later, when making bugs of this sort, soak each strip in water, to which a little glycerine has been added, until the strip is pliant. With the tail fastened on, there remains only to tie the body in place and fasten on the wings. Taper one edge of the strip and tie it to the shank. Wind the strip around the shank, fasten it with the working silk, tie on the wings and the bug will be complete. The hair will project nearly at right angles to the body and will weave back and forth when the bug is retrieved.

By following the foregoing directions you will be able to modify any particular style by combining it with other styles to produce nearly any kind of hair lure. Individual effects such as legs, feelers, sideburns or knobby knees can be devised to suit your own fancy.

Chapter Thirteen

AQUATIC INSECTS AND CRUSTACEANS

The fisherman with a knowledge of aquatic insects and the important relationship they bear to the fish he wants to catch is better equipped with a single fly than is the man who knows nothing of such things though he sports a jacket full of fly-boxes stuffed with crisp, unmouthed flies of every description. The man with an understanding of aquatic life knows how and where to place his casts, fishing those places his knowledge tells him suit the lure and the fish, whereas the other fellow will cast at random, forever changing flies, fondly hoping that eventually he will discover a fly of some sort that will catch a fish.

It is better to fish a fly that will catch a trout than to hunt a trout that will take a fly.

The fly-dresser in particular is obliged to know as much as he possibly can about the life cycles of the insects his flies are designed to represent. The more he knows about their aquatic and aerial stages, the more intelligently he will design, balance, and dress the copies. Local fly-makers have a surprisingly strong influence on the anglers they serve and for this reason have a responsibility to be both honest and reasonable about the products they offer. In this connection, it is good management to know the appearance at each stage and the duration of these stages in natural insects to satisfy those serious-minded anglers who carefully fish the "hatch." This does not mean that exact imitation of "naturals" is always necessary, however; many flies resembling little if anything in nature are phenomenal fish catchers.

The study and classification of stream-inhabiting insects has been a source of interest to anglers for hundreds of years. Both simple and complex systems of classification have been developed to aid the anglers to identify stream insects and in some manner associate them with artificials. Some of these systems have been very useful; others have been merely confusing. Among them certain inconsistencies are apparent, making comparison of them difficult if not impossible. Few have been complete enough to enable the fisherman to identify properly the nymphs and larvae with their respective adults since, in the majority of cases, the emphasis was placed almost entirely on describing the color and size of the adults alone, with the consequence that the mention given immature insects was, for the most part, superficial.

Two of the most earnest attempts to associate angling flies with supposed prototypes were those developed by two Englishmen, Prof. L. C. Miall and Michael Theakston. Although these two methods of identification were originated many decades ago, they prove how profitably scholarship and practical streamside observation

152

can be combined into angling "know-how." Both Miall and Theakston, while they do not at all agree generally, are most instructive and even their differences of opinion are conducive to a better understanding about natural insects. It was Theakston, an angler of note, who classified the "spinner," which we associate with May flies, as belonging to the crane flies. Miall, on the other hand, placed the "spinner" under the category of May flies, which is in keeping with correct zoological listings.

These two systems have left far-reaching influences. Since American fly-fishing customs originally were patterned to a large extent on British opinions and fly patterns, both Miall and Theakston were accepted in this country without question. This accounts for the frequent use of the word "spinner" to describe a crane fly in some parts of our country, while in other parts the same term is accepted to mean the final stage of the May fly.

It is interesting to compare these two systems. Each has its merits and both are examples of the creditable work which has made the study of fly-fishing the absorbing subject it is. It should be remembered that this description deals only with those insect classifications associated with fishing or arranged for the fisherman's benefit.

MIALL'S SYSTEM OF CLASSIFICATION

This consists of five classes, associating certain insects with the names given the corresponding artificial fly by anglers.

Notice that Miall's system differs from more recent classifications in that it includes the blue dun and sand fly, both of which are May flies, in the Caddis class.

1. *2-Wing flies* (diptera): Golden dun midge.
2. *Caddis flies* (trichoptera): Blue dun, little red spinner, sand fly, grannom, turkey brown, dark spinner, silver horns, cinnamon fly.
3. *Alder flies* (Sialidae): Alder or orlfly.
4. *Stone flies* (Perlidae): Red fly, stone fly, willow fly (Shamrock).
5. *May flies* (Ephemeridae): March brown (dun or brown drake) great red spinner, yellow dun, iron blue dun, jenny spinner, little yellow May dun, sky blue, green drake (May fly), gray drake, orange dun, black drake, dark mackerel, pale evening dun, whirling blue dun, July dun, August dun.

THEAKSTON'S SYSTEM OF CLASSIFICATION

This system classifies anglers' flies into seven groups. Notice the separation of the drakes from the duns which is entirely different from either both Miall's and present-day classifications. It is evident Theakston did not consider "duns" as the first aerial stage of the May fly but preferred to associate them with the caddis fly.

1. *Browns* (Plecoptera): Stone fly, needle brown, early brown, orange brown, yellow brown, yellow Sally.
2. *Drakes* (Ephemeridae): May fly, green drake, black drake, etc.
3. *Duns* (Trichoptera): Caddis fly.
4. *Spinners* (Diptera): Crane fly, black hackle, early spinner, jenny spinner and spiders.
5. *Houseflies* (Diptera): Blue bottle, cowdung, etc.
6. *Beetles* (Coleoptera) and *Bugs* (Hemiptera).
7. *Ants*.

IDENTIFICATION OF FISH FOOD

As has been pointed out, it is good investment of your time to investigate and study stream life. When the strikes have become so few as to make casting merely a mild form of exercise, it is well to spend an hour or two searching for underwater organisms. Line your landing net with mosquito netting and set out to capture whatever you can for study. One or two dips of the net among the weed beds fringing most streams is usually sufficient to scoop up a whole host of wriggling creatures of divers kinds. There are little black things which scoot back and forth, some crescent-shaped, translucent objects, a long dusky worm or two and other sprawling creatures of forbidding appearance. Then, if you turn over a stone or two in the riffles, you will discover an entirely different society. Select one and ask yourself:

(1) Is this a nymph or larvae?
(2) To what order of insects does it belong?
(3) Is it wholly or partially aquatic?
(4) Do fish eat it?
(5) Does it become a fly?
(6) What size will it be?
(7) When does it become an adult?
(8) What are its usual colors?
(9) Are fish partial to the aquatic or the aerial form?
(10) What is the best way to make a successful imitation?

Successful fly fishing is founded on the answers to these ten questions. If you can answer them, you will be able to identify anything of value to the fisherman and have the foundation for intelligent fly imitation. Keep these questions in mind. Their correct answers appear as keys to the identification of the main orders of aquatic insects important to fishing. By using them you will recognize the nymph of the Ginger Quill or the Green Drake, for example, and have a fairly accurate idea of when to expect the emergence of the flying form which we all recognize as the "hatch."

There are surprisingly few insects of wholly aquatic habitat. Among them are the May flies, caddis flies, stone flies, the dragonflies and damselflies. Certain other groups are partially aquatic; that is, one or more phases of their life-spans are spent in the waters of streams, ponds, marshes, etc. The nymph or larva may be a stream inhabitant while the later developed adult may be terrestrial by nature. Or the terrestrial grub or maggot in some field may become an adult that will frequent ponds and streams. So long as some part of the insect's life cycle is for an appreciable time associated with water, that insect can be classified as partially aquatic and of interest to the fly fisherman. Only those insects of wholly or partially aquatic habitat are considered in this book, since no attempt to include insects other than those of angling value has been made.

It will be noticed that in the table on page 157, the individual species are not labeled with their scientific names but are identified by the names common to anglers. Aliases are included for the purpose of associating many regional names for insects with the true "natural." In cases involving British names which have been handed down, identification of the angling fly is likewise made with the "natural." Only the orders are listed according to their formal titles. This is done for the single purpose of showing that, in nearly every case, the translation of the formal name applied to the order gives the key characteristics of the order.

METAMORPHOSIS

Entomologists refer to the life cycle of an insect involving several forms as its metamorphosis. There are two kinds of metamorphoses: *complete,* in which the transformation from the larva through the pupa stage to the adult is most pronounced; *incomplete,* in which the transformation from the nymph to the adult is least pronounced. In the first type, little similarity of appearance exists between the larva, pupa and adult. In the second type, an appreciable similarity exists between the nymph and adult.

It will be noticed that the immature stage of the *incomplete* metamorphosis is called a nymph, whereas in the *complete* the counterpart of the nymph is known as a larva. Therefore, we now have the beginning of identification. In the Table of Insects, Aquatic and Partially Aquatic, it will be seen that the metamorphoses have been subdivided and listed under the headings Incomplete and Complete. How, then, is it possible to classify the insect you are examining into either of these two groups for further breakdown and subsequent naming? Simply by looking for wing pads.

If wing pads are present, the insect is a nymph. If not, it is a larva. Let us suppose the creature you are looking at *does* have wing pads. Then we know it belongs to one of the groups listed under the subdivision *incomplete.* Thus you have obtained a factual answer to the first question, Is this a nymph or a larva?—and a leader toward the answer to the second question, To what order does it belong?

TABLE OF INSECTS
Aquatic and Partially Aquatic

ORDER	METAMORPHOSIS			
	Incomplete (2-Phase)	Complete (3-Phase)	Wholly Aquatic	Important to Angler
1. *Ephemeroptera*: May flies	X		X	X
2. *Plecoptera*: stone flies (perlids)	X		X	X
3. *Trichoptera*: caddis flies		X	X	X
4. *Diptera*: crane flies, midges		X		X
5. *Neuroptera*: hellgramites, alder flies, fish flies		X		X
6. *Odonata*: dragon flies and damsel flies	X		X	X
7. *Coleoptera*: beetles (parnids)		X		
8. *Hemiptera*: waterbugs	X			
9. *Hymenoptera*: ants, bees		X		
10. *Lepidoptera*: moths		X		
11. *Thysanura*: springtails		X		

It should be mentioned here that for the benefit of the fisherman I have taken the liberty of qualifying the terms *incomplete* and *complete* in the tables because these terms are only relative and somewhat vague. What the fisherman must know is that an insect which undergoes an incomplete metamorphosis is actually a "two-phase" insect, meaning that two types of artificial flies will simulate its existence. Similarly, an insect which undergoes complete metamorphosis is a "three-phase" insect, and three types of artificial flies will simulate its existence. In both cases the egg stage is left out of account.

Table on page 157, entitled Recognition Features, illustrates the use of these substituted terms in connection with tracing the nymph or larva to a definite order.

ORDERS

Insects have been classified according to specific orders because of certain structural characteristics. The character of the wings, their number, the kind of feet, tails, abdomen, or other peculiarities, set one order apart from the other orders. Some irregularities exist, naturally, but not to the extent that they make identification impossible. Insects within each order are distinguished by similarities of structure. Consequently recognition of an insect belonging to any one order will suggest similar characteristics to look for in other insects belonging to that same order.

Now back to the second question. To what order of insects does it belong? You give the nymph a cursory examination. It has tails, legs, and the other usual equipment. But what is the one distinguishing characteristic by which this nymph can be classified? A second examination reveals other facts: that there is a single claw on each foot, that there are three, flexible tails. By referring to the table on page 157, you can readily see that nymphs possessing one claw on each foot are of the order Ephemeroptera or May flies. If the nymph in question had been equipped with paired claws on each foot, the nymph would have been of the order Plecoptera or Odonata, requiring more detailed examination to determine to which order it belonged.

The table on page 157 gives primary recognition features only, which are adequate to trace a nymph or larva to the proper order. These key features are easily detected and are consistent with the true entomological orders so that further study of aquatic insects can be made without altering information already learned. Each of the six orders of prime importance to the fly angler, therefore, can be studied and their member insects recognized by comparison. When identifying nymphs and larvae, it should be remembered that "It isn't what an insect is—it's what it isn't . . . " that counts.

The six orders illustrated in the table comprise the essentials of trout diet. Other insects are eaten in varying degrees of frequency but, because of their small size or unfavorable habitat, they are not especially valuable to fish the size the angler wishes to catch.

The third question: Is it wholly or partially aquatic? cannot be answered by examination. So we refer to the table on page 155 again, to find that the Ephemeroptera or May-fly group is a wholly aquatic class. This third question is important from the fishing standpoint. If the nymph and adult forms are wholly aquatic, the entire life cycle is available to the fish. Therefore, the fly-dresser is required to know the stages of development and the relationship of one stage to the others in connection with periods of emergence and duration.

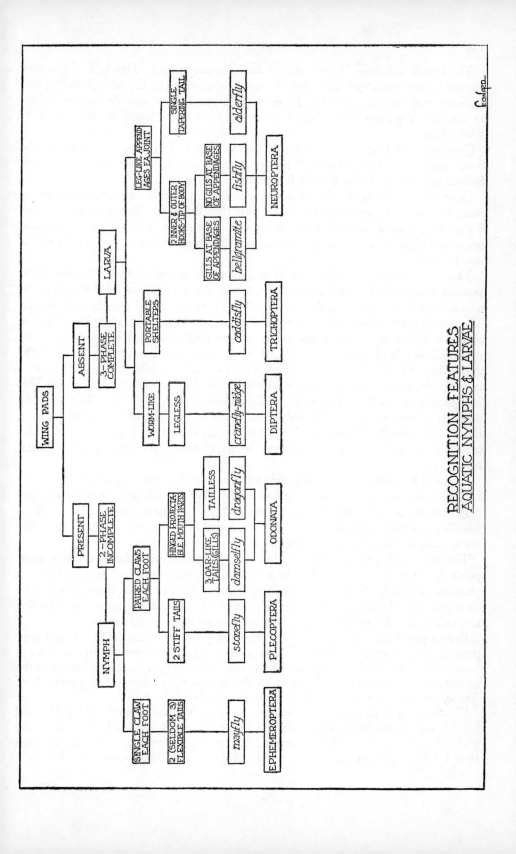

RECOGNITION FEATURES
AQUATIC NYMPHS & LARVAE

The fourth question: Do fish eat it? almost answers itself. Hardly a creature of aquatic habitat exists that a fish will not eat. In our example, the table indicates that Ephemeroptera is a major order. To verify this, just observe how the stream springs to life with the surge of feeding trout whenever a dun "hatch" or spinner "fall" takes place.

Question five: Does it become a fly? Yes. With very few exceptions, such as the water beetles and bugs, almost all aquatic nymphs and larvae are eventually transformed into flying insects. Only a few adults are wingless.

Question six: What size will it be? cannot be answered by examination since, in many instances, the underwater form is larger than the adult. Therefore, comparisons with descriptions of each order that follows must be made. This applies to questions seven and eight as well, namely, When does it become an adult? and, What are its usual colors?

The ninth question: Are fish partial to the aquatic or aerial form? is one involving years of study and observation to answer. Streamside examination of the contents of a trout's stomach is, perhaps, the only possible means of determining the real answer. Those with years of successful fishing behind them will agree that nymphs and larvae comprise by far the greatest percentage of the food consumed by trout over any measured length of time. Seasonally, there is some variation depending upon the availability of aerial forms; but on the whole, most fish are more aware of the creepers, nymphs, and worms on the stream bottom than they are of the flying adults. This is especially true with regard to larger fish. Usually these large fish "hole up" and concentrate on more easily obtainable underwater food. The older a trout becomes the more he remains hidden, feeding cautiously on bottom food, unless a freshet discolors the water; then he will cruise more boldly, realizing he is hidden by the murkiness of the water.

It should be mentioned that any individual stream may have a peculiar food problem, such as continuously lessening hatches, a condition incident to pollution. But despite many attempts to effect the transplanting of nymphs and larvae, the efforts have been unsuccessful, and it has been concluded by the natural scientists that they are a waste of time, money and energy.

The tenth and, perhaps, the most interesting question from the fly-dresser's viewpoint: What is the best way to make a successful imitation? is best answered after a practical knowledge of the anatomy of each particular insect has been gained. The descriptions of the insects belonging to each order follow in sequence with detailed methods of simulating the many special features peculiar to each order.

Record your findings, and if you can sketch or paint, illustrate the insects you have preserved, or photograph them. Those anglers who are entomologists or have a smattering of knowledge of aquatic insects can contribute invaluable assistance to the betterment of fish culture as well as to the techniques of fly-making, provided, of course, that their findings are based on accurate observations.

Conservation departments will be glad to help. Various journals and books will furnish keys to enable you to study the insect life of all streams in general or the pools of your own favorite little stream. And maybe the reason why you can catch trout from it and others cannot is your knowledge of food sources; only you know.

PRESERVATION OF INSECTS

It is a fascinating pastime to capture aquatic insects for the purpose of preserving them for study or copying. An old but wonderfully effective preserving solution is made up as follows: Add 1 part glycerine and 1 part vinegar to 8 parts grain alcohol. The glycerine minimizes the tendency of the insect parts to become brittle when exposed to the air. Hence, later examination can be made with a minimum of damage to the insect. Interesting and worthwhile files can be kept by placing single specimens, or a few of the same kind, in small corked tubes. It is not practical to preserve insects by pinning them onto boards. In time the specimens will have deteriorated beyond recognition; moreover, moth larvae will go through specimens arranged in this manner like rabbits through a vegetable patch.

RECOMMENDED DRESSINGS

Throughout the descriptions of the following insects it will be noticed that the nymphs and larvae are described but are not compared with imitations, while the adults are. The designing of nymph flies is still in the experimental stages; therefore, your own ingenuity may evolve something better than those already made. The chapter on nymphs describes in detail the many individual characteristics common to most nymphs. With this information it is possible to devise everything necessary to imitate aquatic nymphs and larvae, if imitations are at all practical from the viewpoint of size and usefulness.

Table on page 160 entitled Recognition Features, Adult Aquatic Insects, is a breakdown of winged insects that should be readily understood and is based on the properties of the wings, themselves. In the majority of cases anglers describe first the color and size of an insect's wings, perhaps because the wings are the most noticeable part of an insect's anatomy. This table was prepared as a supplement to the table on page 157. Both are arranged with a view to simplifying the recognition of any stage of an insect's life span.

EPHEMEROPTERA

NAME SOURCE: "Ephemeros"; enduring but one day or less.

PHASES: Two, nymph and adult, but adult has two forms, the sub-imago called "dun" and the imago called "spinner."

RECOGNITION FEATURES:

Nymph, single claw each foot and three (occasionally two) tails; gills on back or sides. *Adult* (dun), dull color, tails comparatively short, leaves water laboriously in a nearly vertical position and flies *away* from the stream toward bushes and trees; two short wings behind two long wings; (spinner), brilliant color often glassy, tails long and delicate, returns to water surface gracefully; always flies *toward* the stream unless lost because of strong winds; egg-laden females dip and rise over water during ovipositing; wings held upright over back when resting.

ANGLERS' NAMES: May fly, lake fly, drake, day fly, sand fly, shad fly, sailor, cocktail, caughlan (Irish).

The life histories of all May flies are similar and seem to fall into a pattern that is quite invariable. Generally dry-fly dressings are based on May flies, a fact to which the names of many patterns will attest. For example, the ginger quill, blue quill,

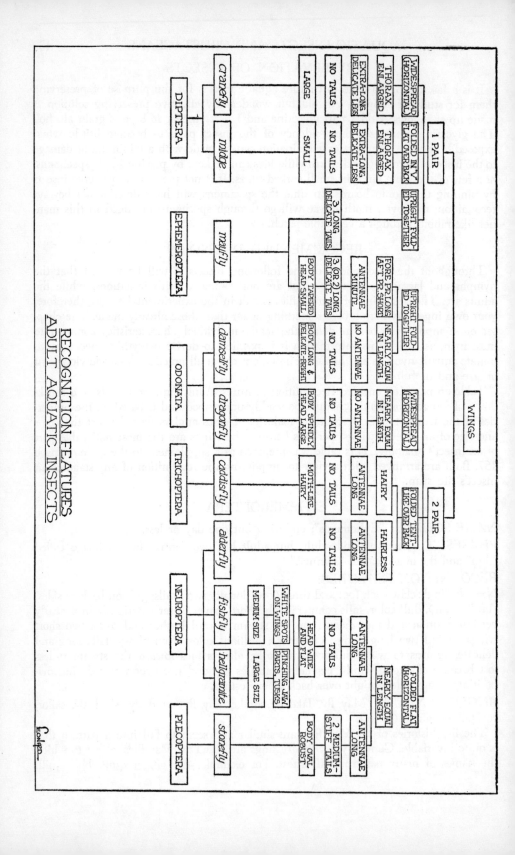

RECOGNITION FEATURES
ADULT AQUATIC INSECTS

iron blue dun, pale evening dun, olive spinner and hundreds of others are names given to ephemerids. Dry-fly fishing was founded on the attempted imitations of May flies. It was not until recent years that anglers became aware to any great extent of the value of copying other kinds of surface food, so strong was their inclination to concentrate on May flies.

These insects differ from others in that they molt after becoming adults. Most fishermen are familiar with the terms "dun" and "spinner" as applied to May flies. These terms are of British origin and are used by American anglers.

The dun is the stage that emerges from the water, where it sheds its nymphal skin to fly in an almost vertical position with seeming difficulty to lift itself from the water surface. Eventually it reaches the protective foliage along the shore and disappears under a leaf or twig to dry. Some hours pass, perhaps a day or in some cases even longer, then the "spinner," a delicate and brilliantly colored creature crawls from the dull, pithy skin that was once the dun and gracefully floats through the air in its return journey to the stream where it will mate and shortly afterward die.

PHASE 1: May-fly nymphs are found in nearly all streams and ponds and are probably the most abundant of all the aquatic insects. Hundreds of species belong to this order and are of many colors and several sizes. Generally they prefer riffles and well-aerated water, but certain of them burrow in the soft bottom of quiet waters. The period of their subsurface existence may be as long as one year or more, during which time they are very active, especially since the trout are ever-mindful of their presence. Some of these nymphs can swim with remarkable speed while others not so endowed seem to travel erratically. However, either type of locomotion suggests the origin of the old and familiar methods of retrieving a wet fly.

In keeping with the character of two-phase insects, the May-fly nymph is shaped like the adult it will become, although the coloration is different, most often a darker hue of little if any brilliance. As the nymph grows it molts its former skin and assumes a larger one of identical kind except for size, since the skin cannot stretch to make room for the enlarging body. Otherwise there are no physical changes during this process. This does not constitute a transformation and should not be considered one. Molting of the nymph in the manner described may be repeated as the growth of the enlarging nymph may determine.

For the most part, there are two distinctly different nymph shapes in this order. One is flattened to deflect strong currents (this is the basis for compressed-body artificial nymphs) and the other is roundish. Most nymphs of this order have three tails, but a few have two.

The keys for identifying May-fly nymphs are few. The first thing to look for is the presence of one claw on each foot and the second, the three tails. If you chance to be examining an ephemeral insect with only two tails, rely on the single claw to identify the nymph.

PHASE 2: When the time is right, the nymph will swim to the water's surface where its case will split between the wing pads. Almost at once a dull dun will pull itself from the nymphal case. It will rest a few moments, during which time it becomes a choice morsel for any foraging trout, then laboriously leave the water's surface. Invariably the "dun," as this stage is known to fishermen, and the "sub-imago" to the entomologist, flies in a vertical position since it is heavy and awkward. This characteristic makes it easy to determine if the insect is in the dun stage. Duns always fly away from the stream in this manner and sometimes, during this short flight toward the protection of shore foliage, stagger in mid-ascent but somehow manage to regain their strength sufficiently to continue to safety. The larger duns, such as the green drake, appear to be suspended head upward as though powered by an invisible propeller. Once they have reached the protective shore they remain out of sight until they return to the water as spinners or full imagoes.

The appearance of many duns constitutes the fisherman's hatch, and when a hatch is on, good fishing is certain.

The dun is semi-opaque, has four wings, the first pair being much longer than the second pair, and rather short tails which are about as long as the body. Hatches are most frequent during the morning hours and continue in decreasing amounts throughout the afternoon, although this is not a hard and fast rule. Some of the large drakes, for example, emerge as duns about dark. I have observed intermittent hatches taking place all night long, although this is rather uncommon. It should be remembered that May flies, while they follow a marked pattern in nearly all other respects, have no special regularity in emergence according to the hour of the day.

Spinners are the final form in the metamorphosis of May flies, and at this stage take on the delicate proportions and brilliant colors for which they are well known. The tails are now graceful and mottled. No longer are the wings heavy and awkward, but are now transparent and edged with the palest of pastel shades. The abdomen is slender and ringed, the legs usually mottled and long. These are the insects seen in the early evening swarming over the water surface, dipping and rising in erratic movements. This maneuver has been referred to as the dance of the May flies by many writers and is an excellent analogy. This dance is really the act of the females leaving their eggs on the water surface. In the case of some species, the female will descend below the water to deposit her eggs. Naturally this suggests the fisherman's use of the winged wet fly. At such times when the female is scurrying below the surface, a reasonably close imitation of correct size will catch fish.

These spinners can appear in unbelievable numbers. One evening on Penn's Creek in Pennsylvania the quill gordons appeared in such quantity as to tint the whole stream area with their color. The air was virtually a fluttering cloud of pinkish gray. The trout began to gorge themselves in a completely reckless manner and took everything on the surface with rare abandon. I have never since witnessed anything to compare with that fall of spinners. It offered ample proof of the abundance of May flies.

Sometimes trout will show a preference for female May flies. This may be due to two causes: the attraction of the erratic flight of the female as she dips and rises during the process of ovi-positing or the fact that she is larger than the male. When such preference is observed, it is well to switch to an egg-sac fly if strikes have been few. Determining the sex of a May fly is not difficult. Since spinners are concerned principally with the process of mating they will always be near the surface of the stream, usually immediately above it, the male and female frequently joined in flight. Females carry their eggs near the tip of the abdomen, hence the so-called "egg-sac" of chenille or wool on the artificials. The males are almost always smaller and have large, often metallic-looking eyes.

After mating, both male and female spinners fall to the stream's surface (while in the final spinner stage they cannot take food and are thus weakened and short-lived) and become an accessible source of food to surfacing fish. Although the insect is physically the same and has not been transformed, it is now called a "spent-wing" which it truly is. With wings outstretched it will drift as willed by the current until quietly sucked into the jaws of a feeding fish. The female survives only long enough to relieve herself of her egg sac.

It is obvious from the foregoing that the May fly is made available to fish in various forms, and while it is strictly a two-phase insect, there are three distinct stages in the appearance of the adult. First it is a dun (sub-imago), then a spinner (imago) and finally a spent-wing (imago). It would seem, therefore, that the fly-fisherman should be equipped with five types of artificials to imitate every phase of the May fly available to fish. A nymph, dun, spinner (male and female), a winged wet fly representing that female spinner which descends beneath the water to lay her eggs, and a spent-wing.

It should also be emphasized here that there are certain, definite means of identifying the presence of each of the five forms characteristic of May flies.

(1) *Nymph*: It is easy to ascertain whether trout are feeding on nymphs. Nymphs are inclined to seek the shelter of the protective bottom. Therefore, whenever feeding trout hunt for them, the fish have to assume an almost vertical position with their tails uppermost. The current tends to make the fish drift away and with quick, powerful thrusts from their tails they maintain their difficult position while probing between the rocks in search of bottom nymphs. These are "tailing" fish and the character of the so-called rise will be an uncertain bulge on the surface of the water nothing like the decisive, neat movement of a surface rise. It is not really a rise but a disturbance created by the tails of the fish.

(2) *Dun* (Sub-imago): The dun flies in a nearly vertical position with its tails hanging downward. It always flies *away* from the stream in a struggling manner. Duns usually appear in groups emerging generally in the morning and early afternoon hours. Large hatches appear on humid days. Duns are dully colored. The rise of a trout for a dun is accompanied by the familiar "chugg" known by all anglers.

(3) *Spinner* (Imago): Spinners are glassy in appearance, delicate and brilliant with long tails. They appear only in the course of their return flight to the stream, and are present just at dusk when they are exceedingly abundant. Trout take this form rather quietly, sometimes inaudibly.

(4) *Spinner* (Imago-female): Certain species of May flies are peculiar in that the female will submerge to deposit her eggs. Detection of this is purely a matter of deduction and of fishing sense. If you observe that there are no hatches of consequence, that there is a return of spinners, that the trout show no interest in surface food but, instead, flash beneath the surface without creating a disturbance, it is logical to conclude that the trout are concentrating on those female spinners which have gone underwater to carry on their mysterious function of egg-laying.

(5) *Spent-Wing* (Imago): At times, when trout are surfacing for spent-wings, there seems to be absolutely no insect life on the water. This is due to the utter collapse of the insect as it lies on the water. It requires extremely acute vision to see a spent-wing if it is further away than a few feet. The rise of the fish is almost imperceptible and may be detected only by the faint rings which appear after the surface has been pierced by the lips of the fish.

The exact identification of any particular May fly is cause for argument among anglers or fly-dressers. Consider the ginger quill for example. It is firmly established that a fly very similar to the commercially known Ginger Quill exists; that the nymph is brownish with dark rings, has a straw-colored belly, rusty-brown tails and yellowish-brown legs; and that the adult is generally ginger-colored. However, commercial adaptations of the ginger quill are numerous as well as various. Patterns such as the Dark Ginger Quill, Light Ginger Quill, Cahill Quill and others and the so-called spinners of each kind make the representation of the ginger quill anything but standard. Therefore, the concept of a single dressing supposed to represent the ginger quill is untenable. Recent developments have given the angler many alternatives for the original patterns, and these bear such definite similarity to the natural insect that they, fundamentally, could also be given the name of the "natural." Fly-dressers are prone to disregard naming their innovations according to any consistent plan and often resort to fanciful titles—sometimes the surnames of their originators. This custom has and always will cause confusion, and for this reason I have chosen to list alternates, both probable and possible, with the descriptions of the individual insects. By this arrangement an attempt has been made to achieve consistency and cohesive descriptions. Likewise, for the purpose of identifying a particular insect, one name has been used wherever possible to cover the nymph, the dun and the spinner forms. This eliminates the confusion which usually accompanies a system in which each of the three forms possesses a different name imposed on it by anglers. An example might be useful. The iron blue dun is well known. However, many anglers do not know that the male spinner form of this dark fly is the light and brilliant jenny spinner. One would find it next to impossible to associate the two by comparing their names. It is much more consistent to consider the insect as the iron blue dun and the iron blue spinner.

Any natural insect frequenting streams and ponds may be recognized by as many as ten or twenty locally popular names. In the great majority of cases, however, the scientific name is the only tenable one. Moreover, freestone and limestone streams markedly affect the colors and sizes of otherwise identical insects, giving rise to disagreement over what those insects might correctly be called. The green drake is a classic example which is dressed in amazing variety, according to each particular region of the country where it is tied.

SPECIAL FEATURES

When a May fly rests upon the water its wings are folded together over its back in typical "sail-wing" fashion. Consequently a trout in a position immediately below the insect can see very little of the wing and should accept a wingless artificial of proper color as readily as a winged pattern. However, if a trout is located laterally to the drift of the insect, it will be in a position to view critically the whole profile, particularly the wings. For this reason it is better design to dress the wings folded together over the back.

Hackle can be arranged in a most lifelike manner and still benefit the buoyancy of the artificial. Before winding the main hackle, fasten a long-fiber hackle by the butt end and wind it one turn around the body. Tie it down, then wind the main hackle. Apply one turn of long-fiber hackle in front of the main hackle and finish as

MAY FLY CALENDAR
PROBABLE DAYS OF EMERGENCE

SIZE	MAY FLY	Apr 18	Apr 19	Apr 20	Apr 21	Apr 25	Apr 26	May 8	May 9	May 10	May 13	May 14	May 15	May 16	May 18	May 19	May 20	May 21	May 22	May 24	May 25	May 26	May 27	May 28	May 29	May 30	May 31	Jun 1	Jun 2	Jun 18	Jun 19	Jun 20	Jun 21	Jun 25	Jun 26	Jun 27	Jul 1	Jul 2	Jul 3
14	Blue Quill-dun	X	X	X																																			
14	Blue Quill-spinner		X	X																																			
12, 14	Red Quill-dun			X	X	X																																	
14	Red Quill-spinner			X	X	X																																	
16	Pale Olive Q.-dun							X	X	X																													
16	Pale Olive Q.-spin.								X	X																													
14	Black Quill-dun										X	X	X																										
14	Black Quill-spinner											X	X	X																									
10	Light Cahill-dun												X	X																									
12	Light Cahill-spin.												X	X																									
12, 10	March Brown-dun														X	X	X																						
12, 10	March Brown-spin.														X	X	X	X																					
14	Pale Evening Dun															X	X	X																					
14	Pale Evening Spin.																X	X																					
8	Brown Drake-dun																X	X	X																				
8	Brown Drake-spin.																	X	X																				
16	Olive Dun																		X	X	X																		
16	Olive Spinner																			X	X	X																	
8	Green Drake-dun																				X	X	X	X															
10	Grn.Dr.Sp.(blk) M*																					X	X	X	X														
8	Grn.Dr.Sp.(gry) F**																				X	X	X																
12	Ginger Quill-dun																				X	X	X																
12	Ginger Quill-spin																						X	X	X														
16	Iron Blue Dun																						X	X	X														
16	Iron Blue Spin.																								X	X	X												
12	Brown Quill-dun																									X	X	X											
12	Brown Quill Spin.																										X	X	X										
12	June Drake-dun																													X	X	X							
12	June Drake-spin.																														X	X	X						
10	Yellow May-dun																															X	X	X					
12	Yellow May-spin.																																	X	X	X			
10	Yellow Drake-dun																																				X	X	X
12	Yellow Drake-spin.																																				X	X	X

* Male   ** Female

usual. These two single turns of hackle add much to the appearance of the fly. When large drakes are returning to the water surface, flies with these extra long fibers will prove exceptionally good.

Tails of May-fly spinners are usually much longer than the tails of duns. The Gray and Black Drakes, for example, have very long tails.

MAY FLIES—Group 1

NAME	USUAL EMERGENCE	SIZE
Black Quill	early May through June	14
Iron Blue	late May	16
Brown Quill	late May	12
Pale Olive Quill	early May	16

The nymphs of these four May flies are approximately one-half inch or less in length and are abundant in water adjoining riffles. The body is roundish and slender, gray-green and olive-brown with yellow-gray to olive legs; the tails are yellowish or yellow-olive.

BLACK QUILL

The Black Quill is one of the first of the May flies to appear each year. It is the prototype for many of the black, blue-black, and gray-brown artificials. It is entirely possible that this insect is often mistaken for the Iron Blues. Although its name would indicate a black color, the insect is really a dark brown with very dark gray-brown areas.

The *dun* emerges during the first days of May and continues to emerge throughout June. The body is dark smoky brown with blackish rings. The tails are also smoky brown with grayish joints. The wings are dark smoky blue-gray; the legs dark smoky brown.

The *spinner* comes into existence after the molting of the dun. Black Quills in this stage are often over the water quite some time before evening, which is a little unusual for May flies as a rule. After the final transformation the wings become glassy, a characteristic of the majority of most of the May-fly spinners, and are now lighter in color with a faint purplish cast. The body has become a ruddy brown with brown rings, the tails a ruddy brown with dark brown joints, and the legs a dull, dark brown with faint rings of a darker hue.

RECOMMENDED DRESSINGS

DUN: *Wings,* dark gray duck. *Hackle,* natural (not dyed) black. *Body,* quill stripped from dark brown turkey quill. *Tails,* coch-y-bondhu hackle fibers.

SPINNER: *Wings,* gray duck. *Hackle,* coch-y-bondhu hackle fibers. *Body,* dark peacock herl quill. *Tails,* guinea fibers dyed dark brown.

REASONABLE IMITATIONS

DUN: commercial Black Quill, Iron Blue Dun (male), silk body Black Gnat.
SPINNER: Quill Gordon.

IRON BLUE

There are perhaps as many variations of the Iron Blue as there are iron blues in your favorite stream. Fly-makers make this fly in shades from light brown to near black. Actually, few imitations even remotely resemble the natural insect. One can purchase Iron Blues from several fly-dressers and be equipped with enough varieties to meet most fishing conditions. The Iron Blue is as necessary to the fly-box as tobacco is to your pipe; therefore, its colors should be known.

The *male dun* emerges during the latter part of May (although this schedule is variable with certain streams) and is transformed into the spinner within two days. The body is a dark grayish-olive, the wings dark grayish-blue, the legs and tails dark blackish-brown.

The *female dun* is very similar except that its body has a purplish-brown cast. Once you have seen this fly taken by trout, you will never forget the pattern.

The *male spinner* has clear wings with a cinnamon tinge near the front, an ivory body with a ruddy brown tip, ruddy, olive-brown legs, and ivory tails with faint cinnamon overcast. This is most popularly known as the jenny spinner.

The *female spinner* has clear wings sometimes suffused with a pale bluish cast, a pinkish-brown body, grayish-brown legs, and cinnamon tails with whitish areas.

It is interesting to note that Theakston called the iron blue spinner (male) the Pearl Drake, a seemingly appropriate name.

RECOMMENDED DRESSINGS

DUN (male): *Wings,* dark gray-blue, preferably coot. *Hackle,* grizzly dyed dark brown. *Body,* dark gray and olive dubbing mixed. *Tails,* mixed fibers of brown and iron blue hackle fibers.

DUN (female): *Wings,* hackle and tails same as the male. *Body,* dark brown and purple dubbing mixed.

SPINNER (male): *Wings,* palest gray mallard. *Hackle,* pale olive brown. *Body,* white porcupine quill, ruddy-brown floss tip (narrow). *Tails,* palest wood-duck breast.

SPINNER (female): *Wings,* palest gray mallard dyed a very pale blue. *Hackle,* pale grizzly dyed light brown. *Body,* raffia dyed a pinkish tan (pink predominating). *Tails,* palest wood duck breast.

REASONABLE IMITATIONS

DUN: Dark Whirling Blue Dun, Dark Cahill, Dark Olive Dun, Iron Blue Quill, Adams; Sherry Spinner for male only.

SPINNER: Jenny Spinner, Whitechurch Dun, plain body male Beaverkill.

BROWN QUILL

There is a possibility that this May fly is sometimes mistaken for the dark ginger quill which it noticeably resembles. The commercially named Dark Ginger Quill, if correctly tied with dark ginger hackle, is a fairly good imitation.

The *dun* appears during the last of May and is somber brown with gray wings mottled with brownish areas. The body is dull brown, the tails and legs grayish with fine cinnamon rings.

The *male spinner* suggests the Mallard Quill, Dark Ginger Quill, Cahill Quill and others of similar appearance. The wings are clear with a faint cream cast, the legs are ruddy tan, the body bright cinnamon with brown rings, the tails cinnamon with brown rings.

The *female spinner* is unmistakable because of the olive-yellow sac of eggs carried near the tip of the abdomen. This feature is generally seen in the imitations representing the fly, hence such names as "the Green Egg Sac" and "Green Tip."

RECOMMENDED DRESSINGS

DUN: *Wings,* wood duck breast. *Hackle,* grizzly dyed brown. *Body,* peacock (herl) quill—not light and dark striped. *Tails,* wood duck breast.

SPINNER (male): *Wings,* Cinnamon (pale) duck. *Hackle,* ruddy ginger. *Body,* Raffia dyed cinnamon. *Tails,* dark wood-duck breast.

SPINNER (female): *Wings,* palest gray mallard. *Hackle,* grizzly dyed ginger. *Body,* peacock (herl) quill, not light and dark striped—with olive-green chenille egg sac. *Tails,* wood duck breast.

REASONABLE IMITATIONS

DUN: Dark Cahill, Dark Cahill Quill, Mallard Quill.
SPINNER: Dark Ginger Quill, Cahill Quill.

PALE OLIVE QUILL

This is another early May fly which usually appears simultaneously with the black quill. It is frequently found in swarms flying low over the shallows.

The *dun* emerges very early in May and is characterized by its small size and pale, almost neutral color. The wings are dull, light gray, the body olive with slightly darker rings, the tails and legs olive again with somewhat darker olive rings.

The *spinner* is slightly lighter in color than the dun, having clear wings, lemon-yellow legs and an olive-yellow body. The tails are brownish with a lemon cast.

RECOMMENDED DRESSINGS

DUN: *Wings,* pale gray duck. *Hackle,* grizzly dyed olive (light). *Body,* raffia dyed yellow-olive. *Tails,* pale gray mallard dyed olive (light).

SPINNER: *Wings,* pale gray mallard. *Hackle,* lemon. *Body,* pale olive raffia. *Tails,* pale-gray mallard dyed lemon.

REASONABLE IMITATIONS

DUN: Watery Dun.
SPINNER: Pale Watery Dun, Pale Olive Dun, Apple Green.

MAY FLIES—Group 2

NAME	USUAL EMERGENCE	SIZE
Ginger Quill	Middle of May	12
March Brown	Middle of May	10
Light Cahill	Middle of May	10, 12

The nymphs from which the adult Ginger Quill, March Brown and Light Cahill come are so similar in all respects that it requires very close examination to determine the slight differences in each. This nymph is a hardy creature and is capable of living comfortably in the fastest waters. Its body is flattened to facilitate movement against the current. Abundant in riffles where it can be captured in a fine-mesh net, this nymph can be recognized by its brownish body with dark rings, and three tails of rusty-brown color. The belly is straw color and the legs are deep yellow mottled with dark brown.

GINGER QUILL

The *dun* can be expected to emerge from its nymphal case near the middle of May. The wings are ruddy gray with indistinct mottlings of a dark brown color, the body ruddy tan with brown rings, the legs and tails ruddy tan.

The *spinner* appears approximately two days after the emergence of the dun. At sundown these beautiful spinners can be seen in unbelievably large swarms during their mating flight. Transformation has caused the heavy, dark wings to become clear with faint tinges of pink near the front. The legs are now a bright, ruddy tan with brown rings, the body is also ruddy tan with darker rings, and the tails cinnamon with tan speckles. The female is lighter, having a body quite yellowish on the underside. The egg sac is bright yellow.

RECOMMENDED DRESSINGS

DUN: *Wings,* wood duck breast. *Hackle,* dark ginger. *Body,* raffia dyed ruddy tan. *Tails,* wood duck breast.
SPINNER (male): *Wings,* palest gray mallard. *Hackle,* light ginger and pale grizzly mixed. *Body,* peacock-eye quill. *Tails,* pale wood-duck breast.
SPINNER (female): *Wings,* palest gray mallard. *Hackle,* light ginger. *Body,* peacock-eye quill dyed palest cream-yellow. *Tails,* light ginger.

REASONABLE IMITATIONS

DUN: Cahill Quill, Light Hendrickson.
SPINNER: Light Cahill Quill, Light Cahill, Golden Spinner.

MARCH BROWN

A complete book could be written on the March Brown. As it is, no other fly has been afforded more attention in angling literature. Early English fishing authors wrote of it and expounded theories on its metamorphosis, variously terming it the great brown, dun drake, red drake, amber drake, and brown drake. The influence of Michael Theakston is responsible for the apparently correct names "March Brown" for the *sub-imago* (dun) and "Red Drake" for the *imago* (spinner). However, the name "Great Red Spinner" has become more popular through the years for the imago and for this reason is recognized by most authorities. The March brown has had applied to it several series of names, one of the most interesting of these being the "mackerel" group. At one time, years ago, the sub-imago (March brown) was known as the dark mackerel and the imago (great red spinner) as the light mackerel. Speculation as to the possible association of the word "mackerel" with the insect has been widespread, although no satisfactory explanation for using this peculiar name has ever resulted.

As a dry or wet fly, the March Brown is a standard requirement on nearly all trout streams. Certain large salmon flies have been designed in accord with its color combinations and, while they do not represent the natural insect because of their large size, they do, however, prove the effectiveness of the colors of the March Brown.

The *nymph* is very similar to the nymph of the Ginger Quill but the tails are slightly darker. The same rusty-brown tone is apparent.

The *dun* (March brown) emerges simultaneously with the dun of the Ginger Quill but is a little darker in appearance. The wings are mottled grayish-brown, distinctly marked, the legs are brownish with brownish-black rings, the back is brown and the belly is ruddy brown with light rings. The tails are dark reddish-brown.

The *spinner* (great red spinner) is often called the Red Drake. Most of the other names it has borne from time to time have been forgotten. This spinner usually sheds its sub-imago case the same day the insect emerges as a dun. The females deposit their eggs a few at a time by dipping and rising repeatedly over the water surface. Trout are ever mindful of the great red spinner when it is available and will take it boldly. The wings are clear with an indistinct brown color along the front edge, the legs are brown with dark brown rings, the body is reddish-brown on the back and ruddy-brown below, and the tails are dark ruddy brown.

RECOMMENDED DRESSINGS

DUN: *Wings,* dark wood duck or preferably brown mallard. *Hackle,* grizzly dyed brown, or brown and grizzly mixed. *Body,* raffia dyed brown counterwound with yellow thread. *Tails,* brown mallard.

SPINNER: *Wings,* gray mallard. *Hackle,* grizzly dyed brown. *Body,* red-brown fox fur dubbing. *Tails,* dark red-brown.

REASONABLE IMITATIONS

DUN: Dark Cahill, Dark Ginger Quill, Hare's Ear.

SPINNER: Great Red Dun, Red Quill, Red Spinner, Red Upright.

LIGHT CAHILL

The Light Cahill is one of the most needed flies in eastern and some mid-western waters. When these large May flies start to emerge the trout usually spring into action to gorge themselves on the light, fluttering insects. This has been one of the "standard" dry flies for many years.

The *dun* and *spinner* are similar. If any difference exists it is merely the additional brilliance of the spinner as compared with the more subdued hues of the dun. The wings are ruddy cream with faint brownish checks, the legs light ginger with slightly darker areas at the base, the body light grayish-cream, the tails ruddy cream with faint ginger spots.

RECOMMENDED DRESSINGS

DUN: *Wings,* wood-duck breast. *Hackle,* pale grizzly dyed cream-buff. *Body,* ruddy cream dubbing. *Tails,* wood-duck breast.

SPINNER: *Wings,* palest wood-duck breast. *Hackle,* pale cream-ginger. *Body,* light ruddy-cream fox fur dubbing. *Tails,* palest wood-duck breast.

REASONABLE IMITATIONS

DUN and *SPINNER*: Little Marryat, Light Hendrickson, Flight's Fancy.

MAY FLIES—Group 3

NAME	USUAL EMERGENCE	SIZE
Pale Evening Dun	Throughout May and early June	14
Olive Dun	Late May	16

The nymphs of the Pale Evening Dun and the Olive Dun are small, inhabit quiet sections of the stream and are more seclusive than most nymphs of Ephemeroptera. Their general coloration is olive to brownish-olive with light olive legs mottled with still lighter areas. The tails are somewhat shorter than the tails of other May-fly nymphs of proportionate size and are dark brownish-olive.

PALE EVENING DUN

The *dun* is a well-known fly, but, like most other imitations of May flies, is dressed variously. Variations range from near white to gray and green, and while various dressings may be effective at various times, it seems unnecessary to mention that all of them cannot represent the prototype. At this stage, the natural fly is characterized by light gray wings with a faint olive cast, a pale yellow-olive body, very pale gray legs and tails.

The *spinner* is that small, ivory and yellow fly that makes trout become so selective at times. Although the trout will always surface eagerly for this small insect, they are often contemptuous of the best imitations. The wings are glassy clear with a slight ivory cast along the edge and the body is a rich cream yellow. The legs are pale yellow and the tails are ivory.

The *female* spinner is very similar to the already-described male, except that the body is somewhat brighter; its color is golden yellow. The egg sac is cream-white.

RECOMMENDED DRESSINGS

DUN: *Wings,* gray mallard. *Hackle,* pale blue dun. *Body,* pale yellow-olive dubbing. *Tails,* pale blue dun hackle fibers.

SPINNER (male): *Wings,* pale gray mallard breast or natural white duck quill. *Hackle,* palest ivory-cream. *Body,* raffia dyed yellow. *Tails,* ivory-cream hackle whisks.

SPINNER (female): *Wings,* hackle and tails same as the male. *Body,* deeper yellow with cream-white egg sac.

REASONABLE IMITATIONS

DUN: Light Hendrickson.

SPINNER: Little Marryat.

OLIVE DUN

The Olive Dun is an old, popular fly often confused with the Pale Olive Quill. These two flies are not similar but, because each possesses some olive color, are frequently considered one and the same.

The *male dun* has medium gray wings, yellow and gray legs, a brownish-red back with ruddy-brown underside, and olive brown tails.

The *female dun* has olive-gray wings, yellow and gray legs, a brownish-olive back with a tannish-olive underside, and olive-gray tails.

The *male spinner* is considerably lighter than the dun. Its wings are glassy with a faint bluish tinge; its body is light olive with brown rings; legs, light olive; tails, olive with lighter olive rings.

The *female spinner* is quite different in color from the male spinner, in that the body is a bright golden-olive and the egg sac is bright lemon.

RECOMMENDED DRESSINGS

DUN (male): *Wings,* medium gray duck quill. *Hackle,* grizzly dyed pale yellow. *Body,* ruddy-olive dubbing. *Tails,* olive-brown hackle fibers.

DUN (female): *Wings,* white duck quills dyed olive-gray. *Hackle,* grizzly dyed pale olive. *Body,* tannish-olive dubbings. *Tails,* olive-gray hackle fibers.

SPINNER (male): *Wings,* gray mallard dyed palest bluish-gray. *Hackle,* pale olive. *Body,* peacock eye quill dyed olive. *Tails,* gray mallard dyed olive.

SPINNER (female): *Wings,* hackle and tails same as the male. *Body,* raffia dyed golden-olive and lemon egg sac.

REASONABLE IMITATIONS

DUN: Yellow Dun.

SPINNER: Yellow Quill.

MAY FLIES—Group 4

NAME	USUAL EMERGENCE	SIZE
Brown Drake	Late May	8
Green Drake	Late May	8
Yellow Drake	Late June	10

BROWN DRAKE

These large insects emerge from the largest nymphs of the order Ephemeroptera. Some of these nymphs measure well over an inch in length, and will average close to 1¼ inches. These are the burrowing nymphs which conceal themselves in the soft parts of the stream bottom. Naturally their equipment for tunneling in addition to their size is a good key to identification. Their long jaws, broad legs and fringed tails leave them unmistakable. Invariably they frequent placid waters and it is from such places that the huge sub-imago will flutter vertically into the air. The nymph body is a dull, pale gray and the legs and tails are whitish with faint cinnamon cast.

The *dun* is cause for disagreement among authorities on fishing flies and has been labeled with many names which frequently have no connection with the "natural" or its characteristics. Perhaps the most logical name is the Brown Drake, since that is what it is called in its final stage. The wings are large and brownish-olive, the body mustard color slightly lighter in the belly. The legs are mustard and the tails are ruddy brown with dark rings.

The *spinner* is the true Brown Drake and usually sheds its sub-imago case after a day or two. In size it parallels the dun except that the tails are longer. The wings are bright brown mottled with dark brown areas. The body is reddish brown with cinnamon colored rings. The legs are cinnamon and the tails are reddish brown with darker mottlings.

RECOMMENDED DRESSINGS

DUN: *Wings,* gray mallard dyed brownish-olive. *Hackle,* grizzly dyed mustard. *Body,* mustard dubbing. *Tails,* dark wood duck.

SPINNER: *Wings,* dark wood duck or brown mallard. *Hackle,* dark ginger. *Body,* raffia dyed reddish brown counterwound with tan thread. *Tails,* brown mallard.

REASONABLE IMITATIONS

DUN and *SPINNER*: Brown Drake seems the only close imitation.

GREEN DRAKE

The Green Drake has long been the cause for wide divergence of opinion among anglers concerning its identity especially in relation to the imago or spinner stage. For this reason, the majority of angling and scientific volumes treating of this large May fly have identified the insect as the Green Drake, its most popular name, and the correct one of the dun stage, to avoid confusion as much as possible. In this instance, the popular names for the male and female spinner at least have some visible relationship to the color of the natural, which is more than can be said for most names given natural insects.

Not all anglers know that the Green Drake is the sub-imago (dun), the Gray Drake the female spinner and the Black Drake the male spinner (both imagoes).

It is interesting to know that the Green Drake figured largely in the first transplanting of ephemeral insects. Taking nymphs from a well-supplied stream and stocking them in waters where these insects were perhaps few or even wholly absent has been done for many years. Mr. A. Nelson Cheney, state fish culturist for the State of New York, referred to this practice before the twentieth century, writing at length in the publications of that day about his successes. He captured the insects as they emerged from the water and placed them in small tins into which small holes had been punched to admit air. Incidentally, from his observations, Mr. Cheney discovered quite inadvertently that some adult May flies live longer than the single day attributed to them by the writers of his day. By this method, the evolution of the Green Drake into the Black or Gray Drake was studied.

Major W. G. Turle, a British angler of merit, performed similar experiments with the Green Drake and later discovered that excellent results could be obtained by capturing the nymphs and relocating them in other parts of the same stream. In one particular account he described that a "hatch" followed in due time, which verified his theory. However, it is probable that eventually the insect returned to those stream areas to which it was more physically suited and which it would naturally select. Mr. Cheney's plan to improve the insect population of thinly populated streams has been followed for many years with varying degrees of success. The present theories are that natural insects will frequent only those waters to which they are attracted unless, of course, they have been destroyed by pollution, in which case they can be restored to that stream if, and only if, the stream has been cleansed of the pollution.

The *dun* (Green Drake) emerges in late May from quiet pools. It is one of the largest of the May flies and has long, yellow-olive wings with irregular brownish-black areas. The back is brownish-olive with straw-color rings, the belly yellow with an olive cast. The legs are light brownish-olive and the tails are olive.

The *male spinner* (Black Drake) is smaller than the dun and has dark brown wings with a mottled lemon undertone. Sometimes they give the appearance of being purplish. The body is pale cream, the legs lemon with whitish and brown areas, and the tails are dark brown with lighter, rather indistinct rings.

The *female spinner* (Gray Drake) has pale olive wings with dark brownish areas, yellow-olive legs with brown joints, an ivory body, and yellow tails with blackish joints.

RECOMMENDED DRESSINGS

DUN: *Wings*, teal dyed yellow-olive. *Hackle*, yellow-olive. *Body*, yellow-olive dubbing. *Tails*, mallard dyed olive.

SPINNER (male): *Wings*, dark, closely marked teal dyed pale lemon. *Hackle*, grizzly dyed lemon. *Body*, raffia dyed cream. *Tails*, brown mallard.

SPINNER (female): *Wings*, teal dyed pale olive. *Hackle*, grizzly dyed pale olive. *Body*, porcupine quill. *Tails*, badger hackle fibers dyed yellow.

REASONABLE IMITATIONS

DUN: Schuylkill Haven Special, Green Shad Fly, Dark Olive, Large Olive Dun.

SPINNER (male): Coffin Fly.

SPINNER (female): Carpenter, Badger Bivisible.

YELLOW DRAKE

The *dun* of the Yellow Drake has grayish wings with small dark-brown mottling. The body is brownish-gray with brown rings. The legs are brownish with brown rings and the tails are grayish-brown with yellowish-brown rings.

The *spinner* is a bright, light-colored fly, the wings of which are pale yellow with small, indistinct darker areas. The body is cream-white with light brown rings, the legs are cream and the tails yellow with dark brown rings.

RECOMMENDED DRESSINGS

DUN: *Wings*, gray mallard dyed light brown. *Hackle*, grizzly dyed buff. *Body*, peacock-eye quill dyed light brown. *Tails*, wood-duck breast.

SPINNER: *Wings*, gray mallard dyed palest yellow. *Hackle*, cream. *Body*, raffia dyed cream-white counterwound with light-brown thread. *Tails*, wood-duck breast.

REASONABLE IMITATIONS

DUN: Golden Spinner.

SPINNER: Light Cahill.

MAY FLIES—Group 5

NAME	USUAL EMERGENCE	SIZE
Red Quill	Late April	12
Blue Quill	Mid-April	12, 14

The nymphs of the Red and Blue Quills are flat, two-tailed and rather small, seldom exceeding ⅜ of an inch in length. The Red Quill nymph is a dull mustard color with darker, reddish areas and has ringed brownish tails. The nymph of the Blue Quill is very similar but has a gray body with brownish areas; the tails are grayish-brown.

RED QUILL

The *dun* of the Red Quill emerges on bright days in late April and easily could be mistaken for a small Ginger Quill. However, from a distance the insect appears quite reddish in color. The wings are cinnamon with slightly darker, irregular areas, the body smoky red-brown, and the tails and legs are grayish-brown.

This is an old, well-known fly, having had dozens of other names at one time or another. One of the most common of these some years ago was the Brown Caughlan, a name of Irish vintage.

The *spinner* invariably appears during the early evening of the same day the dun emerges. It is considerably brighter in this stage and can be recognized by its rich red body. The wings are glassy with a faint grayish cast. The body is reddish, the legs cinnamon, and the tails deep red-brown with light brown rings.

RECOMMENDED DRESSINGS

DUN: *Wings,* wood duck. *Hackle,* grizzly dyed brown. *Body,* peacock-eye quill dyed dull red. *Tails,* grizzly hackle fibers dyed brown.
SPINNER: *Wings,* pale gray mallard. *Hackle,* cinnamon brown. *Body,* raffia dyed dull red. *Tails,* brown mallard.

REASONABLE IMITATIONS

DUN: Dills Choice, Brown Hackle Red.
SPINNER: King of Waters.

BLUE QUILL

The Blue Quill is a perfect example of an insect offering a deceptive color to the fisherman. When viewed from above the Blue Quill is reasonably bluish and seems to be in keeping with its name. However, from the trout's viewpoint, especially in the case of a floating fly, the Blue Quill is anything but blue and is, as a matter of fact, on the ruddy side. Fishermen argue for hours about the exact shade of the hackle and body for the imitation but, at the same time, often fail to realize that the upper side of the fly *they* see is not at all like the underside the *trout* sees. Consequently, the Blue Quill should really be considered a fly having bluish wings but a two-color body.

The *dun* to some degree resembles the Olive Dun. Its wings are medium blue-gray with an olive undertone, especially in sunlight, its legs are dull brownish-gray; the body is bluish gray on the back and pewter color on the underside; the tails are pewter with brownish flecks.

The *male spinner* is appreciably brighter in appearance, having dark blue-gray wings, smoky-gray and brownish legs, a ruddy brown body with a darker brown back, and two dark bluish-gray tails.

The *female spinner* is very similar to the male but generally lighter throughout. The wings are blue-gray (more bluish than the male's), the legs smoky gray with little if any brown, the body ruddy buff with a brown back, and the tails medium blue-gray.

RECOMMENDED DRESSINGS

DUN: *Wings,* medium-gray duck quill. *Hackle,* dull blue gray. *Body,* pale blue-gray dubbing. *Tails,* gray mallard dyed pale-blue dun.

SPINNER (male): *Wings,* gray mallard dyed slate, or coot quill. *Hackle,* mixed blue dun and dark ginger. *Body,* peacock herl quill (not eye quill) dyed dull reddish. *Tails,* blue dun hackle whisks.

SPINNER (female): *Wings,* gray mallard dyed slightly brighter blue than male's. *Hackle,* blue dun. *Body,* peacock herl quill (not eye quill). *Tails,* blue dun hackle whisks.

REASONABLE IMITATIONS

DUN: Blue Dun, Hendrickson.
SPINNER: Quill Gordon, Blue Upright.

MAY FLIES—Group 6

NAME	USUAL EMERGENCE	SIZE
June Drake	Late June	12

The nymph of this fairly large May fly is easily recognized by its humped back and large eyes. The average length is between ½ and ¾ of an inch. These nymphs are generally found in swift water and, being hardy, are well adapted to it. The general color scheme is rusty brown with some lighter amber flecks on the forelegs. The belly is reddish with lighter rings.

JUNE DRAKE

The *dun* of the June Drake emerges during the last days of June and immediately flies toward the bushes lining the stream. It usually reappears as the spinner during the evening of the same day, frequently after darkness has settled. The wings are dark grayish-brown, the legs reddish tan, the body brownish-gray, the tails dark grayish-brown

The *spinner* is so similar to the Light Cahill as to make that imitation ideal. At this stage, the June Drake returns to the riffles sometime after sundown. The wings are clear with the slightest undertone of very pale blue, the legs cream with a brownish cast on the front side of the front pair of legs only, the body ruddy brown with a darker brown back, the tails cream white with some cinnamon at the base.

RECOMMENDED DRESSINGS

DUN: *Wings,* gray mallard dyed brown. *Hackle,* bright ginger or light natural red. *Body,* brown and gray dubbing mixed. *Tails,* gray mallard dyed brown.

SPINNER: *Wings,* palest gray mallard. *Hackle,* cream with one turn of brown in front. *Body,* ruddy-gray fox fur dubbing. *Tails,* wood-duck breast.

REASONABLE IMITATIONS

DUN: Whirling Dun, Dark Cahill.

SPINNER: Golden Spinner, Light Cahill.

MAY FLIES—Group 7

NAME	USUAL EMERGENCE	SIZE
Yellow May	late June, early July	· 10

Despite the many yellow flies attributed to the order Ephemeroptera and called "Yellow Mays" by their designers, there is actually only one May fly of yellowish color that might properly be named the Yellow May or more appropriately, perhaps, the Yellow June, due to the time of its appearance. It is a pretty insect and presents a bright spot in the night air. Being generally a nocturnal insect, the Yellow May is seldom seen during the daytime hours.

The *dun* is a dull-yellow insect resembling the Light Cahill artificial. The wings are light gray with a faint yellowish tinge, the body grayish-yellow, the legs a dull tan, the tails brownish with yellow mottlings.

The *male spinner* has clear wings with a very pale lemon cast along the upper front edge, the legs cream with yellow markings at the base, the body rich cream with light brown rings, the tails yellowish with light brown markings.

The *female spinner* differs from the male in having true yellow wings and being slightly larger, which is typical in the case of most May flies.

RECOMMENDED DRESSINGS

DUN: *Wings,* pale-gray mallard dyed palest yellow. *Hackle,* tan ginger. *Body,* gray and yellow dubbing mixed. *Tails,* wood-duck breast.

SPINNER (male): *Wings,* pale-gray mallard dyed palest yellow. *Hackle,* cream ginger. *Body,* cream-yellow raffia counterwound with light brown thread. *Tails,* pale gray mallard dyed yellow.

SPINNER (female): *Wings,* white duck quill dyed true yellow. *Hackle, body,* and *tails* same as male's.

REASONABLE IMITATIONS

Actual copy preferred although certain pale-yellow flies will work satisfactorily.

PLECOPTERA

NAME SOURCE: "Plecos," folded; and "pteron," wing.

PHASES: Two (nymph and adult).

RECOGNITION FEATURES:

Nymph: Paired claws on each foot; clings upside down to bottoms of rocks; two long bristly tails; mottled coloration—sometimes brilliant yellow and black.

Adult: Two pairs of wings folded flat (horizontally) over back when at rest; awkward in flight; heavily veined wings; antennae.

ANGLERS' NAMES: Stone fly, perlid, willow, sallie, yellow sally, creeper, curler, water cricket, jack.

The stone fly has been fashioned out of feathers, wool and quill for many years, although it is amazing how so many different dressings can apply to a single insect. Perhaps this may be due to the probability that the fly-dressers who first made the

STONEFLY CALENDAR

Size	Species	__APRIL__										__MAY__																				__JUNE__
		14	15	16	17	18	19	20	28	29	30	1	2	3	13	14	15	16	18	19	20	21	22	23	24	25	26	27	28	29	30	
16	Black Stonefly	X	X	X	X	X	X	X																								
10	Light Stonefly								X	X	X	X	X	X																		
8	Dark Stonefly														X	X	X	X														
14	Yellow Stonefly																		X	X	X	X										
14	Green Stonefly																						X	X	X	X						
14	Brown Stonefly																										X	X	X	X	X	

CADDIS FLY CALENDAR
Probable Days of Emergence

Size	Species	_APRIL_					__MAY__																_JUNE_									_JULY_				
		25	26	27	28	29	4	5	6	7	8	14	15	16	17	18	26	27	28	29	30	31	1	2	3	4	16	27	28	29	30	1	2	3	4	5
18, 16	Black Caddis	X	X	X	X	X																														
10	Grannom						X	X	X	X	X																									
14	Spotted Sedge											X	X	X	X	X																				
12	Green Caddis																X	X	X	X	X															
12	Blue Sedge																	X	X	X	X	X	X													
8	Brown Sedge																										X	X	X	X	X					
12, 14	White Caddis																															X	X	X	X	X

conflicting patterns may not have been concerned with *what* stone fly they were attempting to copy. This is not meant to be a reflection on the fly-dressers. They have contributed too much to fishing-fly lore to be criticized for not having known the endless subdivisions of insect families. However there has always been a problem in connection with the naming of flies. For example, a certain stone fly may emerge from any stream of water and be copied successfully by a fly-maker as accurately as possible and duly labeled "stone fly." Its efficacy may prompt widespread adaptations among commercial and individual manufacturers alike. Naturally these will also be labeled "stone fly," but which one? Fly dictionaries are far from standard at this time, and there are no less than ten different dressings for a stone fly. For this reason I have here described the stone flies according to their predominating colors, which, from the angler's viewpoint, makes identification reasonable and logical. Aliases are shown for the purpose of associating information found in other sources with the descriptions in this text, therefore making summation of all pertinent facts easy and definite.

Stone flies are of retiring habits and to many fishermen their activities in the adult phase remain mysterious. The average fisherman could fish for several seasons and seldom see an adult stone fly, mainly because stone flies are nocturnal insects. The nymphs, however, are extremely common to nearly all fast-running streams and their nymphal skins can be found dried and deserted on rocks and on branches of low bushes. These brittle cases are sometimes over 2 inches long, which alone is a good indication of the size and consequent food value of these nymphs. I have seen these cases clinging to objects projecting only a fractional part of an inch out of the water.

Stone-fly nymphs of some genera are strikingly figured and colored. Others range in color from solid straw to brown. The coloration of the adults is nearly always a flat hue: pale green, flat yellow, black, brown and gray. The adults are slow and awkward in flight.

SPECIAL FEATURES

Artificial stone flies should be dressed with flat (horizontal) wings, two short tails and two comparatively long antennae. The two bristly tails peculiar to the nymph can be simulated with the use of two hackle feathers from which all fibers have been stripped. The remaining quill stem will be of sufficient stiffness but at the same time elastic enough not to resist the strike of a fish.

Since stone flies have flat wings, they are not imitated well by the majority of dry flies having upright or spent-wings. Therefore it is advisable to use only those imitations dressed with down-wings or, especially, flat-wings.

PHASE 1: As is characteristic of the other two-phase insects, nymphs of stone flies are quite similar to their respective adults in physical appearance. These insects are mainly inhabitants of mountain streams and cold, clear, well-aerated rivers. They have hardy bodies and average ¾ of an inch in length. It is not uncommon to find stone-fly nymphs in company with May-fly nymphs. The majority are brightly figured in yellow and black or yellow and brown, although several are similarly figured but in green and olive. These insects are partial to the under surfaces of rocks where they cling upside down with their legs straddled. They are two-tailed and have antennae approximately twice the length of the tails. The feet are armed with paired claws which, in themselves, are an excellent key to identification and a means of differentiating between stone-fly and May-fly nymphs, since May-fly nymphs have but one claw on each foot. Wing pads are present. Doubtless every angler who has seined for hellgramites has captured many of these nymphs.

Identification is not difficult. Their location under the stones and their upside-down position are fundamental characteristics. Then the sight of their flattened legs, two long, bristly tails, their feet equipped with paired claws and their stout, husky bodies should leave little doubt as to their identity. The color alone is not entirely reliable for forming a basis of recognition except in the case of the yellow and black or dark-brown figured nymphs. These are unmistakable. However, straw-to-dark nymphs of solid color should be examined further before identification can be positive and the only single, reliable characteristic feature is the paired claws.

After one or two years the nymph becomes fully developed and leaves the water to crawl upon the exposed surfaces of a rock or piece of brush. Then it will emerge from the nymphal case, a dull-hued adult stone fly. This process usually occurs after nightfall.

PHASE 2: The adult is an awkward flier and its flight has an aimless quality. When at rest its wings are folded flat over its body. They are noticeably lined with heavy veins, and extend a little beyond the tip of the abdomen. The head is flattened, the body and wings are hairless, and the antennae are long and straight. Usually there are two short tails present. The males are smaller than the females, a condition which prevails among nearly all of the aquatic insects. Coloration ranges from pale straw to black.

In many regions adult stone flies are of little if any interest at all to fish and consequently to fisherman, since they are less available than their nymphal forms. The yellow-sally stone fly is sometimes an exception, in that it may appear in swarms at dusk if the weather has been hot and humid. The adult female of certain species will submerge to lay her eggs, showing conclusively that flat-wing wet flies have a place in every angler's fly-book.

One adult stone fly is especially important, however. This is the "salmon fly" of Western waters whose nymph is the "big curler." Dr. Paul R. Needham, one of our most eminent zoologists, who checked the technical data in this chapter, states that trout gorge themselves on this adult stone fly during the times of its heavy emergence. Being a large insect of around 2 inches in length, it interests trout to the exclusion of other food sources while it is in evidence.

Don Harger, master fly-maker of Salem, Oregon, considers this particular stone fly very important from the angler's viewpoint. He writes, "It is strictly a special fly and is effective only during the May and early June hatch of these big bugs. At times one can see thousands of them in the air along the Deschutes, Crooked and Metolius Rivers. During that period when they are hatching it is almost useless to use anything else. Once the hatch is over the fly is just so much plunder in the fly-box until the following season. Anyone planning an early season trip to the west should have a few of them."

STONE FLIES

NAME	USUAL EMERGENCE	SIZE
Dark stone fly	Mid-May	8
Green stone fly	Mid-June	14
Light stone fly	Early May	10
Brown stone fly	Late June	14

| Black stone fly | Mid- April | 16 |
| Yellow stone fly | Late June | 14 |

DARK STONE FLY

The *nymph* of the dark stone fly is one of the most common of all nymphs of this order. This insect inhabits riffles, lying sprawled out on the bottom side of rocks. The body is flattened as are the legs and the two tail bristles are stiff and clearly marked. The entire body is spotted in yellow and black or dark-brown areas. Averaging 1 inch in length, this insect is large enough to interest any fish.

The *adult* is large in relation to most artificial dry flies. Its wings are translucent brown with a faint yellowish cast and are folded flat over the body when at rest. The body is muddy brown, the legs blackish with amber areas. The tail bristles are brown and the antennae are gray-brown. The adults are often found hidden under foliage bordering the stream but can be picked up readily.

RECOMMENDED DRESSING

ADULT: Wings, brown turkey tied flat. *Hackle,* grizzly dyed light brown. *Body,* gray and brown dubbing mixed. *Tails,* gray mallard dyed brown. Antennae, gray mallard dyed brown.

GREEN STONE FLY

This stone fly is exceptional for the fact that it appears in the daytime. It is the color of pale-green grass, and is considerably smaller than the majority of stone flies. Its food value to trout is perhaps minor but it is fairly abundant.

The *nymph* is an abbreviated version of the dark stone-fly nymph having similar markings but is of greenish instead of yellowish background. It seldom is longer than ¼ of an inch.

The *adult* is small and of pale green coloration.

RECOMMENDED DRESSING

ADULT: Wings, duck-wing quill dyed pale green (not olive) and tied flat. *Hackle,* pale green. *Body,* yellow and green dubbing mixed. *Tails,* pale green. *Antennae,* gray mallard dyed pale green.

LIGHT STONE FLY

The *nymph* of this fly like others of the order frequents those sections of the stream that are well aerated. The body is ½ inch or slightly less in length and straw colored. The legs are yellowish with light brown spots on the joints. The tails and antennae are straw colored.

The *adult,* although it is not frequently seen by the angler, has been known for years to be an important food for trout (reasonably close imitations are most successful at night). Of all the stone flies, this one is the most important from the angler's viewpoint. The wings are yellowish with a faint lemon cast, the body yellowish with a very pale pinkish tinge on the underside. The legs and antennae are muddy brown.

RECOMMENDED DRESSING

ADULT: Wings, gray mallard dyed mustard, tied flat. *Hackle,* brown. *Body,* raffia dyed pale pinkish buff over padding. *Tails,* brown hackle fibers. *Antennae,* brown hackle fibers.

BROWN STONE FLY

Insufficient information available to the author at the time of this writing makes the description of the *nymph* impractical.

The *adult* has translucent brownish wings and the body is dull gray with an amber underside. The legs and antennae are brown.

RECOMMENDED DRESSING

ADULT: *Wings,* gray mallard dyed dark brown, or brown mallard tied flat. *Hackle,* golden badger or light furnace. *Body,* gray and brown dubbing mixed. *Tails,* brown mallard. *Antennae,* brown mallard.

BLACK STONE FLY

Nymphs of the black stone fly are very small and narrow, approximately ½ inch in length or less.

The *adult* is a small, black fly appearing very early in the season. It is found only during the cold days of early spring and it disappears with the approach of the first warmer days. It seems impractical to base artificials on this very small fly for various reasons but mainly because the season is so cold during the emergence of these stone flies that trout are not interested in anything but worms and perhaps minnows. When conditions require a counterfeit any black fly of small size will suffice.

RECOMMENDED DRESSING

ADULT: *Wings,* duck quill dyed black. *Hackle,* darkest grizzly dyed brown. *Body,* raffia dyed blackish brown. *Tails,* black hackle fibers. *Antennae,* black hackle fibers.

YELLOW STONE FLY

The *nymph* is much like the nymph of the light stone fly and likewise is found in riffles under the stones.

The *adult* emerges during the evening hours usually in the summer months. The wings are pale lemon and the body and legs are yellow. The antennae and the tail bristles are ginger with faint, light markings.

RECOMMENDED DRESSING

ADULT: *Wings,* white duck quill dyed yellow-tan. *Hackle,* cream-ginger. *Body,* pale tan fox fur dubbing or raffia dyed tan. *Tails,* wood duck. *Antennae,* wood duck.

TRICHOPTERA

NAME SOURCE: "Trichos," hair; and "pteron," wing.

PHASES: Three (larva, pupa, adult).

RECOGNITION FEATURES:

Larva: Great majority in portable shelters; wormlike.

Pupa: Two oar-like appendages at sides to propel to surface.

Adult: Two pairs of wings finely haired and held tent-like over back when insect is at rest; moth-like; long delicate antennae; tailless.

ANGLERS' NAMES: Caddis Fly, Caddice Fly, Sedge, Grannom, Fish-moth, stickworm, creeper, carpenter, mason, weaver, case-worm, gravel bug.

Caddis flies as larvae are remarkable for their achievements in building stream-bed shelters, and have been aptly called "architects." With uncanny precision they go about their business of making portable houses almost immediately after hatching from the egg and, when the clever device has been finished, crawl into it, leaving only their heads and legs protruding from the front end. Remarkable, too, is the way these houses are constructed. Leaves, twigs, gravel sand, straw or tiny shells, are cemented together by the use of saliva secreted by the larvae.

The worms comprise three kinds; the *Weavers*, which make nets and fasten their "huts" to the tip end of the net, the *Carpenters* which fasten their cases from bits of twigs and straws in a most orderly manner, and the *Masons* which construct their shelters of gravel and sand. These sturdy dwellings are the key means of identification. These shelters are built after a manner peculiar to each type, and although many of the various types may live together—that is, the carpenters, the masons, and the weavers—each of the three kinds will construct its case according to a pattern set by its predecessors. As one would expect, caddis larvae will seek those regions in the stream that will provide each with the materials it needs for constructing its type of shelter. This suggests the reason why certain of the caddis flies will not be found in all parts of the stream.

Caddis larvae are cylindrical and have no tails but have instead two claws for firmly holding their shelter. They are nearly always found in riffles or along the edges of lakes.

PHASE 1: Caddis worms are abundant in nearly all streams where trout exist. It has been said that places where caddis worms will not thrive are not suitable for trout culture. Brook trout especially and brown trout generally are on the move looking for these worms, and it is not an unusual thing to find a trout's stomach filled with gravel and sand, remnants of the shelters.

Doubtless, all anglers have observed the "stick-worms" clustered on the large rocks and logs found in all streams. At times they can be seen milling about, lugging their cumbersome dwellings, although if touched they will withdraw quickly out of sight and depend on their shelter for protection. Those which do not transport their cases, but affix them permanently between rocks, weave a small circular net in front and thus capture their food. Others live in crevices in rocks and need no cases for protection. These forage by extending themselves a little to capture the minute food drifting in the current. Imitations representing this last type are often productive.

PHASE 2: When ready to pupate (a period of rest) the worms fasten their shelters securely to a rock or similar object, seal the ends of the case, and retire for periods varying according to the climate, environment, and nature of the species. During this time they are of no interest to the angler. However, after the period of pupation is over, the pupa cuts the end of the case with nippers, with which it is equipped for this operation, and struggles to reach the water's surface. This activity immediately suggests the efficacy of the wet fly fished in a similar manner, that is, retrieved in erratic jerks. Shortly after the pupa has reached the surface, it sheds its pupal skin and the adult caddis fly appears. Then it flies to the shore with great effort where it will remain hidden until mating time. This is usually a nocturnal process. Aquatic pupation is peculiar to caddis flies only.

PHASE 3: Although there are some exceptions, caddis flies are usually small. A few are large. The majority are seldom longer than ½ inch and have long, delicate antennae which project forward. The wings, as indicated by the word Trichoptera, are covered with fine hair, are four in number and carried tent-like when at rest. The alias, fish moth, is not entirely unfounded, for the adult does resemble a moth. Colors are most frequently dull gray or brown. Like the May flies, they do not take food in the final adult form and are concerned principally with mating.

The female carries her eggs in the form of a sac at the tip of her abdomen and some species submerge to extrude them. Naturally the females are never seen again. It may be surprising to some anglers to know that there does exist an insect which, when egg laden, swims underwater to deposit her eggs. Some years ago I discounted the feasibility of dressing wet flies with egg sacs on the basis that all adult insects were aerial only, but have long since changed my mind after having used the female caddis wet fly tied with a green egg sac. The imitation of the caddis adult female is an important one to the fly-dresser.

It has been presumed by several authorities that the wet fly was first dressed to simulate the female caddis in her underwater venture. Perhaps this is so. However, it seems more likely to me that the anglers of centuries ago observed the myriad aerial flies and copied them as best they could with the materials available, but fished them wet after the habit of using bait for so many years.

SPECIAL FEATURES

Caddis flies and sedges are of dull color. This is due to the hair covering on the wings. Avoid harsh colors. Antennae improve the overall appearance of the imitation. These are sometimes made of material a little too flimsy to retain the natural shape of the antennae. A handy trick is to moisten the first one-third or one-half of the antennae from their base with varnish (not cement), leaving the remaining portion natural. This does improve the antennae and prevents their curling backward.

Caddis flies, like stone flies, are not well imitated by the general run of dry flies. They are a "down-wing" fly and should be dressed in that way. Some anglers have better than average success using bivisibles of the off-shade colors. During low-water season, when the caddis flies and sedges are abundant, a wet fly made buoyant with fly-floating solution will do as well as anything. Of course, it is not suitable for broken water.

Don Harger of Salem, Oregon, ties one of the most natural and beautiful caddis flies ever made. Don calls this the Buck Caddis. Its wings are made of fine deer hair, producing a finely marked, delicate fly. This fly is described in the Fly Pattern section.

CADDIS FLIES

NAME	USUAL EMERGENCE	SIZE
Spotted Sedge	mid-May	14
Black Caddis	late April	18, 16
Green Caddis	late May	12

White Caddis	late June	12, 14
Grannom	early May	10
Brown Caddis	late June	8
Blue Sedge	early June	12

SPOTTED SEDGE

This insect appears in May generally in the evening and can be recognized by its mottled brown and straw colors. It is a small, delicate fly of retiring habits.

The *larva* of the spotted sedge inhabits riffles and the edges of lakes, and is by nature one of the weavers, building a permanent shelter of fine gravel behind an artfully spun web. It remains immediately behind the funnel-shaped net and retreats into the shelter only for protection, since the greatest portion of its life as a larva is spent waiting for food to be swept through the net. Although this worm seldom exceeds 1 inch in length and averages less than half that size, it is, nevertheless, a staple food for trout because of its extremely wide distribution. Incidentally, the spotted sedge larvae, along with the other larvae that weave nets but do not construct portable cases, are excellent patterns to follow in making artificials. The case worms, or those which construct portable cases, are obscured almost entirely by the case.

The period of the spotted sedge's pupation is passed in a case made of fine sand which the larva fabricates shortly before undergoing the transformation.

The emergence of the pupa to the water surface is usually accompanied by violent struggle. It is this stage of the insect that is very tempting to feeding trout.

The spotted sedge *adult* is locally referred to as the brown sedge, cinnamon sedge, the ginger caddis and sometimes the light caddis, but because the wings are so clearly spotted, the name spotted sedge has been chosen in this description purely for its appropriateness to the fisherman. The wings are cinnamon brown and straw mottled, the body a deep yellow, the legs ginger and the antennae cinnamon with indistinct, smoky spots.

RECOMMENDED DRESSING

ADULT: Wings, hen pheasant tied down-wing style. *Hackle,* light furnace. *Body,* raffia dyed buff. *Antennae,* light wood duck.

BLACK CADDIS

One of the earliest insects to appear over the stream in the spring is the black caddis, a very small fly of deep brown and black coloration. It differs from the majority of caddis flies in the respect that it often flies over the water during daytime hours. Another of the net weavers, the *larva* of the black caddis obtains its food by means of a small, fringe-like net of irregular design, in the center of which is spun a tubular net, the home of the worm. The larva, which approximates ¼ to ½ inch in length, is very abundant and easily found on the bottom sides of stones, and is easily recognized by its true yellow color.

The *adult* is small and appears copiously in early spring. Artificials which simulate the adults are really worth while, although any small, blackish dry fly will serve favorably when the trout are rising to pick the naturals from the surface.

Aliases for this insect are few and quite appropriate. Sometimes it is called the black snow fly by reason of its emergence at times when the snow is still clinging to the banks of the stream. It is also erroneously known as the Black Quill, which, of course, it is not.

The wings are very small and delicate, the body is blackish-brown, the legs dark brown and the antennae velvety black.

RECOMMENDED DRESSING

ADULT: *Wings,* duck quill dyed black. *Hackle,* coch-y-bondhu. *Body,* black and dark brown dubbing mixed. *Antennae,* coch-y-bondhu hackle fibers.

GREEN CADDIS

The green caddis is one of the larger flies of the order Trichoptera, and is distinctive in two respects. As a nymph it constructs no shelter at all and roams the stream bottom at will, making itself available to the fish. The adult female, when laden with eggs, instead of dropping her egg string on the water surface, prefers to descend beneath the surface to deposit her eggs wherever she chooses. This activity is interesting to watch. First the female will fly downstream until she has settled on a rock or other object projecting through the water. Then, very nervously, as though loath to perform the suicidal act, she will cautiously approach the water only to scamper back to safety again. This she will repeat several times in rapid succession, until, finally, after hanging on the brink of decision for several seconds, she will disappear into the water.

The *larva* of the green caddis is extremely abundant in swift waters, and can be found under stones. It is readily identified by the bright green color of its body, which averages about ½ inch in length.

Adults occur in late May and into June. It is a simple matter to determine whether they are in season by looking for their congregations on the rocks and logs, at which time a properly fished wet fly of reasonable resemblance to the "natural" will be apt to take trout.

The wings are brownish-gray. The body is a clean, clear green, the legs olive and the antennae ginger.

RECOMMENDED DRESSING

ADULT: *Wings,* dark-brown mottled turkey. *Hackle,* olive. *Body,* raffia dyed grass-green. *Antennae,* dark-ginger hackle fibers.

WHITE CADDIS

The white caddis is strictly nocturnal; therefore many anglers may never have seen one. It is fairly large and conspicuously white with the exception of the body which is green.

The *larva* is one of the masons and constructs its portable case of grains of sand. The case is shaped like a cow's horn and is pointed at the closed end. This caddis larva is partial to the riffles and can be found on the tops of submerged stones in the faster parts of the stream. The worm averages one-half to three-quarters of an inch and is a grayish-green color.

Somewhat like a moth in appearance, the *adult* might be mistaken for such an insect if it were not for the silvery-green body. The wings are a pure white, the body silvery-green, the legs and antennae pale straw.

RECOMMENDED DRESSING

ADULT: *Wings,* white duck quill. *Hackle,* pale badger. *Body,* light-green floss, silver rib. *Antennae,* wood duck.

GRANNOM

The grannom has been known for many years and is still used according to its original pattern. It is a large caddis fly approximating the length of a size 10 hook and somewhat resembles the spotted sedge except for the wings and the size of the fly itself. The grannom is over the water in June, and during the time of its appearance, which is late evening, the trout will surface readily for it.

Larvae of the grannom are indigenous to cold streams and generally prefer headwaters. These are carpenters and fashion twigs and wood fragments into squarish, tapered cases. When the larva has grown to full size it moves toward the strongest part of the current and remains there until ready to pupate. The cases seldom exceed 3/4 of an inch in length.

The wings of the *adult* are dark-brown mottled, the body is medium-brown, the legs and antennae ginger. In this instance the egg sac of the female is green.

RECOMMENDED DRESSING

ADULT: *Wings,* brown mallard or dark wood duck (*without* black tips). *Hackle,* grizzly dyed ginger. *Body,* yellowish-brown dubbing. *Antennae,* wood duck.

BROWN CADDIS

This is the old "stick-worm" known by anglers for many years, and is so named because of the strangely made hut of bits of wood and leaf stems it carries around with it. The cases are large, sometimes 2 inches long, and the larvae are among the largest of all the caddis worms. Naturally the stick-worm is classed as a carpenter. The larvae are slow and can be seen lumbering over the stream bottom during all seasons.

The *adult* is a large insect of brownish color and emerges from the water in late June. The wings are brown, the legs and antennae ginger, the body brownish-yellow. Also known as brown sedge.

RECOMMENDED DRESSING

ADULT: *Wings,* white duck quill dyed reddish-brown. *Hackle,* dark ginger. *Body,* raffia dyed yellow-brown. *Antennae,* natural red-brown hackle fibers.

BLUE SEDGE

The blue sedge is another of the masons, coming from a worm enclosed in a slightly curved case made of sand grains. It is a small and delicate creature more smoky than blue in appearance.

The *larva* has characteristics similar to those of the white caddis including the general shape of its case. It is an inhabitant of riffles.

The *adult* is typical of all caddis flies with its "down-wings" and delicate antennae. The wings are indistinctly mottled with bluish-gray and soft brown, the body is smoky gray, the legs and antennae indistinctly mottled gray and soft brown.

RECOMMENDED DRESSING

ADULT: *Wings*, closely mottled gray turkey quill dyed blue dun. *Hackle*, grizzly dyed blue dun and grizzly dyed brown, mixed. *Body*, raffia dyed pale bluish gray. *Antennae*, gray mallard dyed blue dun.

DIPTERA

NAME SOURCE: "Dis," apart; and "pteron," wing.

PHASES: Three (larva, pupa, and adult).

RECOGNITION FEATURES:

Larva: Large and small, legless, worm-like in appearance; cylindrical.

Pupa: Filamentous gills around head; looks inverted.

Adult: Two wings, narrow and glassy; no tails, legs appear to hang in flight; enlarged thorax; short antennae.

ANGLERS' NAMES: Crane fly, spinner, swale fly, mosquito, midge, fly, deer fly, horse fly, black fly, gnat, bloodworm, waterworm.

A vast number of insects are comprised in this order, some of which are pests such as the mosquito, black fly and gnat. The larvae are so abundant that it is virtually impossible to estimate their worth as a regular part of trout diet. The adult forms are especially important as surface food. Anglers who have seen the aggressiveness of trout when surfacing for the large crane flies, the largest of this order, will attest to this. Certain of the families are wholly aquatic, while others are not. The larvae are quite diversified in physical structure and may be of many colors, white, yellow, red and green predominating. Size is variable as well between but not among the families—an average would probably be between 1 and 2 inches in length. But with all the diversities peculiar to these insects, certain qualities and characteristics indicate unmistakable parallels which serve to identify them. In no other order of aquatic insects are the larvae devoid of legs. This plus the worm-like appearance of their bodies makes them identifiable. In regard to the adults, they are easily recognized by their single pair of wings, their centralized, seemingly swollen thorax and lack of tails. The wings are veined but appreciably narrower than wings of equal length belonging to insects of other orders.

PHASE 1: *Larvae* of this order abound on the stream bottom and are gregarious. Certain of the smaller ones live in delicate tube-like affairs which they construct, and in this connection are similar to caddis flies, although the tiny tubes of dipterous worms are permanent, not portable like those belonging to the caddis larvae. Some are worm-like and cylindrical. Many of these larvae are not suited to fast currents and are found, therefore, in slack waters where they are found living among the leaves, decaying vegetation and trash attendant on such places. Crane-fly larvae are unmistakably large worms without legs.

PHASE 2: The *pupae* are not especially important to the fly-dresser since most pupae are not available to feeding fish except when they struggle to the surface. At this time a long-hackled wet fly representing the adult will perform as well as anything else.

PHASE 3: Many of the *adults* are biting insects such as the deer and horse flies and mosquitoes. They are all two-winged, and have long legs. Most anglers have observed the large crane flies whirling about over pools (hence the name "spinner" which is inconsistent in consideration of the other dipterous flies). Many of these insects emerge about sundown to embark on their mating flight, when it is not unusual to see joined pairs whirling erratically over the pools and flats. Often the largest trout in the stream will surface with a resounding splash to take these long-legged flies.

Imitations of the various midges, crane flies, the mosquito and occasionally the deer and horse flies are most useful artificials. It is entirely probable that the wide-hackle spread dry flies were developed to imitate the long-legged crane fly. A proper counterfeit of the crane fly is temptation enough to make any trout take a chance.

SPECIAL FEATURES

Midges are best imitated with wings tied flat-wing style with a slight V. This simulates the natural position of the insects' wings when they are at rest. Spider-radius hackle helps to create the appearance of sparseness and daintiness typical of midges. Although they tend to sink the fly more quickly, lacquered bodies are lustrous and, therefore, are quite similar to the bodies of the natural.

Crane flies are unmistakably long-legged and spread-winged. Hackle of spider radius and wings tied spent are the two most important features.

Since these flies are tailless, they are not easy to float properly. One means of overcoming the tendency of the fly to sink tail-end first is this: wind two or three turns of stiff spider-radius hackle around the center of the body, the dull side of the feather toward the rear; repeat this immediately behind the eye of the hook but with the dull side of the feather toward the front. This will brace the fly in much the same manner as a saw-horse supports a board.

The shape of the crane-fly body is important enough to try to imitate it. Before the body surface, which usually is floss, is wound, the hook should be built up with wool thread so that the tip is slightly larger than the mid-section. Avoid lumps or irregular surfaces and taper the body as much as possible. For additional lifelikeness the shoulder can be built up to give a slightly bulbous effect.

Crane flies are quite singular in appearance. For this reason faithful imitations of the "naturals" are theoretically the best. However, wide hackle spreads and spiders are effective, being representative more particularly of midges than of crane flies.

There are many spent-wing flies that bear the name "gnat" and, despite the opinions of some fishermen that these flies are in no way similar to the real gnat, they are logically named. The Equinox Gnat, designed by the Orvis people in Manchester, Vermont, is a good example. This fly, according to Mr. C. W. Schafer, former treasurer of the Orvis Co., copied the "natural" which hatched on Equinox Pond, at the foot of Equinox Mountain in Manchester. Today this fly is popularly called the Mosquito, which it really is. The use of the word "gnat" in connection with artificial flies goes back to English nomenclature. Mosquitoes and similar insects are called "gnats" in England. Since most of the flies used in this country were originally of English design, the patterns remained unchanged for many years. Hence the ever-disputed word "gnat" as applied to American artificials.

MIDGES

NAME	USUAL EMERGENCE	SIZE
Green Midge	intermittently	18
Olive Midge	throughout the	16
Black Midge	season	16, 18

GREEN MIDGE

Larvae of the green and the olive midges are cylindrical, yellowish in color and common to pond and stream waters. They construct seemingly flimsy tubes in which they live throughout their aquatic existence as both larva and pupa.

The green midge appears intermittently throughout the season and is minute in size. The wings are glassy with a slight grayish cast and the body is a lustrous, almost metallic, green. The legs are olive.

RECOMMENDED DRESSING

Wings, pale gray duck quill tied flat-wing V shape. *Hackle,* dyed olive. *Body,* green floss.

OLIVE MIDGE

The olive midge is similar to the green midge and may be a variation of it but, because of its frequency and slightly larger size, it is shown here separately. Seasonal appearance is simultaneous with that of the green midge. The wings are glassy, the body pale yellow-olive, the legs dull gray.

RECOMMENDED DRESSING

Wings, pale gray duck quill tied flat-wing V shape. *Hackle,* badger dyed pale yellow. *Body,* gray-green (light) floss.

BLACK MIDGE

The black midge swarms regularly from spring through summer but, fortunately, is not a biting insect. The larvae are the very common "blood worms" of fresh water, deriving their name from the color of their bodies. These worms are less than 1 inch in length and have the characteristics and the habitat of their relatives, the green and olive midges.

The wings of the adult are glassy, the body black, the legs dark brown.

RECOMMENDED DRESSING

ADULT: Wings, pale gray duck quill tied flat-wing V shape. *Hackle,* coch-y-bon-dhu with wide black center. *Body,* black floss.

PUNKIE, GNAT, BLACK FLY

These obnoxious insects are all of a kind in one respect: they should be exterminated. Where they abound, wear a head net, gloves with the finger tips cut out, and smoke vile-smelling tobacco. If they persist, head for the sleeping bag.

CRANE FLIES

NAME	USUAL EMERGENCE	SIZE
Orange Crane Fly	intermittently	8
Dark Olive Crane Fly	throughout the	8
Yellow Crane Fly	season	14, 12
Gray Crane Fly		10
Badger Crane Fly		10

Crane-fly larvae are large legless worms sometimes as long as 2½ to 3 inches. They are partial to backwaters and the slow sections of streams where they live among the trash on the bottom. Their color is a dull, neutral gray except for the heads, which are grayish to muddy brown.

ORANGE CRANE FLY

Like most dipterous flies, this one emerges in the spring and continues to do so sporadically until fall. It is a large insect of orange and amber colors and has extremely long legs. In some sections this fly is known as the orange spinner after its peculiar manner of flying. Nearly all of the crane flies are most abundant in headwaters especially those which emanate from swamps. The wings are glassy, the body light orange, and the legs are amber.

RECOMMENDED DRESSING

ADULT: Wings, dark grizzly hackle tips tied spent-wing. Hackle, light grizzly dyed ginger, spider radius. Body, orange floss made bulbous at the shoulder.

DARK OLIVE CRANE FLY

This crane fly is a near relative of the orange variety and is one of the largest insects to be seen flying over trout waters. In all other respects this fly parallels the orange crane fly with the exception of color. The wings are glassy with a pale-gray undertone; the body and legs are dull olive.

RECOMMENDED DRESSING

ADULT: Wings, dark grizzly hackle tips tied spent-wing. Hackle, grizzly dyed dull olive, spider radius. Body, gray-olive floss made bulbous at the shoulder.

YELLOW CRANE FLY

The larva of this fly is anomalous in that it constructs a case of net-like material which it fastens to stones. It is approximately 1 inch long and greenish-yellow in color. The adult crane fly appears quite regularly throughout the spring and summer months. When sparsely dressed, imitations of correct size and color are very effective. I have often thought that the small lemon-body Light Cahill, which is so successful during early June, is accepted by the trout for the yellow crane fly. It may seem like straining the imagination a little too far to draw this comparison, especially since may flies and crane flies have very little in common. However, it may show the possibilities of using one type of fly for two or more purposes. This insect is smaller than other crane flies, has wings which are glassy clear with a faint lemon undertone, a bright yellow body, and amber legs.

RECOMMENDED DRESSING

ADULT: Wings, pale badger hackle tips or white dyed pale lemon. Hackle, pale cream-ginger. Body, yellow floss made bulbous at the shoulder.

GRAY CRANE FLY

This large insect is similar to the other crane flies but is outstanding for its reddish gray body and blackish thorax and head. The wings are glassy with a gray cast, the body reddish-gray, the legs dark gray with yellow areas.

RECOMMENDED DRESSING

ADULT: *Wings,* glassy-white hackle tips tied spent-wing. *Hackle,* grizzly dyed brown and white mixed. *Body,* black floss made bulbous at the shoulder.

BADGER CRANE FLY

The most unusual feature about this black and white crane fly is its long, slender abdomen, although it is recognizable by its striking white and black coloration. The wings are glassy with a whitish tinge, the body black with a whitish stripe down the back. The legs are grayish brown with white flecks.

RECOMMENDED DRESSING

ADULT: *Wings,* glassy white hackle tips tied spent-wing. *Hackle,* grizzly dyed brown and white mixed. *Body,* black floss made bulbous at the shoulder.

NEUROPTERA

NAME SOURCE: "Neuron," nerve; and "pteron," wing.
PHASES: Three (larva, pupa, and adult).

RECOGNITION FEATURES:

Larva: Flat; leg-like appendages each body segment behind the true three pairs of legs.
Pupa: Unavailable to fish, therefore of little value in regard to imitation.
Adult: Large, clumsy fliers; two pairs of wings heavily veined and held flat over body with a slight separation between them, V shape; tailless; fairly long antennae; head flatter and wider than thorax.
ANGLERS' NAMES: Hellgramite, conniption-bug, devil, clipper, hell-devil, hell-diver, pinch-bug, dobson, bogart, fish fly, alder fly, orl fly.

The hellgramite, fish fly and alder fly are the most important members of this order from the fisherman's standpoint. There are other members which frequent the water surface only occasionally, being blown there by wind, but these are of relatively little value. In a general way it could be said that this order consists of three kinds and sizes of hellgramites. Technically this is not entirely correct, but will serve as a basis of comparison which will benefit the angler. Many anglers think the smaller, red-headed larvae, which look so much like the hellgramite, are that insect. Actually they are the larvae of the fish fly, a slightly smaller creature easily identified by the absence of the whitish tufts at the base of the leg-like appendages characteristic of the hellgramite. The smallest of the three "hellgramites" is the alder fly larva, which seldom exceeds 1 inch in length. This larva is identified by its single tail which replaces the paired claspers at the tip of the body on both the true hellgramite and the fish fly.

HELLGRAMITE GROUP

NAME	USUAL EMERGENCE	SIZE
Hellgramite	late June	2 to 3 inches*

Fish Fly   late May, early June   1½ to 2¼ inches*
Alder Fly   early May   10

* These dimensions are given in inches rather than in hook sizes as in every other case because these flies are so large that it is impractical to express them in terms of hook sizes.

HELLGRAMITE

The hellgramite, the best known aquatic insect because it is so widely used as live-bait, is the largest of all the insects of value to the fisherman. It has few if any equals as a bait for smallmouth bass with the one possible exception of the crayfish or fresh-water "crab." Unfortunately, however, it is becoming thinned out to an alarming degree by fishermen and should be used as sparingly as possible. It would seem that modern methods of artificial lure-making should be helpful in reducing the increasing demand made on the hellgramite, by offering a suitable imitation that would be effective. However, even the most cleverly molded plastic and soft rubber imitations are of little value. Attempts to produce a successful artificial have been many but none of them has been successful.

PHASE 1: The larva is flat, wide, and of dark brownish-black color. The color is slightly variable, however, being greenish at times. This stone-haunting insect prefers riffles and well-aerated water. It is large and menacing in appearance and can puncture your finger with its sharp, pointed "clippers" jutting from its head. Sometimes attaining a size of more than 3 inches, this larva is eagerly taken by trout, bass, and the majority of panfish. It is unmistakable in appearance. It has six legs, which is typical of all insects, behind which are leg-like appendages on each body segment. The tip of the abdomen is terminated in a pair of claspers. As many as three years or more are spent in the larval stage after which the insect enters pupation, thus becoming unavailable to fish during that time.

PHASE 2: The second or pupal phase is of little value to the angler.

PHASE 3: After several weeks have been passed in the pupal stage, the insect is ready to emerge to the surface as a full-fledged flying adult in a manner which, if once seen, is never to be forgotten. Only one time have I ever witnessed a large "hatch of hellgramites. This took place on the Susquehanna River near Laceyville. The air was truly filled with these huge, awkward insects with their wings flapping audibly. Their inadaptability to sustained flight became evident at once, since they seemed willing to alight temporarily on anything on the water large enough to support their weight. They became a nuisance by crawling over my face, neck and hands, and otherwise made fishing so miserable that it was useless to continue. I had handled thousands of the larvae but did not relish the idea of things so large as hellgramites trying to crawl inside my clothing. I did, however, capture several of the male and female insects for examination and sketching.

The outstanding feature of the male adult is the long, curved mandibles projecting from the head. These are actually harmless since they perform the single function of grasping the female which, incidentally, has retained its pinching jaws. The wings are folded flat over the body when the insect is at rest.

FISH FLY

The fish fly is the "little hellgramite" to many anglers. Many believe that fish-fly larvae are half-grown hellgramites. This error is reasonable because the two insects are similar. Fish-fly larvae, however, are somewhat lighter in color than the hellgramites, especially to the rear of the collar.

PHASE 1: Larvae of the fish fly are blackish with a grayish undertone, are approximately 1½ inches long and prefer deeper, more placid water than the hellgramite.

PHASE 2: Pupation of the fish fly compares with that of the hellgramite.

PHASE 3: Fish flies are conspicuous because of a whitish spot approximately midway in the wing showing so plainly. This fly is darker than the hellgramite and is nearly all black, with the exception of the legs which are darkest brown. It frequents brush bordering the stream.

RECOMMENDED DRESSING

ADULT: *Wings*, black and white barred wood duck tied flat. *Hackle*, coch-y-bondhu. *Body*, peacock herl or black dubbing. *Antennae*, coch-y-bondhu.

ALDER FLY

This is the smallest of the three "hellgramites" and can be recognized by its single tail. In other respects it is similar to the fish fly and hellgramite, with the exception that it prefers slow waters, and is of lighter color.

PHASE 1: The larvae seek safety in the sand in the stream bottom. They are comparatively light in color and seldom exceed 1 inch in length. The body is a dull brown, the legs a dull grayish-yellow.

PHASE 2: The pupae, like the pupae of the hellgramite and fish fly, are not available to the fish, since they burrow in the softer parts of the stream bed.

PHASE 3: Adults of the alder fly differ from the adults of the other members of the order Neuroptera in that they hold their wings in a tent-like position when at rest in much the same manner the caddis fly does. The alder can be identified, however, by the absence of hair on the wings. Since alder flies do not have hairy wings, they should not be confused with caddis flies, which do. Their flight is awkward and aimless, frequently taking place among the alder bushes to which the insects are partial. The females lay their eggs on pillars or stumps rising above the water. One characteristic makes the alder fly especially noticeable: it is averse to water and tends to drown, struggling violently when blown to the surface by a gust of wind. The wings are brown with a blackish tinge, the legs and antennae black, the body black-brown.

RECOMMENDED DRESSING

ADULT: *Wings*, teal breast dyed darkest brown tied flat-wing. *Body*, peacock herl. *Hackle*, black. *Antennae*, black.

ODONATA

NAME SOURCE: "Odonata"; toothed.

PHASES: Two (nymph and adult).

RECOGNITION FEATURES:

Nymph (primary): Hinged, hook-like jaws on lower part of mouth parts. (secondary)

Damsel only, three tail-like gills at tip of body; wing pads develop slightly to rear of last pair legs.

Adult (primary): Long, slender body bright in color; two pairs of long, glassy wings. (secondary) Dragons only, wings held horizontally at all times; dart, have rapid flight. (secondary) Damsels only, wings flutter during flight; wings held vertically over abdomen when at rest.

ANGLERS' NAMES: Snake feeder, dragonfly, damselfly, devil's darning needle, hawk, mosquito hawk, bass bug, perch bug, water cricket.

Dragon and damselflies are known to all fishermen particularly for their annoying habit of perching on rods, hats, pipes, noses, or wherever they are likely to interfere with the business of fishing. Their value as fish food is likely to be overlooked because their rapid, darting flight and cunning in staying well above the water preclude the possibility of the adult being caught by fish. However, the nymphs are abundant and are eagerly taken by trout especially, and frequently by bass. There are many kinds of dragonflies whose nymphs are of assorted shapes and colors and a few kinds of damselflies whose nymphs are less varied. Nymphs of each compete with small fish for food, preying largely on small aquatic forms and even tiny minnows. The larger dragonfly nymphs will attack a small fish with their strong equipment and devour it at leisure. The damselflies are not so abundant in most trout waters and for this reason are of lesser food value than the dragons, which are prolific in nearly all waters.

PHASE 1: Dragonfly nymphs are, for the most part, partial to static waters where they dwell in the ooze of backwater bottoms or among the water weeds. Damselfly nymphs prefer moderately moving waters at the head ends of slicks where they cling to all forms of aquatic vegetation. Both the dragons and damsels have one common characteristic which leaves recognition indisputable: each has a pair of hinged hooks appended to the lower half of the mouth parts with which the nymph clutches the hapless creature it is about to consume. All nymphs of the order Odonata are positively identified by the presence of these hooks. These insects move slowly in their natural habitat but show exceptional agility in attacking and overpowering a victim. It could be truly said that they are the "snapping turtle" of the insect world.

PHASE 2: The adults are of comparatively little value to either the angler or the fish. On occasion a trout or bass will be seen surfacing for one of the glistening insects which has come too near the water for safety. Perhaps, if other surface foods were less abundant, fish would be on the alert for these insects. However, realizing that trout, especially, concentrate on those creatures which they can obtain without showing themselves to disadvantage, it seems a foregone conclusion that damsel and dragonfly adults are hardly worth copying. The majority of imitations are such unwieldy monstrosities as to make casting with them a woeful procedure.

For purposes of recognition only let me state that damselflies are delicate in appearance and fly with their wings held more or less in an upright position. Flight is slow and the wings flap noticeably. Dragonflies fly with their wings held outstretched, seeming to remain motionless while they fairly streak through the air in powerful but erratic darts.

GREEN DRAGON

The nymphs of this insect are sold as bait in many sections of the country and are most often called "bass bugs" or "perch bugs," depending, of course, on which of the two fish is in season. While this genus does not inhabit trout streams to any great extent, it does occur especially in those slow, deeper streams in which lurk the small-mouth bass. It is abundant in ponds and lakes, which should be of interest to bluegill fishermen. Perch or bass bugs are sometimes as long as 2 inches and are a dull, neutral color. They clamber about on the weeds and stems of aquatic growths. The head is broad with large eyes, the body stout and tipped with three short, bristly projections.

This insect emerges as the big green mosquito hawk and is known in most areas as the big green darner. All sorts of legends have been spun about this bug; hence the forbidding sounding names given to it. It strikes quickly while in flight, and is impartial to its victims.

OTHER DRAGONFLY NYMPHS

There are several other dragonfly nymphs indigenous to trout waters that are of some importance to fishermen; the adults, of course, are not. These are similar to the "perch bug" in appearance and habits. One, however, is exceptional in shape. The body is nearly circular, is squat and flat. Development of the wing pads appears to be located well forward in the thorax, instead of behind the point of attachment of the rearmost pair of legs as in the other dragonfly nymphs.

Most dragonfly nymphs can be recognized by the foregoing descriptions.

DAMSELFLY NYMPH

The outstanding recognition feature of the damselfly nymph is the three broad gill plates on the tip of the body. These are anal gills that appear as tails and are used in propulsion in the water. While there are many different species, of which only a few have been copied as flies, there are roughly two general forms. One is long and slender and quite similar to the adult. The other is more like the dragon but shorter, seldom exceeding ½ inch in length.

MISCELLANEOUS AQUATIC INSECTS

The classes that follow are of comparatively small importance to the fly-fisherman, and are therefore taken up in less detail than those previously described.

COLEOPTERA

This order consists of beetles, the larvae of which are not infrequently eaten by small trout. The larvae are quite small, generally less than ⅜ of an inch in length, are blackish, and prefer mossy places. Both larvae and adults are aquatic to a large extent. Beetle larvae are recognized by their similarity to hellgramites and on first examination might seem to be miniature forms of the hellgramite. However, beetle larvae have long, delicate filaments projecting from the sides of the body segments.

Because they are so small, they have relatively little value as a food to mature fish. But they may be taken in exceptional cases. Brook trout are, perhaps, more apt to seek beetle larvae than either the brown or the rainbow trout.

HEMIPTERA

Hemiptera comprise the only true bugs. These are the water-skaters, whirlers, and whirligigs of the fisherman. While they are entertaining to watch, water bugs are of little interest to fish. Most of the water bugs skate or glide on the water surface of placid pools or at the edges of riffs. They are perpetually in motion in search of food.

Certain of this group are curious in that they swim on their backs with their bellies uppermost and are colored in reverse, that is, have a light back and a dark belly.

These insects appear very infrequently among the stomach contents of trout. Analyses have allotted them only a minor role as trout food.

HYMENOPTERA

This is an order consisting of terrestrial insect forms which come to the stream surface strictly by accident. Ants, bees, wasps and sawflies are typical of this order. Naturally all anglers are familiar with them. Dry flies imitating these insects are often producers of good catches. The red and black ants have been imitated very well by some commercial patterns and should be dressed with spent-wings, hackle-tips preferred. The bee has been represented in the form of the McGinty. In small sizes this fly is excellent for dry-fly fishing.

LEPIDOPTERA

The white moth is typical of this terrestrial order. At times the huge reddish-brown moths the size of a butterfly are present over the water and will always attract the larger trout, panfish and bass. The "twitch-and-wait" method of bug fishing is founded on the action of these large moths.

Caterpillars, or the larvae of this order, are usually taken by trout. Some long-shank Palmer flies have been very successful as imitations.

ORTHOPTERA

The order Orthoptera includes the grasshoppers, locusts, katydids and crickets. These insects are so well known that they need little if any description here. Crickets have been recognized as good brook-trout bait for years. Grasshoppers are so well known for brown trout that many fly-dressers have spent years trying to perfect their imitations.

These are all terrestrial insects and have no functions to perform near the water. Their presence on the stream is accidental.

DISTRIBUTION OF INSECTS AND CRUSTACEANS

NYMPHS AND LARVAE

There is definitely a reason why one fly, or one type or pattern of fly, will not interest fish consistently. It may work well in a riffle or perhaps a pool but not in both; or it may catch fish near the surface but not down deep. The reason is obvious: the efficacy of a fly depends on the distribution of the natural fly which it imitates.

Throughout this chapter emphasis has been placed on the habitat of the natural insect. It should be firmly established in the reader's mind that a nymph or larva has a natural preference for a specific environment. Therefore, a knowledge of the distribution of each nymph or larva is of great value to the serious angler.

Many articles have appeared in magazines describing how a certain fly on a certain day on a certain stream became the "one-and-only" of the day; how the old line favorites such as the Hendrickson, Cahill, Quill Gordon, Adams, Ginger Quill and others were totally ignored by the trout. But, and here is the nub of the thing, this same fly which produced all the trout was, thereafter, a failure on other streams. Why? Simply because it was used that first day in water which produced "naturals" of similar appearance but later used in water which, because of its flow, depth, vegetation and other environmental factors, did not contain insects similar to that fly.

It should be remembered that the word "similarity" does not especially mean "similarity of color." The word is more properly used, in this case, with reference to shape and size. If you will consider that spent-wing flies will take trout when flat-wing flies will not, and that bivisibles will often out-fish an upright-wing, in spite of the fact that the colors of each may be similar, the logic of the distinction becomes quite evident.

To take time out from actual fishing to study the aquatics in different kinds of water will be one of the best investments you can make. The results may bring you to conclusions entirely contrary to your expectations in many instances. For example, you will find insects in pools that you will not find in strong currents and others in the currents that you will not find in the pools. It is possible and valuable to learn the aquatics in your own streams and to divide them into two classes: those common to pools, and those common to currents or riffles.

Keep in mind that dry-fly fishermen, while they are usually as well informed about insects as wet-fly fishermen are, have the tendency to fall into the practice of using cne style, size or pattern of fly and, consequently, are more apt to cast unsuccessfully over a rising fish that might have taken another type of fly than wet-fly fishermen are.

Few zoologists have contributed as much authentic information for the benefit of anglers as Dr. Paul R. Needham, Professor of Zoology at the University of California. His work has been exhaustive, and the results comprehensive, and easily understandable. Fortunately, Dr. Needham has reduced much of his findings to tabular form which is of inestimable value to fly fishermen. Being an expert fly-fisher, himself, he has arranged these tables in such manner as to make rapid comparisons of aquatics possible. The tables on pages 199-202 are summaries of the most important facts of interest to fishermen and fly-dresser alike, since they give food analyses of brook, brown, and rainbow trout, the direct ratios of the quantities of aquatic to land-inhabiting forms eaten by trout, and the availability of all forms. These summaries are, of course, results gained from analyses of streams in certain areas but, nevertheless, are representative to a large extent of all streams. It is true that individual drainage areas may present different ratios between the orders of insects and other food types. The majority, however, will compare favorably with facts contained in these tables.

The table on page 199, Comparison of Available Fish Foods From Riffles and Pools, gives an excellent idea of what to expect in fast and quiet waters. Notice that the May-fly nymphs are quite evenly distributed in both rapid water and pools.

A little checking against previously learned facts may prove interesting. For example, Group 2 of the May flies consisted of the March Brown, Ginger Quill, and Light Cahill. These three flies were grouped together because certain of their physical properties were the same. Since their nymphs are flattened and therefore adaptable to fast currents, we would naturally look for them in waters of that sort. Now turn to the table on page 199. Here it is shown that May-fly nymphs inhabiting rapid-water bottoms comprise 36.9 per cent of the total of all rapid-water inhabitants.

Therefore, it can be assumed that these three well-known and effective flies are definitely a large part of that 36.9 per cent since they are so abundant in most streams. Consequently, the use of the artificial nymph representing any of these three flies would do well in those parts of the stream inhabited by the natural.

Comparison of Available Fish Foods From Riffles and Pools (Given in percentages by orders, based on collections of 1927)

ORDER	RAPID WATER BOTTOMS Per Cent	POOL BOTTOMS Per Cent
May-fly nymphs	36.9	41.2
Caddis-fly larvae and pupae	21.3	1.2
Stone-fly nymphs	14.7	4.1
Fly larvae and pupae	13.8	46.7
Beetle larvae and pupae	7.6	2.6
Crayfish and scuds	3.7	.2
Sialis larvae (Neuroptera)	.9	2.1
Snails and clams	.2	.2
Dragonfly and damselfly nymphs	.1	.5
Miscellaneous	.7	1.1

This table from *Trout Streams* by Paul R. Needham, Ph. D., courtesy of The Comstock Publishing Company.

A good example of the may fly inhabiting pools is the green drake of Group 4. We already know that the nymph of this fly is equipped for burrowing in the ooze and sand of quiet water bottoms. The table on this page gives May-fly nymphs of this kind a percentage of 41.2. From this it can be deduced that imitations of the green drake would be best suited to quiet or very slow sections of the stream. And if you will review your notes or at least remember a few experiences, you will agree that this deduction is quite in line with the facts.

The table, Foods Eaten by 46 Brown Trout, gives a clear picture of the relative values of different kinds of food eaten by this trout. At once the very high percentage of 79.3 for may flies is significant and justifies the popular use of May-fly imitations, both wet and dry, for the brown trout. This figure is still more significant when a check of the drift foods is made. Drift foods are reduced to figures in the table on page 202. Observe that may flies do not reach maximum quantity until August. Considering that the table on page 200 was based on stream reports and findings for the months of May, June, and July, it becomes apparent that the percentage of 79.3 would be even higher for the month of August.

Thus far, the indications are that brown trout are unquestionably partial to may flies. The word "partial" is not incontestable, however, since the size of the fish must be taken into consideration. Large brown trout like large food: *big* nymphs and larvae, minnows, grasshoppers, stone flies, dragonfly nymphs and crane flies. The average creel-size brown trout *is* partial to may flies, however. Caddis flies fall into second place, two-winged or dipterous insects into third place.

Foods Eaten by 46 Brown Trout*

CLASS OF FOOD	NUMBER FOUND IN 46 Stomachs	Per Cent of Total
May flies	1,907	79.3
Caddis flies	230	9.5
Two-winged flies	61	2.5
Earthworms	51	2.1
Slugs	30	1.3
Beetles	28	1.2
Ants, bees, and wasps	22	1.0
Stone flies	17	.7
Leaf-hoppers	17	.7
Crayfish and scuds	15	.7
Fish, salamanders	9	.3
Grasshoppers	7	.3
Miscellaneous	10	.4
TOTAL	2,404	

* These trout had an average length of 8″ and ran from 5″ to 12″; they were taken mostly in May, June, and July.

This table from *Trout Streams* by Paul R. Needham, Ph. D., courtesy of The Comstock Publishing Company.

The rainbow trout is not so discriminating as the brown. This is shown clearly in the table on page 201, Foods Consumed by 80 Rainbow Trout. While the May fly is predominant in the listing, the caddis fly and two-winged fly are fairly close. Instead of 79.3 per cent for the may fly, as in the case of the brown trout, the percentage is only 37.1 in the case of the rainbow. The natural food groups which occupy such a minor place on the brown trout list are advanced to a higher standing on the rainbow list. In other words, rainbow trout are not nearly so selective as brown trout. Anglers who have caught both will hardly argue the point.

Brook trout have entirely different feeding habits from rainbow and brown trout. Their principal food is caddis-fly larvae and the adult two-wing flies. It should be taken into consideration, of course, that brook trout are primarily headwaters fish, having greater quantities of caddis-fly larvae available to them than either the brown or rainbow trout which invariably live in the warmer, lowland sections of the stream.

The table on page 201 gives interesting comparisons of available brook-trout foods. See how the percentage of aquatic forms exceeds that of the aerial forms. Here May flies are given only 13.1 per cent for adults and 19.9 per cent for nymphs; stone flies only 0.7 and 2.0. Thus it seems a foregone conclusion that the artificials for brook trout are fished better wet than dry. A glance at the totals given in the table on page 202 seems to prove it.

Foods Consumed by 80 Rainbow Trout*

CLASS OF FOOD	NUMBER FOUND IN 80 Stomachs	Per Cent of Total
May flies	490	37.1
Caddis flies	247	18.7
Two-winged flies	234	17.8
Beetles	105	7.9
Ants, bees, wasps	88	6.6
Stone flies	44	3.3
Moth larvae	17	1.2
Snails	14	1.1
Leaf-hoppers	13	1.0
Crayfish and scuds	13	1.0
Alder-fly larvae	11	.8
True bugs	11	.8
Grasshoppers	7	.5
Fish and salamanders	6	.5
Algae—Cladophora	+	+
Miscellaneous	23	1.71
TOTAL	1,323	

* Average length 6″, running from 3″ to 12″. Most of these were taken in May, June, July. All of these rainbows were taken from streams, none from lakes.

This table from *Trout Streams* by Paul R. Needham, Ph. D., courtesy of The Comstock Publishing Company.

Comparison of Land and Water Foods Eaten by Brook Trout

CLASS OF FOOD	LAND INHABITING FORMS*		AQUATIC FORMS	
	Number	Per Cent	Number	Per Cent
Caddis flies	57	4.1	1,166	43.2
Two-winged flies	304	22.1	451	16.8
May flies	180	13.1	536	19.9
Beetles	213	15.4	55	2.0
Stone flies	10	0.7	51	2.0
Leaf-hoppers	260	18.8	—	
True-bugs	28	2.0	20	0.8
Ants, bees, wasps	123	8.9	—	
Grasshoppers	66	4.8	—	
Water springtails	—		264	9.8
Moth, larvae	26	1.9	—	
Spiders	29	2.1	—	
Millipedes	32	2.3	—	
Crayfish, scuds	—		68	2.5

Snails	3	0.2	32	1.2
Earthworms	47	3.4	—	—
Fish, salamanders	—	—	21	0.7
Miscellaneous	2	0.1	34	1.1
TOTALS	1,380		2,698	

* The adults of aquatic insects are listed as land organisms on page 201 because they have ceased to be aquatic in the adult stage; their gills are lost, wings fully developed for flight, swimming powers gone. It is only in their immature stages that these can be classed as truly aquatic and adapted to life in water.

This table taken from *Trout Streams* by Paul R. Needham, Ph. D., courtesy of The Comstock Publishing Company.

Of especial interest to dry-fly fishermen are the results of drift-net studies given in the table below. This table is based on over five thousand organisms captured during the months of June, July, and August. This information is self-explanatory, showing the rise and fall in quantity of "naturals" on the surface during these three months. The percentage of true-flies or two-wing flies (Diptera) may be surprising to some. However, this includes mosquitoes and gnats which are superabundant pests. The all-important crane flies also belong to the order Diptera and, for this reason, imitations of them do well in July.

Monthly and Total Drift Foods Found in Streams in June, July, and August, 1927*

KIND OF FOOD	JUNE Per Cent	JULY Per Cent	AUGUST Per Cent	TOTAL Per Cent
True-flies	30.95	51.20	24.42	38.46
May Flies	26.97	27.19	37.03	28.94
Plant-lice	23.77	9.52	9.18	14.91
Ants	5.02	1.54	9.49	4.33
Beetles	4.92	2.84	3.94	3.84
True-bugs	4.18	1.09	3.94	2.80
Caddis flies	1.33	0.96	2.73	1.43
Spiders	0.89	0.52	0.81	0.72
Stone flies	0.84	4.54	6.16	3.43
Miscellaneous	1.13	0.65	2.31	1.15

* Based on a total of 5,314 drift organisms; percentage by months based on total number taken each month.

This table from *Trout Streams* by Paul R. Needham, Ph. D., courtesy of The Comstock Publishing Company.

The foregoing tables are practical indices by which the angler and fly-dresser can estimate their requirements for each type. Had they been prepared aimlessly or without scientific foundation, they might be taken lightly. However, since they have been founded on facts, technical studies, and years of stream testing and analysis, they should be given serious recognition by those who would have a better understanding of natural insects, their imitations, and proper fly selection.

CRUSTACEANS

Fresh-water crustaceans are a more valuable food source to fish than the majority of anglers realize. They are extremely important to young and adult fish alike, the lower-class, Entomostraca, supplying unlimited food for fingerlings and the higher class, Malacostraca, furnishing large quantities of food for mature fish. From the angling viewpoint only those crustaceans of the higher-class are noteworthy. These are the crayfish or crab, shrimp, scuds (frequently incorrectly called "shrimp"), and sow bugs. The largest of these is the crayfish, the smallest the scuds.

Interesting state surveys conducted for the purpose of establishing ratios between the kinds of aquatic life eaten by various game fish and the abundance of these forms of life, have shown that salmon, rainbow trout, brown trout, large and small-mouth bass, and panfish, consume great quantities of crustaceans sometimes even to the exclusion of other creatures of equal abundance and comparative size.

It is interesting that certain authorities have estimated that the crayfish probably could survive the greatest demand made on it by fish and fishermen and never become wholly depleted. Although it may vary with the localities in which field tests have been made, it is a generally established fact that smallmouth bass, particularly, eat more crayfish than they do minnows. Other game fish eat lesser amounts. (See second column of the table on page 204 "A General Summary of the Food Habits of Some Adult Connecticut Lake Fishes.")

CRAYFISH

Crayfish have ten legs, the foremost pair of which are large and equipped with lobster-like claws. Like other crustaceans, they have a coat of hard armor which is shed periodically to allow for the growth of the animal. A larger coat is acquired after each molt. It is during the molting period that bass and trout seek crayfish. They are very soft and tender at this time. I have seen the freshly molted crayfish so soft and limp that they could not move their legs or pincers if out of water.

These backward-swimming fellows are found in the quiet waters along the shores of streams and lakes and in riffles under stones. They develop remarkable agility. Nests are indicated by the presence of little mounds of gravel, near which the adult will be found lurking.

The female carries her eggs on the underside of her tail. It should be mentioned here that it is merely good sportsmanship to return females to the water, especially when their sex is made obvious by the presence of the egg cluster.

The lime content of water affects the color of crayfish. I have found them dark greenish-brown, nearly black, sandy-tan, and even pinkish. Generally the "sheds" are as pink as a young field mouse.

Imitations are not too successful since they are apt to be bulky, difficult to cast, and otherwise unsatisfactory. When crayfish are needed they can be found. It is always an easy matter to locate two or three among the rocks along the shoreline.

Size is variable among individuals taken from lime and free-stone streams. Three inches is approximately the maximum length of old crayfish.

SOW BUG

The sow bug is a broad, flat, fourteen-legged crustacean of grayish color about ½ to ⅝ of an inch in length. Its habitat is among soft aquatic plants, especially watercress,

A GENERAL SUMMARY OF THE FOOD HABITS OF SOME
ADULT CONNECTICUT LAKE FISHES

Species	Fish	Crayfish	Plankton Crustacea	Mollusks	Insect Nymphs	Adult Insects	Plants
Round Whitefish			.X.	X	XXX		
Sockeye Salmon			XXX		X		
Rainbow Trout	.X.		XXX		XXX	X	
Lake Trout	XXX						
Smelt	.XX		.XX		XXX		
Common Eel	.XX	.XX		.XX	XX		XX.
Common Sucker			.X.	.XX	XXX		XXX.
European Carp		X	.X.	XXX	XXX		.XXX.
Golden Shiner			XXX	.X	X		.XX.
Common Bullhead	.X.	.XX	X	.XX	XXX		X
Chain Pickerel	XXX	X					
Northern Pike	XXX						
Largemouth Bass	XXX	XXX				.X.	
Smallmouth Bass	.XX	XXX				.X.	
Red-bellied Sunfish				X	XXX	X	
Common Sunfish				X	XXX	X	
Bluegill Sunfish		X		.XX	.XX	XXX	.XXX.
Rock Bass	.X.	.XX		X	XXX		
Calico Bass	.XX		.XX	X	XXX	X	
Yellow Perch	.XX	.XX	.X.	.XX	XXX	X	
Wall-eyed Pike	XXX	X			X		
White Perch	X		.XX		XXX		

The symbol XXX designates food of primary importance; XX and X are foods of respectively lesser importance. Absence of checks does not infer that the organism is never eaten by the fish. The above grouping is necessarily of the most approximate nature and it is also flexible to the extent that the food habits of fishes vary with size, season, and the body of water in which they live. The interest and value lies in pointing out to the angler the food groups upon which the common Connecticut fishes draw most heavily. The relative specialization in diet among species may also be noted to advantage. Wherever possible, data from Connecticut lakes has been used, but in many cases the chart also includes a compilation from various sources.

This chart by Courtesy of Edward L. Troxell, Ph.D., Superintendent, State Geological and Natural History Survey of the State of Connecticut, from "A FISHERY SURVEY OF IMPORTANT CONNECTICUT LAKES," by State Board of Fisheries and Game Lake and Pond Survey Unit, Bulletin No. 63, Section III by Dwight A. Webster, Cornell University.

which is its principal food. Trout consume large quantities of sow bugs which, fortunately, are extremely prolific.

The shell-back nymph described in Chapter 7 is one of the most suitable imitations. A size 10 hook is proportionate to the natural.

SCUD AND SHRIMP

The scud is different from either the crayfish, shrimp, or sow bug in appearance. Although flattened like the sow bug, it is somewhat curved laterally like the shrimp. The color is usually yellowish or lemon-green. This crustacean prefers to live among weeds and aquatic plants of all descriptions which abound in the slower waters.

It is concluded by fish culturists that trout which have an abundance of scuds to eat take on brilliant colors and become hardy and fat. For this reason the scud has been introduced into many waters originally devoid of this crustacean. It is a vegetarian, and thus not competitive with small fish for food and, therefore, is ideal for stocking purposes.

Scuds are found in brackish waters, where they are readily eaten by the game fish frequenting such places.

THE NUMBERS OF EACH TYPE OF BOTTOM ORGANISMS
COLLECTED FROM 22 LAKES AND PONDS BETWEEN
JUNE 1 AND SEPTEMBER 1, 1942.

Name of Lake	Number of Samples	Average Volume in c.c. per sq. meter	Dragonfly Nymphs Odonata	May Fly Nymphs Ephemerida	Midge Larvae Chironomidae	Beetle Larvae Coleoptera	Caddis Fly Larvae Trichoptera	Alder Fly Larvae Sialis	Mosquito Larvae Chaoborus	Water Mites Hydracarina	Snails and Clams Mollusca	Crustaceans *** Crustacea	Worms Oligochaeta	Other Insects ** Insecta	Other Fly Larvae * Diptera	Flatworms Platyhelmintha	Leech Hirudinea	Roundworm Nemathelmintha
Ashfield	10	4.9	7	17	56		3		5		5	9	2	3	2			
Buck	6	7.7	1		2	1						41	22					
Bog	9	2.1	4	23	57	1	3					4	8					
Chapin	5	7.0		2	26	1	8		4		11	6	3					
Congamond	18	5.1	4		162	1	13		4		27	131	10		9	15	9	
Crooked	7	1.3	1	3	47	2	3		50		3		2				3	1
Center	12	2.05		8	45		5		1	13	21	43	64	1				1
Five Mile	7	1.5			27						4	22	19					
Upper and Lower Great	5	5.6	4	14	9						2	4	30		1			
Hampton	6	8.6	1		19		1		1		14							
Hazzard	9	8.6			83			3		3	4	12		5	2		1	
Long	12	5.4	7	3	61	1	2	2	49		26	54	10	1			1	
Loon	5	7.7		3	21	1	4		4		10	7	5		1			
Lorraine	8	3.9		1	18						11	63	63				1	
Nine Mile	12	1.9	1	1	47				15			1	2					
North	9	1.9	3		13	1	3			5	4	1			6			
Norwich	12	3.4	6	27	80		47		44		2	39	25	1			3	
Oxbow	20	3.9		2	114	1			2		1		272	1	5	1	3	1
Plainfield	11	1.3		4	36		5	1			1	145	63			3	3	
South	7	.7	1		49			2	13	2		17	1		4			
Windsor	12	3.0	1		29		8	3	24		10	21	27		1		1	
Yokum	9	13.7	1	16	48	1	6		2	1	199	61	1		3			1
Totals	211		42	124	1049	11	111	11	213	29	374	655	608	12	33	20	25	4

** Hemiptera   * Ceratopogonidae   *** Decapoda–Crayfish
Lepidoptera   Tabanidae   Isopoda–Sowbug
Neuroptera   Amphipoda–Shrimp

This table from "FISHERIES SURVEY REPORT" 1942, Commonwealth of Massachusetts, 1942, by Albert H. Swartz. Courtesy of The Department of Conservation Division of Wild Life Research and Management.

Although the shrimp and the scud are not the same creature, they look much alike. Shrimp are larger than scuds and therefore of greater importance as fish food. Distribution figures in the importance of these crustaceans from the angling viewpoint: scuds are generally distributed in alkaline, spring-fed waters.

LAKE-FISH FOOD

It is sometimes difficult to determine exactly what lake game fish have available to eat. The water is deep, the vegetation and terrain characteristics difficult to cope with; in addition, the lowest stratum of water is often beyond the scope of worthwhile investigation by the amateur. Too, the remnants in the stomach of a bass or other game fish may not reveal very important information, since the recognizable parts of many creatures will already have been digested. Scientific surveys are, perhaps, the best and most satisfactory source for such information. Survey groups have highly specialized equipment with which to carry on this exacting work. It is for this reason that the table on page 204, A General Summary of the Food Habits of Some Adult Connecticut Lake Fishes, and the table on page 205, The Numbers of Each Type of Bottom Organisms Collected from 22 Lakes and Ponds, are included here. These two tables are well arranged, giving invaluable information which, for general purposes, can be used as cross sections of food availability and feeding habits relative to lakes and lake fish.

Chapter Fourteen

DICTIONARY OF FLY PATTERNS

The fly patterns listed throughout the following pages are the product of years of compilation and correspondence. Naturally there will be disagreement among anglers over certain dressings; however, it should be remembered that any individual pattern may be tied in many ways and still be correct according to the locality for which it was intended. In this connection, the dictionary has been arranged as reasonably as possible to show the many alternate dressings available for every pattern.

"Standard" dressings mean little so far as shape and even color are concerned, unless they are associated with the preferred design accepted by local anglers.

While a standard nomenclature has been presented in this book, with the thought that it may be of future value, there are some descriptions in the forthcoming tables which appear not to conform to that standard nomenclature. This is due principally to the slightly different terms used by fly-dressers throughout the world. For obvious reasons, their dressings are recorded exactly as they wrote them. As a whole, however, the differences are so slight as to cause no real confusion.

For ready reference this section has been divided into type groups. This breakdown is based on classifications described in Chapters 5, 6, 7, 8, 9, 10, and 11, and is divided as follows:

Trout dry- and wet-fly patterns.
Steelhead wet flies.
Trout, bass, and salmon streamers.
Salmon wet-fly patterns.
Fancy lake flies.
Salt-water flies.

The letter "W" indicates the preferred dressing for Western fishing.

PATTERN	WINGS	HACKLE	BODY	TAIL
ABBEY	mallard	brown	red floss, gold rib and tip	gold pheasant tippet
ACADEMY	pheasant cock wing	brown Palmer and shoulder	peacock red floss tip	scarlet
ADAMS (female)	grizzly tips tied spent-wing	brown and grizzly	gray dubbing or muskrat fur, yellow chenille egg sac	brown and grizzly
ADAMS (male)	grizzly tips tied spent-wing	brown and grizzly	gray dubbing or muskrat fur	brown and grizzly

ADDER	brown turkey	brown	brown floss, orange floss rib	
ADIRONDACK NO. 1	white	orange	light brown wool, yellow wool tip	
ADIRONDACK NO. 2	brown turkey, red & yellow strips	scarlet	scarlet, gold rib	scarlet and yellow
ADMIRAL	white	scarlet	scarlet floss, gold rib and tip	scarlet
AGGIE BIVISIBLE		dark brown Palmer, ginger front		dark brown hackle tip
ALDER NO. 1	dark gray	gray dun	peacock herl, gold tip	
ALDER NO. 2	brown turkey	black	peacock herl, gold tip	
ALDER NO. 3 (W)	brown turkey	black	peacock herl, gold tip	gold pheasant tippet
ALDER BROWN (W)	brown turkey	brown Palmer	brown floss, red floss tip	brown turkey
ALDER FLAT WING	brown turkey tied flat over back	black	peacock herl, gold tip	
ALDER GRAY NO. 1	gray turkey	grizzly	peacock herl, gold tip	
ALDER GRAY NO. 2	gray	black	peacock herl, gold tip	
ALDER HACKLE		blue dun	brown feather fiber (thick) wound like wool	
ALDER JAMES		dark rusty-blue	dark blue fur, red thread rib	
ALDER RONALDS	speckled hen tied close to shank	brown	bronze peacock herl	
ALEXANDRIA NO. 1 (W)	peacock sword	black	embossed silver, red floss tip	peacock herl, or sword
ALEXANDRIA NO. 2	peacock sword	pale dun	silver, red floss tip	peacock herl, or sword
ALICE	brown turkey	ginger	silver, peacock herl butt	ginger
ALLERTON NO. 1	scarlet	blue Palmer, yellow at shoulder	yellow floss, gold rib and tip	barred wood duck
ALLERTON NO. 2	mallard, guinea strips		black wool, scarlet tip	
AMBER DRAKE	Another name for Great Red Spinner			
ANALOMINK	black	badger or black and white	black rib, orange dubbing	gold pheasant tippet
ANGUS		ginger	red ostrich	red
APPLE GREEN	pale slate	ginger	light green floss	ginger
APRIL GRAY NO. 1		grizzly	yellow wool, black thread rib	grizzly
APRIL GRAY NO. 2		grizzly hen	gray wool, black thread rib	
ARIZONA SPECIAL MOSQUITO (W)	grizzly hackle tips tied spent	grizzly	Javalina quill	gray hackle wisps
ARMY WORM	peacock herl	gray dun	yellow floss, gray floss rib	
ARTFUL DODGER	cock pheasant	red palmer	purple wool, gold wire rib	
ARTHUR HOYT	turkey	brown	green floss, yellow floss rib	brown

ASH DUN	pale slate	gray dun	silver-gray wool	gray dun
ASH FLY NO. 1	light slate	brown	light gray floss	brown
ASH FLY NO. 2	light slate	gray dun	light gray floss, brown floss rib	gray dun
ASH FOX		brown	rabbit's fur, silver tip	dun
ASHEY		gray dun	gray floss	
ASHEY BIVISIBLE		gray dun, white front	gray floss, silver rib	gray dun
ASHY NO. 1 (W)	gray	gray dun	gray floss	gray mallard
ASHY NO. 2		dark slate gray, Palmer	red wool	
ASHY NO. 3		gray dun	gray floss	
ASHY HACKLE	Another name for Ashy			
AUGUST DUN NO. 1	slate	orange	orange wool, gold rib and tip	
AUGUST DUN NO. 2	slate	brown	brown wool, yellow thread rib	grizzly
AUGUST DUN NO. 3	brown turkey	brown	brown wool, yellow thread rib	grizzly
AUTUMN DUN NO. 1	gray turkey	grizzly	black floss, yellow floss rib	black
AUTUMN DUN NO. 2 (Orvis)	gray turkey	gray dun	black dubbing, tan thread rib, gold tip	white
AUTUMN DUN NO. 3	teal breast	gray dun	black floss, yellow floss rib	black
BABCOCK NO. 1	yellow, black strips	black	red floss, gold rib	black and yellow
BABCOCK NO. 2 (W)	yellow, black strips	black	red floss, gold rib	black
BABE FLY	brown and gray turkey, with gold pheasant tippet	brown	yellow wool, gold rib	
BADGER BIVISIBLE		light badger, Palmer		light badger hackle tip
BADGER PALMER		badger, Palmer	light gray wool, silver rib	badger tips
BADGER QUILL NO. 1	slate	badger	peacock quill	badger hackle
BADGER QUILL NO. 2	grizzly tips	badger	peacock quill	black hackle
BADGER RED		badger	red dubbing	badger hackle
BADGER SPIDER NO. 1		badger	black chenille	badger
BAIGENT'S VARIANT	a type of fly featuring extra-long sparse hackle, no particular pattern			
BALDWIN	teal	claret	white floss, silver rib	teal
BANG BIVISIBLE		scarlet Palmer, white front		scarlet hackle tip
BANNOCK CHIEF NO. 1	slate, jungle cock eye shoulder	brown	peacock herl, yellow floss center joint, red floss tip	gold pheasant tippet
BANNOCK CHIEF NO. 2 (W)	slate	brown	peacock herl, yellow floss center joint, red floss tip	
BARBER POLE BLACK (W)		grizzly	black floss, wide silver rib	
BARBER POLE GREEN (W)		grizzly	green floss, wide silver rib	
BARBER POLE ORANGE (W)		grizzly	orange floss, wide silver rib	

BARRETT'S SHAVING BRUSH SPENT GNAT	black cock hackles, spent (bunched)	black	white kapok, black thread rib	black hackle
BARRINGTON	mallard	brown	peacock herl, gold tip	
BEAMER	brown turkey, brown mallard splits	blue scarlet Palmer	blue dubbing, silver rib	scarlet, wood duck and blue
BEAMIS STREAM	brown turkey, brown mallard splits	brown, Palmer	claret dubbing, gold rib	brown mallard and gold pheasant tippet
BEAR PAW (W)		grizzly shoulder fore and aft	orange chenille, yellow floss center joint	
BEATRICE NO. 1	barred wood duck	gray dun, Palmer	yellow dubbing, green floss tip	scarlet
BEATRICE NO. 2	wood duck	yellow	yellow dubbing, gold rib	scarlet
BEAUTY NO. 1	gray turkey	partridge	gray fur, silver rib	gray turkey
BEAUTY NO. 2	gray turkey dyed golden yellow	badger	black dubbing, silver rib	
BEAVERKILL NO. 1	curlew	brown	white and brown floss striped	
BEAVERKILL NO. 2	gray	brown	white floss, brown floss rib	brown
BEAVERKILL (female)	slate (light)	brown	gray dubbing, yellow chenille butt	gray mallard
BEAVERKILL (male)	gray duck	brown, Palmer	white floss,	medium wood duck
BEAVERKILL RED FOX		ginger, pale blue-gray front	blue-gray fox fur dubbing	ginger
BECK SPINNER	gray duck	ginger	lemon-yellow twisted raffia spiral over black floss base	brown
BEE NO. 1	brown cock pheasant	coch-y-bondhu	yellow chenille, black chenille center joint	
BEE NO. 2	white tipped mallard	brown	4 joint chenille, yellow, black, yellow, black	
BEEMAN	gray turkey	brown	green chenille, gold tip	
BELGRADE	white, scarlet strips, jungle cock eye shoulder	claret, Palmer	light olive-green dubbing picked out, gold rib, pk. herl butt	scarlet and white
BEMIS	another name for Beamis Stream			
BEN BENT	gray goose	gray dun	gray chenille, orange tip, gold tag	pale gray hackle tips
BENNETT	light gray	guinea	peacock herl, yellow floss tip	
BICKNELL	dark black-brown turkey	deep scarlet	scarlet floss, gold rib, black ostrich herl head	gold pheasant crest
BIG INDIAN	yellow	white	yellow floss orange floss rib	
BIG MEADOW NO. 1	mallard	brown	peacock herl, gold tip	scarlet fibers
BIG MEADOW NO. 2	mottled brown	brown	peacock herl red floss rib	scarlet fibers
BIG TROUT (W)	medium gray	grizzly	yellow and brown quill	mallard dyed brown
BINO		white	peacock herl	guinea
BISHOP	claret, white shoulder	brown	white floss	red and white feather fibers

BISSET	solid slate guinea wing	pale guinea	peacock herl, gold tip	
BLACK ANGEL	black hackle tips	black	black, smooth floss	black hackles
BLACK ANT NO. 1	black crow	black	reddish black silk, peacock herl butt, gold tip	
BLACK ANT NO. 2	slate gray	black	black silk, black chenille butt	short gold pheasant tippet
BLACK ANT NO.3 (W)		black	black floss lacquered (or plastic) tied on in-hump hook (knobbed at rear)	no tail
BLACK ANT SPECIAL		black	black floss, claret chenille at shoulder	
BLACK BIVISIBLE		black, white front	black floss, gold rib	black hackles
BLACK AND BLUE	gray	black	black dubbing, gold rib	gold pheasant tippet
BLACK AND CLARET	black	black	claret fur, silver rib	gold pheasant tippet
BLACK DOSE	brown turkey, mallard splits	black	black floss, silver rib, yellow floss tip	gold pheasant crest
BLACK DRAGON		black	flat silver tinsel	red fibers
BLACK DRAKE NO. 1	dark teal	badger	ivory white raffia, silver rib	wood duck
BLACK DRAKE NO. 2	black	black	gold-brown floss, black thread rid	black
BLACK FORKED TAIL (W)	See Forked Tail-Black			
BLACK GNAT	dark gray	black	black chenille, silver tip	with or without red fibers
BLACK GNAT (female)	black, white tipped	black	black floss, gold tip	
BLACK GNAT (male)	black	black	black chenille, gold rib	
BLACK GNAT-PEACOCK (W)	dark gray	black	peacock herl	with or without red fibers
BLACK GNAT-SILVER	dark gray	black	silver	black
BLACK AND GOLD	black	black	black floss, gold rib	gold pheasant tippet
BLACK HACKLE-BLACK		black	black chenille, gold tip	
BLACK HACKLE-PEACOCK		black	peacock herl, gold tip	
BLACK HACKLE-RED NO. 1		black	red dubbing, gold rib and tip	
BLACK HACKLE-RED NO. 2 (W)		black	red floss, gold rib	red fibers
BLACK HACKLE-SILVER NO. 1		black	silver, red floss tip	
BLACK HACKLE-SILVER NO. 2 (W)		black	embossed silver	red fibers
BLACK HACKLE-YELLOW NO. 1		black	yellow dubbing, gold rib	
BLACK HACKLE-YELLOW NO. 2 (W)		black	yellow floss, gold rib	red fibers
BLACK JAY	mallard	black, jay front	black fur, silver rib	gold pheasant tippet
BLACK JUNE NO. 1	dark gray	black	peacock herl, silver rib	
BLACK JUNE NO. 2	black crow	black	peacock herl, gold tip	

BLACK MAY	dark gray duck	black	black floss, gold tip	
BLACK MIDGE NO. 1		black	black floss, silver rib	
BLACK MIDGE NO. 2		2 turns of black (spider radius)	short; 2 turns black seal's fur	
BLACK MOOSE	guinea	black, Palmer	green dubbing	green and yellow
BLACK NYMPH		partridge	black herl, gold rib	wood duck
BLACK O'LINDSAY	light gray mallard over peacock sword	brown and blue mixed	yellow wool, gold rib	brown hackle fibers over blue
BLACK PALMER		black, Palmer	black wool or floss	scarlet fibers
BLACK PHANTOM	black hackle tip	black, parachute	black floss	black
BLACK PRINCE NO. 1	black crow	black	black floss, silver rib	scarlet fibers
BLACK PRINCE NO. 2 (W)	dark gray	black	black floss, gold rib	gold pheasant tippet
BLACK QUILL NO. 1	dark gray	black	peacock eye quill	black
BLACK QUILL NO. 2 (W)	dark gray	black	peacock eye quill	red fibers
BLACK QUILL DUN	black	black	peacock herl quill	coch-y-bondhu
BLACK AND SILVER	black	black	silver	gold pheasant tippet
BLACK SILVER TWIST	See Silver Horns			
BLACK SPIDER NO. 1		black, spider radius	black floss, gold tip	
BLACK SPIDER NO. 2 (W)		black, spider radius	short fat black chenille	
BLACK TRANSLUCENT	black processed silk	black	black-dyed translucent rubber	black hackle
BLOCK HOUSE	scarlet	scarlet	yellow floss, gold rib	
BLOODY BUTCHER	black	scarlet	silver	scarlet fibers
BLUE BIVISIBLE		blue-gray Palmer, white front	gray floss, gold rib	blue hackle fibers
BLUE & BLACK	See Black & Blue			
BLUE BLOA	See Hare's Ear			
BLUE BLOW	dark gray	black, Palmer	blue floss, gold tip	
BLUE BOTTLE NO. 1	crow	black	blue floss, gold rib and tip	
BLUE BOTTLE NO. 2	gray (dark)	black	blue floss, gold tip	
BLUE BOTTLE NO. 3 (W)	gray	black	royal blue floss, gold tip	black hackle fibers
BLUE CLARET	brown turkey (fine mottle)	blue, Palmer	claret dubbing gold tip	
BLUE DUN NO. 1	pale gray	pale blue dun	pale blue fur	pale blue dun
BLUE DUN NO. 2 (W)	medium gray	light blue	gray wool	light blue hackle
BLUE DUN-PALE	See Pale Blue Dun			
BLUE DUN-SILVER	gray	blue dun	silver	blue dun hackle
BLUE DUN SPIDER		2 blue dun, reverse sides	muskrat fur	blue dun hackle fibers
BLUE FOX	grizzly hackle tips	grizzly	blue dun fox dubbing	grizzly hackle

BLUE GORDON	mallard	ginger Palmer down fore body	½ ginger dubbing fore, ½ blue floss aft, gold tip	hen pheasant
BLUE HONEY DUN	wood duck	blue honey dun	buff fox fur dubbing	blue honey dun hackle
BLUE JAY NO. 1	blue jay over black and white	black	silver thread tinsel, scarlet chenille butt	barred wood duck
BLUE JAY NO. 2	blue jay over black and white	red	red floss, gold rib and tip	red
BLUE JAY NO. 3	blue	grizzly dyed orange	orange floss, gold rib	orange hackle
BLUE MILLER	blue	blue	blue chenille, gold tip	blue hackle
BLUE MONTREAL	See Montreal-Blue			
BLUE OLIVE		olive, blue dun face	brown feather fiber, gold wire rib	olive
BLUE PROFESSOR	See Professor-Blue			
BLUE QUILL NO. 1	medium gray	blue dun	peacock quill	blue dun hackle
BLUE QUILL NO. 2	medium gray	blue dun	peacock quill dyed light blue	blue dun hackle
BLUE QUILL NO. 3 (W)	light gray	light blue	gray quill	light blue hackle
BLUE QUILL NO. 4	blue dun hackle tips	blue dun	alternating dark and light moose mane	blue dun hackle fibers
BLUE QUILL VARIANT	blue dun hackle tips	blue dun, long spider	peacock quill	blue dun hackle fibers
BLUE ROOSTER	wood duck	blue Andalusian	condor quill	wood duck
BLUE UPRIGHT NO. 1	same as Blue Quill			
BLUE UPRIGHT NO. 2 (W)	light gray	light blue	peacock quill	light blue hackle
BLUE UPRIGHT-GRAY (W)	light gray	grizzly	peacock quill	silver pheasant tippet
BLUE UPRIGHT-HARRISON		blue dun	pale lemon yellow floss, black thread rib	3 blue dun hackle fibers
BLUE UPRIGHT-SILVER	gray	blue dun	silver	blue dun hackle
BLUE VARIANT	light gray	blue grizzly	peacock quill	blue grizzly
BLUE VARIANT-GOLD		blue multi-color variant	gold	blue multi-color variant hackle
BLUE WING OLIVE	blue dun hackle tip	golden brown	olive-green dubbing	brown hackle
BLUE WING OLIVE (female)	bluish gray	olive	brown floss, olive thread rib	dark olive-brown hackle
BLUE WING OLIVE (male) NO. 1	bluish gray	olive	red-brown floss	brown hackle
BLUE WING OLIVE (male) NO. 2	medium gray	blue dun-olive	olive quill, gold wire rib	blue dun-olive hackle fibers
BLUE WING OLIVE SPINNER (female)	blue dun hackle tip	pale olive	olive-brown quill, yellow egg sac	olive
BLUE WING OLIVE SPINNER (male)	grizzly hackle tips, dyed blue dun	grizzly dyed olive	dark olive quill	grizzly dyed olive hackle
BLUE ZULU		blue	black dubbing, silver rib	scarlet fibers, blunt
BOB LAWRENCE	scarlet, jungle cock each side	guinea	cinnamon dubbing, silver rib	scarlet and barred wood duck
BOB SLEE SPECIAL (W)	light gray	orange	peacock quill	orange hackle

BOG FLY	dark slate	claret	peacock herl, thick	gold pheasant tippet
BOLUS		badger	ostrich herl, dyed yellow	guinea dyed yellow
BONNIE VIEW	gray	brown	olive-brown dubbing, gold rib and tip	gray fibers
BOOT'S BLACK	black	black	red dubbing, gold rib and tip	gray mallard
BOUNCER	white tip turkey dyed yellow	orange	black floss, orange dubbing butt, gold tip	
BOWMAN	gray duck	gray dun	natural quill	gray dun
BRADLEY (W)	furnace hackle tip	brown and grizzly	macaw quill	brown neck guard hackle fibers
BRADLEY SPECIAL	gray mallard	brown	blue-gray and red dun mixed, dubbing	brown hackle fibers
BRANDRETH	gray mallard	yellow Palmer, scarlet front	yellow dubbing picked out, gold rib	scarlet hackle fibers
BREADCRUST NO. 1		grizzly	Rhode Island Red quill (hackle)	
BREADCRUST NO. 2		pale blue dun Palmer	tan raffia	
BRIGHT FOX NO. 1	slate gray duck		fox fur dyed yellow, picked out	dun hackle
BRIGHT FOX NO. 2	white	brown	yellow floss, gold tip	
BRONZE COACHMAN	See Coachman-Bronze			
BROWN ADDER NO. 1	dark brown turkey	dark brown	claret floss, gold rib	gray dun hackle
BROWN ADDER NO. 2	brown turkey	brown, Palmer	brown floss, gold tip	brown turkey
BROWN ANT NO. 1	brown turkey	brown	brown floss, peaocock herl butt, gold tip	
BROWN ANT NO. 2	medium slate gray	coch-y-bondhu	deep garnet silk, peacock herl butt	
BROWN ANT NO. 3 (W)	dark gray	brown	henna floss, peacock herl butt	gold pheasant tippet
BROWN BEETLE	See Coch-y-bondhu			
BROWN BIVISIBLE		brown Palmer, white front	brown floss, silver rib	brown hackle
BROWN CAUGHLIN	gray duck	brown	red floss	black hackle
BROWN COFLIN	dark gray	gray dun	brown floss	
BROWN DRAKE	brown turkey	brown	dark brown floss, gold rib	mallard
BROWN DUN NO. 1	gray duck	brown	brown dubing	brown hackle
BROWN DUN NO. 2 R. B.	blue-gray bucktail, flat	brown	blue-gray fur	
BROWN DUN BIVISIBLE		brown Palmer, white front	red floss	wood duck
BROWN GNAT	cinnamon turkey		red-brown chenille	
BROWN GRUB (W)		brown	black chenille, white chenille butt	
BROWN HACKLE		brown	peacock herl, gold tip	gold pheasant tippet
BROWN HACKLE BROWN		brown	brown dubbing, gold rib	
BROWN HACKLE-ORANGE		brown	orange dubbing, gold rib	
BROWN HACKLE-PEACOCK (W)		brown	peacock herl, gold tip	red hackle

BROWN HACKLE-RED NO. 1		brown	red dubbing, gold rib	
BROWN HACKLE-RED NO. 2 (W)		brown	red floss, gold rib	red hackle
BROWN HACKLE-SILVER NO. 1		brown	silver, red tip	
BROWN HACKLE-SILVER NO. 2 (W)		brown	embossed silver	red hackle
BROWN HACKLE-YELLOW NO. 1		brown	yellow dubbing, gold rib	
BROWN HACKLE-YELLOW NO. 2 (W)		brown	yellow floss, gold rib	red hackle
BROWN HEN	mottled brown hen	brown	peacock herl, gold tip	
BROWN MALLARD	brown mallard	brown	brown dubbing, picked out gold rib	brown mallard
BROWN MAY FLY (female)	pale mallard dyed brown	brown, partridge front	gold-brown floss, gold rib	brown mallard
BROWN MAY FLY (male)	pale mallard dyed brown	brown, partridge front	yellow floss, gold rib	brown mallard
BROWN MILLER	brown mallard	gray	orange dubbing, gold rib	brown mallard
BROWN MOTH	brown hen	brown	brown chenille, gold tip	
BROWN NYMPH		chestnut partridge	brown herl	wood duck
BROWN OLIVE NO. 1	gray	olive	brown-olive dubbing, gold tip	olive
BROWN OLIVE NO. 2	medium gray	dark brown	olive quill	blue dun-olive hackle fibers
BROWN PALMER (W)		brown Palmer	peacock herl	red hackle
BROWN PALMER-BIVISIBLE		brown Palmer ginger front	gold	brown hackle
BROWN PALMER-DARK		brown Palmer	peacock herl, gold tip	gold pheasant tippet
BROWN PALMER-LIGHT		brown Palmer	yellow dubbing, gold rib	
BROWN PENNELL HACKLE		brown	red thread or raffia	brown hackle
BROWN QUILL SPINNER	gray	brown	peacock quill	brown hackle
BROWN SEDGE NO. 1	brown hen or dyed brown	brown	brown floss, gold rib and tip	
BROWN SEDGE NO. 2	brown turkey	brown Palmer	dun dubbing, gold rib	
BROWN SEDGE NO. 3	pheasant	brown	gray wool, black floss rib	
BROWN SEDGE NO. 4 (W)	pheasant	brown Palmer	brown floss	pheasant fibers
BROWN SPIDER NO. 1 (W)		brown, spider radius	short, fat brown chenille	
BROWN SPIDER NO. 2		brown, spider radius	brown floss	
BROWN SPINNER	See Early Brown Spinner			
BROWN STONE	See Stone-Early Brown			
BROWN TRANSLUCENT	natural processed silk	brown	dyed brown translucent rubber	wood duck
BROWN TURKEY	brown turkey	brown	brown dubbing, gold tip	
BUMBLE BEE	See Bee			
BUNTLING	white	black	black floss, silver tip	
BUSTARD & BLACK	bustard	black	black dubbing, silver rib and tip	gold pheasant tippet
BUSTARD & ORANGE	bustard	orange	orange dubbing, gold rib and tip	gold pheasant tippet

BUTCHER		grizzlly dyed yellow	scarlet floss, yellow floss rib	scarlet fibers
BUTCHER-DARK	yellow and black	dark red	scarlet dubbing, brown silk rib	brown hackle
BUTCHER-KINGFISHER	dark gray	orange	gold tinsel, gold wire rib	kingfisher blue
BUTCHER-SILVER	blue black mallard	black	silver, silver wire rib	scarlet fibers
BUZZ FLY		grizzly, fore and aft	½ gold fore, ½ silver aft (embossed)	red hackle
CADDICE	See Caddis			
CADDIS NO. 1	gray duck	brown-red (natural)	brown floss, gold rib and tip	gray fibers
CADDIS NO. 2 (W)	light gray	brown	peacock herl	pheasant
CADDIS-BLACK NO. 1	black	black	½ peacock herl fore, ½ black dubbing aft	
CADDIS-BLACK NO. 2	black	coch-y-bondhu, Palmer	orange dubbing	red fibers
CADDIS, BLACK, Little	See Little Black Caddis			
CADDIS BUCK	light gray or brown deer body hair 1½ X hook length	furnace Palmer	deep orange seal fur	
CADDIS-DARK	gray duck	brown	peacock herl, brown floss tip	
CADDIS-FLYING	gray	brown Palmer	yellow floss	brown hackle
CADDIS-FLYING OLIVE	gray	olive Palmer	yellow dubbing	wood duck
CADDIS-GREEN	slate	yellow Palmer	green floss	
CADDIS-LIGHT NO. 1	dark gray	brown	peacock herl, orange floss tip	brown mallard
CADDIS-LIGHT NO. 2 (W)	gray	brown	peacock herl, orange floss tip	gold pheasant tippet
CADDIS-WHITE	white	white	green floss	
CAHILL BIVISIBLE		brown Palmer white front	gray dubbing, gold tip	wood duck
CAHILL-DARK	wood duck	brown	muskrat or hare's fur dubbing, gold tip	wood duck
CAHILL-GOLD	wood duck	brown	gold	wood duck
CAHILL-LEMON	wood duck	ginger	lemon floss, gold tip	wood duck
CAHILL-LIGHT	wood duck	light ginger	red fox belly fur (cream)	wood duck
CAHILL-LIGHT (Black Rib)	wood duck	ginger	buff dubbing, black thread rib	black hackle
CAHILL PALMER (Light)	wood duck	light ginger Palmer	cream fur dubbing	wood duck
CAHILL QUILL-DARK	wood duck	brown	peacock quill	wood duck
CAHILL QUILL-LIGHT	wood duck	light gray-dun	peacock quill	wood duck
CAHILL-STRAW	wood duck	brown	straw	wood duck
CAHILL-WHITE	wood duck	ginger	white dubbing	wood duck
CALDER	brown turkey with peacock over	furnace	orange floss, gold rib, peacock herl butt	barred wood duck
CALDWELL	brown turkey	brown	brown floss, yellow thread rib	brown mallard
CALIFORNIA (W)		badger	3 joint floss, gray tip, black center, red fore	
CALIFORNIA HACKLE NO. 1 (W)		badger	3 joint floss, red tip, yellow center, blue fore	
CALIFORNIA HACKLE NO. 2		badger	3 joint floss, red tip, white center, purple fore	
CALIFORNIA MOSQUITO (W)	See Mosquito, California			
CAMLET DUN	female brown mallard side	pale gray	gray dubbing, scarlet rib	gray duck fibers

CAMPBELL'S FANCY	teal	coch-y-bondhu	flat gold tinsel	gold pheasant crest or yellow hackle
CANADA NO. 1	brown turkey	brown	red floss, gold rib and tip	claret fibers
CANADA NO. 2 (W)	gray turkey	brown	red floss, gold rib	mallard
CANDY BIVISIBLE		scarlet and white Palmer		scarlet and white hackle
CANNON	See Oak Fly			
CAPERER NO. 1	light brown mallard	brown	scarlet dubbing, gold tip	
CAPERER NO. 2	hen pheasant	scarlet	brick red dubbing	
CAPERER NO. 3 (W)	gray turkey	brown	red floss, red tip	pheasant
CAPTAIN NO. 1	gray	brown	white floss, peacock herl butt	scarlet, yellow and mallard
CAPTAIN NO. 2	white	brown	black floss, gold tip	gold pheasant tippet
CAPTAIN SCOTT	gray turkey	black	dark brown floss, red floss tip	
CARDINAL NO. 1	gray turkey dyed red	ginger	silver	
CARDINAL NO. 2	scarlet	light red	scarlet dubbing, gold rib and tip	scarlet
CARLETON	gold pheasant tippet	olive-green	yellow floss, gold thread rib and tip	
CARMEN	blue, white tip mallard	black, short scarlet Palmer hackle	claret floss, gold rib	scarlet (blunt)
CARMICHAEL (W)	grizzly hackle tips	brown and grizzly mixed	pink fur	brown neck guard hackle
CARPENTER	wood duck	badger	cream dubbing	wood duck
CARTER HARRISON	teal (flat wing)	ginger	purplish-black wool, silver rib	scarlet fibers
CARTER'S FAVORITE	brown mallard, over green center strip	blue	light blue floss, silver rib, yellow wool tip	gold pheasant tippet
CASSARD	green, yellow and scarlet over barred wood duck	scarlet, yellow Palmer	scarlet dubbing, gold rib, peacock herl butt	barred wood duck, green, yellow and scarlet
CASSIN	black-white tip dyed yellow	brown	yellow floss, gold rib	peacock herl, and scarlet
CATOODLE BUG	See Toodle Bug			
CATSKILL NO. 1	mallard dyed orange	brown	orange floss, gold rib	orange mallard
CATSKILL NO. 2 (W)	mallard dyed brown	brown Palmer	red floss	
CAUGHLIN	gray turkey	claret Palmer	claret dubbing	gray turkey
CHAMBERLAIN	brown turkey	brown	orange dubbing, gold rib, black floss tip	gold pheasant crest
CHANTRY NO. 1	partridge	black	peacock herl, gold twist rib	
CHANTRY NO. 2	See Brown Hen			
CHATEAUGAY	mallard	brown	yellow floss	brown mallard
CHAUNCEY (W)		brown and grizzly mixed, Palmer		red fibers
CHENEY	mottled pheasant body feather	yellow	½ yellow floss, gold thread rib, aft; ½ scarlet dubbing, fore	wood duck, black and green
CHERRY SPINNER (female) NO. 1	brown hackle tips	brown	yellow floss, red floss tip, black ostrich herl at shoulder	brown hackle

Name				
CHERRY SPINNER (female) NO. 2	cherry-red hackle tips	cherry-red	dark brown floss, gold rib, black chenille at shoulder	cherry-red hackle
CHERRY SPINNER (male)	cherry-red hackle tips	cherry-red	black quill	cherry-red hackle
CHICAGO	dark red goose	dark red (dyed)	thick scarlet dubbing, gold and silver rib showing alternately	white fibers
CHIPPY (W)	red over white	black	orange floss, gold rib	
CHOCOLATE SPINNER		coch-y-bondhu	chocolate-brown chenille	mallard
CINNAMON NO. 1	cinnamon turkey	cinnamon	cinnamon dubbing	gray dun hackle
CINNAMON NO. 2	cinnamon turkey	black	lemon and black dubbing, gold rib	gold pheasant tippet
CINNAMON NO. 3	plain dyed cinnamon	brown	brown floss, gold rib	
CINNAMON & GOLD	cinnamon brown	cinnamon brown	gold, gold wire rib	gold pheasant tippet
CINNAMON QUILL	cinnamon	ginger	peacock quill (light)	ginger
CINNAMON SEDGE	cinnamon cock	ginger	cinnamon dubbing	
CLAPE	yellow, scarlet splits	scarlet	yellow chenille	scarlet and yellow
CLARET	deep claret	black	scarlet floss, gold rib and tip	
CLARET BIVISIBLE (W)		claret Palmer, white front		claret hackle
CLARET & BLACK	deep claret	black	black floss, gold rib and tip	
CLARET & BLUE	deep claret	blue	blue floss, gold rib and tip	
CLARET, BLUE & GROUSE	grouse, green strips	blue Palmer grouse throat	claret, silver rib	gold pheasant tippet
CLARET GNAT NO. 1	dark gray	claret	claret dubbing gold rib	
CLARET GNAT NO. 2 (W)	gray	claret	claret chenille, gold tip	claret hackle
CLARET & MALLARD	brown mallard	claret Palmer, light blue front	claret dubbing, gold rib	gold pheasant tippet
CLARET MOTH	claret	claret	claret chenille, gold tip	
CLARET & OLIVE	woodcock	guinea dyed claret, olive throat	olive dubbing, gold rib	gold pheasant tippet
CLARET PALMER		coch-y-bondhu Palmer, ½	claret ostrich herl	coch-y-bondhu
CLARET QUILL NO. 1	brown turkey	claret	peacock quill dyed claret	claret
CLARET QUILL NO. 2	gray	black	claret floss, gold wire rib	black hackle
CLARET & YELLOW	brown mallard	blue	yellow dubbing	gold pheasant tippet
CLYDE		red-brown fore and aft over peacock herl sections	peacock herl, red floss center joint	red-brown hackle
COACHMAN NO. 1	white	brown	peacock herl, gold tip	
COACHMAN NO. 2	white	brown	peacock herl, gold tip	gold pheasant tippet
COACHMAN NO. 3 (W)	white	brown	peacock herl, gold tip	red hackle
COACHMAN BIVISIBLE		brown, white front	peacock herl, gold tip	brown hackle
COACHMAN-BLACK	white	brown	black chenille, gold tip	gold pheasant tippet

COACHMAN-BRONZE (W)	bronze pheasant	brown	peacock herl, claret floss center joint	gold pheasant tippet
COACHMAN-BUFF	white	ginger	peacock herl, red floss tip	
COACHMAN-CABIN	Andalusian hackle tips spent	grizzly and brown	peacock herl	red hackle fibers
COACHMAN-CALIFORNIA NO. 1 (W)	white	yellow	peacock herl, yellow floss center joint	w/wo gold pheasant tippet
COACHMAN-CALIFORNIA NO. 2 (W)	white	brown	red floss, peacock herl center joint	brown mallard
COACHMAN-CALIFORNIA ROYAL (W)	white, scarlet splits	brown	peacock herl, gold tip	gold pheasant tippet
COACHMAN-EMERALD	white	brown	emerald green floss, gold tip	gold pheasant tippet
COACHMAN-ENGLISH	white	ginger	bronze peacock herl	
COACHMAN-ENGLISH ROYAL	white, red splits	black	black chenille, gold tip	
COACHMAN-GILT (Gold)	white	brown	gold, peacock herl butt, gold tip	gold pheasant tippet
COACHMAN-GREEN	dark gray	green	peacock herl, gold tip	
COACHMAN-LEADWING (or Dark)	gray duck, dark	brown	peacock herl, gold tip	gold pheasant tippet
COACHMAN-MURRAY	gray duck	brown	peacock herl, red floss center joint	white fibers
COACHMAN-ORANGE	white	orange	peacock herl, orange floss center joint, gold tip	gold pheasant tippet
COACHMAN-QUEEN (W)	white	brown	peacock herl, royal blue center joint	gold pheasant tippet
COACHMAN-RED	white	brown	red floss, gold tip	
COACHMAN-ROYAL NO. 1	white	brown	peacock herl, red floss center joint	gold pheasant tippet
COACHMAN-ROYAL NO. 2 (W)	white	brown	peacock herl, red floss center joint	red hackle
COACHMAN-ROYAL (Bivisible)		brown, white front	peacock herl, red floss center joint	gold pheasant tippet
COACHMAN-ROYAL BLACK	white	black	black chenille, red floss center joint	gold pheasant tippet
COACHMAN-ROYAL GINGER	white	ginger	peacock herl, red floss center joint	gold pheasant tippet
COACHMAN-SILVER NO. 1	blue	black	peacock herl, silver center joint	gold pheasant tippet
COACHMAN-SILVER NO. 2	white	brown	peacock herl, silver center joint	gold pheasant tippet
COACHMAN-SILVER ROYAL	white	brown	peacock herl, silver center joint	silver pheasant tippet
COACHMAN-UTAH ROYAL	white	brown	peacock herl, red floss center joint, red floss tag	gold pheasant tippet
COACHMAN-YELLOW	yellow	brown	peacock herl	
COB FLY	See March Brown			
COBLER	barred wood duck	brown	brown dubbing, gold rib	wood duck

COCH-Y-BONDHU		coch-y-bondhu	peacock herl, gold rib	
COCKTAIL	dark gray	brown	brown dubbing	
COFFIN FLY NO. 1	teal (dark barred)	badger	white raffia lacquered	any white feather having alternate black bands
COFFIN FLY NO. 2 (Green Drake Spinner)	teal breast	dark slatish black	ivory fur	cock pheasant
COLONEL FULLER NO. 1	yellow, red splits	yellow	yellow floss, gold rib	yellow and black
COLONEL FULLER NO. 2	yellow, red splits	yellow	yellow floss, gold rib	scarlet hackle
COLONEL MONELL		grizzly Palmer	peacock herl, scarlet floss rib	
COMBINATION	gray, scarlet and mallard splits	claret	claret dubbing at shoulder picked out, yellow at tip	scarlet and mallard
CONCHER	green, scarlet splits	green	green floss	scarlet fibers
CONNEMARA-BLACK	brown mallard	blue and black mixed or all black	black floss, silver rib	gold pheasant crest
CONOVER		light gold badger	lamb's wool, rabbit fur and scarlet	light gold badger
CONROY	black, white tip	green, guinea over	claret floss, peacock butt	
COOMBE'S BLUE HACKLE VARIANT		olive blue	medium blue-gray dubbing, white thread rib	olive-blue hackle fibers
COOPER	brown turkey	black	orange dubbing	
CORNELL	black	black	black floss, gold rib	black hackle
COTY-DARK	dark blue-gray hackle tips	dark blue-gray	blue-gray and scarlet wool mixed	dark blue-gray
COTY-LIGHT	light blue-gray hackle tips	light blue-gray	blue-gray and scarlet wool mixed	light blue-gray
COWDUNG (W)	white dyed light brown	brown	olive floss, gold tip	
COWDUNG-DARK NO. 1	gray	brown	greenish-yellow mohair, gold tip	
COWDUNG-DARK NO. 2	dark gray	brown	dark olive-green dubbing, gold tip	
COWDUNG-LIGHT NO. 1	light cinnamon turkey	ginger	brown mohair, gold tip	
COWDUNG-LIGHT NO. 2	hen pheasant	ginger	light green dubbing, gold tip	
COWDUNG-ORANGE (W)	cinnamon	brown	orange floss, gold tip	
CRESCO	black	olive green	light brown dubbing, yellow egg sac	black hackle
CRITCHLEY FANCY	grizzly hackle tips and scarlet	yellow and gray	yellow floss, gold rib and tag	yellow fibers
CROSS SPECIAL	wood duck	light blue dun	light cream fur dubbing	wood duck
CULLY	dark gray	brown	black dubbing, silver rib	brown hackle
CUPSUPTIC NO. 1	yellow duck	brown	red floss, silver rib	gold pheasant tippet
CUPSUPTIC NO. 2	brown turkey, guinea over	scarlet Palmer	silver	blue fiber and peacock

CUTTHROAT (W)	white	black	claret chenille, gold tip	black hackle
DANCER BIVISIBLE		blue dun Palmer, white front		blue dun hackle tip
DARK CLARET	dark claret	dark claret	claret dubbing, gold tip	claret fibers
DARK FOX	dark gray		fox fur picked out at shoulder, silver tip	dun hackle
DARK MACKEREL	See March Brown			
DARK MAY FLY (female)	brown mallard	brown	brown floss, yellow thread rib, chenille yellow egg sac	brown mallard
DARK MAY FLY (male)	teal dyed brown	coch-y-bondhu	brown floss, gold rib	black hackle
DARK MAY-FLY SPINNER (female)	grizzly hackle tip	brown	gold brown floss, gold rib, yellow chenille egg sac	brown hackle
DARK MAY-FLY SPINNER (male)	brown hackle tip	coch-y-bondhu	brown floss, gold rib	coch-y-bondhu
DARK MULTI-COLOR VARIANT	grizzly hackle tips	brown, black and blue-gray mixed	black floss	blue-gray, black and brown mixed
DARK OLIVE	dark gray	coch-y-bondhu	dark olive quill	coch-y-bondhu
DARK OLIVE DUN (female)	blue dun	dark blue dun	blue quill, gold rib and tip	olive-green hackle
DARK OLIVE DUN (male)	blue dun	dark blue dun	blue floss, brown thread rib	dark olive hackle
DARK PIED DUN	See Silver Horns			
DARK SAND	brown turkey	dark grizzly	dark gray dubbing	
DARK SEDGE NO. 1		blood red	dark green dubbing, gold wire rib	
DARK SEDGE NO. 2	dark gray	coch-y-bondhu, Palmer	black dubbing	
DARK SPINNER	dark gray	purple	claret floss, purple thread rib	purple hackle
DARK WATCHET	See Iron Blue Dun			
DARK WHIRLING DUN	dark gray	coch-y-bondhu	brown dubbing, gold tip	coch-y-bondhu
DARLING	brown turkey, gold pheasant tippet and blue over	furnace	black dubbing, orange floss tip	gold pheasant crest
DAVIDSON HACKLE		light brown, yellow over	dark orange fur (thick)	
DEACON	mallard	scarlet, yellow Palmer	yellow dubbing	
DEAD CHICKEN NO. 1	yellow hackle tips	yellow	yellow chenille	
DEAD CHICKEN NO. 2 (W)	light brown	ginger	tan chenille, gold tip	pheasant
DEER FLY NO. 1	white duck	white	green floss, gold tip, red head	black hackle
DEER FLY No. 2	gray	grizzly	gray dubbing	
DEER FLY No. 3 (W)	grizzly hackle tips	brown	gray chenille, gold tip	brown hackle
DENNISON	wood duck, green, yellow and scarlet	yellow Palmer	orange floss	wood duck, green, yellow and scarlet
DESPAIR	brown partridge	dark brown	peacock herl, orange floss rib	2 Amherst pheasant, 1 orange hackle fiber
DEVIL	partridge, red strip sides	black	black floss, gold rib	brown mallard
DEVIL BIVISIBLE		scarlet Palmer, white front		grizzly hackle tip dyed scarlet

DEVONSHIRE DOCTOR		black	black wool, gold wire rib	coch-y-bondhu
DICKY		black	peacock herl	guinea
DILL'S CHOICE	gray	brown	garnet floss	wood duck
DOLLY VARDEN (W)	cinnamon	brown	white floss, gold rib	cinnamon
DONNELLY VARIANT (Dark) (W)	badger hackle tips	brown and grizzly mixed	muskrat fur	brown throat guard hackle fiber
DONNELLY VARIANT (Light) (W)	honey dun hackle tips	brown and honey dun mixed	Russian gray squirrel tail	brown throat guard hackle fiber
DORSET	pale mallard	brown	olive-green floss, gold tip	brown hackle
DOWNHILL FLY	See Oak Fly			
DOWNLOOKER NO. 1	See Oak Fly			
DOWNLOOKER NO. 2	brown and black	brown Palmer	brown floss	furnace hackle
DR. BRECK NO. 1 (W)	scarlet and white	scarlet	silver	gray mallard
DR. BRECK NO. 2 (W)	mallard	red	silver (embossed)	red hackle
DR. GRANT (W)	gray	black	tan floss, tan floss tip	wood duck
DRAGON FLY		guinea	dark green floss, gold rib	guinea
DUN DRAKE	See March Brown			
DUN MAY	dark gray	gray dun	yellow dubbing	
DUN & GOLD NO. 1	blue dun hackle tips	blue dun	gold	blue dun hackle
DUN & GOLD NO. 2 (W)	gray	brown	gold	yellow hackle
DUN & SILVER	blue dun hackle tips	blue dun	silver	blue dun hackle
DURHAM RANGER	gold pheasant tippet, jungle cock eye sides	claret	claret floss, gold rib, peacock herl butt, yellow floss tip	gold pheasant crest
DUSTY MILLER NO. 1	gray turkey	grizzly	gray dubbing, gold tip	brown hackle
DUSTY MILLER NO. 2	gray turkey	grizzly	gray mohair, gold wire rib	gray turkey
DUSTY MILLER NO. 3 (W)	pheasant	brown partridge	silver (embossed)	red hackle
DUNHAM (R.B.)		grizzly dyed silver-doctor blue, furnace back	quill of blue and yellow macaw	reddish-brown golden pheasant crest
EARLY BROWN SPINNER	gray	coch-y-bondhu	brown dubbing	wood duck
EARLY GOLD SPINNER (female)	grizzly hackle tips	natural black	gold-brown floss, yellow chenille shoulder	natural black hackle
EARLY GOLD SPINNER (male)	ginger hackle tips	grizzly dyed brown	gold-brown floss, gold wire rib	ginger hackle
EARLY MAY DRAKE (female)	ginger hackle tips	ginger	cream floss, yellow ostrich herl shoulder	ginger
EARLY MAY DRAKE (male)	ginger hackle tips	ginger	brown floss, gold wire rib	ginger hackle
EDANDON	cinnamon cock	furnace	tan wool, peacock herl center joint	gold pheasant tippet
EDDY'S CHOICE	dark gray	brown	peacock herl	
EDMONSON'S WELSH	woodcock	partridge	brownish orange dubbing	
EDRINGTON	black, white tipped	brown	orange chenille, black thread rib	
EDWIN	gold pheasant tippet	yellow Palmer	yellow dubbing, black floss rib, scarlet floss tip	gold pheasant crest
EGG	gray duck		gold, yellow dubbing picked out at shoulder, gold tip	gray duck fibers

Name				
EIGHTH LAKE	guinea over white tipped black	claret	black dubbing, silver rib, claret tip	guinea and brown mallard
EKWANOK	See Equinox Gnat			
ELLIOT	mallard, scarlet splits	green	white chenille	gold pheasant crest and scarlet
EMERALD	brown mallard	light brown	light green dubbing, gold rib and tip	
EMERALD DUN	gray	gray dun	green floss, gold tip	
EMERALD GNAT	gray duck	brown	green floss, gold tip	brown hackle
EMIDA-BADGER	stubby, dark gray	badger Palmer	tan hair (clipped), silver (embossed) tip	
EMIDA-BROWN	stubby, dark gray	brown Palmer	tan hair (clipped), silver (embossed) tip	
EMIDA-CLARET	stubby, dark gray	claret Palmer	tan hair (clipped), silver (embossed) tip	
EMMA	jungle body feather	scarlet	red floss, gold rib	scarlet hackles
EMMET	black, blue; splits	black	black dubbing, gold rib, peacock herl butt	gold pheasant crest
ENGLISH ADMIRAL	white	red	red floss, gold rib	red hackle
EPTING NO. 1	gray mallard	black	red, orange and yellow mohair sections	gray mallard
EPTING No. 2 (W)	gray mallard	black	yellow floss, red floss tip	orange hackle
EPTING HACKLE		coch-y-bondhu	red silk, gold rib	
EQUINOX GNAT NO. 1	teal	grizzly	peacock quill	black hackle
EQUINOX GNAT NO. 2	teal	gray dun	dark peacock quill	
ESMERALDA	mottled partridge	brown, brown Palmer ½	gray wool, green-blue floss tag, gold tip	
ETHEL MAY	barred gray turkey	black	green floss, gold rib and tip	black hackle
EVAN'S RED ANT NO. 1 (W)	See Red Ant-Evans No. 1			
EVAN'S RED ANT NO. 2 (W)	See Red Ant-Evans No. 2			
EVENING DUN NO. 1	light gray	yellow	yellow dubbing, silver tip	yellow hackle
EVENING DUN NO. 2	gray	blue dun	buff mohair, gold tip	blue dun
FERN NO. 1	gray duck	pale gray dun	pale orange floss, silver rib and tip	
FERN NO. 2	dark gray	ginger brown	orange floss	
FERGUSON	brown turkey tail, yellow and red	light green	yellow floss, silver rib, scarlet tip	yellow and scarlet
FETED GREEN	green	green	green	green
FIERY BROWN NO. 1	bronze turkey	Rhode Island Red rooster	golden brown, gold rib and tip	gold pheasant tippet
FIERY BROWN NO. 2 (R.B.)	brown bucktail (flat)	grizzly	fiery brown wool	
FIN FLY	white duck	coch-y-bondhu	scarlet floss, gold tip	brown hackle
FIRE FLY	light gray	guinea	black dubbing, red tip, silver rib	
FIRE HOLE	teal	grizzly and black mixed	cream fur	grizzly and black mixed
FISHER	white tipped black, jungle cock eye	claret	yellow dubbing picked out, gold rib	wood duck

Name	Tail	Hackle	Body	Wing
FISHERMAN'S CURSE		grizzly	gray fur, brown floss rib	
FISH HAWK	brown turkey, jungle cock eye	brown	gold, brown thread rib	brown turkey
FITZMAURICE	mallard	yellow	red chenille, black chenille butt	peacock herl
FLAGGER	gray	grizzly	yellow floss, gold rib	
FLAMER	scarlet	brown	gold, brown chenille butt	scarlet
FLETCHER	brown turkey	grizzly Palmer	black floss, silver tip	mallard, guinea, red and yellow
FLIGHT'S FANCY	gray duck	ginger	cream-yellow floss, gold rib	ginger hackle
FLYING ANT (female)	black hackle tips	black	black floss, black chenille shoulder	black hackle
FLYING ANT (male)	black hackle tips	black	brown floss	black hackle
FLYING UPRIGHT	gray	grizzly Palmer	gray wool	gray fibers
FORKED TAIL NO. 1 (W)	gray	grizzly	light brown dubbing, gold rib	gray fibers (forked)
FORKED TAIL NO. 2 (W)	dark gray	black	black floss, black floss tip	red fibers (forked)
FORKED TAIL-BLACK (W)	See Green Forked Tail			
FORKED TAIL-GREEN (W)	See Green Forked Tail			
FORKED TAIL-RED (W)	See Red Forked Tail			
FORKED TAIL-YELLOW (W)	See Yellow Forked Tail			
FORSYTH	yellow, brown strips	yellow Palmer	yellow dubbing, light blue floss tip	
FORTNEY	blue dun hackle tips	grizzly	pink floss, gold rib	barred wood duck
FOSNOT	light gray	light blue	yellow dubbing	
FOWLER	red and white	red	white floss	red
FRANCIS FLY NO. 1	jungle cock wing (not eye)	gray dun	peacock herl, red floss rib, gold tip	
FRANCIS FLY NO. 2	grizzly dun hackle		peacock herl, red floss rib	
FRATILLEY	guinea, yellow strips	orange	claret dubbing, gold rib	
FURICH	yellow, guinea strips	yellow Palmer	yellow dubbing picked out, silver rib	gold pheasant tippet
FURNACE	gray duck	furnace hackle, coch-y-bondhu Palmer	scarlet floss	
FURNACE BIVISIBLE		furnace Palmer white front		
FURNACE BROWN		furnace	brown dubbing, gold rib	
FURNACE DUN	gray	furnace	brown and orange dubbing, gold tip	furnace
FURNACE HACKLE NO. 1		furnace	peacock herl	w/wo red hackle
FURNACE HACKLE NO. 2		furnace Palmer	orange floss, gold tip	
GALLAGHER SPECIAL		dark brown	black fur, gold rib	dark brown hackle
GENERAL HAMILTON	See Hamilton			
GENERAL HOOKER	dark gray duck	light brown hackle	yellow floss, green floss rib, gold tip	
GEORGE HARVEY		2 black reverse, 1 brown reverse, 1 brown standard	peacock herl, or black ostrich	brown hackle

GETLAND	mallard	brown	green floss, gold rib	cock pheasant
GINGER PALMER		ginger Palmer	yellow floss, silver rib	
GINGER QUILL-DARK	dark gray	ginger	peacock quill (dark)	ginger
GINGER QUILL-DUN	wood duck	ginger	peacock quill	ginger hackle
GINGER QUILL HACKLE		ginger	peacock quill	ginger
GINGER QUILL-LIGHT	light gray	ginger	peacock quill (light)	ginger
GINGER QUILL SPINNER	ginger hackle tips	ginger	peacock quill	wood duck
GINGER TEASER	1 ginger hackle tip	ginger (parachute)	black floss, gold rib	ginger hackle
GINGER TRANSLUCENT	natural processed silk	ginger	dyed tan rubber translucent	pale lemon wood duck
GOGEBIC	white, scarlet strips	scarlet	yellow floss, scarlet floss tag, gold tip	scarlet and white
GOLD BODY MULTI-COLOR VARIANT		cree (spider)	narrow gold (tinsel)	cree (sparse)
GOLD MIDGE		blue dun	pale green dubbing, gold rib	
GOLD MONKEY	dark gray duck	grizzly	yellow silk floss, gold rib	
GOLD PHEASANT	gold pheasant tippet	orange	orange floss, gold rib	gold pheasant tippet
GOLD PROFESSOR	See Professor-Gold			
GOLD STORK	gray mallard	brown	gold	gray mallard
GOLD STRIKE	1 brown hackle tip	brown (parachute)	black floss, gold rib	brown hackle
GOLD VARIANT NO. 1	gray	blue dun	gold	
GOLD VARIANT NO. 2	gray	light blue dun	orange-gold floss	light blue dun
GOLDEN BUT	yellow	yellow	brown floss, gold rib	yellow hackle
GOLDEN DEMON NO. 1	hen pheasant, jungle cock eye shoulder	orange	gold, round	gold pheasant crest
GOLDEN DEMON NO. 2	orange and white hair	orange and white	orange wool, silver rib	orange and white hackle
GOLDEN DOCTOR	brown turkey, mallard, blue and red	claret	gold tinsel	green, yellow and red
GOLDEN DUKE	scarlet	black	1/3 black dubbing at shoulder, balance gold	scarlet fibers
GOLDEN DUN NO. 1	light gray	ginger	gold, gold wire rib	mallard
GOLDEN DUN NO. 2	gray	gray	orange floss	brown mallard
GOLDEN DUN MIDGE	light gray	light gray dun	pale green dubbing, gold rib	gray hair
GOLDEN EYE GAUZE WING NO. 1	green	white	green floss	
GOLDEN EYE GAUZE WING NO. 2	pale green	blue dun	pale yellow floss, green floss rib	blue dun
GOLDEN GROUSE	grouse	yellow	golden-yellow floss, gold rib	brown partridge hackle
GOLDEN IBIS	scarlet	scarlet	gold	scarlet
GOLDEN MIDGE	dark gray	brown	yellow dubbing	
GOLDEN MONKEY	dark gray duck	guinea	green dubbing, gold rib and tip	
GOLDEN OLIVE	cinnamon cock	olive-brown	golden-brown dubbing, gold rib	olive-brown hackle
GOLDEN ROD	jungle body feather	orange	orange dubbing, peacock herl butt, gold rib, gold tip	scarlet fibers

GOLDEN SPINNER NO. 1	dark gray duck	dun-brown	golden-yellow floss, gold rib and tip	wood duck
GOLDEN SPINNER NO. 2 (W)	gray	brown	embossed gold tinsel	brown hackle
GOLDEN SPINNER (female)	white dyed golden-brown	ginger	raffia, natural	wood duck
GOLDEN SPINNER (male)	white dyed golden-brown	ginger and grizzly	raffia, natural	wood duck
GOOD EVENING	white tipped mallard	brown	scarlet floss, gold rib and tip	orange hackle
GORDON NO. 1	barred wood duck	grizzly	yellow mohair, gold tip	wood duck
GORDON NO. 2	barred wood duck	badger	yellow floss, gold thread rib	barred wood duck
GORDON-BLUE	barred wood duck	grizzly	blue mohair, gold tip	wood duck
GORDON QUILL	wood duck	blue dun	peacock quill, gold wire rib	blue dun
GORDON QUILL (female)	wood duck	blue dun	peacock quill, gold wire rib, yellow egg sac	blue dun
GOSLING NO. 1	mallard dyed yellow	yellow	yellow dubbing	yellow duck fiber
GOSLING NO. 2	gray	grizzly	green dubbing	
GOVERNOR	dark brown turkey	brown	peacock herl, red floss tip	
GOVERNOR ALVORD	cinnamon over black	brown	peacock herl, gold tip	scarlet fibers
GOVERNOR-IMPROVED	brown turkey	brown	peacock herl, red tip gold stripe	red hackle
GOVERNOR-RED TIP	dark brown turkey	brown	peacock herl, red floss tip	red (blunt)
GOVERNOR-ROYAL	cock pheasant tail	brown	peacock herl, green floss center joint, gold tip	brown hackle
GRACKLE	scarlet	black Palmer	peacock herl, silver tip	scarlet fiber
GRANNOM NO. 1	dark brown turkey	brown	brown dubbing, bright green butt	blunt brown-green tail
GRANNOM NO. 2	grouse	dark gray dun	green floss, black rib, gold tip	
GRANNOM (female)	brown turkey	chestnut partridge	brown floss, green chenille egg sac	
GRASSHOPPER	gray	furnace	yellow dubbing, gold tip	
GRAVEL BED	wood duck	black, 1 turn only	dark gray floss	
GRAY BIVISIBLE		grizzly, white front	gray dubbing, silver rib	grizzly tips
GRAY BODIED ASHY	gray dun		gray dubbing picked out at shoulder	gold pheasant tippet
GRAY COFLIN	dark gray	yellow	pink floss, yellow floss tip	gray fibers
GRAY COUGHLIN	dark gray	brown and grizzly	rabbit's fur, yellow floss tip	gray fibers
GRAY DOLLY	light gray	dun	gray dubbing, silver rib	gray fibers
GRAY DRAKE NO. 1	mallard	badger	white floss, black thread rib	
GRAY DRAKE NO. 2	mallard	palest gray or white	white floss, black thread rib, silver tip	black hackle
GRAY DRAKE NO. 3	mallard	gray dun	white floss, black rib	gray mallard

Name	Tail	Wing	Body	Hackle
GRAY DRAKE NO. 4 (Coombes)		black, teal feather face, wound hackle-wise	cream fur, narrow gold rib	2 cock pheasant tail fibers
GRAY DUKE	black	grouse	red floss ½ aft, black floss ½ fore, all gold rib	
GRAY DUN	dark gray	light grizzly	gray dubbing, silver tip	
GRAY FOX	dark gray	grizzly	dark gray fox fur, silver tip	dark gray fibers
GRAY FREAK		guinea	yellow floss	
GRAY FLY	brown turkey; mallard, pheasant and blue strips	grizzly Palmer	gray dubbing, orange floss tip, silver rib	gold pheasant tippet and mallard
GRAY GNAT NO. 1	light gray	light grizzly	rabbit's fur	
GRAY GNAT NO. 2 (W)	gray	gray dun	gray quill	gray dun hackle
GRAY & GREEN		grizzly	green dubbing, silver rib	grizzly hackle
GRAY GRUB (W)		grizzly	white chenille, black chenille butt	
GRAY HACKLE-GRAY NO. 1		grizzly	gray dubbing, gold rib	
GRAY HACKLE-GRAY NO. 2 (W)		grizzly	gray floss, gold rib	red hackle
GRAY HACKLE MAY		teal	light straw, gold rib or red floss rib	3 teal whisks
GRAY HACKLE-ORANGE		grizzly	orange dubbing, gold rib	
GRAY HACKLE-PEACOCK		grizzly	peacock herl, gold tip	gold pheasant tippet
GRAY HACKLE-RED NO. 1		grizzly	red dubbing, gold rib	
GRAY HACKLE-RED NO. 2 (W)		grizzly	red floss, gold rib	red hackle
GRAY HACKLE-SILVER NO. 1		grizzly	silver, red tip	
GRAY HACKLE-SILVER NO. 2 (W)		grizzly	embossed silver	red hackle
GRAY HACKLE-YELLOW NO. 1		grizzly	yellow dubbing, gold rib	
GRAY HACKLE-YELLOW NO. 2 (W)		grizzly	yellow floss, gold rib	red hackle
GRAY & LEMON		grizzly	lemon dubbing, gold rib	grizzly hackle
GRAYLING BIVISIBLE		blue dun Palmer, white front	gray dubbing, gold tip	brown hackle
GRAYLING FLY	dark brown mallard	coch-y-bondhu	claret dubbing, gold rib	
GRAY MARLOW	gray duck	gray dun	red dubbing, gold rib and tip	
GRAY MIDGE	mallard	badger Palmer	scarlet floss	mallard
GRAY MILLER	gray duck	gray dun	gray dubbing	
GRAY MONKEY	mallard	black	gray fur, silver rib	3 black hackles
GRAY MOTH NO. 1	widgeon	gray dun	gray floss, gold thread rib	yellow hackle
GRAY MOTH NO. 2 (W)	gray	grizzly	gray chenille, gold tip	grizzly hackle
GRAY PALMER BIVISIBLE		grizzly Palmer, white front	gray dubbing, gold rib, scarlet tip	
GRAY PALMER-DARK	dark grizzly hackle tied Palmer with any of the gray hackle bodies			
GRAY PALMER-LIGHT	light grizzly hackle tied Palmer with any of the gray hackle bodies			
GRAY QUILL	light gray	badger	peacock quill	badger hackle
GRAY-SCARLET MIDGE	mallard	scarlet	scarlet floss, gold tip	
GRAY SPIDER NO. 1		blue dun	gold tinsel	blue dun

GRAY SPIDER NO. 2		grizzly	gray dubbing	
GRAY TOWSER	gray	dun gray	cream floss ½ aft, gray floss ½ fore, all silver rib	
GRAY TRANSLUCENT	natural processed silk	pale blue dun and grizzly	natural rubber, translucent	black hackle
GRAY TURKEY	gray turkey	guinea	½ red chenille fore, ½ blue aft, silver tip	scarlet fibers
GREAT BROWN	See March Brown			
GREAT DUN NO. 1	dark gray	grizzly	brown dubbing	brown mallard
GREAT DUN NO. 2	dark gray	brown	brown floss, gold rib and tip	brown hair
GREAT DUN NO. 3	dark gray duck	black	dun bear hair dubbing, gold tip	gray duck fiber
GREAT RED SPINNER NO. 1	dark gray duck	brown	claret dubbing, gold rib and tip	
GREAT RED SPINNER NO. 2	gray duck	brown	red floss, gold rib	brown and white hackle
GREEN BIVISIBLE		green, white front	olive dubbing, gold rib	green hackle
GREEN DRAKE NO. 1	gray mallard dyed pale green-yellow	grizzly dyed pale yellow	cream fur	ring neck tail feather
GREEN DRAKE NO. 2	wood duck	brown	white floss, black thread rib, gold tip	wood duck
GREEN DRAKE NO. 3	duck dyed lemon	brown	brown dun dubbing	black hackle
GREEN DRAKE NO. 4	dyed yellow-olive	partridge and ginger	raffia dyed pale lemon, brown floss rib	brown mallard
GREEN DRAKE NO. 5	mallard dyed yellow	green	olive-green floss, black thread rib	yellow mallard
GREEN DRAKE-SPINNER	See Coffin Fly			
GREEN FORKED TAIL	gray	grizzly	green floss	green hackle, forked.
GREEN GROUSE	See Grouse & Green			
GREEN HACKLE		green	green floss, gold rib	
GREEN HECKUM	See Heckum-Green			
GREEN INSECT		cream	peacock herl	
GREEN MANTLE	mallard	green	green dubbing	green fiber
GREEN MAY FLY (female)	pale mallard dyed pale green	brown, grouse front	yellow floss, red thread rib, gold tip	brown mallard
GREEN MAY FLY (male)	pale mallard dyed pale green	olive, grouse front	yellow floss, brown thread rib	brown mallard
GREEN MIDGE	dark gray	black	dark green floss, gold tip	black
GREEN NYMPH		green	green dubbing, gold rib	green hackle
GREEN OLIVE	brown mallard	dark olive	dark olive-green wool, silver rib	
GREEN PALMER		grass green Palmer	green thread or raffia	gold pheasant tippet
GREEN PENNEL HACKLE		green	light green floss (not tapered), gold tip	green hackle
GREEN PROFESSOR	See Professor, Green			
GREEN SEDGE	light sand feather tied flat	grizzly	gray feather, green floss rib	
GREEN SPINNER	gray	olive	dark green floss, gold tip	black
GREEN TRANSLUCENT	lemon processed silk	olive-green	dyed green translucent rubber	olive-green hackle
GREEN VALE	mallard	black Palmer	green dubbing, silver rib	

GREENWELL'S GLORY NO. 1	gray	brown	olive-green dubbing, gold rib	gold pheasant tippet
GREENWELL'S GLORY NO. 2	cock pheasant or woodcock	coch-y-bondhu	olive-green dubbing, gold rib and tip	
GREENWELL'S GLORY NO. 3	wood duck	furnace	olive dubbing, gold rib	yellow hackle
GREENWELL'S GLORY-ENGLISH	dark gray	coch-y-bondhu	dark olive quill, gold wire rib	
GREENWOOD LAKE	See "Fancy Lake Flies"			
GREY WULFF	brown bucktail	blue dun	rabbit wool	brown bucktail
GRIFFITH	black crow, gold pheasant crest topping, jungle cock eye	black	black mohair, yellow floss rib, yellow seal fur butt, gold tip	
GRIZZLY HACKLE		grizzly	red floss	
GRIZZLY KING NO. 1	gray mallard	grizzly	green dubbing, gold rib	scarlet fibers
GRIZZLY KING NO. 2 (W)	gray mallard, red strips	grizzly	green floss, gold rib and tip	scarlet hackle
GROUSE BIVISIBLE		grouse Palmer, white front		grouse
GROUSE HACKLE		grouse	red wool, gold rib	
GROUSE PROFESSOR	See Professor, Grouse			
GROUSE SPIDER		grouse	orange floss, gold rib	
GROUSE & BLACK	grouse	black	black dubbing, gold rib and tip	gold pheasant tippet
GROUSE & CLARET	grouse	claret	claret mohair, gold rib and tip	gold pheasant tippet
GROUSE & GREEN	grouse	ginger	green dubbing, gold rib and tip	gold pheasant tippet
GROUSE & ORANGE	grouse	orange	orange dubbing, gold rib and tip	gold pheasant tippet
GROUSE & PEACOCK NO. 1	grouse	dark red	peacock herl, gold rib and tip	gold pheasant tippet
GROUSE & PEACOCK NO. 2 (Harrison)		brown, grouse face	peacock herl	
GROUSE & PURPLE	grouse	black	purple dubbing, gold rib and tip	gold pheasant tippet
GROUSE & YELLOW	grouse	yellow	yellow dubbing, gold rib and tip	gold pheasant tippet
GROUSER		ginger	yellow ostrich herl	ginger fibers
GRUMPY		badger	light yellow dubbing, black thread rib	
GUINEA BIVISIBLE		guinea Palmer, white front		guinea
GUINEA FLY NO. 1	guinea	scarlet	scarlet floss	white fibers
GUINEA FLY NO. 2	guinea	brown	green floss, gold rib	cock pheasant tail
GUINEA HEN	See Guinea Fly			
GUNNISON NO. 1	gray turkey	brown	green floss, white floss rib	mallard
GUNNISON NO. 2	gray	brown	olive-green floss, yellow floss rib	gold pheasant tippet
HACKLE-BLACK		black	peacock herl, gold tip	red hackle
HACKLE-CLARET		claret	claret floss, gold rib	claret hackle
HACKLE CURSE		badger	black floss, silver tip	
HACKLE-OLIVE		olive	light green floss, gold rib	olive hackle
HACKLE-RED		red	red floss, gold rib	red hackle
HACKLE-RED SPINNER		coch-y-bondhu	bright red wool, gold rib	3 brown hackle fibers

Name	Wings	Hackle	Body	Tail
HACKLE-WHITE		white	white floss, gold rib	red hackle
HACKLE-YELLOW		yellow	yellow floss, gold rib	yellow hackle
HACKSTAFF HACKLE		grizzly	white chenille, orange floss tip	
HALF STONE	woodcock	honey dun	yellow dubbing	
HALFORD SPENT MAY (female)	blue dun hackle tips spent	blue dun	pale yellow straw, narrow black floss rib	3 brown hackle fibers
HALFORD SPENT MAY (male)	dark speckled dun hackle tips spent	partridge dyed olive front, olive back	white straw, narrow red floss rib	3 brown hackle fibers
HAMILTON	brown shoulder hackle	brown	scarlet floss, gold rib and tip	
HAMLIN	white duck	black	dark quill, gold tip	white tipped mallard
HAMMOND'S	wood duck	ginger	light brown, gold rib and tip	
HAMMOND'S ADOPTED	grouse	brown Palmer	bright brown dubbing	
HARDY'S FAVORITE NO. 1	gray turkey	brown	red floss, peacock herl rib	black hackle
HARDY'S FAVORITE NO. 2 (W)	pheasant	brown	red floss, peacock herl rib	gold pheasant tippet
HARE'S EAR NO. 1	gray		hare's ear dubbing picked out	brown hackle
HARE'S EAR NO. 2	hen pheasant		hare's ear dubbing picked out	brown mallard
HARE'S EAR-GOLD RIB	gray		hares ear dubbing picked out, gold rib and tip	rabbit hair
HARE'S EAR HACKLE NO. 1			hare's ear dubbing picked out at shoulder, gold tip	rabbit hair
HARE'S EAR HACKLE NO. 2		brown, gray dun front	hare's ear dubbing, gold wire rib	log rabbit hair fibers
HARE'S EAR QUILL	gray	hare's ear picked out	peacock quill	rabbit hair
HARE'S EAR & CLARET	gray over grouse	claret	hare's ear, gold rib	claret hackle fibers
HARE'S EAR & WOODCOCK	woodcock		hare's ear dubbing picked out, gold tip	rabbit hair
HARE'S FLECK	See Hare's Ear			
HARE'S PLUCK	See Hare's Ear			
HARLEQUIN NO. 1	gray duck	black	scarlet aft, blue fore, silver rib and tip	
HARLEQUIN NO. 2	dark gray	black	black floss fore, orange floss aft, gold rib	gold pheasant tippet
HAWTHORNE NO. 1	light gray duck	black	black ostrich herl	black hackle
HAWTHORNE NO. 2	black crow	black	black floss, silver rib and tip	black hackle
HAZLE FLY	See Coch-y-bondhu			
H. C. S.	guinea	brown	scarlet floss, gold rib	
HEATHER MOTH		dun Palmer	rabbit's fur, silver tip	brown mallard
HECKMAN-RED	mallard	brown	scarlet dubbing, gold rib	cock pheasant tail
HECKUM-GREEN	black, white tipped	brown	green dubbing, silver rib	gold pheasant tippet
HECKUM-RED	black, white tipped	brown	scarlet dubbing, gold rib	gold pheasant tippet

HECKUM-YELLOW	woodcock	brown	yellow dubbing, gold rib	gold pheasant tippet
HECKUM PECKHAM GREEN	black, white tipped	brown	green wool, gold rib	yellow gold pheasant body feather
HECKUM PECKHAM RED	black, white tipped	brown	red wool, gold rib	yellow gold pheasant body feather
HECKUM PECKHAM RED & YELLOW	black, white tipped	brown	½ aft yellow, ½ fore red dubbing, gold rib	brown hackle fibers
HECKUM PECKHAM YELLOW	black, white tipped	brown	yellow wool, gold rib	yellow gold pheasant body feather
HELLGRAMITE NO. 1	gray	grizzly	brown dubbing	grizzly hackle
HELLGRAMITE NO. 2 (W)	gray	grizzly	gray quill	mallard
HELLGRAMITE-LIGHT	gray	grizzly	buff dubbing	grizzly hackle
HEMLOCK	brown turkey	brown	dark gray floss, white floss rib	
HEMSWORTH	brown hen, jungle cock eye	olive and scarlet	olive dubbing, gold tip, herl butt	
HEN GUINEA	guinea	red	red dubbing, gold rib and tip	scarlet hackle
HENDRICKSON	barred wood duck	blue dun and brown	tannish gray fox fur	wood duck
HENDRICKSON-DARK	dark wood duck	dark blue dun	dark fox belly fur	wood duck
HENDRICKSON EGG SAC	dark wood duck	dark blue dun	dark fox belly fur, yellow egg sac	wood duck
HEDRICKSON-LIGHT (original)	wood duck	blue dun, pale	light fox belly fur (cream)	wood duck
HENSHALL NO. 1	gray mallard	light gray dun	peacock herl	peacock herl
HENSHALL NO. 2 (W)	mallard	white	yellow floss, peacock herl butt	peacock sword
HERB'S FAVORITE	badger hackle tip	badger (tied parachute)	black floss, gold rib	badger hackle
HERMAN FLY	light gray	brown	red dubbing, gold tip	
H. G. S.	See H.C.S.			
H. HOWARD	white bucktail (flat)	badger	black wool	
HOD	cinnamon turkey	brown	green dubbing, gold rib and tip	
HOD VERMILYE	dark gray	brown	dark green dubbing	
HOFLAND'S FANCY NO. 1		brown	peacock herl, gold rib, red tip	
HOFLAND'S FANCY NO. 2	snipe	brown	orange-brown dubbing	dun-brown hackle
HOFLAND'S FANCY NO. 3	brown and yellow	brown	dark red	brown hackle
HOFLAND'S FANCY NO. 4 (W)	brown turkey	brown	brown floss	brown hackle
HOLBERTON NO. 1	peacock, scarlet, mallard, wood duck, yellow, brown turkey	scarlet	peacock at shoulder, orange floss aft, gold rib	peacock, scarlet, yellow, wood duck, mallard
HOLBERTON NO. 2	See Bass & Lake Fly List			
HONEY SPIDER		honey (spider radius)		
HOPATONG	brown turkey, jungle cock eye sides	black Palmer	silver	scarlet and yellow fibers
HOPKIN'S VARIANT	slate, short and heavy	red-brown, faced with silver doctor blue	condor quill	red-brown hackle
HORSE FLY NO. 1	black hackle tips	black	black chenille, gold tip	

HORSE FLY NO. 2 (W)	black hackle tips	grizzly	black chenille, gold tip	
HOSKINS NO. 1	gray mallard	gray	yellow floss, gold tip	yellow hackle
HOSKINS NO. 2	light gray	grizzly	yellow floss	gold pheasant crest
HOUSE FLY NO. 1	dark gray	black	dun quill	
HOUSE FLY NO. 2	light slate gray	brown	black chenille or peacock	
HOWELL	white tipped turkey	claret	peacock herl, gold rib and tip	scarlet fibers
HUDSON	brown turkey	orange	dark brown dubbing, gold rib, orange floss tip	green fibers
HUMBLE BEE	light gray	brown	4-joint chenille black and yellow alternately	
HUNT FLY	cinnamon turkey	brown	green floss, yellow floss rib	
HUNTER	brown mallard, red strips	orange at shoulder, claret Palmer	dark gray dubbing mixed with claret, silver rib	brown mallard and scarlet
IBIS	See Ibis-Scarlet			
IBIS-GOLD	white, scarlet strips	yellow and scarlet	gold	scarlet and white fibers
IBIS-GUINEA	scarlet	scarlet	yellow floss, silver rib	guinea
IBIS-HACKLE		scarlet	white floss, silver rib	
IBIS-SCARLET	scarlet	scarlet	scarlet floss, gold rib	scarlet fibers
IBIS-SILVER	scarlet	scarlet	silver	scarlet fibers
IBIS-SPLIT	scarlet, white split	scarlet	silver	white and scarlet
IBIS-TINSELED	scarlet, barred wood duck up sides	scarlet	silver, gold rib	scarlet and barred wood duck
IBIS-WHITE NO. 1	scarlet and white	scarlet and white	scarlet floss, gold rib and tip	scarlet and white
IBIS-WHITE NO. 2 (W)	white, red strips over	red hackle	½ fore red floss, ½ aft white floss	red hackle
IBIS-WHITE SHOULDER	scarlet, white strips	white and scarlet	scarlet floss	scarlet fibers
IBIS-WOOD	black	orange Palmer	claret dubbing	orange and brown mallard
IBIS YELLOW	scarlet	scarlet	yellow floss, gold rib	scarlet fibers
IDAHO (W)	gray turkey, red, yellow, and blue strips	bright blue	white floss, gold rib	gold pheasant tippet
IDANHA (W)	gray	brown	yellow floss, black floss rib	red hackle
IKE	brown mallard	brown	yellow floss, white floss tip	brown mallard
ILEN BLUE	bright kingfisher blue	claret	blue floss, silver rib	gold pheasant tippet
IMBRIE NO. 1	gray duck jungle cock eye shoulder	brown	yellow floss, gold rib, black chenille butt, gold tip	gold pheasant crest
IMBRIE NO. 2	gray duck	light red	white floss, gold rib and tip	gold pheasant tippet
IMPROVED GOVERNOR	See Governor-Improved			
INDIAN ROCK	mallard over scarlet	scarlet Palmer	peacock herl, silver tip	scarlet and mallard
INDIAN YELLOW NO. 1	gray duck	brown	scarlet floss, gold rib and tip	brown hackle
INDIAN YELLOW NO. 2	grouse	ginger	light brown dubbing, yellow rib	ginger hackle

INFALLIBLE		dark blue dun	2/3 dark blue fur fore, 1/3 red floss aft.	
INGERSOL	gray turkey	brown	green chenille, gold rib	gold pheasant tippet
INVICTA	partridge	guinea dyed blue, sparse yellow throat	yellow dubbing, gold rib	gold pheasant tippet
INVICTA-SILVER	gold pheasant tail	blue jay over ginger	flat silver, silver wire rib	gold pheasant crest
IRISH BIVISIBLE		light green Palmer, white front		light green hackle tip
IRISH GROUSE	peacock herl	grouse	orange floss, gold rib	
IRISH TURKEY	brown turkey	brown	green floss, yellow floss rib	yellow hackle
IRON BLUE DRAKE	See Iron Blue Dun			
IRON BLUE DUN NO. 1	coot	iron blue dun	brown and deep red dubbing mixed	iron blue dun
IRON BLUE DUN NO. 2	coot	pale blue dun	gray dubbing, gold tip	coot fibers
IRON BLUE DUN NO. 3	coot	dark coch-y-bondhu	blue-gray dubbing, red floss tip	coch-y-bondhu hackles
IRON BLUE DUN NO. 4	coot	iron blue dun	iron blue dun dubbing	iron blue dun hackle
IRON BLUE DUN (female)	coot	brown	brown floss, gold rib	brown hackle
IRON BLUE DUN (male)	coot	grizzly dyed brown	dark peacock quill (from herl)	dark olive hackles
IRON BLUE DUN QUILL	brownish olive	dark olive-brown	dark blue quill	dark olive hackle fibers
IRON BLUE HACKLE		black	dark red quill	olive hackle fibers
IRON BLUE QUILL NO. 1	blue dun hackle tips	iron blue dun	dark iron blue quill	dark blue dun
IRON BLUE QUILL NO. 2	coot	coch-y-bondhu	dark peacock quill (from herl)	coch-y-bondhu
IRON BLUE SPINNER (female)	blue dun hackle tip	brown	dark red floss	brown hackle
IRON BLUE SPINNER (male)	pale yellow hackle tip	cream ginger	pale gray floss, red floss tip	pale yellow hackle
IRON BLUE VARIANT	short dark blue fish skin	dark iron blue	raffia dyed dirty red	iron blue hackle
JAMES	brown turkey	claret	silver	scarlet fibers
JAMES ALDER	See Alder James			
JAMISON'S McGINTY	See McGinty			
JENNIE LIND-BLUE	bright blue duck	scarlet	yellow floss, gold rib	bright blue duck fibers
JENNIE LIND-LAVENDER	light lavender duck	scarlet	yellow floss, gold rib	light lavender
JENNIE SPINNER NO. 1		white	white floss, scarlet floss tip	
JENNIE SPINNER NO. 2	white	white	3 joint floss, black, white, black	
JENNIE SPINNER NO. 3		gray dun	dun-brown quill	
JEWELL	dark gray duck	brown	yellow floss, gold rib	
JOCK SCOTT NO. 1	mallard; blue, scarlet, peacock strips, jungle cock eye	guinea	black floss ½ fore, yellow floss ½ aft, gold rib	gold pheasant tippet and crest
JOCK SCOTT NO. 2	yellow and gray turkey; mallard and scarlet strips, jungle cock eye	guinea	yellow floss, white floss rib, black tip	yellow and scarlet fibers

JOCK SCOT NO. 3	mallard, gold pheasant crest top; blue, scarlet and jungle cock eye strips	guinea	silver, black chenille butt	scarlet and gold pheasant crest
JOCK SCOT NO. 4	gray turkey, scarlet and yellow strips	grizzly	yellow floss, gold rib	gold pheasant crest
JOCK SCOT NO. 5 (W)	brown turkey, peacock sword top; red, yellow, blue, orange, mallard strips	guinea	½ black floss fore, ½ yellow floss aft	red hackles
JOCK SCOT-MONTANA (W)	brown turkey, red and yellow strips	guinea	black floss fore, yellow floss aft, gold rib	scarlet hackle
JOE KILLER	yellow and white, peacock sword and jungle cock eye	red bucktail	silver	barred wood duck
JOE'S GRASSHOPPER	brown turkey lacquered	grizzly dyed brown, brown Palmer	yellow wool	red hackle
JOHN MANN	brown turkey	brown Palmer	yellow floss, gold rib, red tip	brown turkey
JOSEPHINE	scarlet goose	brown	peacock herl, gold tip	gold pheasant tippet
JULY DRAKE (female)	ginger hackle tips	ginger	tan floss, white chenille at shoulder	ginger hackle
JULY DRAKE (male)	ginger hackle tips	grizzly	brown floss, gold wire rib	ginger hackle
JULY DUN NO. 1	gray duck	dark blue dun	yellow dubbing	dun hackle
JULY DUN NO. 2	dark gray		rabbits fur picked out at shoulder	gray hackle
JUNE	brown turkey	black	4-joint white and scarlet chenille	
JUNE BUG (W)	peacock sword	black	orange floss, gold rib	peacock sword
JUNE QUILL (female)	olive-ginger hackle tips	ginger	black floss, black chenille at shoulder	ginger
JUNE QUILL (male)	olive-ginger hackle tips	ginger	black floss, gold rib	ginger
JUNE SPINNER (female)	iron blue dun	badger	black floss, yellow egg sac	
JUNE SPINNER (male)	black	black	black floss, silver rib	
JUNGLE	jungle body feather	grizzly	silver	scarlet fibers
JUNGLE COCK NO. 1	jungle cock body feather (full)	black	silver	gold pheasant tippet
JUNGLE COCK NO. 2	jungle cock body feather (full)	badger	scarlet floss, gold rib	barred wood duck
JUNGLE COCK NO. 3	dark brown turkey, jungle cock eye	claret	blue-gray dubbing, gold rib	scarlet fibers
JUNGLE COCK NO. 4 (W)	mallard	black	red floss, gold rib	black hackle
JUNO	See Bass & Lake Flies			
KAMALOFF	brown turkey	grizzly	yellow dubbing, red floss tag, gold tip	brown mallard
KATOODLE BUG NO. 1	brown turkey	brown	3-joint floss, dark blue tip, yellow center, orange fore	brown mallard
KATOODLE BUG NO. 2	brown turkey	brown Palmer	3-joint floss, green tip, yellow center, orange fore	gray mallard

KATYDID	green duck	green	green floss, gold wire rib	green hackle
KENDALL	brown mallard	scarlet	claret chenille	scarlet hackle
KENNETT BLUE SPENT GNAT	spent blue dun hackle tips	blue dun	pale yellow straw, red floss rib	3 fibers black hackle
KIFFE	brown mallard	scarlet	green floss, gold rib	scarlet
KIMBRIDGE SEDGE	woodcock	brown	white floss, gold rib	
KINDON	See Kingdom			
KINEO	black white-tipped; gray turkey and scarlet	orange scarlet Palmer strips	scarlet dubbing picked out, silver rib	scarlet and gray turkey
KING OF THE WATERS NO. 1	mallard	brown Palmer	scarlet floss, silver rib	
KING OF THE WATERS NO. 2	mallard	brown	scarlet floss, gold rib	mallard
KINGDOM	brown turkey	brown	fore joint peacock herl, aft white floss with blue floss rib	
KINGFISHER NO. 1	gray turkey	light blue	silver	
KINGFISHER NO. 2	gray turkey	brown	scarlet dubbing, gold rib	
KINGFISHER NO. 3 (W)	mallard	brown	red floss, white floss rib	
KITSON	yellow and black	claret	yellow dubbing, gold rib	black hairs
LA BELLE	white	blue	light blue floss, scarlet tip	
LA BRANCHE	gray duck	blue dun	blue-gray dubbing, gold rib and tip	gray hackle
LADY ANDERSON	wood duck	light brown	yellow with black head	wood duck
LADY BEAVERKILL	See Beaverkill (Female)			
LADY GRAY	jungle body feather	scarlet Palmer	rabbit's fur, silver rib	scarlet and gold pheasant tippet, lemon wood duck
LADY MARTHA	white duck	black	peacock herl, gold tip	scarlet duck fibers
LADY MERTON	mallard	scarlet, black Palmer	rabbit's fur, silver rib, claret tip	gold pheasant crest
LADY MILTON	brown turkey, mallard, blue, scarlet and wood duck	blue Palmer	rabbit's fur, black chenille butt, scarlet tag, gold tip	wood duck, scarlet, blue and green fibers
LADY NYLO (W)		brown nylon (monofilament)	nylon-brown aft, ¾ white front, orange stitched belly, black herl head	
LADY OF THE LAKE	white duck	white	peacock herl, silver center joint	peacock sword
LADY SUE	black crow	white (sparse)	scarlet floss, gold rib and tip	white duck fibers
LAKE EDWARD NO. 1	brown turkey	scarlet	brown dubbing	gold pheasant crest
LAKE EDWARD NO. 2	dark bronze turkey; yellow and purple splits	claret	red-brown mohair, silver rib	gold pheasant crest
LAKE GEORGE NO. 1	gold pheasant tippet, brown mallard strips	orange Palmer claret at shoulder	gold, silver wire rib	gold pheasant crest
LAKE GEORGE NO. 2	white and scarlet strips	white	scarlet floss, gold rib	white and scarlet
LAKE GREEN	mallard	brown	yellow floss, green floss rib	

LANGIWIN	yellow	yellow	black floss, yellow thread rib	yellow fibers
LANNIGAN NO.1	mallard	claret Palmer	white chenille	black fibers
LANNIGAN NO. 2	brown turkey, blue strips	brown	scarlet dubbing (picked out), yellow tip	gold pheasant tippet
LARAMIE NO. 1	mallard	dark blue	scarlet floss, silver rib	scarlet fibers
LARAMIE NO.2	dark teal	black	dark red dubbing, gold rib	blunt red fibers
LARAMIE SPINNER	brown mallard	grizzly	yellow floss, black floss rib	
LARGE DARK OLIVE DUN (female)	olive-brown hackle tips	olive-brown	peacock quill (from herl), gold tip	olive-brown
LARGE DARK OLIVE DUN (male)	olive-brown hackle tips	olive	raffia dyed olive, blue thread rib	olive
LARGE DARK OLIVE SPINNER (female)	blue dun hackle tips	yellow-olive	olive-green quill, yellow egg sac	yellow-olive
LARGE DARK OLIVE SPINNER (male)	blue dun hackle tips	olive	peacock quill, dyed olive-green	guinea dyed olive
LARIMIE SPINNER	brown mallard	brown	orange floss, black floss rib	brown hackle
LARRY ST. JOHN	gray mallard, gold pheasant tippet shoulder	grizzly	lavender dubbing, gold rib	grizzly
LAST CHANCE	light gray	brown	yellow floss, black thread rib, gold tip	scarlet fibers
LAWRENCE	See Bob Lawrence			
LEMON FISH HAWK		light badger	lemon floss, gold tinsel rib	with or without badger
LIBERTY	scarlet	white	blue floss, gold rib	scarlet, white and blue
LIGHT BLOW	brown turkey	scarlet	peacock quill	brown turkey
LIGHT FOX	dark gray	yellow	white dubbing, picked out, yellow tag, gold tip	
LIGHT MACKEREL	See Great Red Spinner			
LIGHT POLKA	guinea	white	white chenille	
LIGHT TRANSLUCENT	natural processed silk	cream	natural rubber translucent	pale lemon wood duck
LIGHTNING BUG	dark gray	grizzly	black floss, brown floss rib, orange floss tip	
LILLIE	dark gray turkey	scarlet Palmer	gray dubbing, yellow floss tip	gray turkey fibers
LITTLE BLACK CADDIS	coot or black	coch-y-bondhu	black fur	
LITTLE BLACK STONE-FLY	black	black	brown and black dubbing	black
LITTLE BROWN SPINNER	brown mallard	brown	brown floss, gold rib	brown mallard
LITTLE DARK BLUE	See Iron Blue Dun			
LITTLE DARK DUN	See Iron Blue Dun			
LITTLE EGG	gray	yellow	orange floss, gold tip	blue fibers
LITTLE LEHIGH SPECIAL		golden badger Palmer	olive floss, gold rib	badger hackle
LITTLE MARRYAT NO. 1	pale gray quill	cream	Australian opossum	cream hackle
LITTLE MARRYAT NO. 2	light gray duck	ginger	dark green dubbing, gold tip	brown hackle
LITTLE RED MIDGE	brown turkey	brown	red floss, gold rib	
LONG TOM	cinnamon; brown mallard sides; barred wood duck top	dun Palmer, claret shoulder	rabbit's fur picked out, silver rib	gold pheasant crest
LORD BALTIMORE NO. 1	black	black	orange floss, black floss rib	black hackles

LORD BALTIMORE NO. 2	black, jungle cock eye	black	orange floss, black floss rib	black
LOTTIE	black white-tipped; brown mallard strips	orange Palmer	silver, gold rib	guinea and gold pheasant tippet
LOWERY	light brown	brown	peacock herl, orange floss tip	
LOWRY	cock pheasant tail	brown	peacock herl, yellow floss tip	
LOYAL SOCK	black	black	yellow floss	
LUMN		black	peacock herl	peacock herl (2 fibers)
LUNN'S FLY	2 blue dun hackle tips flat	brown	brown hackle stem tied quill	4 brown hackle fibers
LUZERNE	mallard	black	claret floss	
MACINTOSH-BROWN (effective for Nova Scotia Salmon)	fox squirrel tail (down-wing)	thick brown	black working silk	
MACINTOSH-GRAY (effective for Nova Scotia Salmon)	gray squirrel (down-wing)	badger or grizzly, thick	black working silk	
MADSEN	grizzly (sail wing)	grizzly; brown Palmer	bright green wool	wood duck fibers
MAGALLOWAY	peacock herl	furnace	light brown dubbing picked out, black chenille butt	yellow fibers
MAGPIE NO. 1	white-tipped mallard	black	black dubbing	black hairs
MAGPIE NO. 2	white tipped mallard	brown	brown floss, gold rib	brown hackle
MAINE JUNGLE	jungle feather	claret	claret dubbing, gold rib, green floss tip	scarlet fibers
MAJOR	mallard; brown turkey and blue strips	orange; scarlet Palmer	purple dubbing, gold rib, blue floss tip	gold pheasant tippet
MAJOR PITCHER	white with bright blue strips	brown Palmer	red floss, yellow floss tip	
MALLARD	brown mallard	brown	yellow dubbing, gold rib	brown mallard
MALLARD & AMBER	brown mallard	light red	amber floss, gold rib and tip	gold pheasant tippet
MALLARD & BLACK	brown mallard	black	black dubbing, silver rib	gold pheasant tippet
MALLARD & CLARET	brown mallard	light red (natural)	claret dubbing, gold rib and tip	gold pheasant tippet
MALLARD, CLARET & YELLOW	brown mallard	claret	yellow dubbing, gold rib and tip	gold pheasant tippet
MALLARD & GREEN	brown mallard	light red (natural)	green dubbing, gold rib and tip	gold pheasant tippet
MALLARD & RED	brown mallard	light red	red dubbing, gold rib and tip	gold pheasant tippet
MALLARD & YELLOW	brown mallard	furnace	yellow dubbing, gold rib	gold pheasant tippet
MALLARD QUILL	brown mallard	brown	peacock quill	mallard
MANCHESTER	peacock sword	yellow	brown chenille, gold rib	peacock sword
MARBLE	gray	yellow	scarlet dubbing picked out, yellow tip	mallard
MARCH BROWN NO. 1	dark brown turkey	brown	gray-brown dubbing, yellow floss rib, gold tip	brown hackle
MARCH BROWN NO. 2	pheasant	brown partridge	gray wool, yellow floss rib	brown partridge
MARCH BROWN (female)	brown mottled turkey	chestnut partridge	olive-green dubbing, gold rib	partridge fibers
MARCH BROWN (male)	partridge	partridge	brown dubbing, gold rib	partridge

MARCH BROWN-GINGER	brown mottled turkey	ginger	brown fur	ginger hackle
MARCH BROWN HACKLE		partridge	brown dubbing, gold rib	partridge fibers
MARCH BROWN-LIGHT	light partridge	chestnut partridge	olive and brown dubbing mixed	partridge fibers
MARCH BROWN-SILVER	partridge	partridge	silver	partridge
MARCH BROWN SPIDER		partridge	dark brown dubbing, gold rib	partridge
MARCH DUN	light gray		green dubbing picked at shoulder, gold tip	
MARKHAM	white-tipped brown turkey	scarlet	yellow floss	scarlet and yellow fibers
MARLOW BUZZ	See Coch-y-bondhu			
MARQUIS MAY STRADDLE BUG		teal over dyed olive over ginger	pale yellow straw, gold rib	3 fibers black hackle
MARQUIS WINGED MAY	mallard	teal over dyed olive over ginger	pale yellow straw, gold rib	3 fibers black hackle
MARSTERS	mallard	scarlet	white floss, gold tip	mallard
MARSTON'S FANCY	white, black strips	black	white chenille, silver rib, red floss tip	white tipped black mallard
MARTIN	mallard	yellow	yellow floss, gold rib	yellow and black fibers
MARTINEZ		furnace; grizzly dyed blue front	blue and yellow wing quill	gold pheasant red breast feather fibers
MASCOT	dark gray	black	peacock herl, yellow floss tip	scarlet hackle
MASSASSAGA	guinea dyed yellow	yellow	scarlet ibis green floss or	fur, gold rib
MATHER	gray duck	grizzly	peacock herl; green floss center joint, red tip, gold tag	peacock herl
MAURICE	gray mallard	yellow	scarlet floss aft, black floss gold rib fore	scarlet duck fibers
MAXWELL BLUE		light blue	gray dubbing, silver rib	light blue hackle
MAY FLY	dark gray	yellow	yellow floss, gold rib	gray duck fibers
MCALPINE	scarlet and peacock herl	guinea	claret dubbing, gold rib	scarlet and barred wood duck
MCBRIDE	cinnamon	brown Palmer	yellow dubbing (picked out), silver rib	scarlet fibers
MCGINTY	white tipped mallard	brown	black and yellow 4-joint chenille	scarlet hackle and teal
MCKENZIE	gray turkey	brown	light olive-green dubbing, gold rib	brown hackle
MCKENZIE SPECIAL (W)	light gray	grizzly	green floss, green floss tip	gold pheasant tippet
MCQUARRIE		cream (sparse spider radius)	silver tinsel	cream hackle fibers
MCSNEEK	white fan-wings	black	dyed black peacock herl, silver tinsel center joint	black hackle
MEALY MOTH	white	white	light gray dubbing, silver rib	
MEDIUM SEDGE	gray	natural red Palmer	orange-brown dubbing	
MEGALLOWAY	See Magalloway			

MERSHON	white-tipped mallard	black	black floss, silver rib and tip	black hackle
MERSHON-WHITE	duck dyed dark blue	black	white floss	black hackle
MILLER	white	white	white floss, gold rib	scarlet fibers
MILLER SPECIAL	grizzly hackle tips	grizzly (sparse)	yellow fur, gold wire rib	gold pheasant crest
MILLS' RIPPLE		grizzly Palmer	gray wool, red floss rib	red hackle
MISSIONARY	teal with prominent bars	white (cut short)	white fur picked out, silver rib	white hackle tip
MOHAWK	brown turkey	brown Palmer	claret floss	brown hackle
MOLE	brown turkey	brown Palmer	dark brown floss, gold rib	brown hackle
MOLE CHUNKEMUNK	brown mallard	furnace	orange floss, silver rib	
MOLE HACKLE		grizzly and brown Palmer	brown mole fur, gold rib	
MONTREAL-BLUE	blue	claret	claret floss, gold rib	blue fibers
MONTREAL-CLARET (W)	brown turkey dyed claret	claret	claret floss, gold rib	claret
MONTREAL-DARK	brown turkey	claret	claret floss, gold rib	scarlet hackle
MONTREAL-LIGHT NO. 1	gray turkey	claret	scarlet floss, gold rib and tip	gray turkey
MONTREAL-LIGHT NO. 2	mallard	scarlet	scarlet floss, gold rib	mallard
MONTREAL-ORIGINAL	mallard	ginger	scarlet mohair, gold rib, black head	
MONTREAL-SILVER	brown turkey	claret	silver	scarlet fibers
MONTREAL-WHITE TIP	black white tipped	claret	claret floss, gold rib	claret fibers
MONTREAL-YELLOW	brown turkey	claret	yellow floss, gold rib and tip	scarlet fibers
MOORHEN & YELLOW		moorhen	yellow floss	
MOOSE	yellow and barred wood duck, gold pheasant tippet	guinea	yellow floss, silver rib	
MOOSE HEAD NO. 1	gold pheasant tippet mallard over	white scarlet Palmer	scarlet floss	gold pheasant crest
MOOSE HEAD NO. 2	gold pheasant tippet mallard over	orange, claret Palmer	claret dubbing	gold pheasant crest
MORMON GIRL (W)	mallard	grizzly Palmer	yellow floss, red floss tip	
MORMON GIRL-WILSON'S (W)	1 gray (concave side toward front)	grizzly	yellow floss, red floss tip	
MORRISON	black crow	black	garnet floss, black thread rib, gold tip	black duck fibers
MOSQUITO NO. 1	gray turkey	grizzly	light gray floss, silver rib	mallard
MOSQUITO NO. 2	gray	gray dun	gray quill	mallard
MOSQUITO NO. 3	badger hackle tips	badger	gray quill	badger hackle
MOSQUITO-ALLEN (W)	grizzly hackle tips	grizzly	gray quill	mallard
MOSQUITO-CALIFORNIA (W)	gzizzly hackle tips	grizzly	white floss, black floss rib close	mallard
MOSQUITO HACKLE (W)		grizzly	peacock quill	grizzly
MOSQUITO-ROSS (W)	See Mosquito-California			
MOSQUITO-SPECIAL ARIZONA (W)	See Arizona Special Mosquito			

MOSQUITO-YAKIMA (W)	grizzly hackle tip, fine speckled	grizzly	peacock quill	mallard
MOTH	white	white	white chenille, silver tip	
MOUSE HACKLE (W)		grizzly and brown	peacock herl, gold tip	red hackles
MOWRY	black white tipped	black	black floss, gold tip	black white tipped
MURRAY	brown turkey	orange Palmer	black floss, silver rib	wide scarlet fibers
NAMELESS	peacock, wood duck, mallard	orange	brown chenille, gold rib, orange floss tip	blue and yellow
NATION'S TURKEY WING	turkey	guinea hen	black, silver rib	
NEEDLE BROWN		dark brown	orange dubbing	
NEEDLE FLY	See Willow			
NEVERSINK NO. 1	mallard	yellow	yellow floss, gold tip	black hackle
NEVERSINK NO. 2	teal	yellow	pale cream dubbing, gold tip	black hackle
NEVERSINK SKATER (E. R. HEWITT)	extra spider with long hackles			
NEW PAGE	turkey dyed deep red	brown	yellow floss, gold rib	mallard
NEWVILLE MIDGE	See Black Quill			
NEZ PERCE	close-mottled gray turkey	brown	white chenille, black chenille butt	
NICKERSON	scarlet, brown turkey and mallard	brown Palmer	yellow dubbing	
NICKOLSON	brown mallard, blue strips	claret Palmer, blue shoulder	claret dubbing picked out	mallard and gold pheasant tippet
NICOMEKL	grouse and tippet	short brown	claret, yellow tip	tippet or yellow
NIGGER TRUDE	black hair	black	black wool, silver rib	
NIGHT HAWK	double grizzly hackle tips	grizzly	peacock quill, light	grizzly
NINEKOGEN	brown turkey	brown turkey	brown wool aft, yellow wool fore, tinsel tip, dressed fat	
NONPAREIL	white	black	black chenille, gold tip	
NO NAME (W)		brown Palmer	black wool on long-shank hook	
OAK	woodcock	brown	orange floss, black thread rib	black
OAK FLY NO. 1	woodcock	brown	yellow floss, silver tip	gold pheasant tippet
OAK FLY NO. 2	woodcock	brown	brown floss, yellow floss rib	brown
OAK FLY NO. 3 (W)	brown turkey	brown	orange floss, black floss rib	brown turkey
ODDER	brown turkey, brown mallard sides, peacock herl top	guinea, yellow Palmer	brown dubbing, gold tip	
OLD CLARET	mallard	scarlet	claret dubbing, gold tip	mallard
OLD JOAN	See Red Fly			
OLD JUDGE NO. 1	brown turkey, red, blue & yellow strips	orange	silver	brown hackles
OLD JUDGE NO. 2	white, yellow strips, jungle cock eye	white, yellow Palmer	gold	yellow and white fibers
OLIVE DUN	light blue gray	olive dun	olive dubbing, gold rib	olive dun hackles

Name				
OLIVE DUN, DARK (female)	dark bluish gray	dark olive dun	dark olive-blue dubbing, gold tip	medium olive hackle
OLIVE DUN, DARK (male)	dark bluish gray	dark blue dun	dark blue dubbing, gold rib	dark olive hackle
OLIVE DUN, LIGHT (female)	bluish gray	olive	brown floss, yellow egg sac	olive hackle
OLIVE DUN, LIGHT (male)	bluish gray	olive-brown	peacock quill (from herl)	olive-brown hackles
OLIVE GNAT NO. 1	coot	iron blue dun	dark olive dubbing, gold tip	
OLIVE GNAT NO. 2	green	furnace	olive-green dubbing, gold tip	
OLIVE GNAT NO. 3 (W)	gray	olive	peacock herl, gold tip	gold pheasant tippet
OLIVE QUILL NO. 1	light gray-ish olive	olive	peacock quill dyed olive	guinea dyed olive
OLIVE QUILL NO. 2	dark gray	olive	olive floss, dark olive thread rib	olive hackles
OLIVE QUILL, PALE	light gray	palest olive	peacock quill	palest olive hackle
OLIVE RED SPINNER (female)	light blue-gray	olive-brown	red peacock quill	olive-brown
OLIVE RED SPINNER (male)	light blue-gray	olive	brown peacock quill	coch-y-bondhu
OLIVE, SPECKLED	mallard dyed olive	grizzly dyed olive	peacock quill dyed olive	mallard dyed olive
OLIVE SPINNER (female) NO. 1	blue dun	olive	olive floss, yellow dubbing tip	olive-brown
OLIVE SPINNER (female) NO. 2	olive-brown hackle tips	olive-brown	yellow-olive floss, black chenille butt, red floss tip	olive-brown hackle
OLIVE SPINNER (male)	blue dun	ginger	olive floss, red floss tip	ginger hackle
OLIVE VARIANT	woodcock	dark olive	dark peacock quill (from herl)	dark olive hackle
OLIVE WREN	light brown turkey	furnace Palmer	brown dubbing, silver rib	
ONANDAGO	black, white tipped	black	black dubbing, white tip, silver tag	black, white tipped
OQUOSSAC	dark gray	claret	claret dubbing, pink thread rib, yellow floss tip	gold pheasant crest and mallard
ORANGE ASHER		dark grizzly	orange floss, gold rib	dark grizzly hackle
ORANGE BIVISIBLE		light orange Palmer, white front		orange hackle tip
ORANGE-BLACK	black crow	black	orange floss, gold rib	gold pheasant tippet
ORANGE BUMBLE		brown	orange, black, orange 3-joint chenille	teal
ORANGE CRANE FLY	pale yellow hackle tips	pale yellow	orange dubbing	
ORANGE DUN NO. 1	pale hen pheasant	brown Palmer	orange floss	
ORANGE DUN NO. 2	gray turkey	orange	gray dubbing	yellow hackle
ORANGE DUN NO. 3	gray	brown	orange dubbing	brown hackle
ORANGE FISH HAWK		light badger	orange floss, gold rib	w/wo badger
ORANGE FLY	brown turkey	brown Palmer half way down body	scarlet floss	
ORANGE GROUSE		grouse	orange dubbing	
ORANGE GUINEA	brown turkey, guinea strips	yellow, orange Palmer	gray floss, silver tip	guinea and scarlet
ORANGE MILLER	white	white	orange floss, gold rib	white hackle
ORANGE QUILL NO. 1	light gray	furnace	orange peacock quill	furnace hackle

ORANGE QUILL NO. 2 (W)	light gray	orange	peacock quill	orange hackle
ORANGE SEDGE NO. 1	red & brown	brown Palmer	orange floss, gold rib	
ORANGE SEDGE NO. 2	brown hen	brown Palmer	orange floss, gold rib	
ORANGE TAG		ginger	peacock herl, orange tip	orange floss (tag-tail)
ORANGE WREN	brown turkey	brown	orange floss, gold tip	mallard
ORANGE & GREEN GROUSE	grouse	grouse	½ orange aft, ½ green fore, all silver rib	brown hackle fibers
ORIOLE NO. 1	orange	orange	black floss, gold rib	orange hackle
ORIOLE NO. 2	yellow	black	black floss, gold rib	yellow hackle
ORVIS CRANE FLY		black (spider radius)	yellow silk	
ORVIS GRAY	white tipped black	dun	olive dubbing, gold rib and tip	dun hackle
PAGE FLY	guinea, scarlet strips	scarlet	scarlet floss, gold rib	scarlet hackle
PALE BLUE DUN NO. 1	dun	dun	gray dubbing, yellow floss rib	dun
PALE BLUE DUN NO. 2	pale blue hackle tips	palest blue	pale bluish dubbing	palest blue
PALE BUFF	pale buff	pale buff	pale buff dubbing	pale buff
PALE EVENING DUN NO. 1	light gray	white	cream-yellow dubbing, gold tip	white hackle
PALE EVENING DUN NO. 2	light gray duck	yellow	yellow dubbing, silver rib	mallard
PALE EVENING DUN NO. 3	light gray duck	pale blue dun	lemon dubbing	palest mallard
PALE EVENING DUN NO. 4 (R.B.)	mallard or teal	mixed pale blue-gray & light cream-honey	pale green fur	mixed blue-gray and light cream-honey
PALE EVENING SPINNER	white hackle tips	pale badger	pale cream floss	badger
PALE MAY FLY (female)	wood duck	honey-dun	cream dubbing, white egg sac	honey dun
PALE MAY FLY (male)	wood duck	grizzly	cream dubbing, yellow thread rib	wood duck
PALE MAY FLY SPINNER (female)	light grizzly hackle tips	ginger	cream dubbing, gold wire rib	ginger hackle
PALE MAY FLY SPINNER (male)	ginger hackle tips	ginger	white floss, yellow thread rib	mallard
PALE OLIVE	medium gray	medium olive	olive quill	olive hackle fibers
PALE SULPHUR	palest cream	palest yellow	palest yellow dubbing	palest yellow hackle
PALE WATERY	gray	pale yellow	olive dubbing	yellow hackle
PALE WATER DUN (female) NO. 1	pale gray	dirty white	pale yellow quill	pale yellow hackle
PALE WATER DUN (female) NO. 2	pale gray hackle tips	pale olive-green	brown peacock quill (from herl), peacock herl at shoulder	pale olive-green
PALE WATER DUN (male)	pale gray	yellow	yellow dubbing	yellow hackle
PALE WATERY QUILL	gray	pale yellow	peacock quill	yellow hackle
PALE WATERY SPINNER (female)	pale gray	cream-ginger	pearl gray dubbing	cream-ginger
PALE WATERY SPINNER (male) NO. 1	pale gray	pale yellow	pale yellow floss, red floss tip	pale yellow
PALE WATERY SPINNER (male) NO. 2	white hackle tips	white	yellow floss, red thread rib	white hackle
PALE YELLOW	pale yellow	yellow	yellow dubbing	
PARADISE	black	grizzly	black floss, white egg sac	black hackle
PARKER	guinea spoon	brown	scarlet floss, gold rib	guinea

PARK FLY	black	black	scarlet floss, gold rib	
PARMACHENE BEAU NO. 1	white, scarlet strips, jungle cock eye	scarlet and white	yellow mohair, gold rib, peacock herl butt	scarlet and white
PARMACHENE BEAU NO. 2 (W)	white with black strips	white	yellow floss, gold rib	red hackles
PARMACHENE BELLE NO. 1	white, scarlet strips	scarlet and white	yellow mohair, gold rib, peacock herl butt	scarlet and white
PARMACHENE BELLE NO. 2	white, scarlet strips	scarlet	yellow floss, gold rib	scarlet hackle
PARMACHENE BULL (W)	white with black strips	black and white	yellow floss, gold rib	black hackle
PARSON NO. 1	bronze turkey	black	silver, silver wire rib	gold pheasant tippet
PARSON NO. 2	light brown turkey	black Palmer	black dubbing, silver rib, orange floss tip	gold pheasant crest
PARTRIDGE, GREEN	partridge	partridge	green dubbing, silver rib	gold pheasant tippet
PARTRIDGE, ORANGE	partridge	partridge	orange dubbing, gold rib	gold pheasant tippet
PARTRIDGE, YELLOW	partridge	partridge	yellow dubbing, gold rib	gold pheasant tippet
PATHFINDER	light gray	furnace	scarlet dubbing, gold rib	
PATTON	guinea	brown	brown floss, gold rib	
PEA JAY	scarlet, white strips	orange	white chenille, gold rib, red chenille butt	yellow fibers
PEACOCK	dark gray duck	black	peacock herl, gold tip	
PEBBLE BEACH	orange	black, brown Palmer	claret dubbing, picked out, silver rib	
PELEE ISLAND	scarlet	black	scarlet floss, gold rib, black chenille butt	black fibers
PENNELL HACKLE	sparse slender hackle flies (yellow, brown & green colors) type only			
PERCH FLY	yellow red and white goose	yellow	white floss, gold rib	
PERKINS' IDEAL	mallard	black	scarlet floss, gold rib, black chenille butt	black fibers
PERKINS' PET	dark gray	brown Palmer	silver	
PERKINS' SPECIAL	white	brown	peacock, silver center joint	gold pheasant tippet
PERRY	black, white tipped	black	black chenille, pink chenille butt, silver tip	
PETER ROSS NO. 1	dark teal	ginger	scarlet dubbing, gold tip	gold pheasant tippet
PETER ROSS NO. 2		light ginger	yellow floss, narrow gold tinsel rib	gold pheasant tippet
PETER ROSS NO. 3	teal	black	red floss silver rib ½ fore, silver ½ aft	gold pheasant tippet
PETRIE'S GREEN EGG SAC	woodcock	partridge	peacock quill (from herl), pale green chenille egg sac	partridge
PFIFF		grizzly	ostrich herl dyed light green	ostrich herl (light green) 2
PHEASANT	ruddy pheasant body plumage	brown	yellow floss, gold rib	
PHEASANT, GOLD	hen pheasant	partridge	gold, gold wire rib	gold pheasant tippet

PHEASANT, SILVER	hen pheasant	partridge	silver, silver wire rib	gold pheasant tippet
PHEASANT TAIL		honey dun	pheasant tail (twisted), gold wire rib	3 cock pheasant fibers
PHEASANT & YELLOW	hen pheasant	partridge	yellow floss, gold rib	gold pheasant tippet
PICKET PIN (W)	gray squirrel or impala	brown Palmer	gold twist	gold pheasant tippet
PIKER	white	brown	orange dubbing, gold tip	
PINK LADY BIVISIBLE NO. 1		ginger Palmer, pale olive-yellow front	gold	ginger hackle
PINK LADY BIVISIBLE NO. 2		ginger Palmer, white front	pink floss, gold rib	
PINK LADY HACKLE		badger	pink floss, silver rib	gold pheasant tippet
PINK LADY, WINGED	gray	ginger	pink floss, gold rib and tip	ginger hackle
PINK WICKHAM'S	mallard	brown Palmer	pink floss	brown hackle
PIXIE	grizzly dyed green	mixed pink and white	mixed pink and white wool picked out	gold pheasant crest
PLATH	gray turkey	scarlet	green dubbing, silver tip	scarlet fibers
PLOTH	See Plath			
PLUMB FLY	guinea and wood duck	scarlet	black dubbing	guinea and wood duck
POLICEMAN	dark gray	grizzly and brown Palmer	gray quill	grizzly hackle
POLKA	guinea	scarlet	scarlet floss, gold rib and tip	scarlet hackle
POORMAN	mallard		rabbit's fur picked out, silver tip	mallard
POORMAN'S FLY NO. 1	mallard	ginger	brown dubbing	ginger hackle
POORMAN'S FLY NO. 2	Plymouth Rock wing quill	brown	light brown dubbing, gold tip	
POPE'S NONDESCRIPT	cinnamon	dark ginger	dark green dubbing, gold rib	dark ginger hackle
PORTLAND	teal	scarlet	scarlet floss, gold rib	teal
POST	brown turkey	black Palmer	pink floss, gold rib	scarlet
POTATO BUG	dark brown turkey	dark brown	dark maroon dubbing, gold rib	
POTOMAC	cinnamon	brown	green floss, yellow floss rib	
POTTER	gray duck	brown	green floss, black floss rib	
PREMIER	white, red strips	scarlet	scarlet floss, gold rib	scarlet
PRESTON'S FANCY	white spotted teal	brown	gold	brown hackle
PRIEST		badger	silver, silver wire rib	scarlet ibis
PRIME GNAT NO. 1	black crow	black	black dubbing, scarlet floss tip	black duck fibers
PRIME GNAT NO. 2	dark gray	brown	brown dubbing	
PRINCE WILLIAM OF ORANGE	brown mallard	orange, black Palmer	black dubbing, silver rib, red floss tip, gold tag	yellow hackle
PROCTOR	mallard	brown	pale pink chenille, olive-brown chenille tip	
PROFESSOR (W)	mallard	brown	yellow floss, gold rib	scarlet duck fibers

PROFESSOR, BLUE	mallard	brown	blue floss, gold rib	scarlet duck fibers
PROFESSOR, GOLD	mallard	brown	gold tinsel	scarlet duck feathers
PROFESSOR, GREEN	brown turkey	green	yellow floss, gold rib	scarlet duck fibers
PROFESSOR, GROUSE	grouse	brown	yellow floss, gold rib	scarlet duck fibers
PROFESSOR, ROYAL	mallard	brown	peacock herl, yellow floss tip	gold pheasant tippet
PROFESSOR, TURKEY	brown turkey	brown	yellow floss	scarlet duck fibers
PROFESSOR, WOODCOCK	woodcock	brown	yellow floss, gold rib	scarlet duck fibers
PROFESSOR, YELLOW	mallard dyed yellow	brown	yellow floss, gold rib and tip	scarlet duck fibers
PROUTY	mallard, yellow and red	furnace dyed yellow tied Palmer	½ aft silver twist, ½ fore black herl, orange floss tip, silver tag	gold pheasant crest and blue jay
PUFFER	black crow	brown	dark green dubbing, light green floss rib, gold tip	scarlet duck fibers
PURPLE QUILL	gray	purple	peacock quill	purple
QUACK DOCTOR	brown turkey	scarlet	silver, silver wire rib, black ostrich herl head	scarlet fibers
QUAKER NO. 1	light gray turkey	grizzly	light gray dubbing, gold tip	
QUAKER NO. 2	light gray turkey	badger	gray floss, silver rib	gray mallard
QUEBEC TRUDE	gray squirrel	brown	green floss, gold rib	scarlet hackle fibers
QUEEN O' THE LAKE	mallard, jungle cock eye	brown	scarlet floss, gold rib	gold pheasant tippet
QUEEN OF THE WATERS NO. 1	mallard	brown, brown Palmer	orange floss, gold tip	gold pheasant tippet
QUEEN OF THE WATERS NO. 2	mallard	brown	orange floss, gold rib	gold pheasant tippet
QUEEN OF THE WATERS LIGHT	mallard	ginger	pale orange floss, gold rib	gold pheasant tippet
QUILL GORDON	See Gordon Quill			
QUINN'S FANCY (Orange)	brown mallard	dirty white	orange floss, silver rib, brown herl butt and head	brown hackle fibers
RAINBOW	cinnamon	grizzly	black floss, gold rib, white floss tip	scarlet fibers
RAINBOW SPECIAL	gray duck	blue dun	pale pinkish fur	blue dun hackle fibers
RANGELEY NO. 1	barred wood duck; scarlet and turkey strips	claret	claret dubbing, gold rib	scarlet and wood duck fibers
RANGELEY NO. 2	gray turkey and mallard	claret Palmer	orange floss	yellow fibers
RANGELEY BELLE	mallard, barred wood duck strips	claret	claret dubbing, picked out, gold rib	barred wood duck and scarlet
RAQUET	gold pheasant tippet, guinea strips	black Palmer	black dubbing, gold rib, orange dubbing tip	gold pheasant crest
RAVEN	black	black	black chenille	gold pheasant tippet
RAY BERGMAN	gray duck	brown	reddish orange wool	brown mallard
R. B. BLUE FOX	grizzly hackle tips	grizzly and blue-gray	blue-gray fox fur dubbing	grizzly hackle
R. B. FOX	mallard	honey and ginger	gray fox fur dubbing	honey hackle

Name	Tail	Hackle	Body	Wings
RECKLESS WILLIAM	pheasant tail dyed green, gold pheasant crest topping	orange	½ pink floss fore, ½ flat silver aft	gold pheasant crest
RED ANT NO. 1	gray	brown	red floss, peacock herl butt	gold pheasant tippet
RED ANT NO. 2	gray duck	brown	red floss, peacock herl butt, gold tip	
RED ANT, EVANS (W) NO. 1		brown	in-hump hook (red-knobbed at rear) lacquered or plastic	
RED ANT, EVANS (W) NO. 2	white, red strips	furnace	red floss, peacock herl butt, red floss tip	
RED ANT (female)	gray hackle tips (spent)	brown	red floss, white chenille butt	
RED ANT SPECIAL		brown	red dubbing at shoulder, black dubbing aft	
RED ANT, WILSON (W)	white (single)	ginger	red thread, red thread tag	peacock sword
RED ASH	mallard	dark gray dun, dun Palmer	scarlet floss	
RED DEVIL	red	red	red chenille	white fibers
RED DRAGON		magenta	oval gold tinsel	red fibers
RED DRAKE	marllard, scarlet strips	scarlet and white	red and white chenille wound together, silver tip	
RED FLY	pea-hen wing	claret	dark red squirrel fur fore, claret mohair aft on brown working silk	
RED FORKED TAIL	gray	grizzly	red floss, red floss tag	red hackle forked
RED FOX NO. 1	gray duck	brown	pale fox belly fur dubbing, gold tip	wood duck
RED FOX NO. 2	teal	red-brown (natural)	reddish-brown fox fur	lemon wood duck
RED GROUSE	grouse	furnace	red floss, gold tip	
RED HACKLE, BLACK		natural red-brown	black floss, gold rib	
(All Red Hackles also tied with scarlet hackle as alternate)				
RED HACKLE, MAY		mallard front, red-brown back	yellow straw, gold wire rib	3 brown hackle fibers
RED HACKLE, PEACOCK		natural red-brown	peacock herl, gold tip	
RED HACKLE, RED		natural red-brown	red floss, gold rib	
RED HACKLE, YELLOW		natural red-brown	yellow floss, gold rib	
RED HEAD	teal	brown	gold tinsel thread, gold tip, red head	scarlet fibers blunt
RED HECKUM	See Heckum Red			
RED IBIS	See Scarlet Ibis			
RED-LEGGED MARCH FLY	coot	coch-y-bondhu	peacock herl	
RED MIDGE	brown turkey	brown	red floss, gold rib	
RED MILLER	white	white	scarlet floss, gold rib	scarlet fibers
RED PALMER	white	scarlet Palmer	scarlet floss, gold rib	scarlet fibers
RED QUAIL	mottled quail	scarlet	red dubbing, gold rib	scarlet fibers

RED QUILL NO. 1	gray	natural dark red	red peacock quill (dyed)	natural dark red
RED QUILL NO. 2	wood duck	rusty dun	red peacock quill dyed (or red hackle quill dyed)	rusty dun
RED QUILL NO. 3 (W)	gray	red	peacock quill	red hackle
RED QUILL SPINNER	blue dun hackle tips	natural dark red	red peacock quill (dyed)	natural dark red
RED ROBIN	brown turkey	green	yellow floss, gold rib	scarlet
RED SPIDER		natural dark red	gold	
RED SPINNER NO. 1	dark gray	brown	red dubbing, gold rib and tip	brown hackle
RED SPINNER NO. 2(W)	gray	red	red floss, gold rib	red hackle
RED TAG		brown	peacock herl, red floss tag	red fibers
RED TAG, PALMER		brown Palmer	peacock herl, gold tip	red wool tail tag
RED TURKEY	brown turkey	scarlet	red dubbing, gold rib	scarlet
RED UPRIGHT	gray	brown	peacock quill dyed red	
RED UPRIGHT HACKLE		red-brown	peacock quill	
RED VARIANT	wood duck	coch-y-bondhu variant radius	peacock quill (from herl)	
RED WORSTED JEM	furnace		peacock herl	red wool tail tag
RENEGADE (W)		white fore, brown aft	peacock herl	
REUBEN WOOD	mallard	brown	white chenille, red floss tip	gray mallard
REYNOLD'S FANCY (W)	gray	brown	1/3 black aft, 2/3 red fore (floss)	
RIBBLE	brown turkey, scarlet strips	black; scarlet Palmer	dark yellow floss, dark blue floss tip, silver tag	barred wood duck and scarlet
RICHARDSON	brown mallard	black Palmer	light blue floss, silver tip	brown mallard
RICH WIDOW	black	yellow Palmer	black floss, gold rib	yellow fibers
RILEY	mallard	brown	white dubbing, black tip	
RILEY FLY	mallard	scarlet	white chenille, red chenille butt	
RIO GRANDE KING NO. 1 (W)	white	yellow	black chenille, gold tip	yellow hackles
RIO GRANDE KING NO. 2 (W)	white	brown	black chenille, gold tip	gold pheasant tippet
RIO GRANDE KING, BLACK (W)	white	brown	black chenille	red hackle
RIO GRANDE KING SPECIAL (W)	white	brown	brown fore, yellow aft (floss)	gold pheasant tippet
RIO GRANDE QUEEN (W)	white	black	black chenille, red floss tip	yellow hackles
ROCK WORM		badger	tan linen	
ROMAINE	barred wood duck	black	dark green dubbing, gold tip	barred wood duck
ROMEYN	barred wood duck	gray dun	green floss, gold rib, scarlet tip, gold tag	wood duck
ROOSEVELT	gray	orange	yellow dubbing tip, claret dubbing fore	brown mallard
ROSS	brown mallard, peacock herl topping	furnace	brown floss, gold rib	green fibers, and gold pheasant tippet

Name				
ROSS McKENNEY	white over red bucktail, jungle cock eyes		brown wool, gold rib and tip	barred wood duck
ROUGH OLIVE	gray	dark ginger	olive dubbing	dark ginger hackles
ROUND LAKE	brown turkey, jungle cock eye	orange	claret dubbing picked out, silver rib, orange dubbing tip	silver pheasant dyed blue
ROYAL PROFESSOR	See Professor, Royal			
ROYAL VARIANT	upright white hackle tips	brown (parachute)	peacock herl, red floss joint	gold pheasant tippet
ROYAL WULFF	white bucktail	brown	peacock herl, scarlet floss center joint	brown bucktail
RUBE WOOD	See Reuben Wood			
RUBY SPINNER (female)	deep red hackle tips	deep red	white floss, gold rib, black chenille at shoulder	deep red hackle
RUBY SPINNER (male)	deep red hackle tips	deep red	peacock quill (from herl)	deep red hackle
SAGE (W)	mallard	olive	yellow wool, gold tip	red, yellow & green hackle
SAGE FLY	widgeon or teal	orange	yellow dubbing, silver rib	teal, green & scarlet fibers
ST. LAWRENCE	dark black and white mottled turkey	scarlet	yellow floss, gold rib, scarlet floss tip	scarlet fibers
ST. PATRICK	peacock herl	grizzly	silver	peacock herl
ST. REGIS	brown mallard, gold pheasant tippet strips	orange & guinea; brown Palmer	cinnamon dubbing, silver rib	gold pheasant tippet & guinea
SALMON FLY NO. 1		badger	salmon dubbing, gold tip	
SALMON FLY NO. 2 (W)	cinnamon	brown	brown floss, gold rib	cinnamon
SALTOUN NO. 1	gray duck	ginger	black floss, silver rib	ginger hackle
SALTOUN NO. 2	gray duck	black	black floss, silver rib	ginger hackle
SAND BIVISIBLE		brown Palmer blue dun front		brown hackle
SAND FLY, DARK	brown turkey	brown	gray dubbing	white tipped mallard
SAND FLY, LIGHT	light brown hen	light ginger	bright brown dubbing	light ginger hackle
SARANAC	gold pheasant tippet, brown mallard sides	claret	claret dubbing, gold rib	gold pheasant crest
SASSY CAT	yellow, red cheeks	yellow	peacock herl	scarlet fibers
SAW FLY	gray	grizzly	black floss, gold wire rib	
SCARLET GNAT	light gray	scarlet	scarlet dubbing, gold tip	
SCARLET HACKLE		scarlet	scarlet floss, gold rib	
SCARLET MIDGE	brown mallard	black	scarlet dubbing, silver tip	mallard
SCARLET PALMER	brown mallard	scarlet Palmer	scarlet dubbing, silver tip	mallard
SCHAFFER	brown turkey		yellow dubbing picked out	yellow wool tail tag
SCHAIN FLY	close-barred dark turkey	brown	yellow floss, black thread rib, gold tip	gray mallard
SCHUYLKILL HAVEN SPECIAL	mallard dyed green	light ginger	red fox fur dubbing	3 long black hairs
SEAHAM (W)	See Seeham			
SEAL HACKLE		brown and grizzly mixed	brown seal fur, gold rib	brown and grizzly hackle

SEDGE, LIGHT	hen pheasant	ginger	light cream dubbing	
SEEHAM (W)	mallard	black	yellow floss, red chenille butt	gold pheasant tippet
SETH GREEN	gray turkey	brown	green dubbing, yellow thread rib	
SETH GREEN, CLARET	gray turkey	claret	green floss, yellow thread rib	
SETH GREEN, TURKEY	brown turkey	brown	green floss, gold rib	gold pheasant tippet
SGT. JONES (Harrison)	brown, grouse front		peacock herl, gold tip	3 olive-brown hackle fibers
SHAD FLY NO. 1	dark brown turkey	brown	peacock herl, gold center joint, gold tip	
SHAD FLY NO. 2 (W)	gray	badger	gray wool	
SHAD FLY (female) NO. 1	gray turkey	ginger	orange dubbing, brown thread rib, green chenille butt	
SHAD FLY (female) NO. 2	See Green Drake			
SHAD FLY (male)	See Green Drake			
SHERRY SPINNER (female)	gray	ginger	sherry floss, gray thread rib	ginger hackle
SHERRY SPINNER (male)	dark gray	coch-y-bondhu	deep garnet peacock quill (dyed)	coch-y-bondhu
SHOEMAKER NO. 1	wood duck	brown	pink & gray alternate rib (floss)	wood duck
SHOEMAKER NO. 2	mallard	brown	gray floss, white floss center joint	mallard
SHOEMAKER NO. 3 (W)	gray	brown	white floss, gold tip	teal (forked)
SHOOKUM	jungle body feather	black	yellow dubbing	scarlet and white
SHOSHONE CHIEF (W)	gray	brown	2/3 fore yellow floss, 1/3 aft peacock herl butt, red floss tip	
SILVER BLACK	mallard	grizzly	black dubbing, silver rib	mallard
SILVER BROWN	gray	brown	silver	
SILVER CREEK SPECIAL (W)	pheasant	ginger	peacock quill	ginger hackle
SILVER DEMON	orange & white hair	orange & white	silver	orange & white hackle
SILVER DOCTOR NO. 1	mallard; red, blue and yellow splits	silver-doctor blue	silver-embossed	gold pheasant tippet
SILVER DOCTOR NO. 2	brown turkey, red, yellow, green & blue splits	blue over guinea	silver	yellow, blue, green and scarlet
SILVER DOCTOR NO. 3	brown turkey, blue and scarlet strips	silver-doctor blue, guinea face	scarlet floss, silver rib, yellow chenille butt, silver tip	gold pheasant tippet
SILVER DOCTOR NO. 4	turkey, mallard barred wood duck, red, yellow blue & green	silver-doctor blue	silver, silver wire rib	same as wing
SILVER DOCTOR, IDAHO (W)	gray turkey, red, yellow & blue strips	silver-doctor blue	white floss, gold rib	gold pheasant
SILVER DRAGON		black	flat silver	red fibers
SILVER DRAKE	mallard	badger	silver	mallard
SILVER DUN	gray	blue dun	gray dubbing, silver rib	blue dun
SILVER FAIRY	brown mallard	claret Palmer	silver	scarlet hackle

SILVER GNAT	black	black	silver	gold pheasant tippet
SILVER HORNS	black crow	black	black ostrich herl, silver tip	teal
SILVER JUNGLE NO.1	jungle cock body feather	guinea	silver	scarlet hackle
SILVER JUNGLE NO. 2	black, jungle cock eye	black Palmer	silver	scarlet hackle
SILVER MILLER	white	white	silver	white hackle
SILVER MONKEY	gray	pale guinea	white floss, silver rib	
SILVER NAIL	jungle cock	badger	silver	
SILVER SEDGE NO. 1	cinnamon cock wing	ginger, ginger Palmer	white floss, silver rib	
SILVER SEDGE NO. 2	brown hen (light)	brown Palmer	silver	
SILVER SEDGE NO. 3	medium gray	brown, brown Palmer	white floss, gold rib	
SILVER STALK	mallard	badger	silver	mallard
SILVER STORK	teal	brown	silver	teal
SILVER TRUDE	brown turkey	brown	silver	scarlet hackle
SILVER TURKEY	gray turkey	green and yellow	silver, scarlet floss rib and tip	scarlet and yellow fibers
SILVER ZULU		black	silver	red (blunt)
SIMONDS	gray mallard	scarlet	scarlet floss, gold rib	scarlet
SIR SAM DARLING	mallard	brown	white chenille, black floss tip	brown mallard or wood duck
SKUES'	black, white tipped	badger	black floss	badger hackle
SKUNK BIVISIBLE		black Palmer, white front		black hackle tips
SLIM JIM, GOLD (W)	grizzly hackle tips	brown	gold	brown hackle
SLIM JIM, GRAY (W)	grizzly hackle tips	grizzly	black, silver rib	red hackle
SLIM JIM, RED (W)	grizzly hackle tips	scarlet	scarlet floss, gold rib	red hackle
SLIM JIM, SILVER (W)	grizzly hackle tips	grizzly	silver	red hackle
SLIM JIM, UTAH (W)	grizzly hackle tips dyed red	ginger	black floss, gold rib	red hackle
SLIM JIM, YELLOW (W)	grizzly hackle tips	grizzly	yellow floss, gold rib	red hackle
SMALL DARK SEDGE (female)	dark grouse	coch-y-bondhu	dark brown dubbing, yellow dubbing tip	
SMALL DARK SEDGE (male)	dark grouse	coch-y-bondhu	dark red-brown dubbing	
SNIPE & GREEN		snipe	green floss	
SNIPE & ORANGE		snipe	orange floss	
SNIPE & PURPLE		snipe	purple floss	
SNIPE & RED		snipe	red floss	
SNIPE & YELLOW		snipe	pale yellow dubbing	
SNIPE HACKLE		snipe breast	gold	
SNO FLY (W)	A number 18 Black Quill. See Black Quill for dressing.			
SNOB		ginger	black ostrich	guinea
SNOW FLY	See Coch-y-bondhu			
SOLDIER GNAT	light brown hen	brown	scarlet floss, gold tip	black hackle
SOLDIER PALMER		brown Palmer	red floss, gold rib	
SOULE	white, red strips	red	yellow floss, peacock herl butt	red hackle
SOUTHSIDE	mallard	brown	orange dubbing, gold tip	

Name				
SPECIAL BLACK ANT	See Black Ant Special			
SPECK		black	black ostrich herl	guinea
SPECKLED DOLLY	guinea	scarlet Palmer	silver	white & scarlet hackle
SPENCER		coch-y-bondhu badger Palmer	gray dubbing, yellow dubbing tag, gold rib	
SPENT BROWN DRAKE (female)	brown hackle tips	dark ginger	red-brown floss, yellow chenille egg sac	ginger
SPENT BROWN DRAKE (male)	brown hackle tips	dark ginger	brown floss, gold rib	brown hackle
SPENT GNAT (female)	brown hackle tips	brown	brown floss, wide yellow floss rib	brown mallard
SPENT GNAT (male)	brown hackle tips	brown, partridge front	yellow floss, brown thread rib	brown hackle
SPENT YELLOW	yellow badger	pale yellow	pale yellow dubbing	pale yellow hackle
SPIDER NO. 1		mallard breast	yellow dubbing	
SPIDER NO. 2	dark gray turkey	black	dark gray floss	
SPIDER NO. 3	brown turkey	furnace Palmer	light blue floss, gold tip	
SPOTTED SEDGE	light brown turkey	ginger	warm brown floss, gold wire rib	
SPRATLEY	body cock pheasant rump feather fibers	grizzly	black wool, gold rib, black herl head	grizzly
STARLING	light gray	dun	peacock quill	dun
STEBBINS NO. 1	gray turkey	furnace	green dubbing, gold tip	teal
STEBBINS NO. 2	dark gray duck	grouse	bright green dubbing, gold tip	grouse
STEBBINS NO. 3	gray	grouse	peacock herl	mallard
STONE, DARK NO. 1	dark gray	gray	gray dubbing, yellow floss rib	
STONE, DARK NO. 2	brown mallard or dark turkey	brown	dark brown seal fur, yellow floss rib and tip, gold tag	brown mallard
STONE, EARLY BROWN	grizzly (tan) tips tied flat	blue dun and brown	reddish brown fur	pheasant tail fibers
STONE, ENGLISH	hen pheasant	brown	gray dubbing, yellow dubbing tip	
STONE, LIGHT NO. 1	gray duck	gray	yellow silk floss	gray fibers
STONE, LIGHT NO. 2	light gray	yellow	gray dubbing, yellow floss rib	gray fibers
STONE, LITTLE BLACK	See Little Black Stone Fly			
STONE, YELLOW	gray	yellow	gray dubbing, gold rib	yellow hackle
STONE HACKLE		badger, Palmer down 1/3 of body	brown floss, gold rib	
STORER	mallard	brown	silver, gold tinsel rib	
STRACHAN	gold pheasant tippet; blue & yellow splits	blue; black Palmer	cinnamon floss, gold rib	brown mallard
STRANGER	brown turkey over gold pheasant tippet	brown	brown dubbing, gold rib	brown mallard
STRAWBERRY	grass green	white	scarlet chenille	
STURTEVANT	jungle cock body feather	green Palmer	black dubbing, silver rib	mallard and scarlet
SUN FLY		coch-y-bondhu	rabbit fur, gold rib	coch-y-bondhu
SUNSET	white	yellow	yellow floss, green floss tip	

SWANK SPECIAL	teal	dark ginger	lemon yellow twisted raffia spiral over black background	brown hackle
SWIFTWATER NO. 1	white	brown	peacock herl, orange floss center joint	gray mallard
SWIFTWATER NO. 2	white	brown	peacock herl	gray mallard
SYLER'S SPECIAL		brown	black dubbing, silver rib	
TEAL & BLACK	teal	black	black dubbing, silver rib	gold pheasant tippet
TEAL, BLUE & SILVER	teal	deep blue	silver	gold pheasant crest
TEAL & CLARET	teal	claret	claret dubbing, gold rib and tip	gold pheasant tippet
TEAL & GOLD	teal	dark brown	gold	gold pheasant tippet
TEAL & GREEN	teal	black	green dubbing, gold rib	gold pheasant tippet
TEAL & ORANGE	teal	olive	orange dubbing, gold rib	gold pheasant tippet
TEAL & RED	teal	olive	dark red dubbing, gold rib and tag	gold pheasant tippet
TEAL & SILVER	teal	badger	silver	gold pheasant tippet
TEAL & YELLOW	teal	yellow-ginger	yellow dubbing, silver rib	gold pheasant tippet
TERMITE		yellow	in-hump hook (pale olive, knobbed at rear) lacquered or plastic	
TETON BEAUTY	light gray; jungle cock eye sides	brown	yellow floss, gold rib	brown hackle
THISTLE NO. 1	gold pheasant tippet; long jungle cock eye sides	scarlet; yellow Palmer	green floss, gold rib, black chenille butt, yellow floss tip	scarlet, gold pheasant tippet & crest
THISTLE NO. 2	yellow	green	claret dubbing, gold rib	scarlet hackle
TIC		ginger	ginger ostrich herl (dyed)	guinea dyed yellow
TIGER FLY	barred turkey tail dyed yellow; jungle cock eye	red	yellow floss, gold tip	guinea
TIPPET & BLACK	gold pheasant tippet	black	black dubbing, silver rib	gold pheasant tippet
TIPPET & RED	gold pheasant tippet	dark brown	red-brown dubbing, silver rib	gold pheasant tippet
TIPPET & SILVER	gold pheasant tippet	badger	silver, silver wire rib	gold pheasant tippet
TOMAH-JO	barred wood duck	scarlet & yellow	silver; peacock herl butt	yellow hackle
TOMLINSON	cinnamon turkey	brown	claret dubbing, silver rib	scarlet hackle
TOOCA	black; orange strips	orange ½ body Palmer	black floss, silver rib	mallard and orange
TOODLE BUG NO. 1	brown turkey	brown Palmer	orange and yellow dubbing alternate rib	scarlet fibers
TOODLE BUG NO. 2	brown turkey	brown	3-joint floss, blue tip, yellow center, brown fore	brown mallard
TRANSLUCENT, BLACK	See Black Translucent			
TRANSLUCENT, BROWN	See Brown Translucent			
TRANSLUCENT, GINGER	See Ginger Translucent			
TRANSLUCENT, GRAY	See Gray Translucent			
TRANSLUCENT, GREEN	See Green Translucent			
TRANSLUCENT, LIGHT	See Light Translucent			

TREEHOPPER NO. 1	gray		rabbit's fur silver tip	mallard
TREEHOPPER NO. 2	gray	grizzly	green floss	
TROUT FLY	gray turkey	grizzly	scarlet floss, silver rib	gray turkey
TROUT FLY, WILSON'S	white with 1 black spot, concave side facing front	medium ginger	peacock herl, red thread rib, red thread tip	
TROUT KILLER, WILSON'S	See Wilson's Trout Killer			
TRUDE	squirrel tail	brown	red wool, silver rib	
TUP'S INDISPENSABLE NO. 1		honey dun	yellow	honey dun
TUP'S INDISPENSABLE NO. 2		ginger, white front	yellow floss, pink dubbing tuft at shoulder	dark ginger hackle fibers
TURKEY	brown turkey	brown	yellow dubbing, gold rib	scarlet hackle
TURKEY, BROWN	brown turkey	brown	brown dubbing, red thread rib, gold tip	scarlet
TURKEY PROFESSOR	See Professor, Turkey			
TYCOON	white; black strip top, scarlet side strips	claret; yellow Palmer	orange floss, gold rib, scarlet floss tip	white & scarlet
UNDERTAKER	black, white tipped	black	white floss	black, white tipped
UTAH (W)	cinnamon turkey	ginger	cinnamon floss, gold tip	
VAN PATTEN	barred wood duck	brown	yellow floss, gold tip	scarlet fibers
VOLUNTEER	gold pheasant tippet	green	yellow floss, gold rib	scarlet
WAKE VARIANT	short slate fish skin	pale lavender	pale lavender floss	pale lavender
WALKER	white; gray turkey strips	yellow	white floss, black floss rib	scarlet & white
WALKER HAYS	gray	brown	yellow floss, red floss rib	
WALLA-WALLA (W)	cinnamon turkey	brown	yellow dubbing, gold tip	
WALTON	light woodcock	brown	light brown dubbing, gold twist rib	
WARWICH	See Warwick			
WARWICK	black and peacock sword	orange	peacock herl, gold rib, silver tip	orange hackle
WASP NO. 1	light brown hen; 'black crow splits	grouse	alternate rib black and brown chenille, orange floss tip	
WASP NO. 2	black	brown	yellow chenille, gold rib	
WATER CRICKET NO. 1		black, black Palmer trimmed to ⅛ inch	pink floss	
WATER CRICKET NO. 2		black	orange dubbing, black thread rib	
WATSON'S FANCY NO. 1	black hackle tips	black	red and black dubbing, gold rib (black fore, red aft)	gold pheasant tippet
WATSON'S FANCY NO. 2	brown mallard, jungle cock eye	black	black dubbing ½ fore, orange dubbing ½ aft, gold rib	gold pheasant crest
WELLINGTON	gray	black	blue floss, silver rib	3 black hackle fibers
WELSHMAN'S BUTTON (female) NO. 1	rail bird	coch-y-bondhu	dark brown dubbing, yellow fur egg sac	

WELSHMAN'S BUTTON (female) NO. 2	rail bird	furnace	peacock herl	
WELSHMAN'S BUTTON (male) NO. 1	rail bird	natural red-brown	red-brown floss, black thread rib	
WELSHMAN'S BUTTON (male) NO. 2	grouse	black	peacock herl, gold tip	
WEST BRANCH	scarlet	black Palmer	silver	
WESTERN BEE (W)	gray	brown	orange and black 4-joint chenille	
WESTERN SALMON (W)	fox squirrel tail tied flat	furnace trimmed top and bottom	natural raffia (flattened) over kapok	fox squirrel
WHIMBREL	originally curlew, now hen pheasant	brown	brown dubbing, gold tip	
WHIRLING BLUE DUN	dark gray	ginger-brown	blue-gray dubbing, gold tip	brown hackle
WHIRLING CRANEFLY	grizzly hackle tips	olive	yellow-green dubbing	
WHIRLING DUN	light gray	brown	brown floss, gray floss rib	brown hackle
WHIRLING DUN-DARK	dark gray	brown	green-gray dubbing	brown hackle
WHISKERS		coch-y-bondhu Palmer	peacock herl, gold tip	coch-y-bonhu
WHITCRAFT (W)	grizzly hackle tips	grizzly and brown mixed	2 brown and 1 deep yellow heavy moose mane hairs	brown throat guard hackle
WHITE ANT	white	black	white floss, peacock herl butt	silver pheasant tippet
WHITECHURCH DUN NO. 1	light gray	ginger	yellow floss	gray mallard
WHITECHURCH DUN NO. 2	dark gray	ginger	white floss	ginger hackle
WHITE-FISH MAGGOT-NATURAL (W)		grizzly	natural translucent (fairly large diameter)	
WHITE-FISH MAGGOT-OLIVE (W)		grizzly	olive (pale) translucent (fairly large diameter)	
WHITE-FISH MAGGOT-RED (W)		medium dark ginger	red translucent (fairly large diameter)	
WHITE-GLOVED HOWDY (Wetzel)	gray	badger	red-brown dubbing	silver pheasant tippet
WHITE HACKLE	See Hackle-White			
WHITE JUNGLE	white jungle cock eye sides	orange	brown Palmer, orange floss, gold rib	white, black and scarlet fibers
WHITE MILLER NO. 1	white	white	white chenille, orange floss tip	
WHITE MILLER NO. 2	white	white	white floss, silver rib	
WHITE MILLER NO. 3 (W)	white	white	white floss, gold rib	silver pheasant tippet
WHITE MOTH NO. 1	white	white	white chenille, silver tip	
WHITE MOTH NO. 2 (W)	white	white	white chenille, gold tip	black, white tipped fibers
WHITE PALMER		white; white Palmer	white dubbing	
WHITE WICKHAM'S	gray	white palmer	white floss	brown hackle
WHITE WING	white	brown	bright green ostrich herl (dyed)	
WHITE WULFF	white bucktail	light badger	cream fur dubbing	white bucktail
WHITNEY	dark gray; yellow strips	green Palmer	green floss, silver rib	green fibers
WICKHAM'S FANCY	slate gray quill	brown; brown Palmer	gold tinsel	brown hackle

Name				
WICKHAM'S, PINK	See Pink Wickham's			
WICKHAM'S, WHITE	See White Wickham's			
WIDDICOMB	light blue dun hackle tips, spent	golden badger	peacock quill	wood duck
WIDGEON	widgeon	black	orange floss, gold tip	widgeon
WIDOW NO. 1	black; white strips	black	black floss, white floss rib	
WIDOW NO. 2	black	black	purple floss, white thread rib	
WIDOW NO. 3	gray duck	darkest badger	purple dubbing, silver rib	
WILLIAM'S FAVORITE		black	black floss, gold rib	black hackle fibers
WILLOW NO. 1	dark gray	brown	green dubbing, yellow thread rib	
WILLOW NO. 2	dark gray	brown	dark gray floss, gold tip	
WILLOW NO. 3	mallard dyed yellow	olive	olive-green floss, gold rib	
WILLOW, BLUE NO. 1	gray mallard	blue dun	dark gray dubbing	gray mallard
WILLOW, BLUE NO. 2 (W)	gray	brown	blue floss, gold tip	brown hackle
WILLOW, BROWN NO. 1	brown mallard	brown	dark brown dubbing	brown hackle
WILLOW, BROWN NO. 2 (W)	gray	brown	brown floss, gold tip	brown hackle
WILLOW, COLORADO (W)	gray	brown	gray chenille, gold tip	brown hackle
WILLOW SPECIAL	hen pheasant	black	dark red floss	black
WILLOW SPIDER		dun front, brown back	mixed green and dun wool	
WILSON (W)	teal	orange	orange dubbing	
WILSON'S ANT	brown hen	brown dun	brown dun dubbing, peacock herl butt	
WILSON'S MORMON GIRL (W)	See Mormon Girl-Wilson's			
WILSON'S RED ANT (W)	See Red Ant-Wilson's			
WILSON'S TROUT FLY (W)	See Trout Fly-Wilson's			
WILSON'S TROUT KILLER	teal	grizzly	yellow floss, peacock herl rib, red floss tip	
WIPER		dark blue dun	gray fur, yellow floss rib	3 brown hackle fibers
WITCH		badger	bronze peacock	
WITCH, GOLD		badger	gray dubbing, gold rib and tip	scarlet fibers
WITCHER	dark gray; widgeon strips	black Palmer	black dubbing, silver rib, yellow floss tip	gold pheasant crest
WOODCOCK	woodcock	brown	yellow floss, gold rib	gold pheasant tippet
WOODCOCK FLY	See Oak Fly			
WOODCOCK PROFESSOR	See Professor-Woodcock			
WOODCOCK & BLUE	woodcock	natural black	blue dubbing, silver rib	gold pheasant tippet
WOODCOCK & GOLD	woodcock	ginger	gold, silver rib	gold pheasant tippet
WOODCOCK & GREEN	woodcock	green	green dubbing, silver rib	gold pheasant tippet
WOODCOCK & ORANGE	woodcock	ginger	orange dubbing, gold rib	gold pheasant tippet
WOODCOCK & RED	woodcock	natural red-brown	red dubbing, silver rib	gold pheasant tippet
WOODCOCK & YELLOW	woodcock	woodcock	yellow dubbing, silver rib	gold pheasant tippet

Name				
WOOD DUCK NO. 1	barred wood duck	green	green dubbing, gold rib	yellow fibers
WOOD DUCK NO. 2	barred wood duck	yellow	yellow dubbing, gold rib	
WOODRUFF	grizzly or white	brown	olive-green dubbing, gold tip	
WOOLY WORM		Palmer (badger, furnace, or grizzly hackle)	black, yellow or brown chenille bodies	red tail
WOOLY WORM, NEW MEXICO (W)		yellow Palmer	yellow floss, dyed yellow ostrich herl head	yellow hackle
WOPPINGER	dark gray	grizzly Palmer	dark gray floss, silver tip	slate fibers
WORM FLY		ginger	peacock herl	
WREN NO. 1	fine brown turkey	grouse	dark gray floss, yellow floss rib	mallard
WREN NO. 2	fine brown turkey	grouse	orange dubbing, gold rib	
YANKEE	white	scarlet	blue dubbing, silver rib	white fibers
YAKIMA WHITE FISH FLY		brown Palmer	yellow floss	
Y. B.	grouse	ginger	orange floss, black thread rib	yellow fibers
YELLOW BIVISIBLE		yellow; white front	yellow dubbing	
YELLOW, BLACK	black	black	yellow floss, gold rib	
YELLOW DOLLY	light gray		yellow dubbing, picked out, gold tip	
YELLOW DRAKE NO. 1	brown mallard	scarlet	yellow dubbing, silver rib	brown mallard
YELLOW DRAKE NO. 2	mallard dyed yellow	yellow	yellow floss, gold rib	black hackle
YELLOW DRAKE NO. 3	white duck dyed yellow	yellow	yellow floss	black hackle
YELLOW DRAKE, COOMBES		yellow; mallard dyed yellow face wound hackle-wise	cream floss, narrow gold rib	2 cock pheasant tail fibers
YELLOW DUN NO. 1	light gray	honey dun	yellow dubbing,	honey dun
YELLOW DUN NO. 2	mallard dyed yellow	yellow	gray dubbing, yellow floss rib	
YELLOW FINCH	yellow; mallard dyed yellow strips	guinea; yellow Palmer	yellow dubbing, silver rib	gold pheasant crest and blue
YELLOW FORKED TAIL NO. 1	hen pheasant	grizzly	yellow chenille, gold tip	gold pheasant crest (forked
YELLOW FORKED TAIL NO. 2	gray	grizzly	yellow floss, yellow floss tag	brown mallard sides or red hackle (forked)
YELLOW GROUSE	brown turkey	dark grouse	yellow floss, gold rib	
YELLOW HACKLE	See Hackle-Yellow			
YELLOW JACKET NO. 1	dark gray	brown	4-joint yellow, black, yellow, black chenille	
YELLOW JACKET NO. 2	light gray	yellow	yellow floss, black floss rib	yellow hackle
YELLOW MAY NO. 1	white duck dyed yellow	yellow	yellow floss, gold rib	black hackle
YELLOW MAY NO. 2	mallard dyed yellow	yellow	yellow floss, black thread rib	yellow mallard
YELLOW MILLER NO. 1	white	white	yellow dubbing, herl butt, gold tip	
YELLOW MILLER NO. 2	yellow	yellow	yellow floss, gold rib	
YELLOW MOTH	yellow	yellow	yellow chenille, gold tip	
YELLOW PALMER		badger dyed yellow (Palmer)	yellow dubbing	yellow hackle

YELLOW PARROT	white; yellow strips	yellow	yellow floss, gold rib	scarlet fibers
YELLOW PENNELL HACKLE		yellow	yellow thread or raffia	yellow hackle
YELLOW PROFESSOR	See Professor-Yellow			
YELLOW QUAIL	mallard dyed yellow	red and blue mixed	blue floss, scarlet floss center joint	
YELLOW QUILL	gray	yellow	peacock quill dyed yellow	yellow hackle
YELLOW ROBIN	gray	yellow	yellow chenille	
YELLOW SALLY	duck dyed yellow	ginger	yellow dubbing, gold rib	yellow hackle
YELLOW SPIDER		yellow (spider radius)	yellow dubbing	yellow hackle
YELLOW SPINNER	mallard dyed yellow	yellow	black floss, silver rib	
YELLOWSTONE NO. 1 (W)	black	orange	yellow chenille, gold tip	yellow hackle
YELLOWSTONE NO. 2 (W)	dark gray	yellow	yellow chenille	black hackles
YELLOW TAIL		grizzly	½ yellow chenille aft, ½ peacock herl fore	
YELLOW TURKEY	brown turkey	brown	yellow dubbing picked out, gold rib	
ZULU NO. 1	black	black	peacock herl, red tip, gold tag	
ZULU NO. 2		black	black dubbing, silver rib	scarlet fibers blunt

STEELHEAD WET FLIES

ALASKA MARY: *Wing,* polar bear hair, jungle cock eye shoulder. *Body,* white chenille, silver wire rib. *Tail,* red hackle fibers.

BADGER PALMER: *Wing,* none.*Hackle,* long badger tied Palmer. *Body,* yellow wool. *Tail,* scarlet and badger hackle fibers.

BAIR'S BLACK: *Wing,* white goose, red center strip. *Hackle,* black. *Body,* thick black chenille, red floss tip. *Tail,* red hackle fibers.

BELLAMY: *Wing,* brown over yellow over white hair. *Hackle,* brown beard. *Body,* copper wire. *Tail,* red goose.

BLACK DEMON No. 1: *Wing,* black polar bear hair. *Hackle,* badger or black. *Body,* oval silver tinsel. *Tail,* silver pheasant crest.

BLACK DEMON No. 2: *Wing,* black bucktail. *Hackle,* orange. *Body,* oval gold tinsel. *Tail,* gold pheasant crest.

BLACK GNAT: *Wing,* black polar bear hair. *Hackle,* black. *Body,* black chenille, gold tip. *Tail,* silver pheasant crest.

BOBBIE DUNN: *Wing,* brown over red over white hair. *Hackle,* none. *Body,* copper wire. *Tail,* red bucktail.

BOSQUITO: *Wing,* white hair. *Hackle,* black. *Body,* yellow chenille, gold tinsel tag. *Tail,* red hackle fibers.

BRASS HAT: *Wing,* black over yellow over white hair. *Hackle,* none. *Body,* brass wire. *Tail,* yellow goose.

BROWN DRAKE: *Wing,* teal, brown hair over. *Hackle,* coch-y-bondhu. *Body,* pale olive green floss, black thread rib. *Tail,* teal.

BUCK CADDIS—DARK: *Wing,* brown deer hair. *Hackle,* furnace Palmer. *Body,* orange wool. *Tail,* furnace.

CARSON No. 1: *Wing,* white goose, red center strip. *Hackle,* brown. *Body,* peacock herl, red floss center joint. *Tail,* gold pheasant tippet.

CARSON No. 2 (Donnelly): *Wing,* white hair over scarlet, a few brown whisks over top. *Hackle,* brown. *Body,* peacock herl, scarlet floss center joint, gold tinsel tag. *Tail,* scarlet hackle fibers.

CARTER'S DIXIE: *Wing,* white goose. *Hackle,* scarlet. *Body,* gold cord and tag. *Tail,* gold pheasant crest.

COACHMAN: *Wing,* white bucktail. *Hackle,* brown. *Body,* peacock herl, gold tip. *Tail,* gold pheasant tippet.

CUMMINGS: *Wing,* brown bucktail, jungle cock eye shoulder. *Hackle,* claret. *Body,* ½ aft yellow floss, ½ fore claret wool, gold tinsel rib.

CUTTHROAT: *Wing,* white bucktail. *Hackle,* black. *Body,* claret chenille, gold tip. *Tail,* black hackle fibers.

DONNELLY'S PARTRIDGE: *Wing,* chestnut partridge. *Hackle,* chestnut partridge. *Body,* yellow floss, embossed gold tinsel rib and tag. *Tail,* gold pheasant tippet.

DUSTY MILLER No. 1: *Wing,* red squirrel or Impali. *Hackle,* brown partridge. *Body,* embossed oval silver tinsel. *Tail,* silver pheasant crest.

DUSTY MILLER No. 2: *Wing,* brown turkey tail. *Hackle,* guinea. *Body,* flat silver tinsel and tag. *Tail,* red hackle fibers.

GOLDEN DEMON: *Wing,* brown bucktail, jungle cock eye shoulder. *Hackle,* orange. *Body,* gold tinsel. *Tail,* gold pheasant crest.

GRIZZLY KING: *Wing,* gray squirrel. *Hackle,* grizzly. *Body,* green wool, silver rib. *Tail,* red hackle fibers.

HARDY'S FAVORITE: *Wing,* mottled gray pheasant. *Hackle,* guinea. *Body,* peacock herl, red floss rib and tag. *Tail,* orange hackle fibers and guinea.

JOE O'DONNELL: *Wing,* badger hackles (divided), jungle cock eye shoulders. *Hackle,* yellow and red mixed. *Body,* white chenille. *Tail,* red hackle fibers.

JOCK SCOT: *Wing,* gray squirrel (sparse), toppings of red, yellow and blue hair. *Hackle,* guinea. *Body,* ½ fore black wool, ½ aft yellow wool, all gold rib. *Tail,* gold pheasant tippet and crest.

MARCH BROWN: *Wing,* red squirrel. *Hackle,* brown and grizzly mixed. *Body,* brown-gray dubbing, gold thread rib. *Tail,* red hackle fibers.

McGINTY: *Wing,* gray squirrel-white tipped. *Hackle,* brown. *Body,* 4 joint black and yellow chenille. *Tail,* red hackles and teal.

MICKEY FINN: *Wing,* yellow over red over yellow hair. *Body,* embossed silver tinsel.

MONTREAL: *Wing,* gray squirrel-white tipped. *Hackle,* claret. *Body,* claret wool, gold rib. *Tail,* claret hackle fibers.

ORLEANS BARBER: *Wing,* none. *Hackle,* grizzly. *Body,* red chenille. *Tail,* thick red hackle fibers.

PARMACHENE BELLE: *Wing,* white over red over white hair. *Hackle,* red. *Body,* yellow wool, gold rib. *Tail,* red and white hackle fibers.

PRINCESS: *Wing,* gray squirrel over orange hair over yellow hair. *Body,* gold tinsel or brass wire. *Tail,* polar bear dyed orange.

PAINT BRUSH: *Wing,* brown over red over yellow hair. *Body,* brass wire. *Tail,* red goose.

PROFESSOR: *Wing,* gray squirrel. *Hackle,* brown. *Body,* yellow wool, gold rib. *Tail,* red hackle fibers.

QUEEN BESS: *Wing,* gray squirrel over yellow hair. *Hackle,* gold pheasant tippet throat. *Body,* silver tinsel. *Tail,* gray squirrel.

QUEEN OF THE WATERS: *Wing,* gray squirrel. *Hackle,* brown Palmer. *Body,* orange wool, gold rib. *Tail,* gold pheasant tippet.

RAILBIRD No. 1: *Wing,* teal, jungle cock eye shoulder. *Hackle,* claret Palmer, yellow face. *Body,* claret wool or seal's fur. *Tail,* red hackle fibers.

RAILBIRD No. 2: *Wing,* dark barred teal, jungle cock eye shoulder. *Hackle,* yellow. *Body,* flat silver tinsel. *Tail,* claret hackle fibers.

RED OWL-EYE OPTIC: *Wing,* red bucktail. *Hackle,* none. *Body,* heavy oval silver tinsel. *Head,* large black with large orange eye, large black pupil.

ROGUE: *Wing,* polar bear hair over white deer, jungle cock eye shoulder. *Hackle,* grizzly. *Body,* green chenille, oval silver rib. *Tail,* red hackle fibers.

ROYAL COACHMAN: *Wing,* white bucktail. *Hackle,* brown. *Body,* peacock herl, red floss center joint. *Tail,* gold pheasant tippet.

SHRIMP: *Wing,* white polar bear. *Hackle,* orange. *Body,* orange fur. *Tail,* red hackle fibers.

SILVER ANT: *Wing,* skunk or black bucktail. *Hackle,* crimson. *Body,* silver tinsel. *Tail,* yellow hackle fibers.

SILVER DEMON No. 1: *Wing,* guinea, gold pheasant crest topping. *Hackle,* orange. *Body,* flat silver tinsel. *Tail,* sparse polar bear hair.

SILVER DEMON No. 2: *Wing,* gray squirrel-white tipped. *Hackle,* orange. *Body,* oval silver. *Tail,* orange hackle fibers.

SILVER DOCTOR: *Wing,* barred wood duck with brown mallard over, 3 peacock sword feathers for topping. *Hackle,* silver-doctor blue, guinea face. *Body,* silver tinsel, red wool butt, silver tinsel tag. *Tail,* red hackle fibers, gold pheasant crest and peacock sword.

SILVER LADY: *Wing,* 2 blue hackles, strip of barred wood duck each side, gold pheasant crest topping. *Hackle,* badger. *Body,* flat silver tinsel. *Tail,* gold pheasant tippet.

SILVER ORANGE: *Wing,* yellow polar bear hair. *Hackle,* orange. *Body,* flat silver tinsel. *Tail,* none.

STEVENSON'S SPECIAL: *Wing,* yellow bucktail. *Hackle,* guinea dyed yellow. *Body,* ½ aft oval gold, ½ fore black chenille. *Tail,* guinea dyed red.

THOR: *Wing,* white bucktail. *Hackle,* brown or brown bucktail. *Body,* red chenille. *Tail,* orange hackle fibers.

UMPQUA: *Wing,* red polar bear over white polar bear hair, jungle cock eye shoulder. *Hackle,* coch-y-bondhu. *Body,* ½ fore red chenille, ½ aft yellow wool, silver tinsel rib and tag. *Tail,* red polar bear hair over white polar bear hair.

VAN LUVEN: *Wing,* white bucktail. *Hackle,* brown. *Body,* red wool, oval silver rib. *Tail,* red bucktail.

WELLS' SPECIAL: *Wing,* teal, strips of brown mallard, red, blue and yellow; jungle cock eye shoulder. *Hackle,* yellow. *Body,* ½ aft oval silver, ½ fore peacock herl.

YELLOW FORKED-TAIL: *Wing,* hen pheasant. *Hackle,* grizzly. *Body,* yellow chenille, gold tag. *Tail,* 2 gold pheasant crest concave sides outside.

YELLOW PHEASANT: *Wing,* Chinese pheasant cock side plumage with black end spot, tied folded flat. *Hackle,* yellow. *Body,* yellow floss, gold rib. *Tail,* gold pheasant crest.

TROUT, BASS AND SALMON STREAMERS

ABBEY: *Wing*, grizzly streamers, jungle cock eye shoulders. *Hackle*, brown. *Body*, red floss, gold rib and tip. *Tail*, gold pheasant tippet.

ALECK'S WONDER: *Wing*, blue, yellow and claret saddles or neck hackles, jungle cock eye shoulders. *Hackle*, blue first, scarlet over. *Body*, gold. *Tail*, barred wood duck and blue chatterer.

ALLAN'S FIRST CHOICE: *Wing*, blue center, yellow outside saddles or neck hackles. *Hackle*, red first, yellow over. *Body*, gold, gold wire rib. *Tail*, barred wood duck and blue.

ALLAN'S LAST CHOICE: *Wing*, blue center, grizzly outside. *Hackle*, magenta first, grizzly over. *Body*, gold, gold wire rib. *Tail*, barred wood duck and blue.

ANDROSCOGGIN: *Wing*, green saddles or neck hackles. *Hackle*, long white bucktail. *Body*, claret floss, silver rib.

ANSON: *Wing*, white bucktail, barred teal shoulder, jungle cock eye cheek. *Hackle*, red. *Body*, silver tinsel, peacock herl rib. *Tail*, red hackle fibers.

ARNOLD: *Wing*, red and white bucktail center, grizzly outside. *Hackle*, white. *Body*, silver, silver wire rib.

AUNT IDER: *Wing*, yellow bucktail center, grizzly outside, silver pheasant shoulder. *Hackle*, peacock herl first, white bucktail over. *Body*, silver, gold wire rib.

B & B: *Wing*, white with black on top (saddles or neck hackles).

BARIBEAULT No. 1: *Wing*, red, white, yellow and orange bucktail. *Body*, red chenille, gold wire rib. *Tail*, barred wood duck.

BARIBEAULT No. 2: *Wing*, white bucktail center, red bucktail over. *Body*, embossed silver. *Tail*, barred wood duck.

BARIBEAULT No. 3: *Wing*, gray squirrel. *Body*, silver, silver wire rib. *Tail*, white hackle tips.

BARNES' SPECIAL: *Wing*, yellow center, grizzly outside. *Hackle*, white. *Body*, silver, silver wire rib.

BARTLETT'S SPECIAL: *Wing*, white, orange and blue saddles or neck hackles. *Hackle*, yellow. *Body*, black floss, gold rib. *Tail*, orange hackles.

BAUMAN: *Wing*, white bucktail first, then yellow bucktail, peacock herl horns. *Hackle*, red. *Body*, gold. *Tail*, barred wood duck.

BEAN'S SPECIAL: *Wing*, white saddles or neck hackles. *Hackle*, red and yellow. *Body*, white floss, silver rib. *Tail*, barred wood duck.

BI-PLANES (Plympton & Johnson): streamers tied horizontal.

BLACK PANTHER: *Wing*, 3 gray dun hackles over 1 badger over 1 iron blue. *Hackle*, yellow over red beard, black collar sparse and long. *Body*, peacock herl. *Tail*, blue over red over yellow hackle fibers.

GRAY CHARM: *Wing*, 4 gray dun hackles. *Cheek*, silver pheasant tippet. *Hackle*, red (sparse) beard over sparse blue beard. *Body*, orange wool, silver embossed tinsel rib. *Butt*, peacock herl. *Tip*, silver embossed tinsel. *Tail*, yellow over red hackle fibers.

SMELT: *Wing*, 1 white neck hackle over 1 gray dun over 1 blue over 1 white. *Cheek*, silver pheasant tippet sparse. *Hackle*, red over yellow beard (sparse). *Body*, white wool, silver embossed rib. *Tag*, silver embossed. *Tail*, yellow over red hackle fibers.

BIG DIAMOND: *Wing,* badger dyed yellow, wood duck shoulders, red splits. *Hackle,* blue bucktail. *Body,* gold. *Tail,* red feather.

BILDOW: *Wing,* white polar bear hair. *Body,* yellow wool picked out, silver rib, red wool tag.

BLACK DEMON: *Wing,* black, saddles or neck hackles. *Hackle,* orange. *Body,* gold tinsel.

BLACK DEMON No. 2: See Wounded Minnow dressings.

BLACK DEVIL: *Wing,* badger saddles. *Cheek,* jungle cock eye. *Hackle,* short red beard. *Body,* black floss, silver rib. *Tail,* peacock sword.

BLACK DOG: *Wing,* blue dun saddles or neck hackles. *Cheek,* jungle cock eye. *Head,* black. *Hackle,* black with yellow duck (small piece) at throat. *Body,* black floss, narrow silver rib. *Tail,* yellow and black hair.

BLACKBIRD: *Wing,* black bucktail, jungle cock eye cheeks. *Hackle,* black bucktail under hook. *Body,* black floss, narrow gold rib.

BLACK DOSE: *Wing,* 2 black saddles in center, 2 red grizzly saddles outside. *Hackle,* red grizzly. *Body,* black wool, silver rib. *Tail,* gold pheasant crest.

BLACK GHOST: *Wing,* 4 white saddles. *Hackle,* yellow feather at throat. *Body,* black floss, silver rib. *Tail,* yellow feather.

BLACK PANTHER (bi-plane): See Bi-Planes.

BLACK SKUNK: *Wing,* black skunk tail, jungle cock eye cheek. *Head,* optic. *Body,* heavy black chenille, silver rib.

BLACK AND YELLOW: *Wing,* black bucktail over yellow. *Body,* silver. *Tail,* gold pheasant crest.

BLUE DEVIL: *Wing,* blue and orange neck hackles, peacock herl topping, black and white barred shoulder, jungle cock eye cheek. *Hackle,* white hair, long under body, blue throat. *Body,* black floss, silver rib.

BLUMARABOU: *Wing,* blue marabou with grizzly hackle on top. *Body,* silver.

BOLSHEVIK: *Wing,* coch-y-bondhu, white hair under. *Hackle,* red. *Body,* silver.

BOURBON BUCK: *Wing,* white bucktail. *Hackle,* red. *Body,* gold, gold wire rib. *Tail,* red hackle feather.

BRENNAN: *Wing,* 3 badger hackles, wood duck shoulders, jungle cock eye cheeks. *Hackle,* long silver pheasant crest, short guinea. *Body,* gold, round gold rib. *Tail,* gold pheasant crest, and red hackle.

BRIGHT ANGLE NIGHT RIDER (W): *Wing,* black saddles or peacock herl, jungle cock eye cheek. *Hackle,* polar bear hair. *Body,* gold tinsel.

BROSSEAU: *Wing,* silver pheasant tippets, jungle cock eye cheeks. *Hackle,* guinea, red beard. *Body,* silver. *Tail,* gold pheasant crest.

BROWN BUCKTAIL: *Wing,* natural brown bucktail. *Body,* silver.

BROWN GHOST: *Wing,* brown neck hackles, gold pheasant crest topping. *Hackle,* yellow. *Body,* brown floss, gold rib. *Tail,* gold pheasant crest.

BROWN HACKLE: *Wing,* brown saddles or neck hackles. *Hackle,* brown. *Body,* peacock herl.

CAIN RIVER: *Wing,* 2 red saddles in center, 2 yellow saddles outside. *Hackle,* yellow over blue. *Body,* gold, round gold rib. *Tail,* gold pheasant crest.

CAREY SPECIAL: *Wing,* body cock pheasant rump feathers, long, tied hackle-wise, tied down. *Body,* dark bear hair. *Tail,* dark bear hair.

CARMICHAEL'S MALLARD STREAMER (W): *Wing,* long mallard side plumage wound hackle-wise and tied down. *Body,* deep yellow yarn (heavy), gold rib. *Tail,* red hackle fibers.

CATSKILL: *Wing,* red over white bucktail, peacock herl topping. *Body,* silver, round silver rib.

CHAMP'S SPECIAL: *Wing,* yellow hair center, grizzly outside. *Hackle,* white bucktail long, peacock herl over. *Body,* silver. *Tail,* red hackles, short.

CHIEF NEEDABEH: *Wing,* yellow saddles, jungle cock eye cheeks. *Hackle,* red (sparse) top and bottom. *Body,* red, silver rib and tip.

CHINESE SPECIAL: *Wing,* brown and white Chinese deer tail, peacock herl topping, jungle cock eye cheeks. *Body,* silver.

COLONEL CAREY: See Carey Special.

COLONEL FULLER: *Wing,* yellow saddles or neck hackles, red pheasant breast cheeks. *Hackle,* long yellow at throat. *Body,* silver, round silver rib.

COLONEL PHEASANT: *Wing,* white saddles, gold pheasant tippet shoulder. *Body,* silver, oval silver rib.

COLONEL WHITE: *Wing,* white saddles, red cheeks. *Body,* silver.

CONGDON: *Wing,* yellow bucktail, wood duck topping. *Body,* blue-green chenille. *Tail,* barred wood duck.

CONGER'S LASSIE: *Wing,* orange saddles in center, grizzly outside. *Hackle,* black. *Body,* silver. *Tail,* gold pheasant crest.

CONNECTICUT RIVER DICK: *Wing,* yellow hair center, teal outside, red strips. *Hackle,* peacock herl, gold tag.

CORN BUCK: *Wing,* red squirrel or impala. *Hackle,* red. *Body,* gold, gold wire rib. *Tail,* red hackle feather.

COSSEBOOM: *Wing,* gray squirrel. *Hackle,* yellow. *Body,* light green wool, silver rib. *Tail,* light green wool.

DANA SPECIAL: *Wing,* white and yellow saddles, red shoulder. *Hackle,* white. *Body,* silver. *Tail,* red feather.

DEACON: *Wing,* short polar bear hair first, then yellow saddles, peacock sword topping, jungle cock eye cheek. *Body,* peacock herl. *Tail,* gold pheasant crest.

DR. BURKE: *Wing,* white gamecock, jungle cock eye cheek. *Hackle,* medium long yellow beard. *Body,* flat silver. *Tail,* thick green peacock sword.

DUNK'S SPECIAL: *Wing,* red and blue saddles. *Hackle,* red and blue. *Body,* silver. *Tail,* barred wood duck and red.

DUSTY No. 1: *Wing,* grizzly. *Hackle,* red at throat only. *Body,* silver, silver round rib.

DUSTY No. 2 (Quimby): *Wing,* grizzly, jungle cock eye cheeks. *Hackle,* peacock herl long under body, brown over white throat. *Body,* silver. *Tail,* peacock herl.

DUSTY MILLER: *Wing,* orange saddles in center, grizzly outside. *Hackle,* guinea and orange. *Body,* silver, round gold rib. *Tail,* gold pheasant crest.

EAST BRANCH: *Wing,* black bucktail on top of white. *Body,* silver, red tag.

EDSON TIGER: See Tiger.

EMERY: *Wing,* grizzly, peacock herl topping at front. *Hackle,* white bucktail long. *Body,* black floss, silver rib.

FAMILY SECRET: *Wing,* white gamecock 3 each side, jungle cock eye cheeks. *Hackle,* long guinea. *Body,* silver, oval silver rib. *Tail,* thick green peacock sword.

FOREST SPECIAL: *Wing,* yellow hair over white hair, black hair on top, jungle cock eye cheeks. *Body,* gold, gold wire rib.

GALLOPING GHOST: *Wing,* Bali, jungle cock eye shoulder. *Hackle,* orange. *Body,* orange floss, silver rib. *Tail,* red quill feather.

GARDWIN: *Wing,* light brown bucktail. *Hackle,* yellow throat. *Body,* yellow wool, silver rib. *Tail,* red feather.

GASPEROUX: *Wing,* red and yellow bucktail, jungle cock eye shoulders. *Body,* silver, oval silver rib.

GENERAL MacARTHUR: *Wing,* white saddle center, blue saddles over, grizzly outside, jungle cock eye shoulders. *Hackle,* red over white over blue throat. *Body,* silver tinsel. *Tail,* red over white over blue hackle fibers.

GOLDEN CATSKILL: *Wing,* yellow bucktail first, brown bucktail on top. *Body,* gold. *Tail,* peacock sword.

GOLDEN KILLER: *Wing,* brown bucktail over yellow. *Body,* gold. *Tail,* gold pheasant tippet.

GOLDEN WITCH: *Wings,* grizzly, gold pheasant tippet shoulder. *Hackle,* peacock herl over white bucktail. *Body, claret* floss, silver rib.

GOVERNOR AIKEN: *Wing,* purple bucktail, peacock herl on top. *Hackle,* red. *Body,* silver. *Tail,* barred wood duck.

GRAND LAKER: *Wing,* brown saddles. *Hackle,* long brown bucktail. *Body,* black floss, gold rib.

GRAY CHARM (bi-plane): See Bi-Planes.

GRAY GHOST: *Wing,* blue dun neck hackles, silver pheasant breast shoulder, jungle cock eye cheek. *Hackle,* sparse white bucktail under hook, 5 or 6 strands of peacock herl, last sparse yellow. *Body,* orange floss, silver rib.

GRAY MOUSE: *Wing,* gray squirrel. *Body,* silver.

GREEN BEAUTY: *Wing,* 4 dark green saddles over 4 peacock herl strands, wood duck shoulder, jungle cock eye cheek. *Hackle,* white hair. *Body,* orange floss, silver rib.

GREEN GHOST: *Wing,* green saddles or neck hackles, silver pheasant breast feather shoulder. *Hackle,* sparse white bucktail under hook, 5 or 6 strands of peacock herl first, gold pheasant crest fastened at throat. *Body,* orange floss, silver rib. *Cheek,* jungle cock eye.

GREEN KING: *Wing,* white hair first, then green, last grizzly on top, jungle cock eye shoulder. *Body,* silver—silver aft hook.

GREEN SPOT: *Wing,* green and white bucktail, 2 dark green saddles on top. *Body,* silver, silver rib.

GREEN'S POT: See Green Spot (this is correct name).

GREGG'S DEMON: *Wing,* grizzly dyed brown, gold pheasant crest topping, jungle cock eye shoulder. *Hackle,* orange. *Body,* silver, gold rib. *Tail,* barred wood duck.

GRIZZLY GRAY: *Wing,* grizzly. *Hackle,* white bucktail. *Body,* silver. *Tail,* orange hackles.

GRIZZLY KING: *Wing,* grizzly. *Hackle,* grizzly. *Body,* green floss, silver rib. *Tail,* red feather.

HANCE: *Wing,* black and brown neck hackles. *Hackle,* black at throat. *Body,* yellow and black joint chenille.

HELL CAT: *Wing,* natural brown bucktail, black tied over it. *Body,* yellow chenille, peacock eyed tail fiber butts fore and aft. *Shoulder,* jungle cock eye. *Tail,* red hackle fibers.

HERMAN'S FAVORITE: *Wing*, red neck hackles, furnace on top. *Hackle*, brown. *Body*, gold. *Tail*, mallard.

HIGHLAND BELLE: *Wing*, orange saddles inside, grizzly outside. *Hackle*, white bucktail. *Body*, gold, silver rib.

HIGHLANDER: *Wing*, yellow saddles inside, grizzly outside. *Hackle*, grizzly. *Body*, silver. *Tail*, barred wood duck.

HOAG FAVORITE: *Wing*, red saddles inside, grizzly outside. *Hackle*, green and grizzly. *Body*, silver.

HOGG: *Wing*, red squirrel. *Hackle*, brown. *Body*, peacock herl, red floss center joint.

HONEY: *Wing*, yellow neck hackles or saddles. *Body*, red floss, gold rib, red ostrich herl butt, gold tag.

HOWE'S FANCY: *Wing*, brown and yellow hair mixed, red head. *Body*, round gold. *Tail*, barred wood duck.

HURRICANE: *Wing*, red hair tied on first, then white hair, grizzly on top. *Hackle*, peacock herl. *Body*, silver ½ body aft black rib. *Tail*, jungle cock eye.

IRIS: *Wing*, white polar bear hair, jungle cock eye shoulder. *Body*, silver, oval silver rib.

IRISH BUCK: *Wings*, green over white hair. *Body*, green floss, gold rib. *Tail*, green feather.

JACK'S SALMO: *Wing*, green saddles on top of white hair, jungle cock eye shoulder. *Hackle*, red throat. *Body*, silver, silver wire rib.

JANE CRAIG: *Wing*, white saddles, peacock herl topping. *Hackle*, white at throat. *Body*, silver, round silver rib.

JAZZ BOA: *Wing*, white and orange. *Hackle*, yellow. *Body*, yellow floss, gold rib.

JESSA BOU: *Wing*, brown saddles, peacock herl topping. *Hackle*, brown. *Body*, silver.

JESSE WOOD: *Wing*, Yanosh feathers (Bali duck), jungle cock eye shoulder. *Hackle*, furnace. *Body*, silver. *Tail*, red feather.

JOCK SCOT: *Wing*, 2 yellow saddles inside, 2 badger outside, peacock sword topping. *Hackle*, guinea. *Body*, black floss fore, yellow floss aft, silver rib all. *Tail*, gold pheasant crest.

JOE KILLER: *Wing*, yellow hair, silver pheasant crest sides, lemon wood duck shoulders. *Hackle*, yellow at throat (hair). *Body*, silver, silver wire rib. *Tail*, barred wood duck.

JOHNSON: *Wing*, thick peacock herl over dark brown turkey, peacock sword shoulder. *Hackle*, red beard. *Body*, thick brown Palmer.

JUNGLE PRINCESS: *Wing*, yellow grizzly, blue chatterer cheeks, long jungle cock eye shoulder. *Hackle*, white. *Body*, gold.

JUNGLE SUPERVISOR: *Wing*, white hair, 2 blue saddles on top, jungle cock eye shoulder. *Body*, silver, silver wire rib. *Tail*, red feather.

KENNEBAGO TROUT FLIES of Kennebago region, Maine:

    No. 1: *Wing*, brown hair on top of white. *Body*, silver.

    No. 2: *Wing*, black hair on top of yellow. *Body*, silver.

    No. 3: *Wing*, red hair on top of white. *Body*, silver.

    No. 4: *Wing*, black hair on top of white. *Body*, silver.

    No. 5: *Wing*, red hair on top of yellow. *Body*, silver.

    No. 6: *Wing*, green hair on top of white. *Body*, silver.

KENT: *Wing*, 4 grizzly dyed yellow, jungle cock eye shoulders. *Hackle*, black beard. *Body*, yellow wool, silver rib. *Tail*, red fibers.

KIDDER: *Wing*, brown saddles in center, grizzly outside. *Hackle*, brown. *Body*, gold. *Tail*, barred wood duck.

KING: *Wing*, white bucktail. *Hackle*, brown. *Body*, peacock herl, wide red floss center joint.

KING SALMO: *Wing*, blue grizzly over red hair over white. *Hackle*, grizzly. *Body*, gold, silver wire rib. *Tail*, gold pheasant crest.

KLONDIKE KATE: *Wing*, white saddles, badger over. *Hackle*, red, olive front. *Body*, silver, oval gold rib.

LADY DOCTOR: *Wing*, black over white hair, red cheek. *Hackle*, yellow Palmer. *Body*, yellow floss, silver rib, red wool tag. *Tail*, gold pheasant crest.

LADY GHOST: *Wing*, badger, copper pheasant shoulder, gold pheasant crest topping. *Hackle*, peacock herl and white hair long, gold pheasant crest fastened at throat. *Body*, silver, oval silver rib. *Tail*, gold pheasant tippet.

LEECH LAKE: *Wing*, white. *Hackle*, sparse red, full white face. *Body*, silver, oval silver rib.

LIGGETT: *Wing*, white hair, sparse red and yellow hairs on each side, jungle cock eye shoulder. *Body*, silver, silver aft hook.

LITTLE WONDER: *Wing*, grizzly over red neck hackles. *Hackle*, yellow. *Body*, gold.

MANSFIELD: *Wing*, orange hair over white. *Body*, black floss, silver rib. *Tail*, gold pheasant tippet.

MARABOU SPECIAL: *Wing*, white marabou, pintail sides 2/3 length of marabou, gold pheasant tippet fibers. *Body*, silver. *Tail*, gold pheasant tippet.

McGINTY: *Wing*, white hair, black streamer 2/3 length of white. *Hackle*, coch-y-bondhu. *Body*, yellow and black chenille alternate twist, gold tip. *Tail*, teal and red hackles.

MEADOW LAKE SPECIAL: *Wing*, double grizzly divided—shiny side out. *Hackle*, brown. *Body*, white chenille, red floss tip ¼ of body. *Tail*, same as wing.

MICKEY FINN: *Wing*, yellow over red over yellow hair. *Hackle*, none. *Body*, silver, silver twist rib.

MICKEY'S STREAMER: *Wing*, yellow and red bucktail. *Body*, red floss, gold tag. *Tail*, black hackles.

MILLER'S RIVER SPECIAL: *Wing*, black bucktail over yellow, gold pheasant crest topping, dyed red cheeks, jungle cock eye shoulder. *Body*, gold, gold wire rib. *Tail*, gold pheasant crest.

MIRAMICHI: *Wing*, red and peacock blue. *Hackle*, red and peacock blue. *Body*, gold. *Tail*, barred wood duck and blue.

MOOSE RIVER: *Wing*, badger over scant white hair, peacock herl topping, gold pheasant tippet cheeks. *Body*, silver.

MORNING GLORY: *Wing*, 4 yellow saddles over 10 long black feather fibers, red gold pheasant body feather shoulder, jungle cock eye. *Hackle*, white hair, blue over black throat. *Body*, red floss, silver rib.

NEW ENGLAND COUNCILLOR: *Wing*, grizzly over white maribou. *Body*, silver, silver wire rib, and tag.

NIMROD: *Wing*, green hair, black hair on top, jungle cock eye. *Hackle*, long yellow hair. *Body*, silver, silver wire rib.

NINE-3: *Wing*, white bucktail first, 3 green saddles flat, 2 natural black edgewise, jungle cock eye shoulder. *Body*, silver, silver aft hook.

ORDWAY: *Wing*, white, red cheeks. *Body*, silver, round silver rib.

PARMACHENE BEAU: *Wing*, red over white, jungle cock eye shoulder. *Hackle*, red over white. *Body*, yellow wool, silver rib. *Tail*, gold pheasant crest.

PARMACHENE BELLE: *Wing*, red over white. *Hackle*, red over white. *Body*, yellow wool, silver rib. *Tail*, gold pheasant crest.

PARMACHENE COCK: See Parmachene Beau.

PEAMARED: *Wing*, white marabou, peacock herl topping, several long red hairs on each side of white, jungle cock eye shoulder. *Body*, silver.

PEAMAROU: *Wing*, gold pheasant crest, white marabou on top, jungle cock eye shoulder. *Body*, silver.

PEET'S FAVORITE: *Wing*, red and white. *Hackle*, brown. *Body*, gold.

PEET'S MASTERPIECE: *Wing*, blue center, yellow outside. *Hackle*, blue over magenta. *Body*, gold. *Tail*, barred wood duck and blue.

PINK PUP: *Wing*, brown hair over red and yellow. *Body*, ½ fore black floss, ½ aft silver, all silver wire rib.

PROFESSOR: *Wing*, gray squirrel. *Hackle*, brown. *Body*, yellow floss, gold rib. *Tail*, red feather.

QUEEN OF THE WATERS: *Wing*, gray squirrel. *Hackle*, brown. *Body*, orange floss, gold rib. *Tail*, gold pheasant tippet tail.

RAINBOW: *Wing*, blue and yellow. *Hackle*, red, yellow front. *Body*, gold tinsel.

RED FIN: See Wounded Minnow.

RED AND WHITE: *Wing*, white hair over red hair over white hair. *Body*, silver. *Tail*, red feather.

RED AND WHITE POLAR BEAR: See Red and White.

RED AND YELLOW: *Wing*, yellow over red over yellow. *Body*, silver. *Tail*, red feather.

REUBEN WOOD VARIATION: See Meadow Lake Special.

ROARING RAPIDS: *Wing*, red and yellow. *Hackle*, blue. *Body*, silver. *Tail*, barred wood duck and red.

ROGER SMITH: *Wing*, 10 or 12 impala hairs. *Body* (slender), gray floss, sparse, fine silver rib. *Head*, large black.

ROSCOE: *Wing*, brown bucktail. *Body*, silver.

ROSS McKENNEY: *Wing*, white, long gold pheasant crest topping, red cheeks, jungle cock eye shoulder. *Body*, silver, silver wire rib.

RYE BUCK: *Wing*, red hair over white hair. *Body*, red dubbing picked out, gold tip. *Tail*, red feather.

SABASKONG: *Wing*, yellow and blue. *Hackle*, yellow and blue. *Body*, gold.

SALMO SEBAGO: *Wing*, white, peacock herl topping. *Hackle*, yellow. *Body*, gold, gold wire rib. *Tail*, red over white hair.

SANBORN: *Wing*, 4 yellow saddles, jungle cock eye shoulder. *Hackle*, yellow. *Body*, black floss, silver rib. *Head*, black with red strip on each side.

SANDERS: *Wing*, grizzly over white bucktail. *Body*, silver.

SCOTCH BUCK: *Wing*, black hair. *Body*, black floss, silver rib. *Tail*, red feather.

SCOTCH LASSIE: *Wing,* blue and yellow. *Hackle,* purple and claret. *Body,* silver, gold wire rib.

SCOTTY: *Wing,* red-brown furnace. *Hackle,* garnet. *Body,* garnet seal fur, black ostrich butt, white floss tip, gold tag. *Tail,* wood duck.

SHEENIC SPECIAL: *Wing,* dark green saddles on top of white hair, jungle cock eye shoulder. *Body,* silver, silver wire rib.

SILVER DEMON: *Wing,* grizzly. *Hackle,* orange. *Body,* silver.

SILVER DOCTOR No. 1: *Wing,* 2 blue saddles, 2 grizzly (grizzly on top). *Hackle,* grizzly over blue. *Body,* silver, round silver rib. *Tail,* silver pheasant tippet.

SILVER DOCTOR No. 2: *Wing,* blue, white and red, peacock sword topping. *Hackle,* guinea over blue. *Body,* silver. *Tail,* red, gold pheasant crest and blue.

SILVER DOCTOR No. 3: *Wing,* grizzly over brown. *Hackle,* grizzly over blue. *Body,* silver tinsel.

SILVER GHOST: *Wing,* 6 white saddles, jungle cock eye shoulders. *Hackle,* yellow beard. *Body,* silver. *Tail,* yellow hackle fibers.

SILVER GRAY: *Wing,* badger. *Hackle,* badger. *Body,* silver, round silver rib. *Tail,* gold pheasant crest.

SILVER SHINER: See Wounded Minnows.

SILVER WHITE: *Wing,* white, teal cheeks. *Hackle,* white hair (long). *Body,* silver, silver wire rib, red tag.

SMELT No. 1: See Bi-Planes.

SMELT No. 2: See Wounded Minnows.

SNEAKY JOE: *Wing,* fox squirrel. *Body,* black chenille. *Tail,* scarlet feather.

SPENCER BAY: *Wing,* 2 furnace hackle feathers over 2 light blue feathers, jungle cock eye shoulder. *Hackle,* blue and yellow mixed. *Body,* silver. *Tail,* gold pheasant tippet.

SPRUCE: *Wing,* double badger hackles divided—shiny side out. *Hackle,* sparse badger. *Body,* peacock herl (thick) over padding, red wool butt ¼ of body. *Tail,* 4 peacock sword fibers ¾" long.

STEVENSON: *Wing,* yellow bucktail over dark red, jungle cock eye shoulder. *Body,* silver.

SUPER IMP: *Wing,* green hair, green saddles over. *Hackle,* white hair sparse. *Body,* silver. *Tail,* red wool tail tag.

SUPER SPECIAL: *Wing,* light blue over white hair, green hackle cheeks. *Body,* silver. *Tail,* red wool tail tag.

SUPERVISOR: *Wing,* white bucktail, 2 light blue and 2 olive neck hackles outside (olive last), jungle cock eye shoulders, peacock herl strip each side. *Body,* silver, silver wire rib. *Tail,* red wool tail tag.

SUPERVISOR SPECIAL: *Wing,* yellow saddles over blue saddles over white hair. *Body,* silver. *Tail,* red wool tail tag.

TIGER-DARK: *Wing,* brown bucktail, peacock herl topping, jungle cock eye shoulder. *Hackle,* red feather (short) at throat. *Body,* yellow chenille, silver tip. *Tail,* barred wood duck.

TIGER-LIGHT: *Wing,* pale yellow hair, short red feather on top, jungle cock eye shoulder. *Body,* peacock herl, silver tip. *Tail,* barred wood duck.

TIGER-YELLOW: *Wing,* bright yellow hair, jungle cock eye shoulder. *Body,* peacock herl. *Tail,* red feather.

TROUT ROCK FLIES originated by Bert Quimby.

No. 1: *Wing*, black over white hair, jungle cock eye shoulder. *Body*, black floss, silver rib. *Tail*, red.

No. 2: *Wing*, yellow hair first, then red hair, then black on top, jungle cock eye shoulder. *Body*, black, silver rib.

No. 3: *Wing*, brown bucktail, jungle cock eye. *Body*, brown wool, silver tip.

No. 4: *Wing*, red hair over white, jungle cock eye shoulder. *Body*, silver, silver wire rib.

No. 5: *Wing*, black hair, jungle cock eye shoulder. *Body*, brown wool, silver tip.

No. 6: *Wing*, squirrel, jungle cock eye. *Body*, red, silver rib.

VAMP: *Wing*, cream neck hackles or bucktail. *Hackle*, badger-collar type. *Body*, white wool, silver tag. *Tail*, black forked fibers.

WADE'S CHOICE: *Wing*, grizzly over red and yellow. *Hackle*, grizzly over yellow. *Body*, silver. *Tail*, barred wood duck and blue.

WARDEN'S WONDER: *Wing*, red and grizzly. *Hackle*, yellow (full). *Body*, silver. *Tail*, red wool tail tag.

WARDEN'S WORRY: *Wing*, brown bucktail. *Hackle*, yellow. *Body*, yellow dubbing picked out, silver rib. *Tail*, red feather.

WATER WITCH: *Wing*, yellow. *Body*, black floss, silver rib.

WELSH RAREBIT: *Wing*, red inside, white outside, peacock herl topping. *Hackle*, guinea at throat. *Body*, silver, round silver rib. *Tail*, red, yellow and blue and peacock sword.

WHITE BUCKTAIL: *Wing*, white bucktail. *Body*, silver.

WHITE MARABOU: *Wing*, white marabou over red hair, peacock herl topping. *Body*, silver, silver twist rib. *Tail*, gold pheasant crest.

WHITE MILLER: *Wing*, white. *Body*, white, silver rib. *Tail*, silver pheasant tippet.

WILKINSON: *Wing*, 2 red saddles, 2 light blue saddles. *Hackle*, red and blue. *Body*, silver, round silver rib. *Tail*, gold pheasant crest.

WIZARD: *Wing*, 1 yellow neck hackle in center, 2 black outside. *Hackle*, scant white, peacock herl over. *Body*, black floss, fine gold rib.

WOUNDED MINNOWS (Plympton & Johnson). These are dressed on one side only.

BLACK DEMON: *Wing*, 2 black streamers outside, white hair top and bottom inside (all on one side of hook). *Hackle*, lemon yellow outside over streamers. *Body*, lemon floss, black floss rib. *Tail*, yellow hair. *Head*, black thread.

RED FIN: *Wing*, badger over 1 green outside with long very sparse red hairs over (all on one side of hook). *Hackle*, red and yellow sparse top and bottom. *Body*, orange wool, gold twist rib, gold tag. *Tail*, badger over yellow over red hackle fibers. *Head*, peacock herl.

SILVER SHINER: *Wing*, 2 white streamers outside, 2 strands peacock herl inside (all on one side of hook). *Hackle*, long, sparse yellow hair beard, short, sparse red top. *Body*, white wool, gold rib, peacock herl butt, gold tip. *Tail*, badger over yellow over red.

SMELT: *Wing*, 1 olive over two white, 1 peacock herl on top. *Hackle*, white beard. *Body*, lemon floss, gold rib, red floss tip, peacock herl butt. *Tail*, 2 short white hackle tips.

YELLOW: *Wing*, fox squirrel, gold pheasant crest. *Hackle*, yellow. *Body*, yellow floss, silver rib. *Tail*, gold pheasant crest.

YELLOW GHOST: *Wing*, yellow, peacock herl topping, bronze mallard or wood duck shoulder. *Hackle*, long white hair. *Body*, black floss, gold rib.

YELLOW MARABOU: *Wing*, yellow marabou, red feather cheek, peacock herl topping. *Body*, gold.

YELLOWSTONE: *Wing*, blue and yellow. *Hackle*, red and yellow. *Body*, gold, oval gold rib. *Tail*, amherst pheasant tippet.

YORK'S KENNEBAGO: *Wing*, badger, jungle cock eye shoulder. *Hackle*, sparse red top and bottom. *Body*, silver, silver wire rib, red tip, silver tag.

SALMON WET-FLY PATTERNS

ABBEY: *Tail*, gold pheasant crest. *Tag*, gold. *Body*, red floss. *Rib*, gold. *Hackle*, brown. *Wing*, gray squirrel.

ACE: *Tail*, gold pheasant crest. *Body*, blue floss. *Rib*, gold. *Hackle*, chestnut partridge. *Wing*, Amherst pheasant tippet dyed red.

AKROYD: *Tail*, gold pheasant crest over gold pheasant tippet. *Body*, ¼ black wool fore, ½ yellow aft. *Rib*, gold and silver. *Hackle*, black spey cock tied long to lay back. *Wing*, brown turkey splits. *Cheek*, jungle cock eye.

ALEXANDRIA: *Tail*, red feather fibers. *Body*, silver. *Hackle*, black. *Wing*, peacock sword.

BAKER: *Tail*, gold pheasant crest. *Tag*, gold. *Tip*, blue floss. *Butt*, black ostrich herl. *Body*, red dubbing. *Rib*, gold. *Hackle*, sparse red Palmer under; guinea over blue at shoulder. *Wing*, gold pheasant tippet, gold pheasant tail over. *Splits*, green, red, yellow and blue (at top).

BARON: *Tail*, gold pheasant crest. *Tag*, silver twist. *Butt*, black herl. *Body*, ½ aft silver (flat), silver twist rib, ½ fore black silk. *Trailers*, Indian crow between fore and aft body. *Hackle*, dark red-claret Palmer; jay throat. *Wing*, mixed swan and gold pheasant tail. *Topping*, gold pheasant crest. *Cheeks*, chatterer. *Horns*, blue macaw. *Head*, black herl.

BEADLE-BROWN: *Tail*, gold pheasant crest. *Body*, black floss. *Rib*, gold. *Hackle*, Palmer, 1/3 aft red, 1/3 center purple, 1/3 fore deep blue. *Wing*, dark brown turkey.

BEADLE-BUFF: *Tail*, gold pheasant crest. *Body*, black floss. *Rib*, gold. *Hackle*, Palmer, 1/3 aft red, 1/3 center purple, 1/3 fore deep blue. *Wing*, white dyed ginger.

BEADLE GRUB: *Body*, black floss. *Rib*, gold. *Hackle*, starting at head ¼ deep blue, ¼ purple, ¼ red, ¼ yellow at tip.

BEADLE-RED: *Tail*, gold pheasant crest. *Body*, black floss. *Rib*, gold. *Hackle*, Palmer, 1/3 aft red, 1/3 center purple, 1/3 fore deep blue. *Wing*, white dyed red.

BEADLE-SPECKLE: *Tail*, gold pheasant crest. *Body*, black floss. *Rib*, gold. *Hackle*, Palmer, 1/3 aft red, 1/3 center purple, 1/3 fore deep blue. *Wing*, gray turkey.

BEADLE-WHITE: *Tail*, gold pheasant crest. *Body*, black floss. *Rib*, gold. *Hackle*, Palmer, 1/3 aft red, 1/3 center purple, 1/3 fore deep blue. *Wing*, white goose or swan.

BEADLE-YELLOW: *Tail*, gold pheasant crest. *Body*, black floss. *Rib*, gold. *Hackle*, Palmer, 1/3 aft red, 1/3 center purple, 1/3 fore deep blue. *Wing*, goose dyed yellow.

BEAUFORT MOTH: See Fancy Lake Flies.

BEAULY SNOW FLY: *Body,* silver-doctor blue wool or seal's fur. *Rib,* gold and silver wound together. *Hackle,* long black hair or heron under body, short orange facing. *Wing,* peacock sword full and long.

BENCHILL: *Tag,* silver twist. *Body,* blue wool. *Rib,* silver. *Hackle,* long black-cock spey fashion. *Wing,* green peacock sword with red feather quill strip up sides.

BENGIE: *Tail,* gold pheasant crest. *Tip,* gold. *Body,* blue floss. *Rib,* silver. *Hackle,* yellow. *Wing,* brown turkey, brown mallard over. *Topping,* sparse blue.

BLACK BEAR: *Tail,* gold pheasant tippet. *Tag,* gold. *Body,* green wool. *Rib,* gold. *Hackle,* guinea beard. *Wing,* black bear hair.

BLACK BOMBER: *Tail,* gold pheasant crest. *Tag,* silver wire. *Tip,* yellow floss. *Body,* black wool. *Rib,* oval silver. *Hackle,* black. *Wing,* black squirrel. *Cheeks,* jungle cock eye. *Topping,* gold pheasant crest.

BLACK DOCTOR No. 1: *Tail,* gold pheasant crest with short blue feather topping. *Tag,* gold. *Tip,* scarlet floss. *Body,* black floss. *Rib,* gold. *Hackle,* guinea. *Wing,* gold pheasant tail, gold pheasant tippet sides. *Strips,* 2 blue goose. *Topping,* gold pheasant crest. *Horns,* gold pheasant tail. *Cheeks,* jungle cock eye. *Head,* black herl with scarlet floss at rear.

BLACK DOCTOR No. 2: *Tail,* gold pheasant crest with short blue feather topping. *Tag,* gold. *Tip,* scarlet floss. *Body,* black floss. *Rib,* gold. *Hackle,* black Palmer on fore half of body, claret hackle front. *Wing,* woodcock, dark mottled black and white turkey over. *Strips,* red at sides, blue upper strips. *Topping,* gold pheasant crest tied low. *Shoulder,* jungle cock eyes.

BLACK DOSE No. 1: *Tail,* red feather and teal married, gold pheasant crest topping. *Tag,* silver. *Tip,* red floss. *Body,* blue dubbing 1/3 aft, black dubbing 2/3 fore. *Rib,* silver. *Hackle,* black Palmer on fore body, deep claret at shoulder. *Wing,* gold pheasant tippet, brown mallard sides. *Splits,* green and red, peacock sword. *Topping,* teal. *Head,* black herl.

BLACK DOSE No. 2: *Tail,* gold pheasant crest. *Tag,* silver wire. *Tip,* yellow floss. *Body,* black floss. *Rib,* oval silver. *Hackle,* black Palmer. *Wing,* brown turkey inner, gold pheasant tail, blue, red, yellow married strips outer, covered lightly with brown mallard and teal. *Shoulder,* jungle cock eye. *Topping,* gold pheasant crest.

BLACK EAGLE: *Tail,* gold pheasant crest, red over. *Tag,* silver. *Body,* black dubbing picked out. *Rib,* silver. *Hackle,* blue Palmer. *Wing,* white tipped metallic turkey.

BLACK HERON: *Tail,* gold pheasant crest. *Body,* yellow wool. *Rib,* gold. *Hackle,* large black. *Wing,* brown mallard.

BLACK PRINCE: *Tail,* gold pheasant crest. *Tag,* silver. *Tip,* dark yellow floss. *Butt,* black herl. *Body,* 3 silver sections with black herl butts between. *Trailers,* black crow top and bottom at each butt. *Hackle,* black. *Wing,* 5 or 6 gold pheasant crest feathers. *Splits,* blue macaw. *Head,* black herl.

BLACK RANGER: *Tail,* gold pheasant crest and Indian crow. *Tag,* silver twist. *Tip,* yellow floss. *Butt,* black herl. *Body,* black seal fur. *Rib,* silver. *Hackle,* black Palmer. *Wing,* 4 gold pheasant tippets overlapping (2 each side). *Cheeks,* chatterer. *Topping,* gold pheasant crest. *Horns,* blue macaw.

BLACK SILK: *Tail,* gold pheasant crest. *Tag,* gold. *Body,* black dubbing. *Rib,* gold. *Hackle,* sparse red, blue in front. *Wing,* sparse silver pheasant tippet inner, gold pheasant tippet and brown mallard outer. *Strips,* red each side.

BLACK SPEAN: *Tail*, gold pheasant crest. *Tip*, yellow floss. *Body*, black floss. *Rib*, silver. *Hackle*, guinea, sparse Palmer down ½ body. *Wing*, brown mallard. *Topping*, blue strip.

BLOODY MARY: *Tail*, gold pheasant crest. *Tag*, gold. *Tip*, blue floss. *Body*, gold-yellow floss. *Hackle*, yellow at throat. *Wing*, sparse staggered gold pheasant tippet. *Topping*, gold pheasant crest and silver pheasant crest.

BLUE CHARM: *Tail*, gold pheasant crest. *Tag*, silver. *Body*, black floss. *Rib*, silver. *Hackle*, light blue. *Wing*, brown mallard and teal, darkest teal strips up sides. *Topping*, gold pheasant crest.

BLUE DOCTOR: *Tail*, gold pheasant crest and gold pheasant tail. *Tag*, silver. *Tip*, yellow floss. *Body*, blue floss. *Rib*, silver. *Butt*, red. *Hackle*, blue, guinea front. *Wing*, brown mallard. *Splits*, blue. *Topping*, gold pheasant crest.

BLUE & GRAY: *Tail*, gold pheasant crest. *Tag*, gold. *Tip*, yellow floss. *Body*, blue seal fur. *Rib*, gold. *Hackle*, yellow throat, blue Palmer. *Wing*, brown mallard. *Splits*, yellow fiber each side.

BLUE & GRAY JAY: *Tail*, gold pheasant crest and short red feather fibers. *Tag*, silver. *Tip*, orange floss. *Body*, blue dubbing picked out. *Rib*, silver. *Hackle*, pale blue and sparse guinea mixed. *Wing*, brown mallard sides over red center strip.

BLUE JOCK: *Tail*, gold pheasant crest long, silver pheasant crest short. *Tag*, silver. *Tip*, yellow floss. *Butt*, black herl. *Body*, ½ aft blue floss, ½ fore black floss. *Rib*, silver. *Center Joint*, black herl. *Trailers*, gold pheasant crest fastened at center joint. *Hackle*, blue with guinea over. *Wing*, white tipped turkey inner; married gold pheasant tail, blue, red and yellow over; brown mallard, yellow and teal married outside. *Cheeks*, chatterer. *Shoulder*, jungle cock eyes. *Topping*, gold pheasant crest and peacock sword.

BLUE MARINE: *Tail*, gold pheasant crest with gold pheasant tippet topping. *Tag*, gold. *Tip*, blue floss. *Butt*, black herl. *Body*, ½ aft yellow floss, ½ fore blue floss. *Rib*, silver. *Hackle*, blue; guinea and claret mixed at throat. *Wing*, gold pheasant tippet center, brown mallard over. *Topping*, gold pheasant crest.

BLUE PALMER: *Tail*, gold pheasant crest and red fibers mixed. *Tag*, silver. *Tip*, yellow floss. *Body*, blue floss. *Rib*, silver. *Hackle*, claret Palmer ½ of body, blue throat. *Wing*, brown mallard. *Cheeks*, blue.

BROWN BOMBER: *Tail*, gold pheasant crest. *Tag*, silver. *Tip*, yellow floss. *Butt*, black chenille. *Body*, brown wool. *Rib*, oval silver. *Hackle*, brown. *Wing*, fox squirrel tail. *Cheeks*, jungle cock eye. *Topping*, gold pheasant crest.

BROWN SHRIMP: *Body*, red-brown dubbing. *Rib*, gold. *Hackle*, red-brown in three clusters—tip, middle and front.

BUCKTAIL DOCTOR: *Tail*, gold pheasant crest. *Tag*, silver. *Tip*, yellow floss. *Butt*, red ostrich herl. *Body*, black wool. *Rib*, flat silver. *Hackle*, guinea. *Wing*, sparse brown (bucktail).

BULLDOG: *Tail*, gold pheasant crest and teal. *Tag*, gold. *Tip*, red floss. *Butt*, black ostrich herl. *Body*, silver ½ aft, black ostrich herl joint, silver ½ fore. *Hackle*, blue Palmer ½ body, guinea front. *Wing*, gold pheasant tippet, teal sides. *Splits*, yellow at each side. *Shoulder*, jungle cock eye. *Topping*, gold pheasant crest.

BULLDOG (Irish): *Tail*, gold pheasant crest. *Tag*, silver. *Tip*, yellow floss. *Butt*, black herl. *Body*, ½ aft silver, black herl center joint, blue floss ½ fore. *Rib*, silver. *Trailers*, gold pheasant crest at center joint. *Hackle*, blue Palmer on fore body, mallard facing. *Wing*, yellow. *Shoulder*, jungle cock eye. *Topping*, gold pheasant crest.

BUTCHER: *Tail,* gold pheasant crest, barred wood duck. *Tag,* gold. *Tip,* yellow floss. *Butt,* black ostrich herl. *Body,* red dubbing. *Rib,* silver. *Hackle,* guinea Palmer ½ body, olive facing. *Wing,* gold pheasant tippet, gray mallard and brown mallard over. *Shoulder,* blue. Gold pheasant crest at sides.

CALIFORNIA: See Fancy Lake Flies.

CANARY: *Tail,* gold pheasant crest and red fibers. *Tag,* gold. *Butt,* black herl. *Body,* flat silver with black herl center joint. *Trailers,* yellow hackle tips each herl butt. *Hackle,* orange. *Wing,* 5 or 6 gold pheasant crests. *Horns,* red.

CANDLESTICK MAKER: *Tail,* scarlet goose and wood duck. *Tag,* silver. *Body,* ½ aft black silk, ½ fore black wool picked out full at the shoulder. *Rib,* broad silver. *Hackle,* golden-olive Palmer, claret at the shoulder. *Wing,* 5 or 6 gold pheasant crests. *Shoulders,* double jungle cock eye each side.

CAPTAIN: *Tail,* gold pheasant tippet. *Body,* black floss. *Tip,* gold. *Hackle,* brown. *Wing,* white hair.

CASSARD: See Fancy Lake Flies.

CAUSAPASCO: *Tail,* gold pheasant crest. *Tag,* silver. *Tip,* claret floss. *Butt,* black ostrich herl. *Body,* yellow seal fur. *Rib,* silver. *Hackle,* yellow. *Wing,* dyed yellow swan. *Cheek,* blue kingfisher.

CHILDERS: *Tail,* gold pheasant crest, gold pheasant tail in center, red feather topping. *Tag,* silver. *Tip,* blue floss. *Butt,* black herl. *Body,* yellow floss. *Rib,* silver. *Wing,* gold pheasant tippet, brown mallard strips at sides and top. *Shoulder,* short blue. *Splits,* sparse red. *Topping,* gold pheasant crest. *Head,* black herl.

CLARET: *Tail,* gold pheasant crest and short red fibers. *Tag,* silver. *Tip,* yellow floss. *Butt,* black herl. *Body,* black dubbing. *Rib,* silver. *Hackle,* claret Palmer, blue throat. *Wing,* brown mallard.

CLARET & BLUE: *Tail,* gold pheasant crest, gold pheasant tippet on top (short). *Tag,* silver. *Tip,* orange floss. *Body,* blue dubbing. *Rib,* silver. *Hackle,* blue Palmer, claret at shoulder, guinea and blue facing. *Wing,* teal, brown mallard sides. *Cheeks,* chatterer.

CLARET JAY: *Tail,* gold pheasant crest. *Body,* red-brown dubbing. *Rib,* gold. *Hackle,* light blue. *Wing,* brown turkey. *Topping,* blue strip.

CLARET JOCK: *Tail,* gold pheasant crest long, silver pheasant crest short. *Tag,* silver. *Tip,* yellow floss. *Butt,* black herl. *Body,* ½ aft claret floss, ½ fore black floss. *Rib,* silver. *Center Joint,* black herl. *Trailers,* gold pheasant crest at center joint. *Hackle,* claret Palmer, guinea front. *Wing,* white tipped turkey inner; married gold pheasant tail, blue, red and yellow over; brown mallard, yellow and teal married outside. *Cheeks,* chatterer. *Shoulder,* jungle cock eye. *Topping,* gold pheasant crest and peacock sword.

CLARET & MALLARD: *Tail,* gold pheasant crest and silver pheasant crest. *Tag,* gold. *Tip,* yellow floss. *Body,* black floss. *Rib,* gold. *Hackle,* claret, blue face. *Wing,* brown mallard. *Cheek,* blue.

CLARET ROGAN: *Tail,* gold pheasant tippet. *Tag,* gold. *Body,* red-brown floss. *Rib,* gold. *Hackle,* bright medium blue. *Wing,* brown turkey, sparse gold pheasant tippet over, silver pheasant tippet sides (sparse).

COINER: *Tail,* gold pheasant crest, short red topping. *Tag,* silver. *Tip,* yellow floss. *Butt,* black herl. *Body,* yellow floss. *Rib,* silver. *Hackle,* orange-red; yellow facing. *Wing,* brown mallard. *Cheek,* blue.

COLD RANGER: *Tail,* gold pheasant tippet. *Body,* gold. *Hackle,* scarlet. *Wing,* gold pheasant tippet, teal strip, over at top, silver pheasant crest sides. *Topping,* peacock sword.

COLONEL FULLER: *Tail,* black metallic turkey and gold pheasant crest. *Tag,* gold. *Body,* yellow floss. *Rib,* gold. *Hackle,* yellow. *Wing,* yellow. *Shoulders,* red. *Topping,* gold pheasant crest and silver pheasant crest topping.

CONNEMARA BLACK: *Tail,* gold pheasant crest. *Tag,* silver. *Tip,* yellow floss. *Body,* black floss. *Rib,* silver. *Hackle,* dark brown Palmer; guinea and blue throat. *Wing,* brown mallard. *Splits,* blue fiber each side.

COOSEBOOM: *Tail,* green hackle fibers. *Body,* green wool. *Rib,* silver. *Hackle,* yellow collar type. *Wing,* gray squirrel tail.

COUND: *Tag,* gold. *Body,* black floss. *Rib,* gold. *Hackle,* yellow. *Wing,* sparse gold pheasant tippet, brown mallard strip outside at top. *Splits,* red each side.

CURRY'S SHRIMP No. 1: *Tail,* gold pheasant red breast feather over bend of hook. *Tag,* silver. *Body,* ½ aft hot orange floss ribbed with fine oval silver and butted at sides with red tanager. Small badger cock hackle wound in butt first at center. Fore half of body black floss ribbed with medium oval tinsel and butted with red tanager feather. Jungle cock feather on top. Large badger cock hackle wound butt first in front.

CURRY'S SHRIMP No. 2: Same as No. 1 except that tail is of gold pheasant gold-olive dyed breast feather. *Body,* gold tinsel. Butts and hackle badger dyed golden.

DANDY: *Tail,* gold pheasant crest and barred wood duck. *Tag,* silver. *Tip,* orange floss. *Butt,* black herl. *Body,* 2/3 aft silver, 1/3 fore blue floss. *Rib,* all round silver rib. *Hackle,* medium blue, guinea front. *Wing,* gold pheasant tippet barred wood duck shoulder. *Cheek,* narrow blue. *Shoulder,* long jungle cock eye. *Topping,* gold pheasant crest.

DEEP WATER DEMON: *Tail,* gray duck fibers. *Tag,* gold. *Body,* ½ fore lemon floss, ½ aft black floss. *Rib,* all gold. *Hackle,* none. *Wing,* gray duck flared outward. *Head,* 2 short peacock herl antennae.

DE WINTON: *Tail,* gold pheasant crest. *Tag,* silver. *Tip,* blue floss. *Butt,* peacock herl. *Body,* red floss. *Rib,* silver. *Hackle,* claret Palmer; sparse guinea front. *Wing,* cock pheasant, teal sides. *Shoulder,* jungle cock eye. *Strips,* blue. *Topping,* gold pheasant crest.

DOUGLAS GRAHAM: *Tail,* gold pheasant crest. *Tag,* silver. *Tip,* red floss. *Butt,* peacock herl. *Body,* ½ aft silver, ½ fore peacock herl ribbed with silver. *Trailers,* silver pheasant crest top and bottom fastened between fore and aft body. *Hackle,* claret Palmer ½ body; blue front. *Wing,* gold pheasant tippet. *Shoulder,* barred wood duck. *Splits,* green, red and gold pheasant crest. *Cheeks,* jungle cock eye.

DUN WING: *Tail,* gold pheasant crest and tippet. *Tag,* silver. *Body,* loose sheep wool dubbing—aft 1/3 yellow, 1/3 center red, 1/3 fore blue. *Rib,* all silver. *Hackle,* black. *Wing,* dun goose.

DUNKELD: *Tail,* gold pheasant crest and jungle cock. *Tag,* gold twist. *Tip,* orange floss. *Butt,* black herl. *Body,* gold tinsel. *Rib,* gold twist. *Hackle,* orange Palmer; jay throat. *Wing,* mallard. *Strips,* 2, peacock wing. *Cheeks,* chatterer. *Topping,* gold pheasant crest. *Horns,* blue macaw.

DURHAM RANGER No. 1: *Tail*, short silver pheasant crest and long gold pheasant crest. *Tag*, silver. *Tip*, yellow floss. *Butt*, black herl. *Body*, claret dubbing. *Rib*, gold. *Hackle*, claret Palmer; blue throat (pale). *Wing*, 2 long, 2 short gold pheasant tippets, jungle cock in center so the eye extends beyond the tippet wings. *Cheeks*, light blue. *Topping*, gold pheasant crest.

DURHAM RANGER No. 2 (Welsh): *Tail*, gold pheasant crest and sparse red fibers. *Tag*, gold. *Butt*, black herl. *Body*, ½ aft yellow floss, ½ fore red floss. *Rib*, all gold. *Hackle*, scarlet Palmer; pale blue front. *Wing*, 2 long, 2 short gold pheasant tippets, jungle cock eye between extending beyond tippet wings. *Cheeks*, narrow blue. *Topping*, 2 gold pheasant crests.

DURHAM RANGER No. 3 (Scotch): *Tail*, short gold pheasant crest and red feather fibers. *Tag*, silver wire. *Tip*, yellow floss. *Butt*, black herl. *Body*, silver tinsel, 1/3 aft plain, 2/3 fore oval silver rib. *Hackle*, scarlet, scarlet Palmer down fore body. *Wing*, 2 long, 2 short gold pheasant tippets, jungle cock eye center extending beyond tippets. *Cheeks*, blue chatterer. *Topping*, gold pheasant crest. *Horns*, blue and yellow macaw.

DUSTY MILLER: *Tail*, gold pheasant crest long and red fibers short. *Tag*, silver. *Tip*, yellow floss. *Butt*, black herl. *Body*, 2/3 aft embossed silver, 1/3 fore orange floss ribbed with silver. *Hackle*, guinea (sometimes tied with orange hackle backing). *Wing*, white tipped turkey inner wing, outer wing married strips of brown mallard, red, teal, yellow and gold pheasant tail covered with sparse wood duck. *Shoulder*, jungle cock eye. *Topping*, gold pheasant crest. *Horns*, blue macaw.

FIERY BROWN: *Tail*, gold pheasant tippet. *Tip*, gold. *Body*, bright-gold-brown dubbing. *Rib*, gold. *Hackle*, blue. *Wing*, uneven segments of sparse gold pheasant tippet. *Strips*, red each side.

GARIBALDI: *Tail*, gold pheasant crest. *Body*, blue fur. *Rib*, silver. *Hackle*, yellow. *Wing*, brown mallard.

GLED: *Tail*, gold pheasant crest. *Tag*, silver. *Tip*, brown floss. *Body*, black dubbing. *Rib*, gold. *Hackle*, partridge. *Wing*, brown hen.

GLEN TANA: *Tail*, red breast of gold pheasant. *Tag*, silver twist. *Butt*, black herl. *Body*, 1/3 aft orange seal fur, 2/3 fore claret seal fur. *Hackle*, black heron Palmer fore body only. *Wing*, white tipped cinnamon turkey.

GOLD FINCH: *Tail*, gold pheasant crest. *Tag*, gold twist and gold floss. *Body*, gold floss. *Rib*, gold tinsel. *Hackle*, yellow; blue jay facing. *Wing*, 5 or 6 gold pheasant crests. *Horns*, red macaw. *Head*, black herl.

GOLD RANGER: *Tail*, same as Black Ranger. *Tag*, silver twist. *Tip*, yellow floss. *Butt*, black herl. *Body*, embossed gold. *Rib*, oval gold. *Hackle*, claret and red Palmer wound together. *Wing*, same as Black Ranger.

GOLDEN DEMON: *Tail*, gold pheasant crest. *Body*, gold. *Rib*, round gold wire. *Hackle*, orange. *Wing*, hen pheasant. *Shoulder*, jungle cock eye. *Topping*, gold pheasant crest.

GOLDEN OLIVE: *Tail*, gold pheasant crest and short red fibers. *Tag*, silver. *Tip*, blue floss. *Butt*, black herl. *Body*, golden olive floss. *Rib*, silver. *Hackle*, golden olive Palmer; blue facing. *Wing*, brown mallard. *Cheeks*, blue.

GOLDEN PHEASANT: See Fancy Lake Flies.

GORDON: *Tail*, gold pheasant crest. *Tag*, silver twist. *Tip*, yellow floss. *Butt*, black herl. *Body*, 1/3 aft yellow floss, 2/3 fore claret floss. *Rib*, all silver. *Hackle*, claret Palmer on fore body. *Wing*, gold pheasant crest, 1 gold pheasant tippet each side backed with peacock sword. *Cheeks*, jungle cock eye.

GREEN GROUSE: *Tail*, gold pheasant crest. *Tag*, silver. *Tip*, red floss. *Body*, light green floss. *Rib*, silver. *Hackle*, grouse at shoulder and Palmer at ribs on bottom. *Wing*, grouse; red and blue married strips outside at top. *Head*, peacock herl.

GREEN HIGHLANDER: *Tail*, gold pheasant crest. *Tag*, silver. *Tip*, yellow floss. *Butt*, black herl. *Body*, ½ aft yellow floss ribbed with round silver; ½ fore green fur ribbed with oval silver. *Hackle*, green Palmer on fore body; yellow at shoulder. *Wing*, gold pheasant tippets, narrow green strip sides, brown mallard outer wing. *Shoulder*, jungle cock eye. *Topping*, gold pheasant crest. *Horns*, yellow and blue macaw.

GREY EAGLE: *Tail*, red gold-pheasant breast. *Tag*, silver twist. *Butt*, black herl. *Body*, alternate bands of yellow, light blue and scarlet seal fur. *Rib*, silver. *Hackle*, long blue-gray. *Wing*, red gold-pheasant backed with 2 strips of mottled brown turkey (white tipped).

GREY WULFF: *Tail*, gold pheasant crest. *Tag*, yellow floss. *Body*, dark gray wool. *Hackle*, guinea. *Wing*, brown bucktail. *Shoulder*, jungle cock eye. *Topping*, gold pheasant crest.

GRIZZLY KING: *Tail*, red hackle fibers. *Body*, green. *Rib*, silver. *Hackle*, grizzly. *Wing*, gray squirrel.

GROUSE-SILVER: *Tail*, gold pheasant crest. *Body*, silver. *Rib*, silver wire. *Hackle*, grouse. *Wing*, gold pheasant tippet. *Topping*, gold pheasant crest.

HARLEQUIN: *Tail*, gold pheasant crest. *Tag*, gold. *Tip*, green floss. Butt, peacock herl. *Body*, 1/3 aft red floss, 1/3 center blue floss, 1/3 fore yellow floss. *Rib*, all gold. *Hackle*, blue, red front. *Wing*, gold pheasant tippet, brown mallard and gold pheasant tippet tail outside on top. *Shoulder*, jungle cock eye. *Topping*, gold pheasant crest. *Horns*, red and blue macaw.

HELMSDALE: *Tag*, silver twist. *Tip*, orange floss. *Butt*, black herl. *Body*, 2 turns of light yellow floss at butt, rest of body yellow seal fur. *Rib*, silver rib. *Hackle*, yellow Palmer, blue throat. *Wing*, white-tipped brown mottled turkey. *Topping*, gold pheasant crest.

HILL FLY: See Fancy Lake Flies.

HIPO: *Tail*, silver pheasant tippet dyed blue. *Body*, blue floss. *Rib*, gold. *Hackle*, blue. *Wing*, silver pheasant tippet dyed blue.

INFALLIBLE: *Tail*, gold pheasant crest. *Body*, brown floss. *Tip*, gold. *Hackle*, brown. *Wing*, gold pheasant tippet dyed brown.

INVER GREEN: *Tail*, gold pheasant crest. *Tag*, gold. *Butt*, peacock herl. *Body*, olive-yellow floss. *Rib*, gold. *Hackle*, olive yellow at shoulder and Palmer at ribs under body. *Wing*, brown mallard; gold pheasant tippet and blue strip side; narrow red strip top.

JEANNIE: *Tail*, gold pheasant crest. *Tag*, silver. *Tip*, orange floss. *Body*, black dubbing. *Rib*, gold. *Hackle*, black. *Wing*, brown mallard. *Shoulders*, jungle cock eye.

JOCKIE: *Tail*, gold pheasant crest. *Tag*, silver. *Body*, black floss. *Rib*, silver. *Hackle*, orange. *Wing*, brown mallard.

JOCK O'DEE: *Tail*, gold pheasant crest and red fibers. *Tag*, silver. *Body*, ¼ aft lemon floss, ¾ fore black floss. *Rib*, oval silver. *Hackle*, long gray Palmer 1/3 of fore body; mallard at front. *Wing*, cinnamon quill.

JOCK SCOT: *Tail*, gold pheasant crest long, silver pheasant crest short. *Tag*, silver. *Tip*, yellow floss. *Butt*, black herl. *Body*, yellow floss ½ aft, black floss ½ fore. *Rib*, all silver. *Center Joint*, black herl between fore and aft body. *Trailers*, gold pheasant crest at center joint. *Hackle*, guinea. *Wing*, white tipped turkey inner wing; outer wing married gold pheasant tail, blue and red and yellow strips; brown mallard, yellow and teal outside at top. *Cheeks*, chatterer. *Shoulders*, jungle cock eye. *Topping*, peacock sword and gold pheasant crest.

JOE BRADY: *Tail*, gold pheasant crest. *Tag*, silver. *Tip*, magenta floss. *Body*, silver. *Hackle*, green. *Wing*, copper pheasant. *Cheek*, red.

JUNGLE COCK: See Fancy Lake Flies.

KATE: *Tail*, blue feather, short gold pheasant crest. *Tag*, silver. *Butt*, peacock herl. *Body*, red dubbing. *Rib*, silver. *Hackle*, yellow. *Wing*, teal. *Shoulder*, jungle cock eye. *Splits*, red. *Topping*, gold pheasant crest.

KENNEDY: *Tail*, gold pheasant crest. *Body*, red-brown dubbing. *Rib*, silver. *Hackle*, black and brown Palmer; black at shoulder. *Wing*, reddish-brown metallic barred turkey.

KEN'S BLACK CREEPER: *Tail*, red wool tail tag. *Body*, black dubbing. *Hackle*, black Palmer clipped short. *Wing*, jungle cock eye.

KILLER-BROWN WING: *Tail*, red gold-pheasant breast. *Tag*, gold. *Tip*, yellow floss. *Butt*, black herl. *Body*, 1/3 aft yellow, 1/3 center red, 1/3 fore blue seal fur. *Rib*, all silver. *Hackle*, long red spey cock Palmer. *Wing*, brown turkey.

KILLER-WHITE WING: Same as Killer-Brown Wing except wing is white swan tied strip wing.

LADY CAROLINE: *Tail*, gold-pheasant red body feather fibers. *Body*, olive-brown dubbing. *Rib*, oval gold. *Hackle*, large light gray dun, teal face. *Wing*, brown mallard.

LAKE GEORGE: See Fancy Lake Flies.

LEE BLUE No. 1: *Tail*, gold pheasant crest. *Tag*, silver. *Body*, dark blue floss. *Rib*, silver. *Hackle*, yellow. *Wing*, gold pheasant red rump feather, teal sides. *Topping*, gold pheasant crest.

LEE BLUE No. 2 (Irish): *Tail*, gold pheasant crest, short silver pheasant crest. *Tag*, silver. *Tip*, yellow floss. *Body*, blue dubbing. *Rib*, silver. *Hackle*, blue Palmer, yellow face. *Wing*, brown mallard sides over gold pheasant tippet, married; blue, red and yellow strips.

LEMON GRAY: *Tail*, short rose feather, long gold pheasant crest. *Tag*, silver. *Tip*, yellow floss. *Butt*, black herl. *Body*, gray dubbing. *Rib*, silver. *Hackle*, lemon. *Wing*, gold pheasant tippet; rose, blue and yellow married strips inside, brown mallard and teal married outside at top. *Cheeks*, blue.

LION: *Tag*, silver twist. *Tip*, yellow floss. *Butt*, black herl. *Body*, flat silver 2/3 aft, 1/3 fore scarlet seal fur. *Rib*, all silver. *Hackle*, natural black, guinea over. *Wing*, gold pheasant tippet, gold peacock sword and bustard inside, 2 brown mallard each side over. *Shoulder*, jungle cock eye. *Splits*, red macaw and peacock herl. *Topping*, gold pheasant crest. *Horns*, blue macaw. *Head*, black wool.

LITTLE INKY BOY: *Tag*, silver. *Tip*, red floss. *Butt*, peacock herl. *Body*, black floss. *Hackle*, badger dyed olive-yellow. *Wing*, brown mallard. *Topping*, gold pheasant crest. *Horns,* fine red macaw.

LIZZIE: *Tag,* silver. *Butt,* peacock herl. *Body,* 5 sections of floss purple, green, red, purple, red. *Rib,* silver between each rib. *Hackle,* blue. *Wing,* yellow, red, green and blue married, teal over. *Topping,* gold pheasant crest.

LOGIE: *Tail,* gold pheasant crest. *Tag,* silver. *Tip,* orange floss. *Body,* brown-red floss. *Rib,* silver. *Hackle,* blue. *Wing,* brown mallard.

MAJOR GRIGGS: *Body,* peacock herl. *Hackle,* white. *Wing,* fine white hair over fine black. *Shoulder,* jungle cock eye.

MAR LODGE: *Tail,* gold pheasant crest and jungle cock eye. *Tag,* silver. *Butt,* black herl. *Body,* silver, black floss center joint. *Rib,* all silver. *Hackle,* guinea. *Wing,* inner: gold pheasant tail, wood duck, gray mallard, yellow, red and brown turkey tail; outer: brown mallard. *Shoulder,* jungle cock eye. *Topping,* gold pheasant crest. *Horns,* blue macaw.

MARCH BROWN: *Tail,* partridge. *Tip,* orange floss. *Body,* brown dubbing. *Rib,* gold. *Hackle,* partridge. *Wing,* brown turkey.

MATADOR: See Fancy Lake Flies.

McGINTY: See Steelhead Wet Flies.

MITCHELL: *Tail,* gold pheasant crest long, short blue feather. *Tag,* silver. *Tip,* yellow floss. *Tip,* red floss. *Body,* black floss. *Rib,* silver. *Hackle,* yellow, black front. *Wing,* black metallic cock tail. *Shoulder,* jungle cock eye. *Topping,* gold pheasant crest.

MOOSE: See Fancy Lake Flies.

MORGAN: *Tail,* gold pheasant crest and tippet. *Tag,* gold. *Butt,* black herl. *Body,* 1/3 aft flat gold, 1/3 center claret floss, 1/3 fore flat gold. *Rib,* all oval gold. *Hackle,* bright claret. *Wing,* red, yellow and blue swan married. *Shoulder,* jungle cock eye. *Topping,* gold pheasant crest. *Horns,* blue macaw. *Head,* black herl.

MUNRO: See Fancy Lake Flies.

MYSTERY No. 1: *Tail,* gold pheasant crest. *Tip,* silver. *Body,* pink floss. *Rib,* silver. *Hackle,* red. *Wing,* yellow, narrow red strip top.

MYSTERY No. 2: *Tail,* gold pheasant crest. *Tag,* silver. *Tip,* yellow floss. *Butt,* black chenille. *Body,* silver tinsel. *Hackle,* brown. *Wing,* fox squirrel. *Shoulder,* jungle cock eye.

NICHOLSON: See Fancy Lake Flies.

NIGHT HAWK: *Tail,* gold pheasant crest with sparse blue jay fibers. *Tag,* silver. *Tip,* yellow floss. *Butt,* red dubbing. *Body,* silver. *Rib,* oval silver. *Hackle,* black. *Wing,* black crow quill. *Cheeks,* blue jay. *Shoulder,* jungle cock eye. *Splits,* red macaw each side. *Topping,* gold pheasant crest.

NOTION, THE: *Tail,* gold pheasant crest long, short blue fibers. *Body,* ½ aft gold, ½ fore brown dubbing. *Hackle,* brown Palmer on fore body. *Wing,* gold pheasant tippet, married strips blue fiber top, brown mallard center, yellow fiber bottom, a strip of wood duck each side. *Cheeks,* blue. *Head,* black herl.

ORANGE GROUSE: *Tail,* gold pheasant crest. *Tag,* silver. *Tip,* blue floss. *Butt,* peacock herl. *Body,* orange floss. *Rib,* silver. *Hackle,* medium blue and grouse mixed. *Wing,* green, yellow and red strips married; brown mallard outside, sparse gold pheasant tippet at top.

PARMACHENE BEAU: *Tail,* silver pheasant tippet, crest and white. *Tag,* gold. *Tip,* yellow floss. *Butt,* black herl. *Body,* yellow floss. *Rib,* silver. *Hackle,* yellow Palmer at ribs on bottom; red and white at shoulder. *Wing,* white. *Shoulder,* jungle cock eye. *Splits,* red each side. *Topping,* silver pheasant crest.

PARMACHENE BELLE: See Fancy Lake Flies.

PHEASANT MILLER: *Tail*, gold pheasant crest. *Body*, yellow chenille. *Tip*, gold. *Hackle*, orange. *Wing*, gold pheasant tippet. *Shoulder*, jungle cock eye. *Topping*, gold pheasant crest.

PINK LADY: *Tail*, silver pheasant crest short, gold pheasant crest long. *Tag*, gold. *Butt*, black herl. *Body*, pink floss. *Rib*, round gold. *Hackle*, pink Palmer. *Wing*, teal. *Shoulder*, jungle cock eye. *Topping*, gold pheasant crest.

PINK SHRIMP: *Tag*, gold. *Body*, brown dubbing. *Rib*, gold. *Hackle*, red-brown in 3 sections, at tip, center and front.

POPHAM: *Tail*, gold pheasant crest long with short silver pheasant trailers. *Tag*, gold. *Body*, yellow floss with three black herl joints (narrow) at tip, center and front. *Rib*, gold. *Trailers*, silver pheasant crest tied top and bottom at each herl joint.

PREMO: *Tail*, silver pheasant crest. *Body*, gold-brown floss. *Rib*, silver. *Hackle*, blue. *Wing*, silver pheasant tippet dyed yellow.

PROSSER'S BLACK: *Tail*, short silver pheasant crest, long gold pheasant crest. *Tag*, gold. *Butt*, black herl. *Body*, silver. *Rib*, silver. *Hackle*, black. *Wing*, gold pheasant tippet, gold pheasant crest sides.

PURPLE KING: *Body*, blue and red mixed wool. *Rib*, gold and silver alternating. *Hackle*, spey cock Palmer crossing over body ribs. *Wing*, 2 strips mallard tied split.

RANKIN SPECIAL: *Tail*, gold pheasant crest. *Body*, red floss fore, black floss aft. *Hackle*, silver-doctor blue. *Wing*, dark brown turkey.

ROSS SPECIAL: *Tail*, gold pheasant crest. *Body*, red wool. *Rib*, oval silver. *Hackle*, yellow. *Wing*, fox squirrel tail. *Shoulder*, jungle cock eye.

SARANAC: See Fancy Lake Flies.

SHERBROOKE: *Tail*, gold pheasant tippet. *Body*, ½ aft orange floss, ½ fore blue floss. *Rib*, all gold. *Hackle*, blue. *Wing*, gray mallard, sparse blue, gold pheasant tippet sides; red strip at top.

SILVER BLUE: *Tail*, gold pheasant crest. *Tag*, silver. *Butt*, black herl. *Body*, silver. *Rib*, round silver. *Hackle*, blue. *Wing*, teal.

SILVER DOCTOR No. 1: *Tail*, gold pheasant crest, short blue sides. *Tag*, silver. *Tip*, yellow floss. *Butt*, red floss. *Body*, silver. *Rib*, round silver. *Hackle*, guinea over silver-doctor blue. *Wing*, gold pheasant tippet and brown turkey inside; blue, red and yellow married strips over at top; brown mallard outer wing. *Topping*, gold pheasant crest. *Horns*, blue and yellow macaw.

SILVER DOCTOR No. 2 (Orvis):See Fancy Lake Flies.

SILVER DOCTOR No. 3 (Shearer): See Fancy Lake Flies.

SILVER DOCTOR No. 4 (Wells): See Fancy Lake Flies.

SILVER GRAY: *Tail*, gold pheasant crest. *Tag*, silver. *Tip*, yellow floss. *Butt*, black fur. *Body*, silver. *Rib*, round silver. *Hackle*, badger Palmer ½ fore body; teal front. *Wing*, inner wing married gold pheasant tail fibers, green, red, yellow and teal; outer wing: brown mallard married to teal. *Shoulder*, jungle cock eye. *Topping*, gold pheasant crest.

SILVER GRAY BOMBER: *Tail*, gold pheasant crest. *Tag*, silver. *Tip*, yellow floss. *Butt*, black chenille. *Body*, silver. *Rib*, oval silver. *Hackle*, speckled guinea. *Wing*, brown and a little white bucktail mixed.

SILVER WILKINSON: *Tail*, gold pheasant crest, silver pheasant crest short, and pale blue fibers. *Tag*, gold. *Tip*, yellow floss. *Butt*, red wool. *Body*, silver tinsel. *Rib*, round silver. *Hackle,* magenta and teal at throat only. *Wing,* married strips yellow over blue over red on each side of gold pheasant tippet; brown mallard over, gold pheasant cock tail fibers each side. *Cheek,* very short gold pheasant tippet with blue feather strip over. *Topping,* gold pheasant crest.

SIR CHARLES: *Tail,* gold pheasant crest. *Tip,* silver. *Body,* orange floss. *Rib,* silver. *Hackle,* blue. *Wing,* teal.

SIR RICHARD: *Tail,* silver pheasant crest. *Tag,* silver. *Butt,* black herl. *Body,* black floss. *Rib,* silver. *Hackle,* guinea. *Wing,* teal, silver pheasant crest sides. *Shoulder,* blue. *Topping,* gold pheasant crest.

STUDLEY: *Tail,* gold pheasant crest. *Tag,* silver. *Tip,* yellow floss. *Butt,* black herl. *Body,* yellow floss, black herl joints at center and shoulder. *Trailers,* blue hackle fibers each herl joint and butt. *Hackle,* yellow. *Wing,* yellow. *Topping,* gold pheasant crest.

THUNDER & LIGHTNING: *Tail,* gold pheasant crest long, short silver pheasant crest. *Tag,* gold. *Tip,* yellow floss. *Butt,* black herl. *Body,* black floss. *Rib,* gold. *Hackle,* orange Palmer at ribs, guinea dyed blue front. *Wing,* brown mallard. *Shoulder,* jungle cock eye. *Topping,* gold pheasant crest. *Horns,* blue and yellow macaw.

TOMAH-JO: See Fancy Lake Flies.

TORRISH: *Tail,* gold pheasant crest and sparse gold pheasant tippet. *Tag,* silver. *Tip,* yellow floss. *Butt,* black herl. *Body,* ½ aft silver, black herl center joint, ½ fore yellow dubbing. *Rib,* silver on fore body. *Hackle,* yellow. *Wing,* cinnamon teal. *Shoulder,* jungle cock eye. *Splits,* red. *Topping,* gold pheasant crest.

TORRISH (Irish): *Tail,* gold pheasant crest. *Tag,* silver. *Tip,* yellow floss. *Butt,* black herl. *Body,* silver tinsel with black herl center joint. *Trailers,* gold pheasant tippet unbarred at center joint. *Rib,* silver. *Hackle,* yellow and orange mixed. *Wing,* teal. *Topping,* gold pheasant crest.

TRUMPETER BLACK: *Tail,* gold pheasant crest. *Tag,* silver. *Tip,* pink floss. *Body,* black floss. *Rib,* silver wire. *Hackle,* guinea and orange mixed beard. *Wing,* black trumpeter swan white-tipped. *Horns,* cock pheasant tail.

WATSON'S FANCY: *Tail,* gold pheasant crest and silver pheasant crest. *Tag,* gold. *Body,* ½ aft orange floss, ½ fore black floss. *Rib,* all gold. *Hackle,* black. *Wing,* brown mallard. *Shoulder,* jungle cock eye. *Topping,* gold pheasant crest.

WILKINSON: *Tail,* gold pheasant crest and short silver pheasant crest. *Tag,* silver. *Tip,* yellow floss. *Butt,* red wool. *Body,* silver. *Rib,* round silver. *Hackle,* blue with red front. *Wing,* brown mallard, gold pheasant tippet sides, red and blue strip outside at top. *Shoulder,* jungle cock eye. *Topping,* gold pheasant crest.

YELLOW BUCKTAIL: *Tail,* gold pheasant crest. *Body,* silver. *Rib,* oval silver. *Hackle,* yellow. *Wing,* yellow bucktail.

YELLOW EAGLE: *Tail,* gold pheasant crest on top, red gold-pheasant breast under. *Tag,* silver. *Butt,* black herl. *Body,* red, scarlet and light blue fur in alternate bands. *Rib,* silver. *Hackle,* long soft yellow Palmer, teal or widgeon face. *Wing,* red gold-pheasant backed with 2 strips of mottled brown turkey (white-tipped).

FANCY LAKE FLIES

(Landlocked Salmon, Squaretails and Bass)

ACADEMY: See Trout Dry- and Wet-Fly Patterns.

ALEXANDRIA: *Wing,* peacock sword, red splits. *Hackle,* gray dun or badger. *Body,* gray floss, silver rib, red floss tip, gold tag. *Tail,* peacock sword.

BABCOCK: See Trout Dry- and Wet-Fly Patterns.

BARNWELL: *Wing*, widgeon, scarlet shoulder. *Hackle*, brown. *Body*, scarlet dubbing, gold rib, blue floss tip, gold tag. *Tail*, scarlet fibers.

BEATRICE: See Brazilian Blue-Wing.

BEAUFORT MOTH: *Wing*, white-spoon wing. *Hackle*, brown. *Body*, peacock herl, gold tip. *Tail*, gold pheasant crest.

BISHOP: *Wing*, scarlet spoon wing, white spoon shoulder. *Hackle*, brown. *Body*, white chenille, gold tip. *Tail*, scarlet and white.

BLACK DUKE: *Wing*, black. *Hackle*, white. *Body*, scarlet chenille. *Tail*, black herl.

BLACK GNAT: See Trout Dry- and Wet-Fly Patterns.

BLACK PRINCE: *Wing*, black goose. *Hackle*, black. *Body*, gold tinsel. *Tail*, scarlet goose.

BLUE BOTTLE: *Wing*, black crow. *Hackle*, natural black. *Body*, blue floss, gold rib.

BOB-WHITE: *Wing*, quail (brownish body feather). *Hackle*, scarlet. *Body*, peacock herl, gold tip. *Tail*, scarlet and white fibers.

"B" POND: *Wing*, gray mallard. *Hackle*, scarlet, yellow over. *Body*, scarlet ½ fore, yellow ½ aft, all gold rib. *Tail*, gray mallard.

BRAZILIAN BLUE-WING: *Wing*, pale blue spoon wings *Hackle*, scarlet. *Body*, yellow floss, gold rib. *Tail*, pale blue, black-tipped.

CAHILL: See Trout Dry- and Wet-Fly Patterns.

CALIFORNIAN: *Wing*, yellow mallard. *Hackle*, yellow. *Body*, yellow floss, black thread rib, gold tip. *Tail*, black and yellow hackle tips.

CASSARD: *Wing*, black-tipped wood duck, gold pheasant tippet shoulders, splits of gold pheasant crest, scarlet and green. *Hackle*, scarlet (sparse), yellow Palmer. *Body*, claret silk, silver rib, black chenille butt, silver tip. *Tail*, gold pheasant crest, scarlet, green and barred wood duck. *Head*, peacock herl.

CHENEY: *Wing*, black edge white-tipped mallard. *Hackle*, yellow. *Body*, red chenille ½ fore, white floss ½ aft, silver rib. *Tail*, green parrot and barred wood duck.

CHIPPY: *Wing*, white, scarlet shoulders. *Hackle*, black and brown mixed. *Body*, orange floss, gold rib and tip.

CLEVELAND: *Wing*, ringneck pheasant black-tipped side feather, ringed body side feather shoulder. *Hackle*, ringed pheasant body side feather (green, black, tan, and white rings). *Body*, gold, pale green chenille butt, scarlet floss tip, gold tag. *Tail*, peacock sword, barred wodduck and gold pheasant crest. *Head*, red.

COACHMAN: See Trout Dry- and Wet-Fly Patterns.

COLONEL FULLER: See Trout Dry- and Wet-Fly Patterns.

CRACKER: *Wing*, black, white, blue and scarlet strips, peacock sword topping. *Hackle*, brown and scarlet. *Body*, blue floss, gold rib, yellow floss tip, gold tag. *Tail*, blue, yellow and peacock sword.

CROPPIE: *Wing*, widgeon. *Hackle*, yellow. *Body*, blue floss, gold rib. *Tail*, scarlet and yellow fibers.

CUNNINGHAM: *Wing*, brown hen spoon wing. *Hackle*, brown. *Body*, dark brown wool, silver rib, silver tip. *Tail*, mallard, scarlet and gray-green goose.

DANDY: *Wing*, black. *Hackle*, white. *Body*, scarlet chenille. *Tail*, black herl.

DARK FLAGON: *Wing*, brown hen. *Hackle*, black. *Body*, peacock herl ½ fore, brown floss ½ aft, gold rib.

DE GEM: *Wing*, widgeon or teal. *Hackle*, yellow. *Body*, scarlet ½ fore, green ½ aft, black thread rib. *Tail*, scarlet fibers.

EPTING: *Wing*, widgeon or teal. *Hackle*, black. *Body*, light orange floss ½ fore, scarlet ½ aft, gold tip. *Tail*, green and yellow hackles.

FERGUSON: *Wing*, woodcock, mallard sides, yellow and scarlet strips. *Hackle*, green. *Body*, yellow floss, gold rib. *Tail*, peacock sword, scarlet and yellow fibers.

F. G. SIMPSON: *Wing*, scarlet ibis. *Hackle*, yellow, scarlet over. *Body*, yellow floss, gold rib and tip. *Tail*, yellow and scarlet fibers.

FIERY BROWN: *Wing*, brown hen. *Hackle*, brown. *Body*, bright brown dubbing picked out, gold tip. *Tail*, scarlet goose.

FIERY DRAGON: *Wing*, gray goose, green split topping, yellow goose shoulder. *Hackle*, green. *Body*, yellow floss, gold rib and tip. *Tail*, yellow fibers.

FRANK GRAY: *Wing*, green teal. *Hackle*, claret. *Body*, orange floss, blue thread rib, blue floss tip.

GOLD PHEASANT: *Wing*, gold pheasant tippet. *Hackle*, 3 turns of Palmer, vermilion. *Body*, vermilion floss, gold rib. *Tail*, sparse black hackle.

GOLDEN DUSTMAN: *Wing*, bronze turkey. *Hackle*, yellow. *Body*, peacock herl, gold rib and tip. *Tail*, gold pheasant crest.

GOLDEN ROD: *Wing*, pointed cock-pheasant brown body feather (mottled), jungle cock body feather shoulder. *Hackle*, orange. *Body*, hot orange dubbing picked out, gold rib, black ostrich butt, gold tip. *Tail*, scarlet goose.

GOVERNOR: See Trout Dry- and Wet-Fly Patterns.

GOVERNOR ALVORD: *Wing*, dark brown hen, cinnamon turkey over. *Hackle*, brown, Palmer ½ of body. *Body*, peacock herl, gold tip. *Tail*, scarlet fiber.

GRACKLE: *Wing*, scarlet goose. *Hackle*, black, 4 turns Palmer. *Body*, peacock herl, gold tip. *Tail*, scarlet goose.

GRASSHOPPER: *Wing*, jungle cock eye (long), yellow and scarlet splits. *Hackle*, claret. *Body*, brown dubbing, light olive-green tip, gold tag. *Tail*, wood duck. *Head*, herl.

GRAY DUKE: *Wing*, deepest gray goose (dyed). *Hackle*, dark partridge or guinea. *Body*, black floss ½ fore, red floss ½ aft, gold rib.

GREEN GLADE: *Wing*, green goose. *Hackle*, scarlet. *Body*, gold, silver rib, gold tag. *Tail*, green and yellow goose. *Head*, peacock herl.

GREEN WEAVER: *Wing*, light grass green. *Hackle*, grass-green, 2 turns of Palmer *Body*, light green floss, silver rib. *Tail*, light green fibers.

GREENWOOD LAKE: *Wing*, wood duck; yellow, red and green splits, peacock herl topping. *Body*, peacock herl ½ fore, yellow floss ½ aft, gold rib. *Tail*, wood duck, scarlet and peacock herl.

GRIZZLY KING: See Trout Dry- and Wet-Fly Patterns.

HAMLIN: See Trout Dry- and Wet-Fly Patterns.

HART: *Wing*, black, teal green over. *Hackle*, orange, sparse guinea and blue over. *Body*, gray dubbing, gold rib, red floss tip, gold tag. *Tail*, gold pheasant crest. *Head*, peacock herl, red floss whip.

HENSHALL: *Wing*, pale blue body feather. *Hackle*, white or pearl gray. *Body*, peacock herl, gold tip. *Tail*, peacock sword.

HILL FLY: *Wing*, gold pheasant tippet, married teal and mallard narrow outer wing, brown turkey strips each side on top, gold pheasant crest center of each side. *Hackle*, black. *Body,* black floss, silver rib, yellow floss tip, silver tag. *Tail,* gold pheasant crest. *Head,* black herl.

HOLBERTON No. 1: See Trout Dry- and Wet-Fly Patterns.

HOLBERTON No. 2: *Wing,* teal or widgeon, scarlet shoulder. *Hackle,* pale gray grizzly. *Body,* light green floss, scarlet tip. *Tail,* scarlet feather.

HORICON: *Wing,* teal or widgeon. *Hackle,* coch-y-bondhu. *Body,* orange floss, gold rib. *Tail,* brown feather.

HUMMING BIRD: *Wing,* white tipped mallard, white and red splits. *Hackle,* red, orange and brown mixed. *Body,* silver, silver wire rib, peacock herl butt, scarlet floss tip, silver tag. *Tail,* red and white fibers. *Head,* light ostrich herl.

IBIS-SCARLET: See Trout Dry- and Wet-Fly Patterns.

JOCK SCOT: See Trout Dry- and Wet-Fly Patterns.

JUNGLE COCK: *Wing,* brown cock-pheasant tail, jungle cock body feather over. *Hackle,* yellow. *Body,* yellow floss, green thread rib. *Tail,* black woodcock and scarlet fibers.

JUNO: *Wing,* scarlet ibis, jungle cock eye shoulder. *Hackle,* scarlet. *Body,* light olive green floss, silver rib and tip. *Tail,* scarlet ibis (goose quill may be substituted for the scarlet ibis).

KING OF THE WOODS: *Wing,* pale mallard, (bottom) married to brown mallard, red strips top each side. *Hackle,* dark green. *Body,* yellow floss, gold rib and tip. *Tail,* scarlet and yellow goose.

KINGFISHER: *Wing,* teal. *Hackle,* brown dun. *Body,* scarlet floss, gold rib, silver tip. *Tail,* gold pheasant tippet.

KLAMATH: *Wing,* black loon with white spots. *Hackle,* brown. *Body,* peacock herl (thick), gold tip. *Tail,* barred wood duck and scarlet. *Head,* black ostrich herl.

KNIGHT'S TEMPLAR: *Wing,* white top, black bottom or wood duck side feather. *Hackle,* white. *Body,* scarlet floss, gold rib. *Tail,* white top, black bottom.

LA BELLE: *Wing,* white goose. *Hackle,* blue. *Body,* blue floss, gold rib, scarlet floss tip. *Tail,* scarlet and white fibers.

LAKE EDWARD: *Wing,* black crow, blue and yellow topping. *Hackle,* claret. *Body,* claret dubbing, silver rib. *Tail,* gold pheasant crest.

LAKE GEORGE No. 1: See Trout Dry- and Wet-Fly Patterns.

LAKE GEORGE No. 2: *Wing,* gold pheasant tippet, brown mallard splits. *Hackle,* claret at shoulder, orange Palmer. *Body,* gold tinsel, silver wire rib.

LORD BALTIMORE: *Wing,* black goose, jungle cock eye shoulder. *Hackle,* black. *Body,* orange floss, black floss rib, gold tip. *Tail,* black goose.

MAID OF THE MILL: *Wing,* Ringneck or Gold pheasant body feather (greenish-blue with mottled brown tip), scarlet fiber, white fiber and 1 peacock sword as topping. *Hackle,* yellow and brown mixed. *Body,* golden brown dubbing, gold rib, red-brown floss tip, gold tag. *Tail,* gold pheasant crest.

MANCHESTER: *Wing,* yellow goose, peacock sword topping. *Hackle,* yellow. *Body,* peacock herl, yellow tip, gold tag. *Tail,* peacock sword.

MARSTON: *Wing,* white spotted loon. *Hackle,* brown dun. *Body,* silver thread, white chenille butts fore and aft, orange floss tip. *Tail,* white tipped mallard.

MASSASAGA: See Trout Dry- and Wet-Fly Patterns.

MATADOR: *Wing,* barred wood duck. *Hackle,* green. *Body,* gold, peacock herl butt, scarlet tip. *Tail,* yellow and black fiber under scarlet fiber.

MATHER: *Wing*, gray goose breast. *Hackle*, gray. *Body*, black ostrich herl, pale green floss center joint, scarlet tip, gold tag. *Tail*, peacock sword.

MAX VON DEM BORNE: *Wing*, none. *Hackle*, pink dubbing picked out, very large. *Body*, yellow dubbing, gold rib, yellow Palmer hackle, peacock herl butt, gold tip, scarlet floss tag. *Tail*, gold pheasant crest.

McCLOUD: *Wing*, grouse, red splits. *Hackle*, yellow. *Body*, green floss, gold rib, scarlet tip, yellow tip, gold tag. *Tail*, scarlet, yellow, mallard and metallic cock-tail feather.

McGINTY: See Trout Dry- and Wet-Fly Patterns.

MOISIC GRUB: *Wing*, none. *Hackle*, guinea. *Body*, yellow dubbing ½ aft, black dubbing ½ fore, sparse black hackle wound between fore and aft body, gold tip. *Tail*, gold pheasant crest.

MONTREAL-CLARET: *Wing*, dark brown turkey dyed claret (no white tip). *Hackle*, claret. *Body*, claret floss, gold rib and tip. *Tail*, scarlet goose.

MONTREAL-WHITE TIPPED: See Trout Dry- and Wet-Fly Patterns.

MOOSE: *Wing*, barred wood duck, gold pheasant tippet shoulders (full). *Hackle*, yellow, sparse guinea over. *Body*, yellow floss, gold rib and tip. *Tail*, yellow goose.

MOOSELUCMAGUNTIC: *Wing*, cinnamon turkey over yellow. *Hackle*, chestnut partridge. *Body*, gray floss, gold rib and tip. *Tail*, cinnamon turkey. *Head*, peacock herl.

MUNRO: *Wing*, brown turkey dyed claret, red splits. *Hackle*, yellow. *Body*, green floss, gold rib and tip. *Tail*, scarlet and yellow (mallard dyed).

NAMELESS: *Wing*, barred wood duck, brown mallard over. *Hackle*, yellow, pale orange (sparse) over. *Body*, gray wool, yellow Palmer hackle, orange floss tip, gold tag. *Tail*, yellow goose. *Head*, black ostrich herl.

NEW LAKE: *Wing*, cock pheasant, scarlet shoulder. *Hackle*, scarlet. *Body*, silver, silver wire rib, scarlet Palmer hackle. *Tail*, mallard and scarlet.

NICHOLSON: *Wing*, brown mallard, blue horn on top. *Hackle*, scarlet, sparse blue over. *Body*, claret floss, scarlet and blue Palmer hackle, gold rib and tip. *Tail*, gold pheasant tippet and mallard.

NO NAME: *Wing*, white goose, scarlet shoulder. *Hackle*, brown. *Body*, yellow floss, silver rib, red floss tip, silver tag. *Tail*, scarlet goose.

OCONOMOWOC: *Wing*, brown mallard or speckled brown hen. *Hackle*, white. *Body*, cream floss, gold rib. *Tail*, brown deer tail.

ONDAWA: *Wing*, ruddy pheasant-cock body feather. *Hackle*, brown. *Body*, orange chenille ½ fore, green floss ½ aft, gold rib aft, gold tip. *Tail*, black fibers.

ORANGE MILLER: *Wing*, orange. *Hackle*, orange. *Body*, orange chenille, gold tip.

ORIOLE: *Wing*, yellow goose. *Hackle*, black. *Body*, black floss, gold rib and tip. *Tail*, black and white fibers.

OQUOSSAC: *Wing*, cock pheasant tail (gold pheasant). *Hackle*, scarlet. *Body*, scarlet floss, scarlet Palmer hackle, yellow floss tip, gold tag. *Tail*, cock pheasant.

OWNER: *Wing*, guinea dyed red. *Hackle*, orange. *Body*, yellow floss, thick yellow floss rib, silver tip. *Tail*, scarlet fibers. *Head*, black ostrich herl.

PARKER: *Wing*, black loon (white spots at tip). *Hackle*, brown. *Body*, peacock herl, gold tip. *Tail*, scarlet and barred wood duck.

PARMACHENE BELLE: *Wing*, white, scarlet over. *Hackle*, scarlet. *Body*, yellow floss, silver rib, yellow Palmer hackle, peacock herl butt, silver tip. *Tail,* scarlet and white.

PLYMOUTH ROCK: *Wing,* Plymouth Rock wing quill. *Hackle,* Plymouth Rock or grizzly. *Body,* silver tinsel, silver wire rib. *Tail,* Plymouth Rock or barred grizzly.

POLKA: *Wing,* guinea. *Hackle,* scarlet. *Body,* scarlet floss, gold rib. *Tail,* brown and white fibers.

PREMIER: *Wing,* white goose breast, scarlet goose shoulder. *Hackle,* scarlet. *Body,* scarlet floss, gold rib and tip. *Tail,* scarlet fibers.

PRINCE EDWARD: *Wing,* scarlet spoon wing. *Hackle,* brown. *Body,* yellow floss, gold rib. *Tail,* scarlet, blunt and full.

PROFESSOR: See Trout Dry- and Wet-Fly Patterns.

QUEEN OF THE WATERS: See Trout Dry- and Wet-Fly Patterns.

RAVEN: *Wing,* black crow. *Hackle,* black. *Body,* black chenille, silver tip. *Tail,* black crow and yellow fiber.

READ: *Wing,* grouse. *Hackle,* brown. *Body,* green chenille, gold tip. *Tail,* scarlet goose.

REUBEN WOOD: See Trout Dry- and Wet-Fly Patterns.

ROYAL COACHMAN No. 1: *Wing,* palest mallard side. *Hackle,* brown. *Body,* scarlet floss center joint, peacock herl butts fore and aft, scarlet floss tag. *Tail,* wood duck.

ROYAL COACHMAN No. 2: *Wing,* white. *Hackle,* dark brown. *Body,* peacock herl, scarlet floss center joint. *Tail,* gold pheasant tippet.

ROMANY REE: See Romany Rye.

ROMANY RYE: *Wing,* barred wood duck, gold pheasant tippet shoulders. *Hackle,* badger. *Body,* silver tag, yellow floss tip, peacock herl butt, silver body, silver twist rib, pink chenille ball behind hackle. *Tail,* peacock herl, red and white feather (married).

SARANAC: *Wing,* gold pheasant tippet, cock pheasant splits. *Hackle,* dull claret. *Body,* claret floss body, gold rib, claret Palmer hackle, gold tip. *Tail,* yellow feather.

SCARLET IBIS: *Wing,* scarlet ibis or red goose breast. *Hackle,* scarlet. *Body,* scarlet floss, gold rib, peacock herl butt, light olive-green tip, gold tag. *Tail,* scarlet and white fibers.

SETH GREEN: *Wing,* cinnamon brown turkey. *Hackle,* medium brown. *Body,* light green floss, gold rib and tip. *Tail,* mallard.

SHEEHAN: *Wing,* mallard. *Hackle,* sparse black. *Body,* yellow floss, sparse black Palmer hackle (2 turns), claret chenille butt, gold tip. *Tail,* gold pheasant tippet.

SILVER DOCTOR No. 1, Orvis: *Wing,* dark brown turkey, red and green splits. *Hackle,* yellow, partridge over. *Body,* silver, silver wire rib, scarlet floss tip, yellow floss tag. *Tail,* green, scarlet, yellow and wood duck.

SILVER DOCTOR No. 2, J. G. Shearer: *Wing,* yellow, red and green married inside; guinea and pink married over, teal outer wing, deep blue splits. *Hackle,* partridge (gray). *Body,* silver tinsel, round silver rib. *Tail,* red and yellow married, guinea on top. *Head,* peacock herl.

SILVER DOCTOR No. 3, H. P. Wells: *Wing,* gray turkey and green married inside; black and white strips, red and gray turkey married outer wing. *Hackle,* silver-doctor blue, guinea over. *Body,* silver tinsel, round silver rib. *Head,* peacock herl.

SILVER IBIS: *Wing,* scarlet Ibis. *Hackle,* scarlet. *Body,* round silver tinsel, peacock herl butt, silver tip. *Tail,* scarlet Ibis and white.

SPIDER: *Wing*, dark brown turkey wing. *Hackle*, black and brown or coch-y-bondhu. *Body*, pale blue floss, gold tip.

SPLIT IBIS: *Wing*, white and scarlet Ibis (split). *Hackle*, brown. *Body*, round silver tinsel, silver tag. *Tail*, scarlet Ibis and gold pheasant crest.

TEASER: *Wing*, pigeon. *Hackle*, gray mallard. *Body*, bottle green chenille. *Tail*, scarlet.

THE SILVER LADY: *Wing*, light gray goose breast, jungle cock eye shoulder, peacock sword topping. *Hackle*, brown. *Body*, silver, white chenille butt, red floss tip, silver tag. *Tail*, peacock sword. *Head*, white chenille.

THE TIM: *Wing*, yellow mallard. *Hackle*, yellow. *Body*, yellow floss, silver rib and tip. *Tail*, scarlet. *Head*, ostrich herl.

TIPPERLINN: *Wing*, guinea. *Hackle*, black. *Body*, white floss, red thread rib, black ostrich herl butt, red floss tip, gold tag. *Tail*, red and yellow fiber and black metallic cock-tail feather.

TOMAH-JO: *Wing*, barred wood duck. *Hackle*, scarlet, yellow over. *Body*, silver thread, peacock herl butt, silver tip. *Tail*, yellow goose.

TOODLE BUG: *Wing*, dark brown turkey. *Hackle*, brown and ginger mixed. *Body*, yellow floss, ginger Palmer, gem-blue tip, gold tip. *Tail*, gray mallard.

TRIUMPH: *Wing*, black goose. *Hackle*, natural black. *Body*, orange chenille ½ fore, green floss ½ aft, gold rib and tip. *Tail*, green fiber.

WEBSTER: *Wing*, fine-mottled guinea. *Hackle*, deep brown. *Body*, black floss, silver rib and tip. *Tail*, gold pheasant crest.

WHITE MILLER: See Trout Dry- and Wet-Fly Patterns.

WHITE MOTH: See Trout Dry- and Wet-Fly Patterns.

WICKHAM'S FANCY: See Trout Dry- and Wet-Fly Patterns.

WM. H. HAMMETT: *Wing*, white, scarlet topping. *Hackle*, green. *Body*, green floss, gold rib and tip. *Tail*, green fiber.

W. T.: *Wing*, pale dun green feather with black spot near shoulder. *Hackle*, dark grizzly. *Body*, claret chenille ½ fore, scarlet floss ½ aft, gold rib, light green tip, gold tip. *Tail*, metallic black cock-tail feather.

YELLOW BETSY: *Wing*, wood duck. *Hackle*, brown. *Body*, orange chenille. *Tail*, wood duck.

YELLOW MAY: See Trout Dry- and Wet-Fly Patterns.

YELLOW MILLER: *Wing*, yellow goose. *Hackle*, yellow. *Body*, yellow chenille, yellow floss tip.

YELLOW SALLY: See Trout Dry- and Wet-Fly Patterns.

SALT-WATER FLIES

(Note: salt-water flies have not been reduced to a common formula at the time of this writing. The following patterns, therefore, are not to be considered a cross section of all the flies or types of flies used in salt water.)

BONBRIGHT: *Body*, silver tinsel. *Streamers*, white. *Cheeks*, red. *Topping*, gold pheasant crests. *Shoulders*, jungle cock.

ENFIELD SHAD FLY: *Body*, silver tinsel. *Wing*, yellow feather or hair. Red bead on leader in front of hook eye; variations are common.

GIBBS' STRIPER: *Body*, silver tinsel. *Wing*, white bucktail (approximately 3½ inches long), narrow blue feather strips up each side. *Cheek*, teal breast. *Hackle*, red, tied beard fashion.

GRESH BONEFISH FLIES: size 1/0 short-shank, nickel hooks.

1: scarlet herl body, white polar bear hair wing with sparse red hair over.

2: silver embossed tinsel body, scarlet polar bear hair wing with sparse white hair over.

3: scarlet floss body, embossed silver tinsel rib, silver tinsel wings. A most unusual arrangement.

4: cream floss body, silver embossed tinsel rib, silver tinsel wing with scarlet polar bear hair wing over.

5: scarlet herl body, Palmer ribbed with scarlet hackle, white polar bear hair wing.

6: yellow herl body, Palmer ribbed with yellow hackle, scarlet polar bear hair wing.

RHODES BONEFISH STREAMERS: size 1 and 1/0 short-shank.

1: Rhode Shrimp Fly. Yellow outside, grizzly and white streamers inside (divided wing style), full salt and pepper yellow-and-white hackle, Palmer style.

2: divided grizzly streamers, thick yellow hackle, Palmer style.

3: divided yellow streamers, thick yellow hackle, Palmer style.

4: yellow polar bear streamer, thick yellow-and-white hackle, Palmer style.

5: divided white streamers, thick red-and-white hackle, Palmer style.

6: white polar bear tail and streamer, red head and body.

MARYLAND SHAD FLIES: size 10, 3X, 4X or 6X long.

1: red hackle streamers, silver body, red fibers for tail, red beard hackle.

2: white hackle streamers, short white hackle (beard style), white chenille body, silver rib, gold pheasant tippet tail; white head, black eyes, white pupil.

3: Silver Doctor: blue hackle streamers between two white streamers, short white hackle (beard style), white chenille body, silver rib, Lady Amherst pheasant tippet; white head, black eyes, white pupil.

Appendix

FAVORITE FLIES

The work of many of the world's best fly-dressers is shown in this chapter, together with their letters, most of which explain why some patterns are preferred to others. It is self-evident that those who earn their living by tying flies must of necessity have first-hand information as to why certain types, colors, and sizes of flies are useful.

From these most interesting letters dependable information can be derived to enable the angler to dress flies for practically any fish, occasion, or region.

Flies illustrated in this section accompany the letters and are especially valuable for the purpose of making comparisons.

In reply to a letter asking for information concerning some patterns which were obscure or little-known, Mr. C. W. Schafer, then treasurer of the Orvis Company wrote as follows:

Manchester, Vermont
August 25, 1948.

As regards the Romany Rye and Romany Ree, it is our opinion that perhaps these two patterns were originally English, rather than American. As you may know, The Romany Rye and Romany Ree are terms which were applied to a Gypsy man and woman by the English in the 18th Century, and earlier.

The following comment is in connection with the Equinox Gnat.

We are wondering if you are familiar with a pattern we have tied for some years. It was originally called the Equinox but is now called the Mosquito. We have sold a great many of these over the years, and the pattern was developed from a gnat which hatched on Equinox Pond, at the foot of Equinox Mountain, here in Manchester.

At a later date Mr. Schafer wrote further concerning the Romany Rye and Romany Ree. His letter follows:

Since writing you sometime ago, we have continued our search for information regarding the Romany Rye and Romany Ree. Only today we succeeded in finding one Romany Rye which had been tied for the exhibit we had at the World's Fair in 1893. We will tie one of these for you . . . as near as we can tell, the Romany Ree is a variation of the Romany Rye, but we can find no information to tell us just how it was tied.

287

When the fly arrived, it was labeled Romany Rye or Romany Ree, and for this reason it appears to be one and the same.

Mr. G. D. Finlay of the Orvis Company sent the six salmon flies which he considers are the "best sellers," and six trout dry flies which are favorites. These are arranged separately in Figs. 34 and 35. Also included were the Orvis selections of flies for trout fishing throughout the United States and Canada. These are listed according to sections.

New England Selection

Wet

Cowdung	Black Gnat	Cahill
Gray Hackle	Coachman	Brown Hackle

Dry

Blue Dun	Black Gnat	Olive Dun
Brown Bivisible	Royal Coachman	Gray Hackle

Mid-Western Section

Wet

Blue Quill	Mosquito	Montreal
Grizzly King	Professor	Hare's Ear

Dry

Blue Quill	Cowdung	Royal Coachman
Iron Blue Dun	Coachman	Pink Lady

Rocky Mountain

Wet

Black Gnat	Cowdung	Grizzly King
Coachman	Cahill	Brown Hackle Red Tag

Dry

Black Gnat	Olive Dun	Mosquito
Ginger Palmer	Blue Dun	Coachman

Canadian Selection

Wet

Parmachene Belle	Royal Coachman	Scarlet Ibis
Montreal	Silver Doctor	Col. Fuller

Dry

Parmachene Belle	Royal Coachman	Pink Lady
Montreal	Silver Doctor	Gray Bivisible

Mr. Harold Gibbs has written me as follows under date of March 13, 1949 (Mr. Gibbs' STRIPER FLY is shown in Fig. 33, No. 4.):

I have fished in all the New England states, New Brunswick, Nova Scotia, Cape Breton, etc., but I do enjoy fishing in the streams of Rhode Island and the nearby waters of Massachusetts.

We have very good brown trout fishing here; my favorite stream is the Moosup River which is in the west central part of Rhode Island and also the Palmer River which rises in Massachusetts and flows into Narragansett Bay.

All our streams are heavily fished but there are some "hold over" trout from previous stockings. The two streams I like to fish are both wide and open for using dry flies.

For wet-fly fishing there is one pattern for which I have a decided preference—the Hendrickson. I like the fly, I have confidence in it and therefore I fish it carefully. To me the body of fur looks particularly attractive and it must have appealed to *some* fish for my best trout fell for it.

In dry flies, while I have tied and fished with about all the patterns there are (and many that grew out of my mind), I like a Light Cahill best of all.

There is another variety of fishing I'd like to write about—taking striped bass on streamer flies and, of course, on a fly rod. Here in Rhode Island we have many salt-water rivers, inlets, coves, rocky points, and the tidal outlets of salt where the currents are fast. In the last ten or twelve years we have had large "runs" of striped bass.

During the war, when it was nearly impossible to get to the salmon rivers in Canada (on account of transportation difficulties and restrictions) I had the idea of taking stripers on flies, to take these fish on light tackle and make the most of the opportunities that were "right under our noses."

The story has been pretty well written up in several books on striped bass fishing and in the fishing papers. In brief, after a lot of experimental fly-tying, I developed a streamer—"The Gibbs Striper" that really took them. This was quite well publicized with the result that hundreds of fly-rod fishermen took up the sport.

This was several years before the book of Ted Gordon's letters was published. (I know that stripers have been taken on flies long before I caught them, and Ted Gordon's description of his "Bumble Puppy" is an excellent pattern. It took stripers besides other species.) My fly did produce, many fly fishermen did take up fly fishing, and it is grand sport—the closest to salmon fishing I know of. A big fish in fast water with plenty of room to run can really put up a battle.

I have taken a lot of 10 to 14 lb. bass; my largest was 16 lbs. 2 oz. So I include the Gibbs Striper as one of my favorite flies. I am enclosing one with the thought it may interest you.

Very truly yours,
HAROLD GIBBS

The following letter was received from Herbert L. Welch:

Moorestown, N. J. and
Mooselookmeguntic, Maine.

Answering your letter of March 10th., I would say the Green Spot streamer is now known as the *Nine-Three*. I am the originator of the Welsh Rarebit, Black Ghost, Jane Craig and Welch Montreal. Fish seemed to be taking green flies at the time I tied the Green Spot.

As you know, I am the originator of the streamer fly way back in 1901.

My favorites are the Gray Ghost and Black Ghost.

All best wishes for success,
HERB

The following from Roger P. Smith tells of fishing in Connecticut waters:

Opening Hill Road
Madison, Connecticut

Connecticut waters, both salt and fresh, abound with fish which may be taken on artificial flies. Among the fresh-water species will be found a well-rounded selection ranging all the way from the humble roach to those kings of fighting fish, the bass, trout, and salmon (although these salmon I speak of are limited to a few lakes in the northwestern sector).

Several of the big rivers and many of the smaller streams that run to the sea are well known for their shad and "buckie" (a kind of herring or alewife) runs in the spring. Although the buckie is not much of a fighter, he will take a fly and provide a lot of sport because of the sheer number of fish that may be caught in a short length of time.

The buckie run precedes the shad run and may be taken as advance notice that the shad will be in soon. In addition to shad and buckies, the white perch also runs up the tidal rivers in the spring and offers real sport on the fly rod.

In the salt water I have caught 17 varieties of fish to date, all on a fly and all from shore! Some of them have never been classed as game fish and the big majority of them have rarely been fished for with flies in the past.

To list a few of these: hake, whiting, sand dabs, flounder, blackfish (but don't try for these on purpose, they raise the devil with your rod), porgy, sea robins, and kingfish.

Weakfish, bluefish (especially snappers), mackerel . . . yes, and hickory shad when you find them . . . are well known for their fly-rod appeal. The striper, too, is joining the ranks. Most Connecticut fishermen, though, are afraid of trying the fly rod on stripers for fear of what the stripers will do to the rod. This fear, however, is unfounded, for the striper is quite easy to subdue with a fly rod.

A trip to one of our local tackle stores will reveal that the most popular flies in these parts conform pretty much to the choice all over the East, a fact which, I believe, can be attributed to fly design from the fisherman's point of view, rather than that of the fish. For fresh-water use, the Royal Coachman, Iron Blue Dun, White Miller, Black Gnat, Hendrickson, and Cahill probably lead the field in wet flies.

Dry flies would go something like this: Royal Coachman, Quill Gordon, Hendrickson, Black Gnat, Brown Bivisible, Badger Bivisible, and perhaps the Yellow May.

Certain of the streams have special flies to which the fishermen have assigned supernatural powers such as the Housatonic Quill which is supposed to be "the only fly to use on the upper Housatonic River." Frankly I don't own one and I've taken a lot of trout out of that wonderful stream.

The Optic bucktail is far and away the most popular in its class and well it might be for it's a killer. Add to this the Mickey Finn, Dark Edson Tiger, Parmachene Belle and, again, the Royal Coachman, and you have the list of commercial patterns most sought by the anglers.

Little is done, comparatively speaking, with nymph fishing. A few Weber patterns, the Rube Cross line and a few local nondescripts seem to suffice.

Shad fishing is 100% addicted to the Enfield Shad Fly and a colored bead. A sample setup is included. I find, though, that many patterns are equally effective. The White Miller, Royal Coachman, and Parmachene Belle, to mention a few. I like white-winged flies pretty well for shad. I do use the bead, too, but I can't tell you why—tradition, I guess.

Next to shad flies, the Trixoreno probably takes more shad on the fly rod than any other lure. Third choice would be some of the very small spinners and spoons, baby Junebugs high on the list.

For salt-water work, I stick mainly to bucktails. Almost any good commercial pattern will do the trick. I do not recommend tinsel decorated numbers because I find that in the presence of salt water a vicious electrolytic action is set up between the tinsel and the hook which results in the hook rotting through.

With regard to sizes, I would list the following as the most popular. Dry flies Nos. 10 and 8, comparatively few No. 12, and rarely Nos. 14 or 16. Personally I like the smaller sizes (even at dusk when it is miserable trying to tie them on the leader). I often use No. 20. Wet flies Nos. 10 and 8 and not infrequently No. 6. Here, again, I much prefer the smaller sizes and tie most of mine on No. 14 hooks. Bucktails, I would say, are most popular from Nos. 6 to 10.

It is singular to note that the fellows who have the full creels are those who use the smaller flies. I believe this is due in a large measure to the fact that pattern details are more easily seen in the larger sizes, consequently a fish once hooked by a big fly knows what to expect and shies away from the big ones after that. How long he will remember it, I don't know. Most of the fish that are hooked and lost are taken on these big flies by novices. Experienced men use small flies and don't lose fish.

There is a limit to the size of a hook that a fly rod should be asked to drive home. I believe it is in the neighborhood of size 4. Many salt-water flies are tied on hooks larger than this, consequently many salt-water fish are lost because the rod could not set the barb of the hook. Most salt-water fishermen have set notions about hook sizes for their pet fishing. This accounts for the disproportionately large flies used in the salt water.

I wish I could count the number of fish I've yanked out of the Sound on bucktails tied on No. 14 long-shank hooks. Everything from three-inch snapper blues to stripers in the four lb. class. Personally I'm a firm believer in small hooks.

Before I leave the subject of hooks, let me say that the sizes I have mentioned represent the average of all the flies purchased. This includes the chain store and dime store junk, as well as those sold in the better tackle stores. I believe that if a survey were conducted on hook sizes in tackle stores only, the average would go a size or two smaller.

So much for the buying habits.

Now, as regards a recommended list of flies for the various branches of fly fishing, you know as well as I, that there are as many "best selections" as there are fishermen. Rather than crush any Connecticut angler's pride by omitting his favorite pattern, let me suggest types of flies for a given season, being careful at the same time to point out that these are the flies I like best, but do not necessarily represent a consensus.

In the early season, give me the dark wet flies and a few Bucktails and I'm perfectly happy. Number one killers would include such flies as the March Brown series, the Montreal, the Alder. . . any of the flies tied with dark turkey wings. Also high on the list would be the Leadwing Coachman, that perennial favorite, the Brown Hackle and the Black Gnat. I use only three Bucktails (I'm somewhat lazy and these are easy to tie) they are, in order of preference, a simple red and white with a silver body and a black head (no painted eye), a similar black and white and the Mickey Finn.

For early season dry-fly work, I believe that nothing equals the Bivisible. Here again, though, I like them small. I tie all of mine on number 14 hooks. For colors, two suffice . . . gray and badger.

As the season progresses, I lean more heavily on the dry fly and turn to the lighter colors and more delicate patterns. Light Cahill, Light Hendrickson, Quill Gordon, Yellow May and a pattern of my own which I have called the Lady Anderson. It has a yellow body, wood duck fibres for tail and wings, light brown hackle and a black head.

The Lady Anderson is also very effective in a wet-fly pattern. Other good wet flies include the Californian Royal Coachman, Parmachene Belle, etc. Sounds as if I run to the yellow and white.

I have a special streamer that I use in the latter part of May when the baby eels are running up the brook. It consists of a slender, tapered body of gray floss, wound very sparsely with fine tinsel to give it just the least bit of flash. Over this is laid just a few (literally only ten or a dozen) black impala hairs. The head is black. I'll send you one.

Any fly that will take fresh-water fish (I'm speaking now of Bucktails) will make a good account of itself in salt water. I've tried most of them with good results. I like the Parmachene Belle, Dark Edson Tiger, any of the well-known salmon streamers and many others. Of special interest is a series of flies designed by Harold Gibbs. They have probably boated more stripers than any other patterns I know about. Then there are three special bucktails I worked out for Gene Edwards, the famous rod builder, for his exclusive distribution.

One pattern that is particularly effective is called the Mossbunker. It is a blue, black, white and silver job tied on a number 1/0 streamer hook. Although as I said before, I do not like tinsel on my salt-water flies. I'd rather tie it on a brightly polished hook for my own use.

I resort to a shrimp pattern of my own creation often. It catches a lot of fish. I believe that the shrimp is to the salt-water fish what the May fly is to the trout. A sample will be sent to you.

Yours very truly,
ROGER

The following was received from Dr. Herbert Sanborn, whose flies are illustrated in Fig. 36:

Waterville, Maine
March 19, 1949

I have quite a bit to say regarding history of my flies, color combinations and favorite patterns but little time to write about it. I have thought seriously about writing a book but just recently my fishing companion on many a trip and a friend of his wrote a book on trolling flies in Maine and although I haven't read it expect it contains many of my theories.

I do however take the *credit* for originating the double hook trolling streamer and getting it on the market for the fishermen to use. I lost many good salmon trolling with a single long shank hook and hence devised the two hook tandem. My theory was that the fish had too much leverage with the long shank and it was, while trolling, a question of them setting themselves. I'll explain later how we troll these flies. The Nine-Three is my own origination, although I've heard of many others that claimed it. It's been told many times how I tie it, but nobody will tie it like I do and that's where they make their mistake. This has been the most effective color combination I have found and when it's tied correctly for fish and not the fisherman's eye it works well.

Wing: bucktail, 3 green feathers tied on flat and two natural black edgewise or the regular way. Jungle cock eye. Both hooks—flat silver tinsel.

The fly doesn't look as neat tied this way because the green feathers go to one side of the other, but when it is wet there is a definite color gradation because the black doesn't cover up the green and the green feathers are in motion and that gives action to the fly that none of the others have.

The first fish I caught on this fly was a salmon (racer). He was 34 inches long and only weighed 9 lbs. 3 oz. and the fellow with me named the fly the Nine-Three.

I don't have time to devote to tying flies but my wife ties many for local dealers and sporting camps thru the state. I have about 6 patterns that I use in trolling and perhaps can give you some history on them.

1. Nine-Three
2. Liggett Special. Tied by a local chap and it's deadly, particularly early in the season. Emile Letoureneau tied it and it's named for his boss in the Hathaway Shirt Factory.
3. Red & White Bucktail.
4. Gray Ghost. Tied originally by Percy Tackle Company in Portland, Maine.
5. Mickey Finn.
6. Green King. Tied by Ed Banghman in Bangor, Maine and was copied from the Nine-Three.

We troll these flies on fly rod and fly line using a six foot Allwyr leader (that's their name). They are invisible in water and made by MacMasters in Portland, Oregon. We use two rod holders. One on either side of the boat and one rod lies in the seats of the boat tip extended over stern of the boat about one foot so that the fly rides in the slip stream of the motor. Use 25 to 30 feet of line on this one and drop one of the side lines back to 40 and the other to 50 feet.

It's difficult to put into words how we do it but our speed varies on different waters . . . conditions, time of year, and whether we are on togue, trout or salmon grounds. It's better to go fast than slow under almost any conditions and I mean 5 to 8 knots. A great many of our fish are caught on turns when the fly has sunk and the boat is coming out of a turn which speeds the fly up toward the surface. These fish hit and set themselves. Sometimes we are holding the rods but going so fast the fish still set themselves. This is why I didn't like single long shank hooks for trolling. This would be different if one were fly fishing and could set the hook.

Back to the Nine-Three. In the spring I use a lot of Bucktail for a *fat* fly. As it warms up I use less of it and make a thinner fly. The color combination of the Nine-Three was derived to imitate the smelts that are in our inland waters.

My favorite dry flies are the Parma Belle and Dark Montreal tied with cocked wings.

As to wet flies, I tie hair flies for myself and prefer them to the others. Nine-Three, Royal Coachman, Red & White, Mickey Finn, Parma Belle (winged), Dark Montreal (winged) and Grasshopper. I'll enclose a couple of these for you to look over.

Yours very truly,

HERBERT SANBORN

Carrie G. Stevens, whose flies are illustrated in Fig. 37, writes as follows:

Madison, Maine.

I was pleased to hear from you and that you are interested in my fly work. At an early date I will make the flies you requested and send them to you. As the Black Ghost pattern was not designed by me perhaps you would prefer that I send another pattern. The first Black Ghost that I saw was sent to me from a fly customer at Middle Dam, Maine. He said it was designed by a guide in Norway, Maine, it was crudely tied but was used successfully and is one of my best sellers today. If you wish I will tie a Gray Ghost, General MacArthur and either one of the following three patterns to take the place of the Black Ghost. Blue Devil, Green Beauty or Morning Glory. I consider these five patterns specially nice salmon flies, also good trout flies.

I am afraid my opinion about flies would not amount to much as I have done very little fly-fishing in late years. The flies mentioned above are attractive to both fishermen and the fish and are included in nearly all of my fly customers orders.

Sincerely,

CARRIE G. STEVENS

The following was received from Lee Wulff:

Shushan, New York,
March 2, 1949.

The best fly I know for bonefish is the Rhode Shrimp fly which is made of three hackles wound around the shank of a No. 1/0 hook with three hackles going out on each side of the shank pointing backward from the bend, a sort of forked tail. This fly has a lot of action in the water and I like it best in natural (or dyed tan) plymouth rock hackles. Homer Rhode, Miami Beach Rod and Reel Club, Hibiscus Island, Miami Beach, Florida designed the fly.

Atlantic Salmon wet flies:

1. Jock Scott, the favorite fly for years and one that works under almost all conditions.
2. Grey Wulff (dark grey wool body, yellow floss tag, brown bucktail wing, guinea hen hackle, golden pheasant crest topping and tail, jungle cock eye), a very effective fly tied generally in the low-water pattern.
3. Blue Charm.

Dry Flies:

1. Grey Wulff.
2. White Wulff.
3. Black Spider, especially for low water. Silver body in sizes 12, 14, 16.

LEE WULFF

The following was received from Fred J. Hogardt:

4 Stimson Street,
W. Roxbury 32

I have found in the past that no two anglers will agree on the right fly for either trout or salmon. Whenever I bring up this subject in any of the various newspapers I edit, I have considerable kickback. Recently I made a check of the ten most active fly fishermen in this area and found that this is their opinion plus my own. All of these anglers were asked their opinions on fishing in only the areas of Maine, New Hampshire and Massachusetts, since there might be some difference in opinion on the other areas of New England.

In this area the greatest number of anglers use worms from the opening date, April 1, to early May as brook trout just do not hit the fly until about the second week of May. During that period over 95% of the fish caught are taken on worms. After that period the choice of the anglers in order named is as follows: Black Gnat, Montreal, Parmachene Belle, Red Tag, Silver Doctor, and Professor. The choice is in the wet fly and in sizes 12 to 14. In the dry flies (size 14) the preference was as follows: Royal Coachman, Grasshopper, and then the Black Spider.

For rainbow trout and brown trout the choice was the same for both—usually on the drab side such as the Cahills, Hendrickson, Gray Hackle, March Brown, Blue Dun, and similar flies in both wet and dry types. The tendency of the older angler is to use sizes 12 and 14 and the new comers the larger sizes.

The choice for landlocked salmon was as follows: streamer flies such as the Grey Ghost, Black Ghost, Supervisor, Lady Doctor, then brown and white bucktails.

All of the above was based on general use as there was some disagreement about weather conditions, time of day, etc.

Respectfully,
FRED J. HOGARDT

H. G. Tapply, editor of *Outdoors Magazine* and author of *Tackle Tinkering*, writes as follows:

FAVORITE FLIES

DARK EDSON TIGER.   Bucktail, size 6, cast and trolled. This pattern has for many years been my favorite for landlocked salmon in Maine, and in size 8 it is also deadly for native brook trout.

NINE-THREE.   Streamer, size 4, trolled. This pattern originated by Dr. Herbert Sanborn of Waterville, Maine, is a most effective trolling fly, used for landlocked salmon, trout and togue (lake trout). It is a close relative to the old Green Spot first tied by Herbie Welch of Haines Landing, Maine.

GEN. MacARTHUR.   Streamer, size 4, trolled. This red-white-and-blue streamer, always tied on an extra-long shank hook, was first tied by Mrs. Carrie Stevens of Upper Dam, Me. Very deadly on landlocks, but abominable to cast. (This fly is relatively little known.)

COACHMAN.   Wet fly, size 10, 12. A popular and widely-used pattern, but my "old reliable" under wet-fly conditions. I fish it *very* slowly and for my own use tie the pattern quite sparsely.

GRAY WULFF.   Dry fly, size 8. Generally a poor fly for browns and rainbows, but very effective on native trout and sea salmon; a useful pattern except during a selective rise.

H. G. TAPPLY

The flies shown in Fig. 38 were developed by R. M. Plympton and Herb Johnson. Without question these are the finest specimens of insect simulation I have ever seen. With bodies made of deer hair and ribbed accurately with working silk, and with legs, antennae and even gills very realistically fashioned, these flies fairly rival nature.

The flies shown in Fig. 39 were prepared by the same team—Plympton and Johnson. The Smelt and Gray Charm are two of several patterns in this series of flies. Bi-plane streamers are dressed with the feathers in a horizontal plane. The Silver Doctor is shown from the left side while the Brown Fairy is shown from the top to illustrate the hackle arrangement peculiar to Glider and Parachute dry flies. The Wounded Minnow Streamer is characterized by the streamer tied on one side only. This tends to impart an erratic action to the fly on the retrieve.

The patterns shown in Fig. 40 are most effective according to Mr. Plympton and are well accepted by many leading salmon anglers. The Rankin Special is a low-water type, having short wings and hackle. It is interesting that these flies are dressed on rather small hooks. The tendency toward smaller hooks is becoming more evident every season, some flies being dressed small as size 10.

Jim Gasque writes me as follows:

1½ Park Square,
Asheville, N. Carolina.

The Tandum Double-header, which I tie for personal use, and for a few others of the fraternity, is one of the best all-season wet bass lures in America—at least I think so. With this fraud I take bass throughout this region (where fishing is good about seven months annually) every month in the year. The reasons why I, and others, think it is the finest of all wet fly-rod lures are as follows:

First, I have fished it in competition with practically everything on the market and with scores of anglers—others have, too—95% of the time it takes the greater poundage of fish. Long experience of fishing about every kind of lure that looked worth fishing, and a careful study of bass and their feeding habits lead to these observations: it looks big to the bass—a bellyfull at one smack; it has a most enticing, weaving action that is lifelike when retrieved properly; its combination of colors—white, cream, salmon, etc., look temptingly juicy and tender, more so than dull, less attractive colors. I might describe its taking qualities this way—a cat, while eating its ordinary food will spring involuntarily to a crippled bird, a passing mouse or ground squirrel, which is evidence the cat has seen something that takes precedence over the regular food. In turn, a wild bird will take off from the backyard feeder tray to capture a large winged insect that comes along only infrequently. Prompted by the same impulse, a bass will rush from his hiding place for this juicy-looking morsel different from anything that ever crossed his window.

Frankly, aside from the colors mentioned, I've nearly forgotten about patterns for bass—they mean little to me. I use much of the natural bucktail and bear hair, dyeing some of the white, of course, to get cream, orange, and salmon.

The colors I use and the order in which they are preferred are: first, white; second, yellow; third, fourth, fifth and sixth about equal in choice for the shorter ties are—salmon, cream, black, and orange.

This elongated streamer fly is made in three sizes. The two larger sizes for lake fishing, the smaller and often the middle size for smallmouth in streams. It may be used with or without a streamer. May I add that this is not the lure for the neophyte with a cheap rod. It's large stuff, requiring a rod of backbone to put it out there before the boat has frightened the bass to other places.

Sincerely,

Jim Gasque

The following is from Bob Moog:

5713 Chilham Rd.,
Baltimore 9, Maryland

In Maryland, flies are used extensively for trout, bass, shad and some species of salt-water fish. Angling for shad with the artificial fly is a relatively new sport and certain fly patterns have come into existence that are proving definitely productive. These flies are of the streamer type and generally resemble the alewife minnows which make up such a large portion of the shad's diet. Rather than prepare any notes on this subject, I thought I would rush you a copy of our next issue of the League of Maryland Sportsmen's monthly Rally Sheet in which I describe these flies in some detail.

Streamer flies are used more widely during the early portion of the trout season as compared to wet flies. Through experience we have learned to tie all streamers on #8 or 10 6X hooks with a lead underbody. Since trout have a tendency on many occasions to strike at the split shot or ribbon lead, the weighted fly is the ideal solution. We stick generally to six or eight hackles for the wing and invariably paint a white and black eye on the head. In addition we deviate considerably from the standard streamer-fly illustrations by tying the wing in such a manner that the tip of the wing rides directly over the bend of the hook rather than trailing out far behind. This one feature is all important since years of bitter experience have taught us that hatchery trout tend to strike short and invariably miss the hook completely when the fly has a long tail or wing. These flies do not look good as a commercial item but are deadly on the water. Another local peculiarity (if one wants to call it peculiar) is the manner of putting tinsel on the flies. Rather than a large stripe which would make about three complete revolutions on a 6X shank, we use a narrow tinsel and make many turns, giving the fly a rather flashy appearance. Am enclosing a typical sample of a Black Ghost tied on a No. 8-6X hook.

Back around 1945 flies were pretty tough to get because of the hook shortage. The majority of us were glad that we tied our own, although the hook shortage was as severe on us as it was on the manufacturers. Consequently, when I landed a box of No. 10-3X hooks, I decided that every fly must count since the hooks might be the last until the end of the war. A friend was consulted and it was his opinion that since the Black Ghost was deadly in his native Pennsylvania, it would be a mistake not to tie up at least a dozen for the coming season. Taking him at his word, I tied some up, substituting yellow hackle fibers for the golden pheasant tail and throat and omitting the jungle cock. The flies proved to be an instantaneous success and permitted me to take several very nice trout out of our local streams. It was quite apparent that trout would come out from their cover to have a look at this flashy fly if for no other reason.

The pattern was shown to several fly-tying friends and soon everyone was proclaiming the Black Ghost to be the best. It is standard equipment down here. Other streamers are still generally on a par with one another insofar as popularity is concerned. The furnace and badger flies are popular as is the Mickey Finn.

The wet- and dry-fly picture is a tough one to describe. On only a few occasions have the trout proven to be really selective, and when feeding trout are not selective, any pattern will work. A Black Gnat wet, or a Cahill or Royal Coachman dry will always do the trick. Trout fishermen are always trying to please their vanity and may carry anything from a Parmacheene Belle dry to a Gray Nymph wet. On the whole, however, dry and wet flies are not too much of a problem. We have repeatedly missed rises to a No. 18 dry fly only to tie on a No. 10 dry and have the same fish rise to it on the next cast.

Cordially yours,
Bob Moog

Note: Bob Moog's Black Ghost is illustrated in Fig. 33, No. 3.

The following list was sent me by Leo W. Young, Durbin, West Virginia:

FAVORITE FLIES

Beaverkill
Cowdung }
Grey Hackle } Divided wing
Willow } wet, size
Red Ant } 10 and 12
Hare's Ear }

These I use on the Greenbrier River, East and West Forks, North Fork and Cheat. Early in the season. For brook and rainbow trout.

Royal Coachman —Fanwing
size 10

For brook and rainbow trout.

Black Gnat, divided wing
Spent Gnat, hair fly
Mosquito, divided wing
Grey Hackle Yellow, hair fly   size
Grey Hackle Green, hair fly   12
Brown Hackle Yellow, hair fly   wet.
Brown Hackle Peacock, hair fly
Rube Wood, hair fly
Cowdung, hair fly

Last week in May till June 20 in above named streams. For brook, rainbow, and brown in the Williams River.

Cowdung
Black Gnat } dry
Queen Waters } size 12 & 14
Hare's Ear } Cook's Four
Wickham's Fancy } Wing Style,
White Miller } except Grey-
Grey Hackle Yellow } Hackle Yellow.

On the above named streams and the Williams till June 20. Brook, brown, and rainbow.

Tuttle Devil Bug, natural, size 1 (dry)
Home-tied bucktail, natural, size 1 (with spinner)
White, red and yellow Bucktail, size 1 (with spinner)

For bass in the Greenbrier. White, red and yellow bucktail for wall eyes.

Sincerely yours,
Leo W. Young

Chas. W. Wetzel writes me as follows:

132 Capitol Trail,
Newark, Delaware,
March 24, 1949.

FAVORITE FLIES

GINGER QUILL DUN, dry, size 12. A fly I am never without.
BLACK ANT, wet, size 8–14. This fly is very simply constructed, being nothing more than two bulges formed on the hook shank by black tying silk, and having a black hackle wound between them.
MIDGE PUPA, wet, size 20. This is another good fly especially during hot

weather when the streams are low and clear. Both the green and white variety are excellent.

FISH FLY LARVAE, wet, size 12 long shank. This is an excellent nymph when fished deep. The fly is fished on the bottom of the stream bed where the old lunkers lie, and is moved very slowly, only about one inch at a time.

RED QUILL, wet or dry, size 12.

BLACK QUILL, wet or dry, size 12.

FAN-WING ROYAL COACHMAN, dry, size 12.

EDSON DARK TIGER, bucktail, size 8 long shank.

YELLOW BODY, GREY HACKLE, wet, size 12.

SAM SKINNER, dry, size 1/0 for bass.

HAIR FROG, dry, size 1/0 for bass.

GASPEROUX, bucktail, size 6 long shank, for salmon.

SILVER DOCTOR, wet, size 8 for salmon.

BLACK DOSE, wet, size 8 for salmon.

Sincerely yours,
CHARLES M. WETZEL

I have the following from Bob Frederick, a young "tyer" from Allentown, Pa.:

1252 Lehigh Street,
Allentown, Pennsylvania,
September 16, 1948.

Although I am only 21, I have been tying and selling fine trout flies for the past six years, and am quite familiar with local patterns.

The Little Lehigh Special made its first appearance about five years ago and has been quite popular ever since. It is primarily an early-season wet fly, being effective until the end of May.

Two other early season wet-fly favorites are the Gallagher Special and the April Grey. These two patterns are excellent until the beginning of May.

Aside from well-known standard favorites, these are the only local patterns which have gained any recognition. They are usually tied sparse and on a number 14 hook.

A bucktail I find especially effective when the waters are cloudy and discolored is one I am selling under the name Black Skunk.

Sincerely,
BOB FREDERICK

M. D. Hart writes me as follows:

Commonwealth of Virginia,
Commission of Game and
Inland Fisheries,
Richmond 13, Virginia,
March 14, 1949.

If I were confined to three trout flies, I would use Royal Coachman dry and wet Black Gnat and Grizzly King. However, I hope this will never happen.

Personally I get great pleasure in trying out different flies and have so many in my fly book I really don't know their names.

I note the insects flying along the stream and have found if I use a fly about the same color I usually get results. I have an idea that it will be almost an impossible undertaking to standardize flies. A great many anglers tie their own flies and now and then some fellow will evolve a fly that works fine on one stream and is no good on another.

One of my greatest pleasures is experimenting with different colored flies. I have had trout take a certain fly in the early forenoon but not in the same afternoon.

Very truly yours,
M. D. Hart,
Executive Secretary

The following is from Bob Carmichael:

Moose, Wyoming,
April 6th, 1949.

I assume you are not acquainted with the Snake River, Jackson's Hole or Yellowstone fishing and will attempt to give you a picture from scratch. This area, unquestionably, is the finest dry-fly fishing country in the U. S. A. and, regardless of time of open season, April 1st to October 31st, trout *can be taken on dry flies.*

First, this is, could I say, a lush country—abundant rainfall, fine stands of timber, lodge pole, balsam, spruce, quaker (aspen), cottonwood, willow, et cetera. Tremendous snows on our high mountains feed countless springs that feed our side streams through our hottest summers. This condition, with purest spring water and an abundance of aquatic insects and other trout food gives quick growth and strength to trout in a remarkably short time. For example, it is not unusual to take Cut-throat (Clarki Lewisii) with small heads that have reached the weight of four pounds yet cannot have reached their fourth year. The Cut-throat is, of course, our "native."

Exotics have done well; in fact we are alarmed for fear the Rainbow will take over our Snake River. 1948 catches on Snake during September and October ran in excess of 20% Rainbow.

There are also hundreds of spring-fed beaver ponds that furnish only fair fishing for Cut-throat. These ponds we planted with Eastern Brook with phenomenal success. Already Jackson's Hole has placed winners in Field and Stream contests and it is the local opinion that the world's record of 14 lb. 8 oz. will be jeopardized.

Added to the above, the planting of Loch Leven in Lewis Lake (headwaters of Snake River) in 1889 by the National Park Service gave us an entirely different species for our dry-fly fishing. Lewis River meadows, one hour's drive from Moose, offers us incomparable fishing for monster trout in crystal clear water. Imagine working over fish from 2 to 9 lbs. with 3X or 4X leaders on dry flies! Fortunately the Lock Leven seldom if ever come down the Snake below Jackson Lake dam so there is no apparent danger of these Lochs taking over our Snake.

In all we have everything from tiny mountain streams to the great Snake River, the famous Grovont River, Fish Creek, Pacific Creek, and dozens of Spring Creeks, dozens of mountain lakes, Leigh, Bradley, Taggart, Phelps in Teton National Park and Lewis, Shoshone and Hart Lakes in Yellowstone easily accessible to Jackson's Hole. These are only some of the leaders.

It has been truthfully said "One thoroughly familiar with the country could fish with flies every single day of our open season, May 1st to October 31st, get good to excellent fishing every day, and *never fish the same water twice."*

I do not claim to have "discovered" Jackson's Hole dry fly fishing but will say that those who preceded me in the area with their drys were very quiet about it. Fishing these waters first in the early thirties, 1931-36, I found fishing too good to be very interesting. Local natives wanting a change of diet would catch a bull head, cut a willow and horse out enough trout to satisfy their immediate needs.

I found from the start trout could be taken on almost any pattern, Quill Gordon, Greenwell's Glory, Blue Upright and Dun, Ginger Quill, Furnace and Badger Spiders were the patterns we used mostly. During 1935-37 we found the Authentic Adams and Adams (Ray Bergman) to be killers. Most of these patterns were tied for me by Don Martinez of California. Not being completely satisfied with the bulkiness of either the Adams or Adams (Ray Bergman) and also the golden pheasant tail (not durable or especially attractive) I had Martinez, then in West Yellowstone, tie for me a macaw quill bodied R. I. red, spike tail, and very sparse mixed (Adams hackle) with Plymouth Rock hackle point, upright wings.

Fact is, the fly embodied what, in my opinion, had everything—best hackle, best body, best wing, best tail.

From the start the pattern was deadly. Many of my customers or "dudes" we were teaching or guiding used it almost exclusively. Fishermen with no dry-fly experience at all took limits consistently. Wanting a name for the new "killer-diller," and already having a "Carmichael" I decided to call it "Whitcraft" in honor of my fishing pal, Tom Whitcraft, the famous fishing superintendent of the Grand Teton National Park. It is our belief that Tom Whitcraft will become immortal from the popularity of this grand dry fly. Incidentally, Martinez, who at that time was tieing flies for me, supplied some of his other customers with the pattern, calling it a "Quill Adams."

Also (this at Martinez' suggestion), he tied for me the identical pattern except for R. I. Red hackle point upright wings. This pattern I named "Bradley" for Bradley Lake, an excellent fly fishing lake just 1½ miles from Grand Teton National Park Headquarters. At this time I was U. S. Government fishing guide, Grand Teton National Park, Jackson's Hole, Wyoming.

Meanwhile (1939-41) our business had grown by leaps and bounds, both in guiding and fly and tackle sales. Reports from New York, Pennsylvania and Maine, even from New Zealand and Chile along with our Pacific states, indicated the opinion of the "Whitcraft" was unanimous, "A remarkable dry fly."

Just before the beginning of the war I was able to get a fine location at Moose, on the banks of the Snake River two miles from Grand Teton National Park Headquarters. Being on the Snake and on the main highway to Yellowstone, I was able to render a better service to my customers and our business prospered proportionately.

Through a mutual friend (whose flies had all the earmarks of having been tied by a master) I made the acquaintance of Roy Donnelly of San Pedro, California, and formed a friendship and business association that has been to our mutual benefit and today, I am able to supply the most exacting and meticulous purist who wades our streams, not only in pattern, but in any quantity he desires.

Donnelly, considered by many as one of the world's master tiers, has hackle knowledge and ways and means of getting materials that are amazing. Hour after hour, day after day, he sits at his vise turning out patterns as one of my customers says, and I quote, "Dry flies balanced so perfectly they seem ready to take wing."

Incidentally this same Donnelly is famous for his steelhead flies and is considered by Kreider and other authorities on steelhead to be one of the finest steelhead fishermen to ever don a felt soled wader.

Donnelly in cooperation with us, and I give him full credit, is responsible for the now famous Donnelly's Variant. The pattern is tied both light and dark. We needed something better than the Ginger Quill. True, the Ginger Quill took fish, but we wanted a pattern of that type and color that would be compelling in its attraction. Continued refusals from big fish to the Ginger Quill and yet something about it that brought these monsters to the surface led us on the right track. Honey-dun hackle was the answer, tied so it would float high and yet sparse enough to look like a natural. The soft fur body took the mucelin well and the water shook out easily on the false or back casts. It was acclaimed from the start; word about it spread like wild fire; Mrs. Robert Carey of Cheyenne, Wyoming (age 66 and one of the finest women dry-fly fishermen in the West) says about it "As succulent a morsel as ever floated over a big trout."

On a "problem stream," such as the Lewis River, the Grovont, or Firehole it has proven its worth and in my opinion no fly box in the Jackson's hole or Yellowstone areas would be complete without the Donnelly's Variant both light and dark from size 14 to size 8.

Summed up, patterns here would be as follows:

Drys:—		
Donnelly's Variant, light	14 to 8	
Donnelly's Variant, dark	14 to 8	
Whitcraft	14 to 8	
Blue Dun	14 to 12	
Greenwell's Glory	14 to 10	
Olive Quill	16 to 14	
Red Variant	16 to 12	
Furnace Spider Quill	18 to 10	
Badger Spider Quill	18 to 8	

These patterns are by no means the only ones that take fish here, but are the backbone of our sales to our best fishermen, and are patterns used most successfully by our guides.

Wet flies in order of effectiveness are as follows:

Blue Dun, grey squirrel tail	12 to 2
Morman Girl, grey squirrel tail	10 to 4
Grizzly King, grey squirrel tail	8 to 4
Professor, grey squirrel tail	8 to 4
Badger Wooly Worm	10 to 4
Alexandria	10 to 6
Carmichael Spider	10 to 4

In finishing I regret to state that business in the shop compels me to cut my guiding to a minimum. I have been very fortunate in obtaining a few very high quality guides who have been with me for years. My method of obtaining guides is to select young outdoor minded fellows and teach them our methods. I might add that seldom during the season are any of my guides idle.

Sincerely,
BOB CARMICHAEL

The following from Ruth M. Evans of the Glen L. Evans Co., whose flies are illustrated in Fig. 41:

Caldwell, Idaho,
December 31, 1948.

We are sending you a small booklet recently compiled by us, showing a list of trout fly patterns. We have marked the patterns most effective in this area.

We are also sending a few samples of patterns especially adapted to the Rocky Mountain region. We hope that this material will be of some value to you.

Sincerely,
RUTH M. EVANS,
Production Manager

For Utah
Bannock Chief
Barber Pole Black
Barber Pole Green
Barber Pole Orange
Mormon Girl
Wilson
Wilson Red Ant
Wilson Trout Fly
Wilson Trout Killer
Slim Jim Red

For Montana
Bear Paw
Big Trout
Jock Scott—Montana
Picket Pin
Sno Fly
Whitefish Maggot

For Rocky Mountain States
Jock Scott
Joe's Grasshopper
McGinty

For Idaho
Black Ant
Bob Slee Special
Evan's Red Ant
Mormon Girl
Red Ant
Termite
Lady Nylo
Renegade

For Washington State
Mosquito Yakima
Whitefish Maggot
Yakima Whitefish Fly

For Colorado
  Grumpy
  Gunnison
  Willow Colorado

For New Mexico
  Chauncey
  Woolly Worm

The following is from V. R. Johnson:

State Game Warden,
Custer, South Dakota

FAVORITE FLIES

ROCK WORM, wet, size 10. Trout of all kinds. This is a very good fly 'till July here in the Black Hills.

BROWN HACKLE, GREY HACKLE, wet, size 10 & 12. Trout of all kinds. These are both good flies all season but better in June and July.

BLACK GNAT, RIO GRANDE KING, wet, size 10, 12. Trout. Both of these flies are good during the season fished either wet or dry. (Upright wings.)

GINGER QUILL, ROYAL COACHMAN, dry, size 10, 12. Trout. Both of these flies are good during the season fished either wet or dry. (Upright wings.)

JACK'S HOPPER, wet or dry, size 8–12. Trout. From the first of July on this is a very good trout getter, one of the best. (Wings lay flat with a little hackle.)

WESTERN BEE, wet, size 10. Trout. Also a good fly after July.

QUILL GORDON, dry, size 10, 12. Trout. This is a good fly all season.

MICKEY FINN, WHITE MILLER, wet, size 8. Crappie. The Miller works best with about a size 7½ shot six inches ahead of the fly. Any fly with white or gold works well here for Crappies.

I tie all my own flies so some of them are a little different from those factory tied. The Rock I tie I believe works far better. I use a black and white variegated fish line for the bodies—gives the fly more gloss and it sinks faster.

V. R. JOHNSON

Utah Fish & Game Dept

FAVORITE FLIES

GINGER QUILL, wet or dry, sizes 8 to 16, for cutthroat trout.

CAHILL, wet or dry, sizes 8 to 16, for brown trout.

HACKLE FLIES: (wet or dry)
  Gray. Size 8 to 16, for trout.
  Brown. Size 8 to 16, for trout.
  Black. Size 8 to 16, for trout.

ROYAL COACHMAN, wet or dry, size 8 to 16, for trout.

BUCKTAIL FLIES, size 2 to 8, all sizes and colors, for trout. Fish on surface or near bottom.

The following from Dan Bailey:

Livingston, Montana,
March 23, 1949.

I am in the fly and fishing tackle business here and feel in a position to act as the voice of the thousands of anglers who come to our shop. As elsewhere, there is a wide divergence in view among the fishermen on what flies are best. The following flies constitute the average preference.

FEATHER WET FLIES: Gray Hackle Yellow, Ginger Quill, Royal Coachman, March Brown, Mosquito, Black Gnat, size 8, 10, 12.

STANDARD DRY FLIES: Adams, Light Cahill, Mosquito, Ginger Quill, Quill Gordon, Olive Quill, sizes 12, 14, 16.

SPECIAL DRY FLIES: Grizzly Wulff, Black Wulff, Gray Wulff, size 10.

SPECIAL FLIES: Black Wooly Worm, size 6. Joe's Hopper Fly (Michigan Hopper), size 8. Red Squirrel Tail, size 6. Sandy Mite, size 8, 10.

There could be many more on the list. The Wulffs are derived from Lee Wulff's original Gray Wulff and the first two patterns are by all odds the best large stream dry flies for these parts. I credit Don Martinez with development of the type of Black Wooly Worm used here. That and the Joe's Hopper are "musts" in the larger flies. The Red Squirrel Tail is standard for the Madison. The Sandy Mite is the best pattern of Hair Hackle Fly developed by F. B. Pott of Missoula, Montana.

Very truly yours,
DAN BAILEY

The following from Bill Hart:

Carbondale, Colorado,
February 9, 1949.

I have been coaching trout fishermen, beginners and advanced beginners for more than twenty years with success. Of course that covers all methods including wet, dry, and nymph flies. I have made it a study for more than thirty-five years of fresh-water fishing.

The information I am furnishing you may be brief, however it is accurate and dependable, I will assure you. I am not for any certain type of fly since the conditions under which one is fishing will often cause the unexpected. I never was the kind of angler to pack around so many patterns. My ideas about hooks are different, thought two or three sizes were sufficient a few years ago but now use around two or three dozen styles and sizes. Each season may cause a change in the fly patterns to a certain degree. A good example is the Rio Grande King and the Rio Grande King Special which are much alike. One season they are proven killers with many anglers, the next season they may not prove nearly so killing.

I am located near four rivers and seventy-five lakes which are all considered good fly fishing at the proper season. The famous Fryingpan River is only a minute away. A good many notables have fished this stream, however, it is not what it used to be. One 9-pounder and few others around 4 to 6 pounds were taken from these waters the past season. I coached a party of Hollywood movie makers on this stream one day and did very well using spinners and bait lures . . .

Sincerely,
BILL HART

FAVORITE FLIES
(DRY FLIES)

ROYAL COACHMAN, upright or fan-wing, size 12 for all trout.
RIO GRANDE KING, GINGER QUILL, BLACK GNAT, GRAY HACKLE (various): upright or fan-wing, size 12 for all trout. Frequently use size 14.

(WET FLIES)

Same patterns as dries, flatwing or upright hackle, size 10, 12.
WHITE MILLER, flatwing or upright hackle, size 10, 12. This pattern is especially effective for brown trout during the day.

(NEW POPULAR FLIES THE PAST SEASON—Colorado's western slope)

BADGER PALMER, upright, size 12.
MAJOR PITCHER, upright, size 10, 12.

(GOOD NIGHT FLIES)

GRAY HACKLE SILVER, flatwing, size 8, 10, 12 for trout. After dark for ordinary size stream.
B&B SPECIAL (Idaho), deer hair streamer, size 1 and 2. After dark for large streams this fly is hard to beat. Has black hair on top and white hair underneath.
BLACK GNAT, upright, size 10, 12; extra good on lakes after dark.

The following from Roy M. Donnelly, some of whose flies are illustrated in Figs. 42 and 43:

San Pedro, California
June 18, 1949.

I cannot claim to have originated any of these flies. The Brown Drake, Brown Partridge, Badger Palmer, and Bosquito I have popularized by proving them excellent fish getters. It is my opinion that the old standard patterns need few additions except to dress them with hair wings for steelhead.

Several years ago I asked Joe Wharton of Grant's Pass, Oregon, what six flies he would choose if he were restricted to that number for steelhead. He replied that he did not need six patterns, that three were enough and named the Royal Coachman, Gray Hackle Yellow body, and the March Brown as his three flies. I did not agree with him then but today we are in close agreement. Instead of the Royal Coachman I would choose the Carson which is the Royal with a red tail and some red in the wing. Instead of the Gray Hackle Yellow I would choose the Badger Palmer Yellow, and for the March Brown I would take the Brown Drake or the Brown Partridge which are not too far off.

The Jock Scott salmon pattern is an excellent fly for the steelheader's fly box, especially when the sun is on the water.

My choice for steelhead are in the following order.

1. Bucktail Carson, 2. Badger Palmer, 3. Brown Drake, 4. Brown Partridge, 5. Bosquito, 6. Thor, 7. Squirrel Tail McGinty, 8. Golden Demon, 9. Joe O'Donnell. For the Umpqua I would include the Umpqua Cummins. The Umpqua is an excellent Klamath River fly, but all around I would prefer the Carson.

The Joe O'Donnell, originated by a northern California angler whose name I believe is Wilson of Arceta, has been a top seller on the lower Klamath.

On any of our steelhead streams we take what we call "chub salmon" which are immature salmon running with the regular run of fish. They take the fly readily and I have found no better fly for them than the Badger Palmer, yellow. We seldom take the regular, mature fish except in the Eel. The reason is probably because the fly does not get down deep enough for the deep-running chinook which run during the summer and early fall. The Eel is another matter. The rains that put the Klamath and Trinity down generally open the Eel. Here it is a matter of pool fishing and getting the fly down to the chinook's level. It is not unusual to include a salmon in our catch of steelhead. These are both chinooks and silvers.

It has been a practice for many years to fish by casting and trolling the fly for salmon in the lower and tidewater pools of the Eel . . . In late years there has been a trend away from the old steelhead patterns to larger flies with metal bodies. They have that added flash and do go down to salmon and steelhead level.

Jim Pray's Optic Flies are a development of the last few years and are killing lots of big fish . . . I have found the enclosed Mickey Finn especially deadly.

My partner and I and two native fishermen had four salmon on at the same time in Singly Pool one afternoon and landed all four. Three were taken on Mickey Finns. These fish were chinooks and weighed 18, 20½, 22 and 33 lbs. . . . No question but what the Cohoe flies of Puget Sound and British Columbia would work well. These are mostly silver-body flies of bucktail and polar bear hair and are tied on large hooks size 2 and over and very long—about 5X.

Yours truly,

ROY M. DONNELLY

The following table and letter were received from Claude M. Kreider, Long Beach, California:

FAVORITE FLIES

Pattern	Type	Size	Kind of Fish	Comments
Royal Coachman	Wet	8-10	All trout	Best all-around. Good bet to try when in doubt.
Grey Hackle Yellow body	Wet	8-10-12	All trout	Just looks like a "bug." So good when in doubt.
Professor	Wet	4-6-8	All trout	A steady producer, good in

Fig. 37, SALMON STREAMERS by STEVENS
1. General MacArthur. 2. Morning Glory. 3. Blue Devil. 4. Gray Ghost.
5. Green Beauty.

Fig. 38, DRY-WET NYMPHS by PLYMPTON and JOHNSON
1. May Fly. 2. Damselfly. 3. May Fly Nymph. 4. Damselfly Nymph.
5. Stone Fly. 6. Stone Fly Nymph.

Fig. 39, SPECIAL TYPES by PLYMPTON and JOHNSON By-plane Streamers: 1. Smelt. 2. Gray Charm. Glider Dry Flies: 3. Silver Doctor. 4. Brown Fairy. Wounded Minnow Streamer: 5. Black Demon.

Fig. 40, ATLANTIC SALMON FLIES by PLYMPTON and JOHNSON 1. Rankin Special. 2. Ken's Black Creeper. 3. Black Bear. 4. Major Griggs. 5. Deep Water Demon.

Fig. 41, TROUT FLIES by EVANS

1. Termite. 2. Red Ant. 3. Lemon Whitefish Maggot. 4. Red Whitefish Maggot. 5. Natural Whitefish Maggot. 6. Joe's Grasshopper. 7. Woolly Worm. 8. Slim Jim, Red. 9. Yakima Whitefish Fly.

Fig. 42, STEELHEAD WET FLIES by DONNELLY

1. Badger Palmer. 2. Bosquito. 3. Brown Drake. 4. Carson (Bucktail). 5. Donnelly's Partridge. 6. Golden Demon (Bucktail).

Fig. 43, STEELHEAD WET FLIES by DONNELLY
1. Joe. O'Donnell. 2. McGinty. 3. Mickey Finn. 4. Thor. 5. Umpqua.

Fig. 44, PACIFIC TROUT FLIES by HARGER
1. Gold Bodied Multicolor Variant. 2. Blue Dun Spider. 3. Blue Quill.
4. Adams (Spentwing). 5. Badger Spider. 6. Black Midge. 7. Cahill.
8. Spruce. 9. Rube Wood Variation. 10. Western Salmon. 11. Caddis
Buck.

Fig. 46, BONEFISH FLIES by RHODE
1. All Yellow. 2. Red and White. 3. White Polar Bear, Red Body

Fig. 45, BONEFISH FLIES by RHODE
1. Grizzly, Yellow and White (Shrimp Fly). 2. Yellow and Grizzly.
3. All Yellow.

Fig. 47, BONEFISH FLIES by GRESH

These flies are un-named, they are identified by the numbers shown above, i.e. Gresh #1, etc.

Fig. 48, SALMON FLIES by CARTILE

1. Black Bomber. 2. Yellow Bucktail. 3. Bucktail Doctor. 4. MacIntosh-Brown (Dry).

Fig. 50, HAIRWING SALMON FLIES by AUCOIN

1. Ross Special. 2. Silver Gray Bomber. 3. Yellow Bucktail. 4. Black Bomber. 5. Mystery. 6. Cosseboom. 7. Brown Bomber.

Fig. 49, HAIRWING TROUT FLIES by AUCOIN

1. Royal Coachman. 2. Montreal. 3. Mickey Finn. 4. Silver Doctor. 5. Black Gnat. 6. Parmachene Belle.

Fig. 51, FEATHERWING SALMON FLIES by AUCOIN
1. Blue Charm (Low Water). 2. Black Dose. 3. Silver Gray. 4. Silver Doctor. 5. Jock Scott.

Fig. 52, SEA TROUT FLIES by GABRIEL-RAY
1. Woodcock and Orange. 2. Peter Ross. 3. Alexandra. 4. Butcher. 5. Mallard and Claret. 6. Heckum and Green. 7. Mallard and Red. 8. Teal, Blue and Silver. 9. Cinnamon and Gold. 10. Teal and Yellow.

Fig. 53, TROUT DRY FLIES by COOMBES

1. Blue Upright. 2. Blue Wing Olive. 3. Brown Olive. 4. Pale Olive. 5. Green Well's Glory. 6. Wickham's Fancy. 7. Silver Sedge. 8. Gray Drake. 9. Yellow Drake.

Fig. 54, SALMON FLIES by COOMBES

1. Silver Wilkinson. 2. Jock Scott. 3. Beauly Snow Fly. 4. Trumpeter Black. 5. Alexandra. 6. Dunkeld.

Fig. 55, PARACHUTE DRY FLIES by MARTIN

1. Olive Quill. 2. Green Well's Glory. 3. Wickham's Fancy. 4. Silver Wilkinson (Salmon). 5. Silver Butcher. 6. Peter Ross. 7. Kingfisher Butcher.

Fig. 56, SALMON and TROUT FLIES by HAYNES

Salmon: 1. Bulldog. 2. Lemon Gray. 3. Jock Scott. 4. Lady Carolyne. Sea Trout: 5. Connemara Black. 6. Claret and Mallard. 7. Orange Grouse.

Flat wing, sparsely dressed		10		lakes when they are feeding on shrimp.
Grizzly King	Wet	6-8-10	All trout	Always good, and also imitates shrimp.
Yellow Pheasant Flat wing	Wet	8-10	Brook trout	Always produces on brookies in the west.
Donnelly's Variants Long hackles	Dry	8-10-12	All trout and killers on the Yellowstone region	Both dark and light patterns. They do not imitate any spe cial hatch and do not need to. They FLOAT.

SPECIAL COMMENTS

WESTERN STEELHEAD: Usually bright flies. I think they can see them better in "big" water and hit them in a fighting mood, as with a spinner. Among these: Thor; Umpqua; Royal Coachman—with jungle cock shoulder; McGinty; Cummings; Golden and Silver Demon. All *No. 4 or 6*, heavy hook.

STEELHEAD, when surface feeding or on nymphs near surface: No. 6— Grizzly King; Brown Partridge; Badger Grey Hackle; Green Drake. These four seem to match the large may fly on western rivers in autumn, and can sometimes be fished dry or barely sub-surface.

I believe strongly in Big water—big fish—big flies. A better chance for the fish to see them, better hooking qualities, better sinking ability when fishing wet. Steelhead flies, ordinarily, must go DEEP.

Western pan fish: Crappie, bluegill, and also bass: Nearly always a red and white streamer; yellow also good. The Mickey Finn is a killer on all these fish out here.

The following received from Don Harger whose flies appear in Fig. 44:

February 2, 1949.
Salem, Oregon,

Enclosed is the listing of flies that I use almost exclusively. Of course, at times I will, as most anglers, try other patterns but usually return to these few and take fish.

1. *GOLD BODIED MULTICOLOR VARIANT.* Dry, sizes 16 and 14 for rainbow and brown trout. This is my favorite under nearly all clear water conditions. It is one of the best all around dry flies for the Central Oregon streams and also on some of the better west-slope Cascade streams. For some reason it is the one fly I always turn to when the going is rough. I have seen brown trout ignore natural insects on the water to come to this fly. It will *always* take fish when other dries have failed. Not good on coastal streams where cutthroat predominate, since they are underwater feeders.

2. *BLUE DUN SPIDER.* Dry, sizes 16 and 14 for brown trout. Very effective when large may flies are hatching. I would rather depend on this fly to take fish when the big blue may flies are on the water than to try to match them closely. It is another of the high-riding dry flies that seem to coax the fish when

they ignore exact or nearly exact imitations. It is especially effective on brown trout in the Deschutes water shed.

3. *BLUE QUILL.* Dry, sizes 14 and 12 for rainbow and brown trout. Most widely scattered hatch in Oregon. Good all around. This fly can be found on most of the streams in various sizes from early season to late. It is probably the most widely used dry fly in the state. Unfortunately I have more luck with the first two patterns and must place the Blue Quill third in my own preference.

4. *ADAMS (SPENT WING).* Dry, sizes 18 and 16 for brown and rainbow trout. Excellent when small gray flies are in evidence. This is one of the best flies in most of the western states when the small gray flies are hatching. A good floater and appealing to the fish for the blending of its colors. It is equally good on lakes in the evening when small flies are in evidence. A must in western fishing.

5. *BADGER SPIDER.* Dry, sizes 14 for rainbow and brown trout. A tempter when fish are a bit choosy mid-day. I usually dress this in two or three different shades of badger from very light to dark. It is a wonderful fly when fish seem to be inactive. It will coax them into rising during mid-day when naturals are being ignored. It is another of the high-riding dry flies that seem to excite the brown and rainbow.

The five patterns listed are the only patterns one will ever find in my dry flies. I can always have an enjoyable day on any of our dry-fly waters with at least one of these patterns. It eliminates the confusion caused by fifty patterns cluttering up the fly box.

6. *BLACK MIDGE.* Wet, sizes 16 and 18 for rainbow trout. Very deadly when fish are feeding on larvae. This should be classed as a nymph, but it has rather long hackles that are not trimmed top and bottom so I will call it a wet fly. It is the answer to the evening fishing when fish are by all appearance surface feeding but will not show interest in any dry fly. Those beautiful head and tail rises sometimes drive an angler nutty but it is usually because he will continue fishing dries. The fish (especially in the Deschutes system and Cascade streams) feed almost exclusively in the summer and fall months on the midge larvae that starts to hatch in the evening. The fish take just before the larvae reaches the surface. By all appearances they are surface feeding. This little black midge will sink just below the surface by greasing the leader all but the tippet. It is referred to in some Oregon circles as the Secret Weapon because of its deadliness during the summer and fall evenings.

7. *CAHILL.* Wet, sizes 10 and 12 for brown and rainbow trout. My choice for best all purpose fly. This fly is as well known if not better known in the east than in the west. It is not too widely used in this area although I cannot understand why. It is one of the most consistent takers of brown trout and at times works equally well on rainbow. Have also used it with success on coastal streams on cutthroat trout but it is not the best fly for the cutthroat who seems to like a bit more color.

8. *SPRUCE.* Wet, sizes 10 and 8 for cutthroat. Best for sea-run cutthroat in coastal streams. This is an Oregon-born fly and is without a doubt one of the most effective coastal stream flies. The big sea-run cutthroat take it with a rush. At times it is weighted by wrapping lead fuse wire under the body so that it will

sink faster and to greater depths. It does not imitate anything I know of yet it is deadly all through the season.

9. *RUBE WOOD VARIATION*. Wet, sizes 10 and 8 for brown and cutthroat trout. Very good in lakes that hold large fish. This variation of the Rube Wood is called locally the Meadow Lake Special. This fly was dressed with the idea of the Spruce in mind but with more color. It has worked very well on cutthroat and in a private club water (Meadow Lake) it has been most effective on brown trout. Several of us have witnessed its power on brownies when all other patterns fail to get a strike. It is fast becoming one of the popular flies in this area.

10. *WESTERN SALMON (STONE FLY)*. Dry, size 8 long shank for brown and rainbow trout. Special early season for hatch duration only. This is my imitation of the big stone fly that hatches in such large quantities in the larger streams of the west. It is strictly a special fly and is effective only during the May and early June hatches of these big bugs. At times one can see thousands of them in the air along the Deschutes, Crooked, and Metolius Rivers. During that period when they are hatching it is almost useless to use anything else. Once the hatch is over the fly is just so much plunder in the fly box until the following season. Anyone planning an early season trip to the west should have a few of them.

11. *CADDIS BUCK*. Dry, size 10 and 8 for brown and rainbow trout. Good during hatch and also to imitate grasshoppers. Although this fly is used by nearly every angler in Oregon from early season to late, I place it as a special in my own box. The caddis hatches almost exclusively at night and the fly itself is not matching anything that may be buzzing around in the daytime. I am convinced that if the fly is dressed on a large hook the early season fish take it for the stone fly. On other occasions I have used it very productively when a strong wind is blowing hoppers to the water surface. The fact that it is a large fly that floats well and is easily watched by the angler probably accounts for its popularity. I have, however, during summer and early fall, found the smaller variants and spiders much more effective. For my own purposes the caddis is to be used only on special occasions, when it is really deadly. Normally it is just another fly.

Sincerely,
Don C. Harger

The following received from C. A. Schoenfeld, 770 Langdon, Madison 6, Wisconsin:

FAVORITE FLIES

PROFESSOR, wet, size 1/0. With spinner for stream fishing for bass. Highly effective during the heat of the day.

GRASSHOPPER, dry, size 8. Stream fishing for trout. A killer in meadow brooks in July and August; this is the fly made by L. L. Bean.

PARMACHENE BELLE, streamer, size 2/0. Lake fishing for northerns; with or without a spinner. A short hank of pork rind often helps.

RED IBIS, YELLOW SALLY, hair minnow, size 6. Lake fishing for panfish.

Vary depth and speed of retrieve considerably until you start getting strikes; large painted eyes seem to add to effectiveness.

HEWITT NYMPH No. 1, wet, size 10. Trout. Down-stream drift very early in the season; probably no more effective on the average than many other nymph patterns.

BADGER VARIANT, dry, size 12. Trout. Peacock herl body, badger tail and hackle, grizzly hackle-tip wings; strictly a personal fancy.

C. A. Schoenfeld

The following from Harold H. Smedley:

Muskegon, Michigan,
February 18, 1949

For about the last ten years I have gone on the theory that flies that will take trout in Michigan will take fish anywhere and I am proving it to my satisfaction. The Adams fly is one of my favorites for the reasons I have outlined in my book, a copy of which I have autographed and is coming forward to you by separate mail. I have taken Grayling in the Yukon territory with that Adams fly as well as Grayling in Manitoba. In fact, I have caught trout on it wherever I have fished with it.

I have taken salmon in Alaska on flies that were tied primarily for brown trout in the Upper Peninsula of Michigan. I have taken baby tarpon in Florida on flies that were tied for speckled trout in the Limestone River in Manitoba, and so it goes, on and on. I do not believe a person can limit himself to a few patterns.

I do have a few pets, one of which is on the order of a Tup's Indispensable. It has a reddish-brown wool body, Andalusian hackle sparsely Palmered, size 12 and 14. I have found it generally successful wherever I go. Another small dry fly is a sparsely tied light Gray Hackle, slightly Palmered, sizes 14 and 16.

Getting back to the Adams for a minute, if the fish are "turning up their noses" at the Adams, the wings can be removed and one has a luscious looking grizzly hackle.

Harold H. Smedley

The following from Don Webb, Ardmore, Oklahoma, March 8, 1949:

FAVORITE FLIES

POPPING BUG. Surface, jumbo size for smallmouth bass. First choice for eighteen years after six years trial of all standard flies. The same lure of largemouth bass.

My twenty-four years of fly fishing, in my book, has proved simply this: for six years I tried everything on the market. Finally settled on a large top-water popper for both largemouth and smallmouth black bass. Personally, I prefer Peck's Jumbo Poppin' Bug Weedless. I get the best results when working 'em slow, and I do mean slow. Effective in reasonably still water around brush, moss, weeds, etc.

Don Webb

The following table and comments were received from Charles C. Niehuis, 1630 West Monroe St., Phoenix, Arizona:

FAVORITE FLIES

Pattern	Type	Size	For What Fish	Comments
Tail gray hackle wisps, gray wings, gray hackle semi-spent. Body Javalina quill	Arizona special mosquito	10 to 16	trout	very durable and dependable
Gray hackle with yellow egg sac—and gray hackle with peacock herl body	Gray hackle	8 to 14	trout	Arizona and Montana waters
Sparse gray hackle in front. Grub body of yellow and white wool tied full	Grub	10	trout	Arizona and Montana waters
Black wool body on long shank, with brown Palmer tied hackle	(no name)	8 to 12	trout	Arizona and Montana waters
Four joints black and yellow chenille, brown hackle spent or divided wing	Western Bee either wet or dry	8 to 12	trout pan fish	Arizona and Montana waters
Gray and mixed gray and black hackles, either dry or wet	Bi-visible	8 to 10	trout smallmouth pan fish	dry or wet or in combination with combination with willow leaf spinner.
Gold tinsel body (black or peacock herl) polar bear hackle and jungle cock	Bright Angel night rider streamer	8 to 10	trout and smallmouth pan fish	
	Black Gnat	12 14	trout pan fish	
	Coachman & Royal	14	trout pan fish	

My experience has been limited to Arizona and Montana waters.

The last few years I tend to use a smaller fly—16-18-20's. I have had exceptional luck with the (no name) woolly worm.

Walter Flesher, 3826 North Tenth Street, Phoenix, Arizonia, is my favorite flytier.

Yours very truly,

Charles C. Niehuis

The following from Herbert Sandusky:

Jackson Daily News,
Editorial Department,
Jackson, Mississippi,
February 15, 1949

In reply to your letter inquiring as to local preferences in bass flies—as you know, Mississippi has no trout—I'm forced to say that this is "bug" fishing territory. I'd be safe in reporting that 99% of the fly fishermen here use bugs in preference to flies.

The favorite colors are red, white, black and yellow, and combinations of these colors.

If the bugs fail to produce, streamer flies are usually the next choice. The following patterns seem to be preferred: Yellow May, Grizzly, Oriole, Parmachene Belle, Raven, and Coachman.

In case you're interested, I might add that a great deal of fly fishing is done here for bluegills. Bugs are again the preference. When flies are used the Black Gnat is the favorite. Others that are used: McGinty, Cahill, Katydid. These are used as both wet and dry flies. No. 8 and 10 hooks are used. Another favorite is the Grasshopper pattern.

I have been out of town for several days, otherwise I would have answered sooner.

Sincerely yours,
HERBERT SANDUSKY,
Outdoor Editor

The following from Earl Wallace:

Division of Game and Fish,
Frankfort, Kentucky,
February 9, 1949

Kentucky does not offer any trout or salmon fishing and the majority of fly fishing done is mainly for large and small mouth bass and the smaller members of the sunfish family such as the bluegill bream.

The most popular and widely used fly patterns for the bream and similar species are: Black Gnat, Brown Hackle, Bee, and the Royal Coachman, the popular size being tied on No. 6, 8, and 10 hooks in both the wet and dry types, the wet being the most popular.

In the past few years the Lord Baltimore pattern tied on either a No. 2 or No. 4 hook and fished with a No. 1 or No. 2 spinner has proven excellent in the smaller streams for both large and small mouth bass and goggle eye. In some of the larger impoundments such as Dale Hollow, Kentucky Lake, and Herrington Lake, streamers are coming into their own, especially the crappie and white bass which are confined within these lakes. This is the conventional type streamer with tinsel body and white hair wings as tied largely by local fly tiers.

I do not know whether you are interested in the patterns of bass bugs, but as they are so important, particularly in the central section of the state, I feel they should be mentioned. The most popular colors are orange bodies and yellow wings as well as brown and black bodies with corresponding colored wings.

Yours very truly,

For the Director, EARL WALLACE,

By, J. T. Cox, Supervisor

The following from Allen Corson on fishing in Florida:

The Miami Herald,
200 South Miami Avenue
Miami, Florida,
February 20, 1949

The area that I discuss runs from Sunny Isles to Naples, thence to Key West. Lake Okeechobee, to the north, could be called the fresh-water terminus of anglers residing in the just described territory.

So you will find more salt- than fresh-water casters. Only an accident created today's fly-rod market. It was found, in June of 1947, that salt-water fish would take a fly. That is, that masses of anglers could do well, on a species no less repected than albula vulpes, the bonefish.

When this news got around, a major shift was involved. The hard core of salt-water fly casters—perhaps no more than 50 to 100 men—took heart. Where, once their deeds went unrecorded, now there was interest. New faces showed up every day. It actually happened this way.

Within five years South Florida will be important to flycasters everywhere. Dozens of flycasters have begun to include Florida in their annual itinerary. Those used to small fish are now catching bigger fish. Those who know well their salmon waters are liking bonefish, tarpon, redfish, snook, jack, and other species.

But insofar as flies go, the old line favorites seem to be out. Dries get almost no play; wets not much more. Standard patterns have been discarded long ago. In their places have crept in an assortment that knows no rules, rhyme or reason. A fellow gets an idea; it works; so he's in business. Only someone else, using the same principle, catches a bigger fish with his creation. A new craze is on.

Generally the formula governing streamer flies would cover the bulk of our working flies. Bastard Yellow Sally's, Mickey Finn's, etc., are the rule. Salmon flies might go well, particularly in all whites, red and whites, or red, yellow and whites. I question if they have yet been tried. The local tyers have had too much fun creating fads of their own. Almost anything seems to go. One standard streamer is the tail hook taken from a Shimmy Wiggler plug.

Very truly yours,
ALLEN CORSON,
Fishing Editor,
The Miami Herald

The following received from Homer Rhode, Jr. (whose flies appear in Figs. 45 and 46) has this to say on color combinations for bonefish flies:

832 *South Greenway Drive*
Coral Gables 34, Florida
June 12, 1949

Divided wing streamer flies tied on a number 1 or 1/0 short-shank hook. My favorite all-year fly is the Shrimp Fly that I developed nineteen years ago after taking my first bonefish. These flies have a yellow, barred rock, and white stiff neck feather (rooster) in each wing with a heavy salt and pepper yellow-and-white hackle.

Next a barred rock divided-wing streamer fly with a yellow, or a yellow and white hackle. Then a straw-color divided-wing streamer fly with yellow or white hackles or a combination of the two. This means a white or barred rock feather between the two straw-color feathers.

After a lapse of around twelve years, deer hair flies in white or yellow and white with a heavy yellow, yellow-and-white or white hackle. These are very effective. The deer hair should be very long in these flies.

Another variation of the above fly is with a tuft of white polar bear hair tied on top and ahead of the deer hair.

Another variation is the same color combination of polar bear flies with heavy yellow, white, or yellow-and-white hackles.

These flies are my own development and I tie them up only on special orders.

I prefer a rustless hook, short shank if possible. They need not be heavy gauge. I use a great number of number 1 and 1/0 Eagle Claw Rustless hooks with about 4/5 of the offset removed.

Other fish that are particularly takeable by the fly rod in saltwater are as follows: tarpon, snook, redfish (channel bass), ladyfish or chiro, trout, crevalle, jack, snapper, bluerunners, mackerel, dolphin, bluefish, and barracuda. In fact, practically every gamefish that can be handled on a flyrod can be taken with an artificial fly. Seriously, a large mullet taken on an artificial fly can give you a scrap that a bonefish need not be ashamed of. So far I have been unable to sell the idea to the boys here; they won't believe it or think it would be worthwhile. Did the same thing for over fifteen years on bonefish, finally got to the point where I was afraid to mention it to myself in my sleep, then bang!—in a year over a thousand nuts took it up.

Yours,
HOMER RHODE, JR

The following received from Earl Gresh whose flies appear in Fig. 47:

St. Petersburg,
Florida

Years ago, when I left my home in Pennsylvania to become a citizen of the state of Florida, I felt I was leaving behind my beloved fly-fishing. Since I knew I was to live in St. Petersburg I realized I would have fishing in salt-water, but even tho I had plug fished in the north my greatest joy was with my fly-rod.

Even before I was settled in a new land I visited the tackle shops to get information as to where to fish and what to fish with. I found the places to fish were plentiful and the accepted method of fishing was with bass casting tackle and plugs or live bait. I was informed I could catch Sea Trout (Weakfish), Redfish (Channel Bass), Robalo (Snook), Bluefish, Tarpon, Crevalle and many other species of salt-water fish. This I found to be true for I started fishing as others did and thus became one of the Florida casters who retrieve by moving the tip of the rod in quick snaps thus making the bait jump in imitation of the movement of a shrimp.

Of course I met and talked to many fishermen and in the course of conversation I always brought up the question of fly-rod fishing, to which all replied it was no good in these waters. I well knew that none of the salt-water fish were fly feeders as there are no hatches of flies on the bay so I started thinking along other lines. Why not tie myself some streamers in the colors of the plugs used in these waters or try and imitate the Sardine minnow or Glass minnow.

I shall never forget my first trip out with a fly-rod and some of the streamers I had made up. I headed for a bayou right in the city, stationed myself at the narrow opening where the bay water entered and started casting directly across the mouth. With short sharp jerks I retrieved the line doing my best to make the streamer act like a Greenback minnow. I must have succeeded for on my third cast a trout struck and struck hard, and thus began a whole new era of fishing for me.

Since that time there has been a vast amount of development and experimentation on rods, lures, lines and methods of presentation. The rod manufacturers have spent many dollars building a rod that will stand up in salt water and after using many different rods I have settled down to a two piece, nine foot, five and a half ounce impregnated rod manufactured by the Orvis Company of Manchester, Vermont. This stick is equipped with stainless steel guides and has all the backbone that is needed to put out a long cast.

Many Florida anglers have spent countless hours under all conditions to develop the all round salt-water fly-rod. Joe Brooks, a famous Florida angler, who has left his wader tracks in the marl of all the Florida Keys, uses a six and a half ounce rod as that is his choice of weight. On the other hand, Bill Steffens of Rutherford, New Jersey who is a close fishing pal of mine, and the most expert and ardent Bonefish angler I know, uses a four and a half ounce rod and handles his fish perfectly with it. It is a delight to see Bill in action when a Bonefish becomes stubborn after that first wild rush; he has an unconscious way of knowing just how much pressure to put on which only comes from hours and hours of practice.

In the matter of the correct line; every angler will want to match the line to the rod he uses. I prefer, for my Orvis rod a Torpedo Head line in a G.B.F. size manufactured by the Ashaway Line Company of Ashaway, Rhode Island and as a backing I use two hundred yards of seven and a half pound braided Nylon. Many times I have thought I didn't have enough backing when a Florida Bonefish started across the flats. Any good make of Salmon reel will do just so it will hold the line and backing but be sure to wash it with fresh water when thru fishing.

As to flies—right here I could start a real argument for no two anglers will ever agree on the same flies for any type of fish or fishing. Along the Keys there are many fly-fishermen each having his choice and swearing by it. I use a short shanked one ought hook for I find that the width of the hook aids me in setting it although some of my friends use a long shanked number six and catch fish right on. My manner of dressing is the result of thirty years of fly-fishing for salt-water fish and I have come to the conclusion that any colors will do just so they are red and white.

I tie white Polar Bear hair on a red wool body or dyed red Polar Bear hair on a white body. However, I have used an all white fly with just a small red cheek very effectively, for after all, as I've said before, there is no such thing as a fly-feeding fish in the Florida salt water so as I see it the idea is to excite the fish in order to make it take the lure. Using the red and white combination I have caught thirty-four different species of salt-water fish, therefore, I really believe it is the presentation of the lure and the manner of retrieving that catches fish.

Some of my northern friends ask me what I think of Florida fish and if there is a real game fish to be caught in the salt water. I answer them by telling them I have fished for Nipigon Brook Trout and Coasters of the shore of Lake Superior; I lived at Doaktown on the Miramichi, New Brunswick, and fished for Bright Salmon from Boicetown to Blackville. For the last six summers I've fished Wyoming, Montana and Idaho for slungling big Rainbows, BUT, angler friend, until you've hooked into an Albula vulpes, Bonefish to you, you don't really know the meaning of Atomic Energy. From the instant the Bonefish takes the fly it is impossible to realize any fish could get started so quickly and take out so much line in so short a time.

Then too, there is a sporting part of this type of fishing that will intrigue any angler. The hazard of mangrove seeds full of small shells that will cut the leader or line; the uncanny sight of the Bonefish which makes it flush quickly and the fact that your quarry is more timid than a deer if the fly is not placed at exactly the right spot. All these things go toward making Bonefishing on the Florida Keys just about the finest fly-rod fishing anyone would want.

EARL GRESH

The following from Roderick L. Haig-Brown:

Above Tide, Campbell River,
B. C., Canada

FAVORITE FLIES

For trout (dry flies). McKenzie River deer-hair patterns such as Yellow and Orange Caddis, Candy Fly, Blue Upright, Purple Upright, etc. Certain sedges, both Parachute and Fanwing Royal Coachman. Bivisibles.

For trout (wet flies). Dark Greenwell, Gammarus Fly, Western Bee, Silver Brown, Silver Lady, Kerry's Special and many others.

For steelhead (winter). Golden Girl, Fiery Ranger, various prawn flies, most Atlantic salmon flies, sizes 4 to 2/0.

For steelhead (summer). Silver Lady, Silver Brown, Lady Caroline, Silver Doctor,

Coquihalla Special, Thunder and Lightning. Most Atlantic salmon flies in smaller sizes (8 or 10 to No. 4).

For cohoe salmon. Polar Bear Flies generally, on 2/0 hooks. Also streamer patterns tied with whole hackles. In fresh water, teal and silver, Parmachene Belle, Silver Doctor, etc., on smaller hooks.

We naturally tend, I suppose, to patterns we think up ourselves, some of which we standardize and name if others want them. Personally I rarely tie two flies exactly the same and I try out many flies that people send me from all over the world. But I think a man could fish B. C. waters with full effect if he were limited to half a dozen patterns, none newer than 100 years old, provided he could tie them on modern hooks with modern materials.

Yours very truly,

RODERICK L. HAIG-BROWN

The following from Sandy Sandiford:

Sandy's Sport Shop,
Kamloops, British Columbia,
Canada

Your letter of March 1st, 1949 addressed to Mr. R. M. Robertson of the Game Department has been handed to me for reply.

The contents of this letter have been studied and I have listed the types of flies which I would recommend in this area. I have given you descriptions and I feel that you will not go wrong in recommending these patterns.

Some of these, no doubt, you know but there are others which you might say are local patterns but they do work throughout British Columbia.

I hope that the information I have given will be helpful. I might add that these patterns are used throughout the interior of British Columbia.

Yours very truly,

"SANDY" SANDIFORD

CAREY SPECIAL: Wet fly size 4 or 6. Cast or trolled. Feathers of this fly open and close. Representing leech or swimming under-water bug life. Largest selling fly in the district.

BROWN SEDGE: Used wet or dry. Size 6. Used as wet fly and stripped approximately 6 inches. Used dry to represent Brown sedge. The brown sedge hatches during late May and June. In some areas they hatch in thousands.

GRIZZLY KING: Wet in size 6. Used generally throughout district from May to September. Every fly box has a Grizzly King.

BLACK O'LINDSAY: Used wet and stripped, also used trolled slowly. Size 6 in May and June, size 4 in Sept. and October.

NATION'S TURKEY WING: Wet fly size 6. Brings excellent results cast and stripped. One of the best fish killers . . . always dependable.

Other patterns used which are standard: Black Gnat, Professor, Cow Dung, Alexandria, Green Sedge, Royal Coachman and Coachman.

Dry flies as Brown and Black Bivisibles good in season.

SANDY

The following from Joe Kendall:

Kamloops, British Columbia,
Canada

Enclosed you will find some of our flies which take them as they are. I have fished here for 36 years and have had some wonderful experiences. Kept a diary and had the same pal as a fisherman all the years. Remarkable—I should say. Sincerely hope for you every success in your venture. I could keep on writing what has happened here as I have stocked many lakes (mostly virgin) and with strange success. We have a small lake just stocked 2 years and 3 months ago and there are already fish 7 lbs. in weight. The biggest growth is usually from the third to fourth year so just what will happen we hope to see.

You ask regarding the Royal Coachman—for night or late evening it works here. For choice a Black Gnat, a March Brown, an Alexandria and a Royal Coachman and I would have been satisfied in years gone past. But now—well is it I or the fish that have changed? Here is one for you. Three of us in a boat . . . all on the green sedge, myself in the bow, my number two friend rowing and trolling a fly, number three friend in the stern casting as myself. All on the same fly. I did not get a rise or a strike or a fish all morning. They did well. After lunch we were out again in the same water. Still number two and three taking fish. At 3:10 P.M. I hooked and landed my first fish that day. After that I had no trouble to take my limit and number two and number three never got a fish. You know I often wonder, don't you?

We find here that the Bumble Bee is very good early in the spring when the willows are in bloom. Well we know the reason there all right. Then the brighter flies come on . . . Jock Scott, Silver Wilkinson, Professor, etc. What a stock a fly-fisherman can gather and I for one waste many hours wondering what to try next. Ha! It's a great life.

As the Poet said:

> "Lord suffer me to bear with grace
> The lies I've listened to,
> Of fish their size, and favourite flies
> And all such Bally Hoo."

Now that's that.

Sincerely yours,
JOE KENDALL,
Known as "The Trout's Nightmare"

Flies enclosed:

SPRATLEY: Use slow and deep. Trolling or on a cast let it sink and retrieve slowly. Size 8.

THE BLACK-O-LINDSAY: Fish same as Spratley. Used very freely here . . . is a good killer. Size 6.

THE COLONEL CAREY: Wet or dry it is hard to beat. When in doubt lead with a Carey. Known as the Dragonfly nymph. Size 6.

GRIZZLY KING: When the green sedge is hatching this is quite a favourite. Size 6. Fish wet and not too deep. Retrieve slowly.

DRY GREEN SEDGE: Fish with very light tackle and keep afloat. This is a good pattern. Size 6.

The following from Peter R. Cartile, some of whose salmon flies appear in Fig. 48:

West Northfield, Nova Scotia,
March 28, 1949

First a word about myself as a fly-tier. I tied my first fly when I was a boy of twelve (that is a hen feather on a hook to catch trout) and I am now thirty-nine years of age and I have been tying flies all these years. For a number of years I have studied the art of tying the fancy English salmon patterns such as "Jock Scott," etc. . . . however the bucktail patterns both wet and dry have proven by far most deadly since introduced a few years ago (the word bucktail also includes any type of hair fly). I have created a number of patterns which my guides thoroughly test. Those that have proven most deadly I am about to describe.

THE BLACK BOMBER: When champion Joe Louis was first named "The Brown Bomber," a bucktail with brown body and hackle, was introduced and called "The Brown Bomber." It was from this pattern I created the Black Bomber which has proved much more deadly and a favorite with many throughout the province.

THE YELLOW BUCKTAIL
THE BUCKTAIL DOCTOR

(Mr. Cartile gives the dressings for these flies which have been included in the Pattern List.)

The three patterns described are my favourite wet patterns in sizes 1/0 to 6.

THE SQUIRREL TAIL DRY FLY (MacIntosh)

This pattern is by far the favourite in dry patterns, so much so that many of my dry-fly fishermen won't use anything else. Fishermen claim if a salmon won't take the fly they will play with it, much as a kitten will with a tassle. I have placed myself in a position not more than five feet from a salmon in low water and, with the aid of a guide serving this pattern to the fish, watched the fish dart almost to the surface, stop suddenly with his nose not more than an inch from the floating fly, as if smelling the fly, then turn and swim slowly back to his original position. This was repeated each time the fly was served to him. The guide did not observe any action whatsoever as the fish did not disturb the surface or touch the fly. Finally the fish darted up and slapped the fly with his tail, thus playing with the fly. The pattern is a simple fly to tie. The body consists only of the waxed tying thread, the wing is taken from the under side of the fox squirrel tail (gingery brown). The wing projects about an inch over the bend of the hook and flat along the shank of the hook. Three neck hackles from a Rhode Island Red rooster (of good stiff quality) complete the fly. The hackles should be large and clipped slightly after the fly is completed. This clipping will add to the stiffness of the hackle which is most important. The hook used for best results is a number 4 regular shank hook even in low water.

I tie trout flies only on request. Some of the popular patterns for trout are the Parma Belle, Silver Doctor, Golden Horn and Purple Quill. My six best selling salmon flies are The Black Bomber, Yellow Bucktail, Bucktail Doctor, Cosseboom, Silver Gray Squirrel, and Wizard. The leading dry-fly patterns are the Mac-

Intosh and two of Halford's patterns The Pink Lady and Greenwell's Glory.

Before closing, this bit of information may be of interest to you in regards to the salmon. Salmon are like people, they have their ideas about the fly they fancy. A fly that will attract one fish will not disturb another at all. They are shy and cunning like the fox. I have seen amateurs fish a pool and the salmon back away, that is slip backwards a few yards and then dart to the shelter of a rock to hide. When things quiet down again they come back to their original position. I have seen salmon maneuver below a dry fly without an offer to take the fly. It occurred the fish was shy of the leader . . . I detached the same fly from the leader and let it float down over the fish and the fish took the fly immediately.

Yours very truly,

Peter R. Cartile

The following from Joe Aucoin whose flies appear in Figs. 49, 50 and 51:

New Waterford, Nova Scotia,
April 5, 1949

Salmon fishing is first and last with me. Trout fishing has no thrills for me anymore.

As regards salmon fishing in Nova Scotia, or anywhere that Atlantic Salmon are fished for with flies, why they take flies is a mystery. They don't feed in fresh water. The answer may be that they take the flies just to destroy them.

For years, hair-wing salmon flies have been favorites for salmon and trout fishing. The only reason I know of is that the hair wings are more lifelike. They have a breathing action in water (any type of water).

During the war years my flies were used in Scotland and proved very successful . . . catching salmon where the old standard fancy patterns failed.

My favorite flies are wet flies for salmon such as the Bomber Series. These are hair-wing type salmon flies such as the Silver Gray Bomber, Brown Bomber, Black Bomber, also the Mystery, Ross Special, Yellow Bucktail and Cosseboom (named after Mr. Cosseboom the original tier). These flies are also my best sellers. I am responsible for the Bomber Series more popularly known as the hair-wing salmon flies . . . that is, tied as I tie them.

My six best sellers for trout are: Mickey Finn, Parmachene Belle, Royal Coachman, Black Gnat, Montreal and Silver Doctor. These hair-wing flies I have enclosed.

I am also enclosing a sample of my favorite fly, the Silver Gray Bomber, which has saved the day and fishing trip for many a time.

Yours truly,

Joe Aucoin

The following table and comments were received from W. R. Maxson, Kelowna, B. C., Canada:

FAVORITE FLIES

NAME	TYPE	SIZE	HOW USED	COMMENTS
GRIZZLY KING	Flat wing, off Mallard flank. Green wool body ribbed with silver or gold. Red Tail & grey hackle.	6 or 7	Wet Sunken	Very effective in the day, when no hatch is on.
GREEN SEDGE	Flat wing, light sand feather, feather body, ribbed with green silk. Brown or Grey hackle.	6 or 7 or 8	Dry	Used especially where the sedge fly is prevalent, in the upland Lakes.
CAREY SPECIAL Brown or Black	Made of, Body-Cock Pheasant Rump feathers, and Bear hair body & tail.	4, 6 or 8	Wet Sunken very slow action.	Used when there is no hatch on the water, and the lake has abundant feed, especially in the Nymph stage.

There are other common flies used, but these above are my favorite. The Montreal, Royal Coachman, Black Gnat, and Cow Dung are also good here, together with several other commonly known flies too numerous to mention.

I am enclosing a sample of the three favorites of mine.

W. R. MAXSON.
Game Warden,
Kelowna, B. C., Canada

The following from Neil M. Lindsay, Shalalth Post Office, B. C., Canada:

FAVORITE FLIES

PATTERN	TYPE	SIZE	KIND OF FISH	COMMENTS
DARK MONTREAL	Wet	8, 10	RAINBOW	ALL SEASON, FLY
LIGHT MONTREAL	Wet	8, 10	TROUT	" " "
HARDY'S FAVORITE	Wet		Ranging in size	Late summer, fall
M'GINTY	Dry, Wet	8, 10	from one to seven	" " "
NICOMEKL	Wet	8, 12	pounds.	Mid-summer
2nd Choice:				
PROFESSOR	Dry, Wet	8, 12		Mid-summer
ZULU	Wet	8, 10		Mid-summer
PAR. BELLE	Dry, Wet	8, 12		Mid-summer
ROYAL COACHMAN	Wet	8, 10		Early summer

SPECIAL COMMENTS

For rainbow trout of this section, the eastern slope of the Cascade Mountains, southern B. C., I prefer a small size fly, usually size 8 or 10. Most attractive patterns are combinations of brown, red, white and yellow, such as the Montreal, Parmachene Belle, Royal Coachman. I like wet flies in the spring and mid-summer and very late autumn. Dries are especially good in late summer and early autumn. All fishing here is in lakes.

Patterns of dry flies that fish take bear little or no resemblance to natural insects on which fish may currently be feeding. Chief food: caddis nymphs, shrimp and crustaceans, to which a wet Montreal bears a reasonable resemblance. Among *dry* flies the more brilliant patterns invariably prove best killers. Streamers are very effective as well as bucktails in the smaller sizes.

Above all I have found beyond all shadow of doubt, that even in this small lake where conditions *seem*, to the casual observer, to vary only slightly from year to year, nevertheless, the fishes' reaction to a given pattern of fly varies greatly from one season to another.

One oddity I have noted in regard to flies here: they become less effective (regardless of pattern) whenever the tail is lost. Checking this, I have found fish biting avidly at a disintegrating fly when wings and body material, unraveling, streamed behind as an elongated tail. Also, have seen fish strike at a fly after the wings came off that otherwise went unnoticed. Without wings the creation seemed a good replica of a nymph.

In wets I have found streamers particularly effective.

Sincerely,

NEIL M. LINDSAY

Grace Gabriel-Ray has sent me the following. Her flies appear in Fig. 52:

April 6, 1949

First of all let me thank you for your very interesting letter and requests, and start in on a personal note. I'm afraid I must disappoint you, and apparently Mr. R. L. Marston too, I am only a mere female, and a housewife at that! So I feel that I cannot be of any great help to you.

It is true, I suppose, that I am considered an expert fly-tier, having tied for over eighteen years for one of England's largest fishing tackle manufacturers. I left business of course when the war ended, and now only tie a limited number of flies mostly for friends, and just to keep my fingers in touch. At the best I am not a good correspondent, being able to express myself better verbally, but I will do my best to give you a few lines, in answer to your questions.

I have not invented any flies, but have several ideas for new patterns. My greatest difficulty is getting them tried out.

As you can imagine every fly-tier varies in her or his construction. I am allergic to flies tied with long legs (or hackles) and short stumpy tails, or vice-versa—or wings that do not have that streamlined look! But mind you the fish are not so particular, my friends tell me they (the fish) sometimes fall for dreadful monstrosities. Personally nothing gives me greater pleasure than to see a fly well balanced.

I have enclosed three lists of flies which I consider are best sellers in their particular group. They are the fisherman's standby on every occasion, and I feel the British fisherman would not go far wrong, if in his box he carried any or all of the flies I have enclosed.

I have favorite flies to make, they would be too numerous to mention here. Perhaps if I am to be perfectly honest with you, when I was going out to business, I (and I was not alone) always admired the American and Canadian flies. Why? You will ask, well simply because they had plenty of colour. Royal Coachman, Parmachene Belle, Pink Lady, Montreal, Queen of the Waters. These real good favourites always gave us great pleasure, there is only one word to describe them—they were really attractive, I only hope they proved so to the fish.

Regarding the usage of flies, there still goes on in England the old argument about Wet or Dry fly fishing. I can add nothing to this as I do not fish myself, but still foster the idea that someday I would like to tie a perfect dry fly that would really float!

As you have probably guessed by now, I do not tie Salmon Flies.

I do hope my flies will reach you in a reasonable condition. May I add that I would be proud and consider it a great honour if any of them were reproduced in your book.

Yours sincerely,
GRACE GABRIEL-RAY

BEST SELLERS

SEA TROUT FLIES

1. Woodcock & Orange
2. Peter Ross
3. Alexandria
4. Butcher
5. Mallard & Claret
6. Heckum & Green
7. Mallard & Red
8. Teal Blue & Silver
9. Cinnamon & Gold
10. Teal & Yellow

SMALL TROUT FLIES (size 13)

1. Olive Dun
2. Coachman
3. Red Quill
4. Greenwell's Glory
5. Wickham's Fancy
6. Cowdung
7. Red Spinner
8. Black Gnat
9. Olive Quill
10. Hare's Ear Gold Rib
11. March Brown
12. Iron Blue Dun

HACKLED TROUT FLIES

1. William's Favourite
2. Red Tag Palmer
3. March Brown
4. Moorhen & Yellow
5. Tup's Indispensable
6. Black Spider
7. Partridge & Orange
8. Snipe & Purple
9. Water Cricket
10. Woodcock & Red
11. Grouse & Orange
12. Coch-y-bondhu.

E. C. Coombes sends me the following. His flies are illustrated in Figs. 53 and 54:

Tenbury Wells, Worcs.,
England

I have enclosed some samples of my own dressings of trout and salmon flies with some of the materials used in a few of the patterns. . .

It is a usual practice of most anglers to carry in their fishing haversack a large assortment of flies. It is a great fault to have too many from which to choose. If in pursuit of trout, I think six well-chosen designs near to the natural flies on the water should be plenty. And that goes for America and most other countries since trout feed in a similar fashion nearly everywhere.

The flies I mention in this letter are successful in the British Isles. None of my own flies are patented, therefore, anyone can make them if they choose.

First we have what I call the main species of river flies. These are the "Olives." The name is taken from their color. Olive Duns are darker in shade in the spring and again in the late summer. In autumn they are light or pale in shade—almost yellow. So I dress the fly I call "Coombe's Blue Variant" which is very near to the natural Dark Olive. It is not too olive in shade nor too grey which is the trouble with most of the imitations of the Dark Olive. This is one of the best killing patterns here and is such right through the season. Fished dry it will kill when any shade of olive fly is on the water.

Then the Hare's Ear is another good dry fly effective when there is a hatch of red spinners. This pattern is also well taken when the Blue Wing Olive flies are out. My version is not dressed like the other patterns of Hare's Ear flies; as a Blue Variant it will get trout all season long.

The Alder is a good fly from May to the end of August and is one of the most used flies here but dressed differently among British anglers. I believe my dressing is more natural looking and it certainly does take trout. It is very similar to the Silver Sedge.

The Silver Sedge is a good evening fly, even better than the Coachman since it can be seen very well even into darkness. I prefer it to the rest of the sedges.

A little fly we call the "Iron Blue," which is one of the Hardy flies, is always dependable, doing good work on the colder days. I prefer this tied with a claret shade of quill body, a rusty dun hackle for the legs and an ink blue shade of hackle for the wings.

The March Brown is a fly used in this country everywhere. It is a world-wide standby.

During July and August when the rivers are low and gin-clear, I like a small (midge) Pale Olive Quill, winged, size 16 or 17. It will often account for ½ dozen decent trout up to 1½ lbs. each, and believe me, during a good season these rivers here are fished hard. Every trout has had many flies pass over it and knows imitations well. Flies have to be dressed like real flies to catch these chaps.

About the third week in May we get the hatch of may flies. These are the Yellow or Green Drake and the Grey Drake. The Yellow is the dun stage, the grey the spinner stage. I prefer the Grey. These are on the water either laying their eggs or dying (spent stage). During the three weeks these may flies are out the trout rise like mad. This is called the "Duffer's Fortnight." The fish are easy to catch.

. . . I will always contend that only if a good imitation is presented in the right way will it catch trout.

The body silk in my design is artificial silk and when oiled it will become the perfect shade of the natural fly.

I have made several patterns of flies used a lot in this country some of which I am sending herewith. My wet flies are based on a few logical deductions of my own. For example, wet-fly fishing is sometimes associated with fishing a drowned surface fly. But this is not so. Wet flies should represent the nymph rising to the surface of the water before hatching into the dun. Some are dressed to appear like a small fry or shrimp.

The Silver March Brown is an excellent wet fly for trout, sea-trout and, in large sizes, for salmon. The Butcher and most all gold or silver body flies represent fry from the trout's point of view. These and a Blue Nymph together with the Tup's Nymph are all of the wet flies any angler really needs . . . Other good patterns are the Mallard and Claret, Grouse and Green, and the Alexandria, the last especially. Good wet casts consist of the Silver March Brown (always) for the tail fly, a nymph for the first dropper, and a fry or fancy fly for the second dropper, say a Butcher, Grouse and Green, Invicta, Mallard and Claret (or orange in place of claret). Change the position of the droppers as required.

As to fly dressing: cock hackles from birds two to three years old if possible, and in natural colors. The better the quality the better the fly floats. The different colors given off by a good hackle adds that extra killing power. For tails I like six to seven fibers which help to cock the fly nicely. Keep the hackles well forward. The body should not be too thick but have slight taper. Hooks should be fine, well-tempered steel not too long in the shank.

Salmon flies. There is not one special. These are all good: Jock Scott, Black Dog, Thunder and Lightning, Silver Wilkinson, Silver Doctor, Black Doctor, Trumpeter Black, Beauly Snow Fly, Mar Lodge and Akroyd.

Sincerely,

E. C. COOMBES

In reply to my letter requesting information on certain obscure pattern dressings for the Dictionary of Fly Patterns, I received the following:

C. Farlow & Co., Limited
11 Pankton Street
Haymarket,
London, SW 1
November 25th, 1948

I have now had time to complete the dressings of the flies on your lists which I return to you enclosed herewith. I hope you will find them useful.

You will observe from the lists that some of the flies listed have no known standard dressings. Many flies are, of course, known by more than one name. In one or two patterns there are alternative dressings which we have given.

We hope you will find the information given to be what you want and of some assistance in compiling the work you have in hand.

Yours faithfully,
for C. FARLOW & Co., LTD.
A. S. Marsh, Director

I received the following letter from C. M. Harrison: The DURHAM RANGER shown in Fig. 33, No. 2, was tied by Mr. Harrison:

C. M. Harrison,
Professional Angler
& Fly-Dresser
Tregaron, Cards.
Wales

I have enclosed a sample of a fly of my own invention . . . Sgt. Jones, which has been the means of catching some really good trout on slow, deep water. Enclosed also are samples of the six best sellers for trout.

I consider a winged dry fly is made to "catch the angler."

The salmon fly most used around here is the Durham Ranger and I enclose a sample.

BEST SELLERS:

1. *WHISKERS*: An extremely good fly from June on and equally good for sea trout.
2. *SUN FLY*: This represents the Olives.
3. *DEVONSHIRE DOCTOR*: Good "all rounder" and very good even on a Chalk stream.
4. *VARIATION BLUE UPRIGHT*: Silk darkens greatly when oiled and I kill most of my fish on it.
5. *GROUSE & PEACOCK*: Good when the Alder is up. If they refuse the true copy of an Alder, they will generally take this.
6. *SGT. JONES*: Deadly in very hot weather, especially in deep pools.

(Dressings for the above flies will be found in the pattern list.)

The firm of Alex Martin whose parachute flies appear in Fig. 55 have sent me the following:

Alex. Martin,
Gun, Rifle and Fishing Tackle Maker
Glasgow, Scotland
and at
Edinburgh, Aberdeen & Stirling

This firm was responsible for development here of the fly dressing method invented by Mr. Brush of Chicago which we called "Parachute." Its feature is tying in a plane parallel to the hook shank to achieve flotation and correct orientation either on or in the water. Enclosed are patterns of six popular flies for trout and one salmon fly. All of these flies are dressed in the above mentioned Parachute style.

The following received from the firm of W. Haynes & Son whose flies appear in Fig. 56:

> W. *Haynes & Son (Cork) Ltd.,*
> *Haynes Fishing Tackle*
> *Cork, Ireland*

Your letter of 10th. inst. arrived here a few days ago, reply was delayed a little due to my absence, the matter being one which required my personal attention.

I am very interested to hear that you are working on a book which is to treat on fishing flies, and I shall look forward to buying a copy of this in due course. I regret, however, that I doubt my ability to provide any information of any value or originality. I have only been in this business for about fifteen years, my father, Mr. Samuel Haynes, would have been able to provide a good deal, I think, had you had need of same a few years sooner, but he is now retired fully, being very blind and senile, and his memory is unreliable. Neither he nor my Grandfather, William Haynes (the founder of this business) kept any notes or memoirs. Both of them certainly contributed ideas and methods to the craft of fly-dressing in their day, as both were absolute masters of the craft as well as of the craft of using the fly in angling. But we have nothing in the way of evidence which I could give you.

In addition to being a fly-dresser, my father was also a specialist in the dying of materials for fly-dressing by the old wood-bark methods, which are now obsolete. It was in this capacity that he often came into contact with other fly-dressers, mostly amateurs, and it is more than likely that many of his ideas may have been borrowed, or improved upon, by the ideas of other dressers who sought his materials, You will appreciate that there was a great deal of give and take between sporting friends in those days, and it was rare for anyone, even those commercially interested, to seek property right in invention, idea, or design.

In Ireland generally, the six best sellers I would name are:

For Salmon: JOCK SCOTT, BLACK DOCTOR, BULLDOG, LEMON GRAY, THUNDER & LIGHTNING, SHRIMP FLY (latter also known as Prawn Fly, or Mephisto).

For Trout: ORANGE GROUSE, MARCH BROWN, OLIVE QUILL, CONNEMARA BLACK, BUTCHER, CLARET & MALLARD.

I personally like the JOCK SCOTT salmon fly the best, but, who in Great Britain doesn't? It is the prince and paragon of all salmon flies, and even though it may not be so well known in the U. S. A. as here, you are nevertheless so sure to know it well there would be little point in my sending you a pattern of it. I am sending you instead some colour plates from a pre-war catalogue, and if any of these illustrations interest you, please let me know and I shall be most happy to send you actual dressings of any of the flies you name.

> Yours very truly,
> JAMES B. HAYNES, Director

The following received from Patrick Curry:

> 22 *Queen Street*
> *Colerain, County Derry*
> *Ireland*
> *May 4, 1949*

Illness prevented my replying to yours received some days ago. I regret not being able to help you about flies or my ideas on angling as I have contracted to let the editor of *Irish Angling* have them in book form sometime in the future.

If it is of any value to you let me state firstly I am a *pro* where angling or flies are concerned. I dress *hundreds* of patterns for my patrons, but when *I* go fishing for salmon, I confine my stock to three patterns. I consider that's enough, in fact *one* pattern of my invention kills 95 per cent of all salmon hereabouts and everywhere it is fished where sizes to suit the water are used. I'm enclosing a sketch and description of this pattern which I call the Curry Shrimp.

As for trout (sea or brown), I consider a half dozen patterns sufficient: Greenwell's Glory, Peter Ross, Wickham's Fancy, Golden Olive, Gold Ribbed Hare's Ear, Butcher.

> Yours faithfully,
> PATRICK CURRY
> (62 yrs. old, 46 fly tying.)

The makers of the flies in the illustrations shown between pages 308-309 may be identified as follows:

Aucoin	Joe Aucoin, New Waterford, Nova Scotia
Cartile	Peter R. Cartile, West Northfield, Nova Scotia
Coombes	E. C. Coombes, Cross Street, Tenbury Wells, Worcs., England
Donnelly	Roy M. Donnelly, 867 West 3rd Street, San Pedro, California
Evans	Glen L. Evans, Inc., Caldwell, Idaho
Gabriel-Ray	Grace Gabriel-Ray, Bromsgrove, Worcs., England
Gibbs	Harold N. Gibbs, A-71 Sowams Road, Barrington, Rhode Island
Gresh	Earl Gresh, St. Petersburg, Florida
Harger	Don Harger, 1245 North 21st Street, Salem, Oregon
Harrison	C. M. Harrison, 7 Well Street, Tregeron, Cards., Wales
Haynes	W. Haynes & Son., Cork, Ireland
Johnson	Herb Johnson, Yarmouth, Maine
Martin	Alex Martin, Glascow, Scotland
Moog	Bob Moog, 5713 Chilham Road, Baltimore, Maryland
Orvis	Charles F. Orvis Company, Manchester, Vermont
Plympton	R. M. Plympton, Morristown, New Jersey
Rhode	Homer Rhode, Jr., 832 South Greenway Avenue, Coral Gables 34, Florida
Sanborn	Dr. Herbert Sanborn, Waterville, Maine
Stevens	Carrie G. Stevens. Madison, Maine

BIBLIOGRAPHY

BIBLIOGRAPHY

CONNECTICUT, State of, Public Document No. 47, A Fishery of Important Connecticut Lakes, by State Board of Fisheries and Game Lake and Pond Survey Unit, Bulletin No. 63, Hartford, 1942.

FISHING TACKLE DIGEST, 1st. Annual Edition, Frank R. Steel, Editor.

FORBES, STEPHEN ALFRED, PH.D., LL.D., and RICHARDSON, ROBERT EARL, A.M., The Fishes of Illinois, Springfield, 1920.

GREGG, E. C., How To Tie Flies, A. S. Barnes & Co., 1940.

INTERNATIONAL GAME FISH ASSOCIATION, Yearbook, 1948.

INDIANA, State of, Indiana Department of Conservation, Investigations of Indiana Lakes and Streams, Vol. III, Indianapolis, 1945.

INDIANA, State of, Indiana Department of Conservation, Investigations of Indiana Lakes and Streams, Vol. II, Indianapolis, 1942.

INDIANA, State of, Indiana Department of Conservation, Investigations of Indiana Lakes and Streams, Vol. III, Indianapolis, 1945.

MARBURY, MARY ORVIS, Favorite Flies and Their Histories, Houghton Mifflin, 1892.

NEEDHAM, PAUL R., Trout Streams, Comstock, 1940.

NEEDHAM, JAMES G. and NEEDHAM, PAUL R., A Guide to the Study of Freshwater Biology, Comstock, 1941.

NEEDHAM, JAMES G. and LLOYD, J.T., The Life of Inland Waters, Comstock, 1937.

NEW YORK, State of, Fisheries and Game Commission Report for 1895, Wynkoop Hallenbeck Crawford, Albany, 1896.

NEW YORK, State of, Fisheries and Game Commission Report for 1896, Wynkoop Hallenbeck Crawford, Albany, 1897.

NEW YORK, State of, Fisheries and Game Commission Report for 1897, Wynkoop Hallenbeck Crawford, Albany, 1898.

NEW YORK, State of, Fisheries and Game Commission Report for 1898, Wynkoop Hallenbeck Crawford, Albany, 1899.

NEW YORK, State of, Fisheries and Game Commission Report for 1899, James B. Lyon, Albany, 1900.

NEW YORK, State of, Forest, Fish and Game Commission Report for 1901, James B. Lyon, Albany, 1902.

SMEDLEY, HAROLD HINSDILL, Fly Patterns and Their Origins, Westshore Publications, Muskegon, 1946.

SWARTZ, ALBERT H., Fisheries Survey Report, The Commonwealth of Massachusetts, Department of Conservation, Division of Fisheries and Game, 1942.

WALTON, IZAAK, The Compleat Angler, fourth edition, 1668.

WETZEL, CHAS. M., Practical Fly Fishing, Christopher, 1943.

INDEX

(NOTE: Only those fly patterns which are important in the text are included in the index. The Dictionary of Fly Patterns, Chapter XIV, lists the patterns.)

A

Abbey, 119
Abel, Joe, 138
Aberdeen, 2
Academy, 124
Acetate enamels, 29
Aelian, Claudius, 32
Aft body, 36
"Airplane" dry fly, 69
Alder flies, 68, 91, 153
Alder fly, angler's name for, 193
  recommended dressing, 193
Alewife, 134
Ambroid cement, 30
American Indians, 35
Amherst pheasant, 26
Amherst pheasant metallics, 28
Angora, 24
Ants, 153, 197
Aquatic adult insects, recognition of, 160
Aquatic nymphs and larvae, recognition of, 157
Arctic fox, 24, 29
Artificial flies, kinds of, 36
Art of Angling, 33
Astraeus (river), 32
A Treatyse of Fysshynge With An Angle, 33
Aucoin, Joe, 322
August Dun, 153

B

Baboon hair, 28
Backing hackle, 38
Badger crane fly, 191
Badger fur, 24
Badger hackle, 22
Badger hair, 22, 28
Bailey, Dan, 306
Bakelite varnish, 29
Bald widgeon wing quills, 27
Bali duck, 27
Ball eye, 7
Ball head minnow, 130
Balsa wood, 30
Barb, 9
Barbless hook, 9
Barker, Thomas, 33
Base wing, 40
Bass bug, 195
Bass Fishing, 97

Bass flies, 127
Beak point, 2, 9
Beard hackle, 38
Bear hair, 28
Beaufort Moth, 127
Beaver fur, 24
Bees, 197
Beetles, 153, 196
Benedictine Nunnery of Topwell, 33
Berners, Dame Juliana, 33
Bishop, 124, 127
Bivisible, 76
Black Bear, 119
Blackbird wing quills, 27
Black bivisible, 121
Black Bomber, 119
Black caddis, 186
Black Dose, 111
Black drake, 153, 166
Black Fairy, 123
Black fly, 34, 188
Black Ghost, 95, 136
Black grouse metallic, 27
Black hackle, 20, 34, 153
Black Louper, 33
Black midge, 190
Black quill, 121, 166
Black Spean, 119
Black stone fly, 182
Bloodworm, 188, 190
Blue Bottle, 153
Blue Charm, 119
Blue Dun, 153
Blue dun hackle, 21
Blue Highlander, 123
Blue jay, 26, 28
Blue Quill, 75, 175
Blue Sedge, 187
Blue wing teal body plumage, 27
Blue kingfisher, 28
Blued finish, 13
Bobbin, 13
Bob White, 125
Body (fly), 36
Body hackle, 22
Body materials, 22
Bodies, picking out of, 18
  tapering of, 40
  wire wrapped, 56

Bogart, 192
"Bonny Red Heckle," 75
Boroea, 32
Branch herring, 134
Brassy dun hackle, 21
Breast and side plumage, 27
Bright Brown, 20, 34
Bright finish, 13
Bronze finish, 13
Brown Bomber, 119
Brown caddis, 187
Brown drake, 172
Brown Fairy, 123
Brown mallard Grand Nashua, 27
Brown Palmer, 121
Brown quill, 167
Brown stone fly, 182
Brush, William A., 122
Bucktail, 29
Bucktail streamers, 103
Bunched wing, 39
Butcher, 111
By-plane streamer, 103

C

Caddis fly, 50, 68, 91, 153, 154, 182, 183
  anglers' names, 183
  calendar, 178
  groups, 184
  recognition features, 182
  recommended dressings, 185
  special features, 184
  worm, 92
Cahill, 75, 121, 125
Cahill Quill, 69, 164
Cain River Streamer, 102
Candlestick Maker, 109
Canvasback duck plumage, 27
Capras, 24, 29
Captain, 119
Caribou hair, 29
Carmichael, Bob, 301
Carpenter (caddis worm), 183
Cartile, Peter R., 321
Case worm, 183
Cassard (pattern), 125
Cassard, William J., 125
Caterpillars, 58, 75, 197
Celluloid enamel, 29
Cement, 29
Center joint, 36, 38
Centripetal bend, 2, 4
Cheek, 36
Cheney (pattern), 127
Cheney, Nelson A., 173
Chenille, 23
Chinese, 1
Chinese goat hair, 24, 29
Chinese mole, 24
Chief Needabeh, 103
Cinnamon fly, 153
Cinnamon Sedge, 121
Cinnamon teal body plumage, 27

Claw point, 9
Cleaning and dyeing hair, 30
Cleveland, 127
"Clipper," 91, 192
Closed wing, 39
Coachman, 119, 121, 125
Cochy-bondhu hackle, 22
Cock Capercailzie wing and tail quills, 26
Cock pheasant wing and tail quills, 26
Coleoptera, 153, 196
Collar hackle, 38
Colonel Monell, 121
Combination streamer, 106
Complete metamorphosis, 155
Condor quill, 25
Conniption bug, 192
Coombes, E. C., 326
Coot, 22, 27
Copper pheasant metallic, 27
Cork, 30
Cork body lures, 139
Cork dust filler, 139
Corson, Allen, 136, 315
Cosseboom, 119
Cotton, Charles, 20, 34
Cowdung, 153
Crab, 203
Cracker, 135
Crane fly, 153, 188
  anglers' names and recognition, 188
  groups, 190
  recommended dressings, 190
  special features, 189
Crawdad hair bug, 149
Crayfish, 193, 203
Cream hackle, 21
Cree hackle, 22
Creeper, 183
Cricket, 197
Crow, 22
Crow quill, 26
Crustaceans, 43, 90, 203
Curry, Patrick, 330

D

Damsel fly, 154
  names and recognition of, 194
Dandy, 116
Dark Mackerel, 153
Dark olive crane fly, 191
Dark spinner, 153
Dark stone fly, 181
De Animalium Natura, 32
Dead drakes, 39
"Dee" wings, 39
Deer fly, 188
Deer hair, 22, 29
Deer hair flies, early, 35
Dennys, John, 33
Detached body, cork, 73
  construction, 72
  hair, 74
  rubber, 72

silk, 74
Devil, 192
Devil's darning needle, 195
Dimensioning wings, 40
Diptera, 153, 188
Distribution of Insects and Crustaceans, 197
Divided wing, 39
Diving bug, 146
Diving disc, 30
Dobson, 192
Donnelly, Roy M., 307
Double barb, 9
Double fiber wing, 62
Down wing, 39
Drake fly, 33, 34
Drakes, 153
Dragon flies, 154
  names and recognition, 194
Drift food, 58
Dry fly, behavior of, 58-60
  bivisible, 76
  definition of, 58
  detached body, 72
  divided wing, 62
  down-wing types, 68
  fanwing, 70
  flatwing types, 70
  fore and aft hackle, 77, 121
  glider, 121
  hackle-tip wing, 66
  hackle types, 74
  hump-body ant, 81
  long shank, 81
  multi-color variant, 78
  Palmer, 75
  Palmer bivisible, 76
  parachute, 78, 121
  proportions, 58
  reverse, 80
  reverse hackle, 77
  reverse quill wing, 68
Dry fly
  rolled wing, 67
  sail wing, 67
  salmon types, 120
  short shank, 82
  spent wing types, 68, 69
  spider, 77
  split wing, 66
  split hair wing, 67
  types of, 62
  upright wing, 62
  variant, 78
  Whitefish maggot, 81
Dry Fly Fishing in Theory and Practice, 34
Dubbing needle, 18
Dubbing, making of, 41
Duck breast, 22
Dun Cutte, 33
Dun fly, 33
Dun hackle, 21
Duns, 74, 153, 159
Durham Ranger, 111

E

Early brown, 153
Early spinner, 153
Edson Tiger, 103, 136
Eggs, depositing of, 43, 53, 162, 170, 180, 184, 186, 194
Egyptian goose body plumage, 27
Egyptians, 1
Elixer, 29
Emerson Hough bug, 138
Emu plume, 25
Ends, hook, 7
Enfield shad fly, 136
English partridge plumage, 27
Entomostraca, 203
Ephemeridae, 153
Ephemeroptera, 159
Equinox gnat, 189
Evans, Glenn L., Inc., 81, 304
Evans, Ruth M., 81
Exact imitation of insects, 35
Experienced Angler, 34
Eye, hook (clearance of), 41
Eyed hook, 7
Eyes, coloration of, 105

F

Face hackle, 38
Fancy body plumage, 27
Fancy lake flies, dictionary of patterns, 279
Fanwing, 34, 39
Farlow, C., & Co. Ltd., 328
Favorite Flies, 125
Feather glazer, 29
Feather streamer, 29
Fiery Brown, 20, 34, 119
Filed point, 9
Finlay, G. D., 288
Fish fly, 91, 192, 193
Fish moth, 183
Fish skin wing, 27, 34, 39
Flathead cork bug, 141
Flat wing, 39
Flatted end (hooks), 7
Fly, 188
Fly and hook proportions, proposed standard, 56, 119
Fly nomenclature, 36
Fly proportions, dry fly, 58
Fly proportions, wet fly, 43
Fly selection, Aucoin, 322
  Bailey, 306
  Carmichael, 301
  Cartile, 321
  Coombes, 326
  Corson, 315
  Curry, 330
  Donnelly, 307
  Evans, 304
  Frederick, 300
  Gabriel-Ray, 325
  Gasque, 297
  Gibbs, 288

Gresh, 316
Haig-Brown, 319
Harrison, 328
Harger, 309
Hart, Bill, 307
Hart, M. D., 301
Haynes, 329
Hogardt, 295
Johnson, V. R., 305
Kendall, 320
Kreider, 308
Lindsay, 323
Martin, 328
Maxson, 322
Moog, 297
Niehuis, 312
Orvis, 288
Plympton, 296
Rhode, 316
Sanborn, 292
Sandiford, 319
Sandusky, 314
Schoenfeld, 311
Smedley, 312
Stevens, 294
Tapply, 295
Utah Fish & Game Dept., 305
Webb, 312
Wallace, 314
Welch, 289
Wetzel, 299
Wulff, 294
Young, 299
Flying caddis, 52
Fore and aft flies, 77
Fore body, 36
Forward wing, 39
Fox tail, 29
France, L. B., 34
Frank Gray, 124
Frederick, Bob, 300
Freestone streams, 164
French thrush wing quills, 27
Frog hair bug, 149
Fur dubbing, 24
Furnace hackle, 22

G

Gabriel-Ray, Grace, 325
Gallinule wing quills, 27
Gasque, Jim, 97, 296
Gibbs, Harold N., 136, 288
Gibbs' Striper, 136
Gill, Emlyn M., 35
Ginger-grizzly hackle, 22
Ginger hackle, 22
Ginger Quill, 99, 154, 169
Glass eyes, 30
Gled, 119
Gnat, 188
Goat hair, 29
Gold-plate finish, 22
Golden Dun Midge, 153

Golden Dustman, 135
Golden pheasant metallic, 28
Golden pheasant wing and tail quills, 26
Goose body plumage, 27
Goose wing quill, 27
Governor Alvord, 125
Grannom, 153, 183, 187
Grasshopper, 34, 197
Gravel bug, 183
Gray crane fly, 191
Gray drake, 153, 173
Gray fox, 29
Gray Ghost, 106
Gray list hackle, 22
Gray Palmer, 121
Gray widgeon wing quills, 27
Gray Wulff, 121
Greased line fishing, 119
Great Red Spinner, 153
Green caddis, 186
Green Dragon, 195
Green drake, 154, 162, 164, 173
Green Ghost, 106
Green Midge, 190
Green Spot, 95
Green's Pot, 95
Green stone fly, 181
Greenwell's Glory, 121
Gresh, Earl, 137, 316
Grizzly hackle, 22
Grizzly King, 119
Ground hog hair, 22
Grouse, 22
Grouse wing and tail quills, 26
Grub, salmon fly type, 120
Guinea, 22
Guinea wing quills, 26

H

Hackle, 21, 36, 38, 41, 44, 60
Hackle flies, 75
Hackle gauge, 60
Hackle pliers, 18
Hackle tip wing, 39
Haig-Brown, Roderick L., 319
Hair bugs, 146
Hair for dry fly wings, 28
Hair for floating bugs, 29
Hair for streamers and wet flies, 28
Hair hackle, 22
Hair wing, salmon fly, 119
Hair wings, 39
Halford, F. M., 34, 73
Harger, Don, 180, 184, 309
Harrison, C. M., 328
Hart, Bill, 306
Hart, M. D., 301
Hawk, 195
Hawthorne, 34
Haynes, W., & Son, Ltd., 329
Head (fly), 38
Hellgramite, 91, 192
Hen mallard body plumage, 27

Hen pheasant wing and tail quills, 26
Hen wing quills, 26
Hell-devil, 192
Hell-diver, 192
Hemiptera, 153, 196
Henshall, Dr. James A., 129, 135, 146
Henshall surface bug, 138, 148
Henshall type wing, 129
Heron, 25
"Hipporous," 32
Hofland, T. G., 34
Hogardt, Fred J., 295
Homer, 32
Honey hackle, 22
Hook, barbs, 9
    bend, 2, 4
    ends, 6, 7
    eyes, 6, 7
    finishes, 13
    gape, 6
    points, 9
    shanks, 4, 6, 7
    shapes, 2
    barbless, 9
    cross section and wire gauge, 6
    early type, 1
    eyed, development of, 1
    parts of, 2
    suitability of, 1
Horns, 38
Hump body ant, 81
Hump shank, 6
Hymenoptera, 197

I

Imago, 159
Impali, 29
Impressionistic flies, 35
Incomplete metamorphosis, 155
Inky Boy, 119
Inner wing, 39
Insects, orders of, 156
Insects, preservation of, 159
Insects, wholly aquatic, 154
In-turn (hook), 2, 4
Inver Green, 111
Iron Blue, 166
Iron Blue Dun, 153, 164

J

Jane Craig, 95
Japanned finish, 13
Jeannie, 119
Jenny Spinner, 153, 164
Jockie, 119
Jock Scot, 114, 119
Johnson, Herb, 103, 121, 296
Johnson, V. R., 305
Joint, 38
July Dun, 153
June Drake, 176
Jungle cock, 28
Juno, 129

K

Kapok, 24
Katydid, 197
Kendall, Joe, 320
Kirbed bend, 4
Knife edge (hook), 9
Knobbed end (hook), 7
Kreider, Claude M., 54, 308

L

Lacquers, 29
Lady Amherst pheasant metallics, 28
Lady Caroline, 119
Lake fish food, 205
Lark wing quills, 28
Larva, 91
Larva, definition of, 155
Leopard fur, 24
Lemon Gray, 119
Lepidoptera, 197
Light Cahill, 69, 170
Light stone fly, 181
Lime content, 203
Limerick, 2
Limestone streams, 164
Lindsay, Neil M., 323
Little Red Spinner, 153
Little Yellow May Dun, 153
Locust, 197
Logie, 119
Long Dee, salmon fly type, 120
Long shank, 4
Low-water fly, purpose for, 53
Low-water salmon fly, 118
Lynx fur, 24

M

Macaw plumage, 26
Macedonians, 32
MacIntosh, 121
Mahogany hackle, 22
Major Griggs, 119
Malacostraca, 203
Malay parrot body plumage, 28
Mallard body plumage, 27
Mallard minnow, 99
Mallard white tips, 26
Mallard wing quills, 27
Mandarin wing quills, 27
Marbury, Mary Orvis, 125
March Brown, 119, 121, 125, 153, 169
Margaree salmon fly, 111
Marked end (hook), 7
Marked shank, 7
Maribou, 27
Married feathers, 39
Marsh, A. S., 328
Marten fur, 24
Martin, Alex, 122, 328
Masons (caddis larvae), 183
Matador, 125
Maure fly, 33
Mavis wing quills, 27

Maxson, W. R., 323
May fly, 34, 153, 154
May fly, Anglers' names for and
    recognition, 159
  calendar, 165
  determination of sex, 162
  dressings and imitations, 166
  groups, 166
  special features, 164
McGinty, 119, 121, 124, 132, 197
Metallic feathers, 28
Metamorphosis, complete, 155
Metamorphosis, incomplete, 155
Miall, Prof. L. C., 152
Miall, system of classification, 153
Mickey Finn, 103
Midge, 188
Midge larvae, 92
Midget streamer, 97
Miniature salmon fly, 118
Mink fur, 24
Model Perfect, 2
Mohair, 24
Mole fur, 24
Mole hackle bivisible, 121
Monkey hair, 29
Montreal, 121, 125
Montreal, silver, 121
Moog, Bob, 297
Moorhen wing quills, 27
Moorish fly, 34
Moose Mane, 25
Moose River, 106
Mosquito, 188
Mosquito Hawk, 195
Muskrat fur, 24
Mystery, 119

N

Needahbeh, Chief, 103
Needham, Dr. Paul R., 180, 198
Needle Brown, 153
Needle eye, 7
Needle point, 9
Neuroptera, 192
New Lake, 124
Nickel finish, 13
Niehuis, Charles C., 312
Nine-three (9-3), 97, 106
No Name, 125
North Carolina Indians, 35, 150
Nymph, compressed body, 90
  definition of, 155
  distribution of, 197
  double wing pad, 88
  Humpback, 86
  shell back, 91
  special features, 85
Nylon, 26

O

Oak flie, 34
Odonata, 194

Offset point, 4
Olive dun, 171
Olive midge, 190
Opossum fur, 24
Optic bucktail, 104
Optic head, 104
Orange brown, 153
Orange crane fly, 191
Orange dun, 153
Orders of insects, 156
Orl-fly, 153, 192
Orthoptera, 197
Orvis, Chas. F., & Co., 125, 189, 287
O'Shaughnessy, 2
Ostrich plumage, 25
Otter, 24
Outer wing, 39
Owl wing and tail quills, 26
Owner, 124

P

Pale Evening dun, 121, 153, 171
Pale Olive Quill, 168
Palmer bivisible, 76
Palmer hackle, 38
Palmer hackle flies, 33
Parachute flies, 78
Parmachene Beau, 114
Parmachene Belle, 119, 121, 125, 127, 136
Partridge, 22
Partridge plumage, 26
Parts of a fly, definition for, 36
Patterns, fly (dictionary of), 207
Peacock body plumage, 22
Peacock eye, 25
Peacock fly, 34
Peacock herl, 25
Peacock quill, cleaning fluff from, 41
Peacock sword metallic, 27
Pearl Drake, 167
Peeler, crab, 134
Perch bug, 195
Perlidae, 153
Pheasant, 123
Pheasant breast, 22
Pigeon wing quills, 27
Pinch bug, 192
Pink Lady, 119
Pink Lady bivisible, 121
Plastacele, 26
Plastics, 23
Plecoptera, 153, 177
Plover wing quills, 27
Plunker bug, 146
Plymouth Rock rooster, 27
Plympton, Ralph M., 103, 121, 296
Polar bear hair, 24
Popham, 111, 116
Porcupine quill, 25
Practical Dry Fly Fishing, 35
Premier, 125
Preservation of insects, 159
Prime, W. C., 34

Pribylof seal fur, 24
Prince Edward, 124, 127
Pritt, T. E., 34
Processed silk wings, 27
Professor, 119, 121, 125
Profile, wet fly, 44, 45
Proportions, dry fly, 58
Proportions, wet fly, 43
Pulman, G. P. R., 34
Pupae, 43, 74

Q

Queen Waters, 52, 121
Quill gnats, 34
Quill Gordon, 69, 162
Quill wing, reverse, 50, 69, 162
Quill wing, spent, 69
Quimby, Bert, 103

R

Rabbit fur, 24
Raffia, 24
Rainbow, 123
Rankin Special, 119
Raven quill, 26
Rayon, 23
Realistic flies, 35
Red-bellied dace, 106
Red Fly, 153
Red fox fur, 24, 29
Red fox tail, 29
Red-grizzly hackle, 22
Red hackle, 22, 32, 75, 121
Red Ibis, 26
Red Quill, 175
Reuben Wood, 121
Reverse bend, 4
Reverse hackle, 38
Reverse wing, 39, 129
Rhode, Homer, 136, 316
Rhode's Shrimp Fly, 136
Ribbing, 38
Ringed eye, 7
Ring-neck body plumage, 28
Ring-neck duck wing quills, 27
Ring-neck pheasant tail, 26
Rocky Mt. goat, 24
Rolla hair, 29
Rolled wing, 39
Romany Ree, 125, 287
Romany Rye, 125, 287
Ronalds, Alfred, 34
Ross Special, 119
Royal Coachman, 67, 69, 70, 119, 121, 136
Royal Coachman bivisible, 121
Royal Wulff, 121
Rubber bands, 26
Rubber translucent, 26
Ruddy fly, 34
Rusty dun hackle, 22

S

Saddle hackle, 27

Sail wing, 39, 164
St. Albans, 33
Salmon fly, "Dee" type, 120
  dictionary of patterns, 269
  dry fly, 77, 120
  grub, 120
  hair wing, 119
  low-water, 118
  Margaree, 111
  Miniature, 118
  spring, 120
  standard, 114
  wet fly, 111
Salt-water flies, dictionary of patterns, 285
Salt-water streamers, 134
Sanborn, Dr. Herbert, 97, 292
Sand fly, 153
Sandiford, Sandy, 319
Sandusky, Herbert, 314
Saw fly, 197
Scaup body plumage, 27
Scissors, 18
Scud, 90, 203, 204
Seagull wing quills, 27
Seal fur, 24
Sedges, 68, 18
Sex, May fly (determination of), 162
Shad, coloration of, 134
Shad fly hatch, 72
Shafer, C. W., 125, 189, 287
Shamrock, 153
Shedder crab, 134
Sheep wool, 24
Shell fly, 33
Shiner minnow, 106
Short shank, 4
Shoulder, 43, 134, 203, 204
Shoulder hackle, 38
Shoveler body plumage, 27
Shrimp, 43, 134, 203, 204
Sialidae, 153
Siberian wolf tail, 29
Silk floss, 23
Silkworm gut, 26
Silver Amherst metallics, 28
Silver Blue, 119
Silver Doctor, 111, 118, 119, 121, 123
Silver fox fur, 24
Silver Gray Bomber, 119
Silver Ghost, 136
Silver Horns, 153
Silver sedge, 52
Silver Wilkinson, 122
Sir Charles, 119
Sizing a fly, 40
Skunk hair, 29
Sky Blue, 153
Sliced shank, 6
Smedley, Harold H., 312
Smelt, coloration of, 134
Smith, Roger P., 134, 136, 390
Snake feeder, 195
Sneck, 2

Snipe wing quills, 27
Soldier Palmer, 121
Sow bug, 90, 203
Spear, 9
Spear point, 9
Speckled Bavarian hackle, 22
Spent wing, 39, 69, 163
Spey, 119
Spiders, 75, 153
Spinners, 39, 153, 159, 188
Split hackle, 38
Split hair wing, 39
Split rolled wing, 39
Splits, 38
Split wing, 40
Spoon wing, 40
Spoon wing lake fly, 127
Spotted sedge, 185
Spring salmon fly, 120
Sproat, 2
Spun fur, 24
Spun wool, 24
Squirrel tail hair, 29
Standard salmon fly, 114
Standards, proposed (Hook and fly), 56, 119
Starling plumage, 26
Steelhead flies, 54, 55
Steelhead flies, dictionary of patterns, 257
Stevens, Carrie G., 294
Stick worms, 91, 183
Stone fly, 33, 34, 53, 70, 88, 153, 154, 177, 178, 179, 180, 181
Straw, 24
Streamer, By-plane, 103
   dictionary of patterns, 260
   bucktail, 103
   combination, 106
   feather, 99
   ideal qualities for, 95
   Maribou, 105
   origination of, 93
   Palmer, 102
   proportions, 98
   special features, 99
   wings, 27
Strips, 38
Strip skin bug, 150
Sub-imago, 159
Supervisor, 106, 135
Swale fly, 188
Swan satinets, 27

T

Tag, 38
Tail fibers, application of, 40
Tail, 38
Tail ruff, 38
Tail tag, 38
Tail topping, 39
Tandum Double Header, 97
Tandy fly, 33
Tapered end (hook), 7
Taper eye, 7

Tapered shank, 7
Tapply, H. G., 295
Tawny fly, 34
Teal body plumage, 27
Teal wing quill, 27
Ten-pin bug, 145
Theakston, Michael, 152, 167, 169
Theakston, System of Classification, 153
The Art of Fly-Fishing, 34
The British Angler's Manual, 34
The Compleat Angler, 34
The Fly-Fisher's Entomology, 34
The Secrets of Angling, 33
Theocritus, 32
Thessalonica, 32
Throat, 39
Throat hackle, 38
Thunder and Lightning, 119 ,123
Tinned finish, 13
Tinsel, 23
Tip, 39
Tomah-Jo, 124
Topknots, 27
Topping, 39
Trailer hook (streamer), 97, 102
Trailers, 39
Translucent, 40
Translucent dry-fly wings, 27
Trichoptera, 153, 182
Trowbridge, George, 135
Turkey Brown, 153
Turkey plumage, 26, 27
Turle, Major W. G., 173
Turn-down eye, 7
Turn-up eye, 7
Two-wing fly (2 wing), 91, 188, 189

U

Under wing, 40
Upper wing, 40
Upright wing, 40
Utah Fish & Game Dept., 305

V

Vade Mecum of Fly-Fishing for Trout, 34
Variant, 75
Variant grizzly hackle, 22
Varnish, 29
Veil, 39, 40
Venable, 34
Vibrator wing, 40
Viking, 2, 4
Vises, types of, 16

W

Wallace, Earl, 314
Walton, Izaak, 33, 34
Warden's Worry, 103
Wasps, 197
Wasp fly, 33, 34
Water bugs, 196
Water cricket, 195
Water skaters, 196

Water worm, 188
Wax, 21
Weaver, 183
Webb, Don, 312
Weedless hair wing, 129
Welch, Herbert L., 93, 289
Welch Montreal, 95, 289
Welch Rarebit, 95, 289
Wells, Henry P., 125
Wet fly, definition of, 43
  closed wing, 50
  divided wing, 45
  flat wing, 53
  hackle tip, 50
  hair wing, 52
  low-water, 53
  Palmer, 52
representation and proportions, 43
  reverse or down wing, 50
  rolled wing, 50
  salmon, 111
  spoon wing, 52
  translucent wing, 53
  vibrator wing, 54
Wetzel, Charles W., 299
Whip finish, 42
Whip finisher, 19
Whirlers, 196
Whirligigs, 196
Whirling Blue Dun, 153
Whirling Dun, 121
Whirling Fly, 131
White caddis, 186
White hackle, 22
White Miller, 136

White mallard blue tips, 27
White moth, 197
Wickham's Fancy, 52, 75
Widgeon body plumage, 27
Wild pigeon wing quills, 27
Williamson, Prof. T. A., 124
Willow fly, 153
Wing feather, removing segments, 41
Wing materials, 26
Wing quills, 25, 26
Wings, dimensions of, 40
Wings, types of, 39
Wood duck body plumage, 26, 27
Wounded minnow streamer, 103
Wulff, Lee, 136, 295

Y

Yanosh, 27
Yellow Bucktail, 119
Yellow Brown, 153
Yellow Crane fly, 191
Yellow Drake, 174
Yellow Dun, 153
Yellow flie, 34
Yellow or greenish fly, 34
Yellow May, 33, 177
Yellow Miller, 123
Yellow Sally, 121, 153
Yellow Stone fly, 182
Yorkshire Trout Flies, 34
Young, Leo W., 298

Z

Zebra pheasant, 26
Zebra pheasant body plumage, 28